CHICAGO

In and Around the Loop

WALKING TOURS OF ARCHITECTURE AND HISTORY

by GERARD R. WOLFE

McGRAW-HILL

New York   San Francisco   Washington, D.C.   Auckland   Bogotá
Caracas   Lisbon   London   Madrid   Mexico City   Milan
Montreal   New Delhi   San Juan   Singapore
Sydney   Tokyo   Toronto

Library of Congress Cataloging-in-Publication Data

Wolfe, Gerard R., date.
    Chicago : in and around the loop / Gerard R. Wolfe.
       p.   cm.
    Includes index.
    ISBN 0-07-071390-1 (pbk. : acid-free paper)
    1. Architecture—Illinois—Chicago—Guidebooks. 2. Loop (Chicago,
Ill.)—Guidebooks. 3. Chicago (Ill.)—Buildings, structures, etc.—
Guidebooks. I. Title.
NA735.C4W67   1996
720'.9773'11—dc20   96-5436
                                               CIP

McGraw-Hill

A Division of The McGraw·Hill Companies

  2 3 4 5 6 7 8 9 0 DOC/DOC 9 0 1 0 9 8 7

ISBN 0-07-071390-1

*The sponsoring editor for this book was Wendy K. Lochner, the editing supervisor was
Stephen M. Smith, and the production supervisor was Suzanne W. B. Rapcavage. It was
set in Times Roman by North Market Street Graphics.*

Printed and bound by R. R. Donnelley & Sons Company.

This book is printed on acid-free paper.

Contents

Note: The following are the landmark symbols used in this guide:

★ Designated City of Chicago landmark (the six-pointed star is adapted from the official flag of the City of Chicago)

☆ Listed on the National Register of Historic Places

Introduction

I am frequently asked by visitors to suggest the best vantage point to appreciate Chicago's spectacular skyline. While the views from atop the John Hancock Center and the Sears Tower provide an all-encompassing panorama for which tourists line up by the hundreds, my favorite spot is in Grant Park, near the Buckingham Fountain, at the crack of dawn, when the first rays of the sun spread across the steel-blue reaches of Lake Michigan. Then, out of the dusk and darkness of the great windswept prairies, Chicago rises suddenly in the morning's first light, soaring skyward in a brilliant fantasy of stone and glass, punctuated with pinnacles of gleaming silver. They are all there—virtually every Chicago skyscraper—each contributing its unique and distinctive profile, creating a luminous and dramatic skyline like no other in the world. There is magic in that unforgettable moment that is uniquely Chicago!

This guide to downtown Chicago's splendid architecture and rich history is divided into 12 walking tours of varying length, which when taken in sequence will provide a reasonably comprehensive overview of how the City of Chicago developed and grew, what and where its most significant buildings and landmarks are, and who were (and are) its most important architects. Some tours are necessarily longer than others because of the number of buildings in the itinerary. Tours 1 and 2, for example, which cover the inner Loop in depth, may each be divided easily into two separate tours; likewise, Tours 3 and 4, which follow the banks of the Chicago River. With the exception of Tours 10 and 12, all starting points are within walking distance of the center of the Loop. Restaurants are not included in this work, except where essential to the text. Excellent eating guides are available in bookstores, and the following free publications are available in most public places: The Chicago Convention and Tourism Bureau's *City Guide; Key—Chicago's Official City Guide* (published weekly); and *Where Chicago Magazine.*

A number of significant lost buildings are included among the illustrations to offer a then-and-now picture of the city and help portray the early skyscraper era. Even before the Great Fire of 1871 eradicated just about every building in the Loop area, the city had already begun to mushroom at a whirlwind pace. The devastating fire proved only a relatively brief delay—some might even say a catalyst—in Chicago's inexorable drive to renew itself and expand.

From a mere frontier trading post in the early 19th century, Chicago grew to become a major city of almost two million people by the beginning of the 20th century. As the primary railroad transportation hub of the country, it became the center for the distribution of grain, lumber, coal, and livestock, and its location at the south end of Lake Michigan made it the ideal transshipment point by water to the Mississippi River and the Gulf of Mexico. Much of the impetus for Chicago's growth came as the result of the Civil War, when demands for food supplies, particularly canned meat, created a burgeoning meat-packing industry, which resulted in the building of the vast Union Stock-yards.

The incredible destruction caused by the Great Fire brought about a dynamic effort to rebuild, attracting architects from around the country to create a new and more permanent metropolis. In a little over a decade after the fire, Chicago rose phoenix-like from its ashes to become one of the foremost cities in America, despite its turbulent politics, corrupt city administrations, and a somewhat exaggerated reputation as the home of tommy gun–toting gangsters. The demand for more office space and the development of structural steel led to the birth of the world's first skyscraper. And while William LeBaron Jenney's Home Insurance Building was only 12 stories high when completed in 1884, in less than a century buildings topping 100 stories were not unheard of. By the early 1890s a whole new Chicago school of architecture had begun to evolve, led by such luminaries as Daniel H. Burnham, John Wellborn Root, Dankmar Adler, and Louis Sullivan, plus a host of others, including Frank Lloyd Wright, who with his unique Prairie style would leave an indelible stamp on building design for years to come. In more recent times, Chicago architects are still recognized as being on the cutting edge of modern building design. When Mies van der Rohe came to Chicago in 1938, his ideas based on the "less is more" of the Bauhaus school, as expressed in his bare-bones International style, created an impact that would endure for over half a century. And while Chicago continues to nourish its own brood of distinguished contemporary architects such as Helmut Jahn, Harry Weese, Skidmore, Owings & Merrill, Bertrand Goldberg, and a bevy of others, the city now attracts architects from around the world who have come to work in this dynamic urban environment that nurtures and esteems innovation and versatility.

Before setting off on a walking tour, it might be a good idea to read through the chapter to get a general idea of the area covered. Although not essential for these tours, each of which has its own detailed map, there are a number of good street maps available; my choices are Pierson Graphics Corp.'s *Chicago Visitor's Guide Map & Bird's Eye View* or Gousha's *Chicago Metromap*. You also might want to photocopy the chapter's tour map, so you won't have to keep flipping pages. For getting around on public transportation—Chicago has one of the best and easiest to use systems of any city in the country—pick up a free copy of the CTA (Chicago Transit Authority) Transit Map at any El station, or phone for one at (312) 836-7000. [Unless otherwise specified, all telephone numbers mentioned in this guide have a (312) area code.] Maps are also available at the Visitors' Information Centers located in the Chicago Cultural Center at 78 E. Washington Street (corner of N. Michigan Avenue) and in the Historic Water Tower, 806 N. Michigan Avenue, as well as at many hotels. For general visitors' information, phone 744-2400 [out of town: 1 (800) 487-2446].

Chicago's downtown is one of the safest and cleanest of any major city in America, and you will find that Chicagoans, being proud of their city to the point of studied chauvinism, will be happy to point you in the right direction. Because of its geography, downtown Chicago is relatively compact and thus extremely walkable. If you are a neophyte architecture buff, you will learn to look at buildings with a new and discerning eye, eventually appreciating the various architectural styles and recognizing the hallmarks of the architects who designed them. Wear comfortable shoes; a hat and sunglasses are advisable on some of the "Windy City's" hot summer days, and take along a notepad to make your own observations. A very important point: to avoid that "run-down feeling" on Chicago streets, be extremely careful of traffic, and don't look up at the tall buildings while crossing intersections! Chicagoans are, as a rule, very helpful and polite to visitors—except when they get behind the wheel of their automobiles.

If, after taking some or all of the tours, you have any questions, suggestions, or corrections, please send them to me in care of my editor, Wendy Lochner, at McGraw-Hill, 11 West 19th Street, New York, NY 10011.

Once you've been "hooked" on Chicago architecture you may want to attend some of the tours, lectures, and exhibitions offered by the Chicago Architecture Foundation (*see* pages 186–188). The Chicago Historical Society also presents a series of exhibits and occasional walking tours (*see* pages 390–393)—and you may even want to enjoy the many benefits of membership in both organizations. Another active organization, the Friends of the Chicago River, offers tours and excursions along the interesting and varied shoreline of the river.

If you would like to learn more about Chicago architecture, the Recommended Readings includes just about every book available in bookstores or your library. In downtown Chicago there is a virtual treasure trove of reading materials in the Chicago Art Institute's Ryerson and Burnham Libraries, the Newberry Library, the Chicago Historical Society, and the Harold Washington Library, to name just a few readily available sources.

Were I asked to make the difficult selection of the most useful titles to begin with, I would recommend the *AIA Guide to Chicago,* which is the most complete compendium of buildings (and their architects) in the city and suburbs; *Chicago's Famous Buildings,* by Franz Schulze and Kevin Harrington, a detailed description with illustrations of the city's and nearby suburbs' most important buildings; *Chicago: A Guide to New Downtown Buildings Since the Sears Tower,* by Mary Alice Molloy, a concise illustrated guide to every Chicago building erected since 1968; *Norman Mark's Chicago—Walking, Bicycling and Driving Tours of the City,* a collection of informal walks that include social history and dining and entertainment suggestions, plus a wealth of humorous anecdotes about Chicago's checkered past; *Lost Chicago,* by David Garrard Lowe, a richly illustrated volume that will bring tears when you see how many magnificent buildings have been demolished through the years, before the advent of the preservation movement; *The Great Chicago Fire,* also by David Garrard Lowe, which will show and tell you everything you'd ever want to know about that incredible holocaust; John Zukowsky's lavish pair of large-format illustrated volumes with informative and interesting text, *Chicago Architecture 1872–1922: Birth of a Metropolis* and *Architecture and Design 1923–1993;* and, if you're *really* serious, *Chicago—Growth of a Metropolis,* by Harold M. Mayer and Richard C. Wade, a comprehensive volume and superb reference (now in paperback) that documents with over 1,000 vintage photographs and brief essays the physical growth and spatial patterns of the city. And for a splendid and comprehensive illustrated work on Chicago's most significant religious edifices, I strongly recommend *Chicago's Churches and Synagogues,* by George A. Lane and Algimantas Kezys. After taking several of the tours in the present work, you'll find it of great interest to go to the library and sit down for a few hours with *The Plan of Chicago: 1909,* by Daniel H. Burnham and Edward H. Bennett, considered by many to be the best urban design scheme ever conceived for a modern city, and one whose visionary precepts endure to this very day.

Now, as you embark on your walks of discovery, I hope that you will come to appreciate Chicago's architectural heritage and share my affection for its buildings and spaces, and at the same time learn more about the city's rich and often tumultuous history.

GERARD R. WOLFE
May 1996

Acknowledgments

In compiling a guide of this nature, one must depend on the advice, suggestions, and contributions of a great many individuals and organizations. I am particularly grateful to the Chicago Architecture Foundation for its encouragement to fulfill the need for a comprehensive walking-tour guide to the Loop area, and for its subsequent endorsement of the completed work.

Among the public and private organizations and institutions that contributed valuable information and materials were the Chicago Historical Society, Friends of the Chicago River, the City of Chicago Department of Cultural Affairs, the Chicago Parks District Communications Department, the Field Museum of Natural History, the Terra Museum of American Art, the Spertus Institute of Jewish Studies, the Wisconsin Marine Historical Society, River City, the First United Methodist Church (Chicago Temple), the Fourth Presbyterian Church, the Seventeenth Church of Christ Scientist, Old St. Mary's Church, St. Peter's Roman Catholic Church "in the Loop," the Loop Synagogue, the "I AM" Temple, the Hotel Inter-Continental, and the Drake Hotel.

There were many individuals in various organizations who made personal contributions "above and beyond": Bertrand Goldberg of Bertrand Goldberg Associates; Deborah Shapiro, Chicago Historical Society; Susan E. Perry, Senior Library Assistant, Ryerson and Burnham Libraries, The Art Institute of Chicago; Meredith Taussig, Landmarks Preservation Specialist, and Janice Curtis, City of Chicago, Commission on Chicago Landmarks; Christopher L. Krueger, Senior Project Director, Chicago Department of Transportation; Violette Brooks, Librarian, Chicago Transit Authority; Kristin Hardin, Collections Assistant, Prairie Avenue House Museums; Bob Wiedrich, McCormick Research Center; Stewart B. Smith, Recorder, Medinah Temple; Robert I. Peak, Chief Photographer, Medinah Temple; John Hoover, Nancy Cutter, and Joe Zijdel of Stein & Company; Richard M. Penner, Manager, Building and Office Services, Inland Steel Industries, Inc.; David A. Mroczkowski, Corporate Communications, USG Corporation; Greg Merdinger, The John Buck Company; Sara E. Feldman, Allerton Hotel; Cindy K. Gountanis, Public Relations Representative, Jardine Water Purification Plant; George Lane, Loyola University Press; Dr. Doren Wehrley, Wisconsin Marine Historical Society; Nicolette Bromberg, The State Historical Society of Wisconsin; and Algimantas Kezys, photographer. Michael Houlahan and Kathleen Oconomou of Hedrich Blessing Photographers deserve a very special note of appreciation; and another thank you goes to Mary Ann Platts, Third Coast Stock Source, in Milwaukee.

I would be remiss if I didn't make special mention of Mary Alice Molloy, Chicago historian and author and specialist on the Prairie Avenue houses, for her invaluable assistance, suggestions, and text revisions of my Prairie Avenue tour; and Bart Swindall, tour guide and archivist of the Auditorium Theatre, for his in-depth personal tours and for sharing his fount of knowledge about this great Adler and Sulivan masterpiece; plus two good friends and former Chicagoans, Val Ginter and David Garrard Lowe, for their advice and encouragement, and for Val's personal anecdotes and unusual background material, and for David's superb and useful books, *Lost Chicago* and *The Great Chicago Fire;* as well as Virginia Palmer, Specialist in Local History and colleague at the University of Wisconsin—Milwaukee, who was always ready with answers to even the most difficult questions on Chicago; and historian Dr. Gareth A. Shellman, Assistant Director, Institute of World Affairs, University of Wisconsin—Milwaukee, for his advice and helpful reference materials.

Others who saw the value of this project and who offered encouragement and support were Matt Smith, Director of Public Affairs, Chicago Department of Planning and Development; Dean Daniel W. Shannon of the University of Wisconsin—Milwaukee; David Dunlap, feature writer, *The New York Times;* Laurie Beckelman, former New York City Landmarks Commissioner; Jack Taylor, President, The Drive to Protect the Ladies' Mile Historic District; Joyce Mendelsohn, teacher and distinguished tour guide; and, particularly, my wife, Caecilia, who pushed me relentlessly to "get it done," and smilingly accepted my long periods of absence while I trod the streets of Chicago.

A special note of gratitude is due to my colleague, Kim C. Beck, who led me patiently through the intricacies of WordPerfect 6.0a and Windows 3.1, without which I could never have completed this work.

A note of recognition is in order for the extraordinarily careful attention to and superb printing of the more than 200 of my negatives which illustrate the text by the skillful technicians of K & S Imaging and Photographics in Milwaukee.

For generous financial support to help purchase the collection of archival photographs in this book, I am deeply indebted to Sybil Parker, publisher at McGraw-Hill. I am also very grateful for the encouragement and advocacy of this project by my sponsoring editor, Wendy Lochner; and for the meticulous attention to every detail and many constructive suggestions, I am much obliged to Stephen Smith, senior editing supervisor.

Finally, for the production of the detailed maps that accompany each chapter, I am deeply indebted to the Cartographic Service of the University of Wisconsin—Milwaukee. The maps were prepared with great care and accuracy from my rough drafts by geography students Joseph Polder and Thomas Vander Velden, under the supervision of Donna Genzmer Schenström, Head Geographer.

                                                                                                    G.R.W.

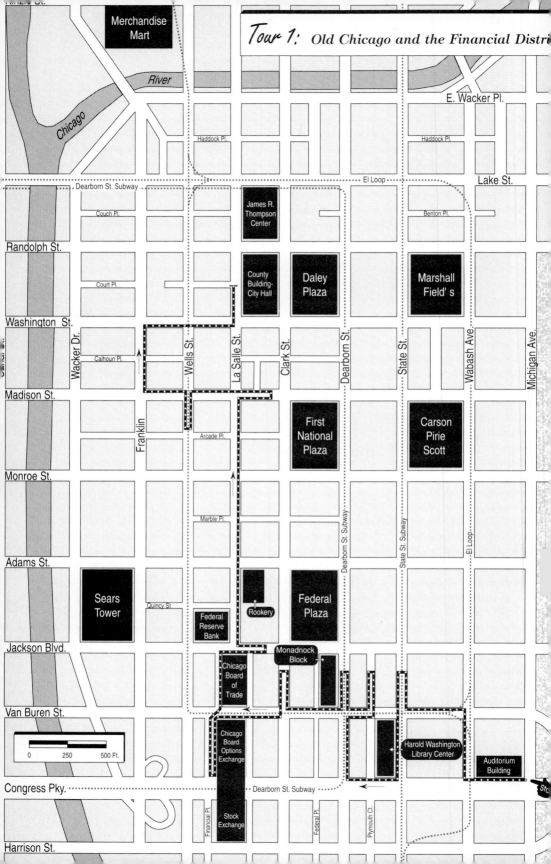

1. The Loop I: Old Chicago and the Financial District

The series of walking tours of downtown Chicago begins at the corner of Michigan Avenue and Congress Parkway, with a visit to the Auditorium Building; it then continues west to the canyons of Chicago's financial district and explores many old and new buildings that have given Chicago the unique reputation as the cradle of modern architecture. Chicago through the years has played host to many of the world's most celebrated architects—Louis Sullivan, Dankmar Adler, John Wellborn Root, Frank Lloyd Wright, and others of the famous Chicago school—as well as to many of the country's most talented and imaginative contemporary building designers. It was here that the skyscraper was born, and where for more than a century Chicago has stood at the forefront and on the cutting edge of modern architectural design.

Before approaching the Auditorium Building, step back across Michigan Avenue into Grant Park to get a broad perspective of the structure and appreciate its scale.

The construction of the **Auditorium Building** came at the time when Chicago was emerging from the incredible devastation of the Great Fire, only 15 years before. It was commissioned in 1886 by Ferdinand Wythe Peck, a

The Auditorium Building, at the corner of S. Michigan Avenue and E. Congress Parkway, rises high above a row of elegant town houses built by some of Chicago's most affluent citizens after the Great Fire of 1871. The photo was taken from what was then Lake Park between 1889, when the Auditorium Building was completed, and 1892, when construction of the Congress Hotel replaced the neat row of mostly Italianate residences. (Chicago Historical Society)

prominent Chicago businessman, lover of the arts, and president of the 1885 Opera Festival. His intent was for the construction of a hotel, an office building, a much-needed opera house and concert hall, convention hall, and place for public events, all to be built under one roof. To carry out the grandiose project, he selected Dankmar Adler, an engineering genius, and his partner, Louis Sullivan, a master of aesthetics, who together had designed a number of music halls, including the highly successful Central Music Hall on State Street. Although it was their first major commission, its subsequent success rocketed them to international fame and contributed immeasurably to their reputation. With Adler's talent in engineering and acoustics and Sullivan's consummate skill as an architectural ornamentalist, they were an unrivaled design team.

The cornerstone was laid on October 5, 1887, and when the building was completed two years later, it set a number of records in the city. With its $3,200,000 price tag, it was the most costly; its 17-story tower made it the tallest; it was also the largest, most massive, and most spacious. Its 110,000-ton weight also made it the heaviest building in the world. The design of the facade was influenced by the then-popular Romanesque Revival style made famous by Boston architect Henry Hobson Richardson, who in 1887 designed Marshall Field's Wholesale Store. Although the style of the Auditorium Building was somewhat similar to the Wholesale Store, the tower was a unique element. The structure is of load-bearing construction, with a base of rusticated granite above which the arched walls are of smooth Bedford limestone.

The 4,200-seat Auditorium Theatre was completely surrounded by the hotel and office sections, and set within a fireproof brick enclosure. It was lavishly adorned with stenciling, stained glass, decorative rows of electric lights, and ornate plaster reliefs. Six huge trusses support the elliptical vault over the theatre, with four successively larger elliptical arches adorned with rows of light bulbs dividing the ceiling and acting as sound reflectors. The acoustics of the theatre are superb and the sight lines uninterrupted, a crowning achievement of Adler's talent. Adler also designed a clever system of iron frames and trusses that "hung" the kitchen and banquet hall above the auditorium. To support the weight of the immense building, Adler sunk a thick support "raft" made of wood beams, rails, and I-beams; and to compensate for the structure's settling into the soft clay, he devised the unusual plan of dumping pig iron and bricks into the lower levels to increase the load on the foundation. The construction of the Auditorium Building has been described as the most important achievement in the history of modern architecture.

Opening night came on December 9, 1889, attended by President Benjamin Harrison and Vice President Levi Morton, who had received the Republican nomination at the site just 18 months before. The Auditorium Theatre immediately became Chicago's cultural center, with both the Chicago Opera and the Chicago Symphony Orchestra taking up residence. In addition to musical events, there were circuses, conventions, sports events, and charity balls with thousands of people dancing on the stage. The hotel section opened in January 1890, together with a business section for offices and stores.

In 1929, both the onset of the Depression and the opening of the rival Civic Opera House (*see* pages 115 and 117) rang the death knell of the hotel and the theatre. With the opera and symphony gone, the corporation went bankrupt, and during World War II, the only tenant was the U.S.O., which used the auditorium stage as a bowling alley. In 1946 Roosevelt University purchased the Auditorium Building and adapted the facilities for classroom and office use.

In 1955 the city widened Congress Parkway, requiring the removal of the sidewalk on the north side. To provide for a pedestrian walk, the entire ground floor of the Auditorium Building facing Congress Parkway was gouged out behind the masonry arches, creating an arcade and eliminating the front of the lobby entrance. The remodeling project was done rather well despite the resultant violence to the original Adler & Sullivan design, and the casual passerby today might conclude that the covered pedestrian passage was always there.

A major restoration project was undertaken by Harry Weese & Associates in the 1960s, and on October 31, 1967, the Auditorium Theatre reopened to a

(Left) The 4,200-seat theatre is the centerpiece of the Auditorium Building. Architect Dankmar Adler designed a truss-framing system to support the great elliptical vault over the orchestra floor. It is composed of a succession of four elliptical arches, each wider and higher toward the rear, dividing the ceiling into smooth ivory panels that act as sound reflectors. The 70- by 100-foot stage was constructed in sections that could be raised and lowered by hydraulic machinery, and was equipped with complex lighting and a 95-foot rigging loft. The upper photo, taken three years after the building was completed, and reproduced from Inland Architect, *Vol. 1, June 1892, shows Sullivan's artistic genius, particularly in the ornamentation of the broad arches and the proscenium. To highlight the arches, each was illuminated with a row of electric bulbs—an extraordinary novelty so soon after the introduction of electric lighting. The lower photo, taken by Richard Nickel 75 years later, reveals only minor changes to the auditorium's appearance, although much of the original decoration had disappeared. (Upper photo, courtesy of the Art Institute of Chicago; lower, Commission on Chicago Landmarks)*

(Below) The talents of Louis H. Sullivan are again revealed in the huge semicircular ornamental panels that adorn the side walls of the theatre. The panel on the left wall serves as a screen for the organ pipes, whereas this one on the right side is a dummy. The photo, which shows considerable peeling paint, was taken prior to the 1967 multimillion-dollar rehabilitation. (Commission on Chicago Landmarks)

packed house for a gala performance by the New York City Ballet. Additional renovations were conducted in more recent times by Skidmore, Owings & Merrill, and the Office of John Vinci, and the theatre, now restored to its former opulence, is again one of Chicago's most popular sites for concerts and dramatic performances. The former hotel's banquet hall/ballroom is now the Rudolph Ganz Memorial Recital Hall, the ornate barrel-vaulted dining room serves as the University's library, and the grand staircase once again leads up to the magnificently restored Ladies' Parlor.

Enter the Michigan Avenue lobby and see the fruits of the years of painstaking rehabilitation. Tours of the theatre complex are available. For information, call in advance 431-2354; $4.00, $3.00 students and seniors.

Now walk west along Congress Parkway to the next corner, Wabash Avenue. (The Congress Hotel, on the south side of Congress Parkway, is discussed in Chapter 6.)

Chicago's **Loop Area** is now generally accepted as the approximately 72-block rectangular grid bordered by Michigan Avenue on the east, the Chicago River on the west and north, and Congress Parkway on the south. The name, however, derives from the original loop of cable-car tracks of the Chicago City Rail Way that encircled part of the downtown area in 1880, and later from the elevated railroad whose more clearly defined loop encompasses a seven- by five-block area bounded by Wabash Avenue and Van Buren, Wells, and Lake streets. By 1900 Chicago had the longest cable car and trolley system in the world.

Turn right (north) on Wabash Avenue one block toward Van Buren Street.

At No. 418 S. Wabash Avenue is the **Prairie Avenue Bookshop,** probably the largest architectural book outlet in the country, and well worth a visit. The bookshop is named for its original location in the Prairie Avenue Historic District, before it relocated here in 1995, and it is a major resource for architects, architecture buffs, and architectural historians.

Occupying the entire blockfront on the east side of Wabash Avenue, from Van Buren Street to Jackson Boulevard, is the distinctive **CNA Center,** actually two separate, but connected, structures (*south tower: 1972, Graham, Anderson, Probst & White; north tower: 1962, C. F. Murphy Associates*), 55 E. Jackson Boulevard, also known as the Continental Center. These are Chicago's "red twins," whose exposed steel framework and extra-wide window bays make them a rather conspicuous landmark on the city skyline. Both have exceptionally wide pedestrian arcades.

Just above, the **Union Loop Elevated Structure** trains make a sharp and squealing turn from Wabash into Van Buren, while a branch continues southward. Although the El is noisy and darkens the streets below and seems almost an anachronism in today's modern city, it is a well-patronized and vital transportation link, and dear to every Chicagoan's heart. A recent proposal to demolish the deteriorating Lake Street El brought howls of protest, and forced the Chicago Transit Authority to decide instead to rebuild it.

Before electrification, Loop elevated trains were pulled by diminutive steam locomotives. Here, No. 41, built by the Baldwin Locomotive Works in Philadelphia for the South Side line, is being oiled by the engineer before the start of his run. (Chicago Transit Authority)

A typical wooden El coach, built in 1892 for the first of several separate lines. The following year, the Chicago & South Side Rapid Transit was extended south to the grounds of the World's Columbian Exposition. The photo, taken many years later, shows restored car No. 1, and in the background, typical El cars used on the Loop around World War I. (Chicago Transit Authority)

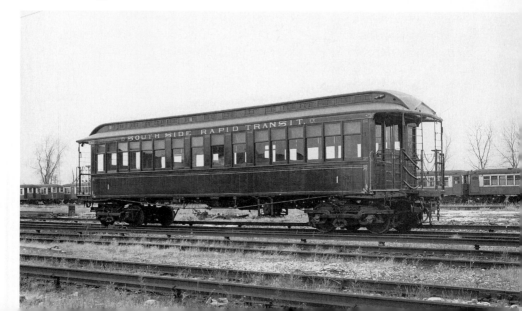

A 1950s-era El train outbound from the Loop to Ravenswood. The "state of the art" cars were built for the CTA by the St. Louis Car Company. (Chicago Transit Authority)

A contemporary scene on the Loop with a Ravenswood-bound train leaving the Randolph/Wabash station, swinging west to its next stop at State/Lake Street. Looming in the background is the ornate 35 E. Wacker Drive Building, formerly the Jewelers Building. (Photo by author)

The double-track El was the brainchild of John Alexander Low Waddell. He foresaw the economic advantages to downtown Chicago of an improved rapid transit system, and he designed the first section in 1892. Several separate companies were involved, the first of which was the Chicago & South Side Rapid Transit Railroad, which ran south to the grounds of the World's Columbian Exposition of 1893 and had wooden coaches pulled by steam locomotives. The next year saw the construction of the Lake Street Line, and in 1895, the opening of the Metropolitan West Side Elevated Railroad, which introduced electric power. Two years later the three independent companies, whose lines did not connect, were merged by transit mogul Charles T. Yerkes into a single "loop" system, the Union Elevated Railway (UER). Yerkes's unquenchable thirst for power and his complete lack of personal integrity was the theme of Theodore Dreiser's 1900 trilogy, *The Financier, The Titan,* and *The Stoic.* Other elevated extensions followed, and in 1924 the UER was taken over by the Chicago Rapid Transit Company, now the CTA. The most recent addition came in 1994 with the opening of the Orange Line which makes a direct connection from the Loop to Midway Airport. The entire Chicago Union Loop Elevated Structure has been determined to be eligible for listing on the National Register of Historic Places.

On the southwest corner of Wabash Avenue and Van Buren Street is **Old St. Mary's Church,** serving Chicago's oldest Catholic parish. Erected in 1961 as the Catholic Information Center, it was remodeled as a church in 1971 to replace an earlier Old St. Mary's at 9th and Wabash, which was demolished. The original church, a wooden structure, built in 1833 on the south side of Lake Street, west of State Street, was the first balloon-frame building ever constructed. Ten years later on the southwest corner of Madison and Wabash the diocese built Old St. Mary's Cathedral, which was destroyed in the Great Fire of 1871. A plaque on the Carson Pirie Scott store's Wabash Avenue Building marks the site. The present structure is the fifth St. Mary's, all having served in the Loop area.

Turn left (west) on Van Buren Street and follow the El to State Street. Cross to the northwest corner and walk north a short distance along the park.

Pritzker Park (*1992*), designed by architect Patrick Shaw, with artist Ronald Jones, is a pleasant oasis and a convenient spot to view the surrounding buildings. The land for the little park was cleared as part of the Harold Washington Library project, one block south. A plaque mounted near the corner gives a detailed explanation and guide to the park's unusual artwork, calling it "a site for the play of imagination, and a haven of green space in the urban environment, intended to complement the Harold Washington Library Center." It also includes a reference to the René Magritte surrealist painting *The Banquet* in the Art Institute, which inspired the planting of the group of trees beyond the granite wall. At the north end is a circular stone seating area based on a council-ring design by the dean of the Prairie style landscape architects, Jens Jensen, who was a contemporary of Frank Lloyd Wright. (A good place to relax for a few minutes.)

Directly across State Street is the splendidly restored, blocklong **DePaul Center** (*1912, Holabird & Roche; renovation 1993, Daniel P. Coffey & Associates*), 333 S. State Street. The glistening white terra-cotta facade and deep bracketed cornice give an excellent idea of the appearance of the building when it first opened in 1912 as Rothschild's Department Store. (Look for the *R*'s on the lower section.) After the demise of Rothschild's, it was the home for many years of Goldblatt's, one of Chicago's most popular department stores, and an emporium that is still sorely missed by many shoppers who loved the variety of merchandise and the bargains. The DePaul Center is now a multiuse building with retail shops and a food court on the lower levels, office space above, and on the upper floors, the classrooms and offices of DePaul University. Note the elaborate cornice. The Jackson Boulevard facade has undergone a complete renovation, rather than restoration; however the modernizations are sympathetic to the original plan. A minipark provides DePaul with a "minicampus."

State Street, nicknamed "The Great Street," was Chicago's prime retail shopping center for almost a century until "The Magnificent Mile" lured away many of the shoppers. (More about State Street and its colorful history can be found in Chapter 2.)

Turn around and walk south, just past Van Buren Street.

On the east side of State Street, extending the full blockfront, is the Second Leiter Building, recently renamed **One Congress Center** (*1891, William LeBaron Jenney*), 403 S. State Street. Designed by the "father of the skyscraper," this eight-story building, sheathed in white Maine granite, was built as a single retail establishment for real estate developer, Levi Z. Leiter, once a partner of Marshall Field, and it fitted his requirements perfectly. (*See* Jenney's First Leiter Building, page 88, and his Home Insurance Building, pages 34–35.) As a building requiring a significant amount of light to display merchandise before the prevalence of electric lighting, Jenney created a solid, steel-frame structure with broad expanses of windows, obviating the need for light courts or atria that were so commonplace in the era of bearing-wall construction. Reputed to have been the largest retail establishment in the world, its 15 acres of floor space made it truly a building ahead of its time, and one which today bears an unmistakable 20th-century look. (Look for Leiter's name and the 1891 construction date just below the cornice.) The first major tenant was the famous Siegel-Cooper & Co., "The Big Store," one of Chicago's largest retail emporiums. In 1896 the company moved to New York, where Henry Siegel, the driving force behind the firm, brought the Chicago tradition with him and built (in the style made famous by the World's Columbian Exposition of 1893) the world's largest department store, until it was eclipsed by Macy's some years later. The most recent occupant was the flagship store of Sears, Roebuck & Company, one of the mainstays of the State Street shopping district for many years, until the street's decline in the 1980s.

Across State Street, and occupying the entire block, is one of Chicago's newest and most important public buildings, and one which embodies much of

The striking Harold Washington Library Center, completed in 1991, is the largest library building in the country. Its unusual postmodern design, which recalls many of the details of the city's most famous Chicago school of architecture buildings, was the winning entry in a widely publicized competition to replace the old Chicago Public Library (now the Chicago Cultural Center). (Photo by author)

the *zeitgeist* of Chicago's architectural environment, the **Harold Washington Library Center** (*1991, Thomas Beeby, of Hammond, Beeby & Babka, with A. Epstein & Sons International*), 400 S. State Street. The Library, whose design was the winning entry in a much-publicized competition for a new facility to replace the former Chicago Public Library (now the Chicago Cultural Center, on Michigan Avenue), is named in honor of Chicago's first black mayor. Its striking 10-story granite and red-brick postmodern facade is reminiscent of several of the city's most famous buildings of the Chicago school of architecture, and visitors gawking at the classic detailing are often astonished to learn its true age; in fact, many call it "Chicago's newest old building." With its Loop location north of Congress Parkway, and its grandiloquent detailing recalling the Beaux Arts style of the "White City" of the World's Columbian Exposition of 1893, the $195 million building fulfills to some extent Daniel H. Burnham's uncompleted 1909 Plan of Chicago which included a grand corridor from Grant Park to the Chicago River. The deeply recessed five-story-tall arched windows recall the Auditorium Building; the rusticated granite base, the Rookery; and the gently sloping mid-section, the Monadnock Building. Because of the scale and size of the massive structure (it is the largest library building in the country) and its ostentatious and unconventional adornment, it has been called many things—a brilliant statement, a monstrosity, an architectural achievement; but whatever *your* opinion may be, it is a modern classic and typically Chicago—big, brash, and forceful!

Even the decorative elements are oversize, as in the incredibly outsize acroteria that mark each roof corner and frame the pedimented glass and steel attic. On the State Street side there is a huge sculpture of an owl, for wisdom, and on the Congress and Van Buren sides there are seed pods symbolic of the natural bounty of the Midwest. To maintain the scale of the building in relation to its older neighbors, the architects kept the cornice even with One Congress Center, across the street. The west wall (facing Plymouth Court), sheathed in glass, where much of the staff works, is in strong contrast to the rest of the building. Not to be overlooked are the huge bronze lanterns, and adorning the interesting facade, several conspicuous icons of the city: the sculptured medallions that depict the "Windy City" and Chicago's "Y" emblem representing the three branches of the river, plus the goddess of grain, Ceres, smiling above the city's motto, *Urbs in Horto* (City in a Garden).

Once inside, however, the effect is no longer overwhelming, and it will immediately become apparent from the throngs of users of all ages and backgrounds that this is indeed a library for the people. Although the central atrium is rather small, and its white marble gives it a cold feeling, the lower lobby is spacious; the facilities are user-friendly, and the conveniently placed escalators, set in maple-paneled enclosures, reach six levels of what is one of the largest open-stack libraries in the world. The visitor is thus whisked from one level to another as if in a modern department store. On the top floor, an impressive glass-enclosed Winter Garden and the administrative offices share the natural light admitted by the metal-framed glass roof.

On the north wall of the main lobby is a mosaic mural entitled *Events in the Life of Harold Washington,* by Jacob Lawrence, which depicts the many stages in the life of the late mayor, represented by pages of books spread across his desk. A large circular well in the center of the lower lobby reveals on the floor below a "design for terrazzo and brass floor installation," illustrating *Du Sable's Journey,* designed by Houston Conwill in collaboration with architect Joseph DePace and poet Estella Conwill Majozo. It celebrates the historical legacy of Chicago as embodied in Harold Washington and Jean Baptiste Point du Sable (Chicago's first settler; *see* page 213), and traces his journey from his native Haiti through the Atlantic Ocean and the Great Lakes. Ask at the main desk for a guide to the Library and for the schedule of tours of the building.

On exiting the Library on the State Street side, walk south to Congress Parkway and turn right (west). Continue past Plymouth Court, glancing back at the west wall of the Library, and proceed one block further to Dearborn Street. Cross to the far side and turn right (north).

Directly across the street is the **Manhattan Building** (*1891, William LeBaron Jenney; renovation 1982, Hasbrouck Hunderman*), 431 S. Dearborn Street. This very impressive early office tower, designed by the first architect to employ an iron skeleton frame to support the outer walls, also boasts another series of firsts: it was the first *entirely* iron-frame building (the columns are of cast iron, and the beams and girders of wrought iron); the first with a satisfactory wind-bracing design; the first building with setbacks; and as the first 16-story building ever to be erected, it was briefly the tallest building in the world. And when it was converted in 1982 to a residential apartment building, it set the record as the largest ever to be so remodeled. Although structural steel had already come into use, the architect considered "Bessemer beams still too expensive." The 10th-floor setback was dictated by the need to lessen the building's load against adjoining smaller buildings. Interesting is the arrangement of the windows on the west facade, with three staggered groups of three bays each, with the wider center-group windows rising seven stories from the fifth level, and the outer-group narrower windows rising five stories from the fourth floor. Note the building's name in Art Nouveau–style letters over the entrance and the sculptured faces in the trumps of the bays.

The adjacent **Plymouth Building** (*1899, Simeon B. Eisendrath*), 417 S. Dearborn Street, was remodeled in neo-Gothic style in 1945 (W. Scott Armstrong) to give a more "collegiate" appearance for a private school; however, the original Eisendrath facade can still be seen around the corner on the Plymouth Court side.

A trio of noteworthy early skyscrapers on S. Dearborn Street just south of the Loop are (left to right): The 17-story Old Colony Building (1894), the only surviving Loop area structure with rounded corner bays; the 1899 Plymouth Building; and the Manhattan Building (1891), the first 16-story skyscraper ever built, as well as the first entirely iron-frame structure, and the largest building ever remodeled for residential condominiums. (Photo by Richard Nickel for the Commission on Chicago Landmarks)

The third member of the 1890s "triumvirate" on the block is the unusual **Old Colony Building** (*1894, Holabird & Roche*) 407 S. Dearborn Street, the only surviving building in the Loop area with rounded corner bays. The attractive and unusual steel-skeleton skyscraper is set on a base of bluish-colored masonry, and sheathed in white pressed brick adorned with terra cotta. Because of its width and 17-story height, a wind-bracing system was required. To solve the problem, the architects came up with a novel plan to use four sets of portal arches, strips which join the steel girders to the columns, and extend them from the foundation to the roof, borrowing a technique from bridge-building technology. The window grid pattern, typical of the Chicago school of architecture, reflects the building's inner skeleton. Holabird and Roche also solved the aesthetics of a wide and a narrow facade by designing strong vertical piers along the Dearborn Street side and broad horizontal spandrels along the Van Buren Street side. The building, commissioned by a Boston lawyer, was named to commemorate the original Massachusetts Bay Colony, as was adjacent Plymouth Court.

Continue north to the northwest corner of Van Buren and Dearborn streets.

Looking across Dearborn Street is the 18-story **Fisher Building** (*1896, D. H. Burnham & Company; Charles Atwood, design architect, and Edward Shankland, engineer*), 343 S. Dearborn Street. Named for developer Lucius G. Fisher, the neo-Gothic-style steel-frame structure, sheathed in yellow terra cotta, presents busy walls of continuous rows of piers framing row upon row of windows. The foundation, set in Chicago's notorious soft clay, required special reinforcement, which came in the form of deep pilings on I-beams buried in cement. This was not completely successful, and on close observation, the south section of the building can be seen to lean against the taller northern section, added in 1906. The facade is covered with an assortment of amusing terra-cotta marine creatures, a humorous reference to the name of the developer, as fish, salamanders, crabs, shellfish, and sea monsters can be seen slithering along the sills and spandrels and among the Gothic detailing of the building. If possible, go up to the second floor to see the original Carrara marble walls and the mosaic flooring.

If you are not in a hurry, take a very brief detour back (east) under the El to Plymouth Court and turn left (north) to midblock.

On the east side, is the narrow, 16-story **Chicago Bar Association Building** (*1990, Tigerman McCurry*), 321 S. Plymouth Court. Particularly notable in this precast concrete structure is the arrangement of paired windows, with tightly spaced pairs on the corners. Rising from each corner of the neo-Gothic upper story are four prominent aluminum finials. Above the entrance is a cast-aluminum sculpture, *Themis,* by Mary Block. To the left, and tied to the Bar Association Building, is the John Marshall Law School Library.

Directly across the street at No. 320 is the **Standard Club** (*1925, Albert Kahn*), an exclusive retreat for members of the upper echelons of the adjoining financial district. The limestone building displays a restrained Renaissance facade.

Return to the Fisher Building at the corner of Van Buren and Dearborn streets.

Facing the Fisher Building, and occupying the entire block, is the famous **Monadnock Block** (*northern half: 1891, Burnham & Root; southern half: 1893, Holabird & Roche*), 53 W. Jackson Boulevard and 54 W. Van Buren Street. The building was erected in two sections, two years apart, with the northern part built first with external masonry bearing walls, while the southern section was erected with a steel skeleton sheathed in terra cotta.

When the northern half was completed, its 16 stories made it not only the world's tallest commercial building, but the tallest stone building as well—a distinction it still retains, as no masonry building was ever built higher! To support its enormous weight, the walls are six feet thick at the base, but interior supports are made of steel. With its walls gently sloping outward to compensate for the load, the graceful shape of the building strongly suggests an Egyptian temple. Note the contrast between the undulating window bays on the north half, with the flat "punched out" rows of windows on the south. The south building still retains its original ornate cornice with elaborate consoles. The twin buildings are connected by a north-south central corridor (which you may want to explore), and each was originally divided into two sections. Since

The landmark Monadnock Block contains the tallest masonry building ever built. Looking south from W. Jackson Street, the northern half of the Block, by Burnham & Root (1891) is the masonry section, while the southern section, by Holabird & Roche, completed two years later, has a steel skeleton sheathed in terra cotta. (Commission on Chicago Landmarks)

they were commissioned by Boston developers, names of New England mountains were given to each section. The north buildings were named Monadnock and Kearsarge (both in New Hampshire); the south buildings, Wachusetts (in Massachusetts) and Katahdin (in Maine). Over time, only the name Monadnock stuck. (A monadnock is a geological term meaning a granite mountain surrounded by a glacial plain.) With the untimely death of Burnham's partner, John Wellborn Root (of pneumonia, at age 41), the contract for the design of the southern half was given to Holabird & Roche.

Return to Van Buren Street, and look briefly south on Dearborn. The imposing tower in the distance is the former Dearborn Street Station, **one of the city's great railroad terminals, now adaptively reused as part of the Dearborn Park development. Turn right (west) past Federal Place to Clark Street.**

On the left, and occupying the entire block south to Congress Parkway, is the **Chicago Metropolitan Correctional Center** (*1975, Harry Weese & Associates*), 71 W. Van Buren Street. Also known as the William J. Campbell U.S. Courthouse Annex, this surprising 27-story reinforced concrete, triangular-shaped tower was not designed simply as a novel and graceful addition to the postmodern vocabulary, but rather as a very functional facility. The shape came in response to the U.S. Federal Prisons' demand for an arrangement of cells around a common area under supervision of an unarmed guard, with corridors of the shortest possible length. Weese's unique triangular plan offered just that, maximum and most efficient use of such space. Notice that the windows on the first nine floors of the administrative section are considerably wider (14 inches) than those on the upper floors. (The gap on the 10th floor is for the mechanical equipment and ventilation units.) The narrow windows above, just five inches wide (the maximum allowed without bars by the Federal Bureau of Prisons, and presumably escape-proof) are for the 44-person self-contained inmate modules which consist of the cells and related facilities. There is also a rooftop exercise yard whose 30-foot-high walls are recognizable by the long horizontal slits. The Center is used to hold those awaiting trial, as well as convicted criminals awaiting transfer to a permanent prison facility. From the little park near the corner, there are fine views of the buildings just seen on the tour.

Turn north on Clark Street, just past the El.

On the east side of Clark Street, and extending to Jackson Boulevard, is the towering, rectilinear **Ralph H. Metcalfe Federal Building** (*1991, Fujikawa, Johnson & Associates*), 77 W. Jackson Boulevard. Its 27 stories of recessed tinted glass and steel mullions and open, glassy lobbies mark it as a harmonious component of the Federal Center to the north, which was one of Ludwig Mies van der Rohe's major Chicago projects, built between 1959 and 1974. The two-story southern extension houses a day-care center and fast-food restaurants. (The Metcalfe Building is discussed in more detail in Chapter 2; *see* pages 73–74.)

The triangular-shaped Chicago Metropolitan Correctional Center, typical of architect Harry Weese's style, is not only a graceful postmodern design, but a functional one as well. The plan responds to the U.S. Federal Prisons' requirement for the arrangement of cells around a common supervised area, with corridors of the shortest possible length. In the right rear are the Sears Tower and the Chicago Board of Trade Building. (Photo by author)

Return to Van Buren Street and turn right (west) to the corner of LaSalle Street.

On the southeast corner is the 17-story neo-Georgian-style **LaSalle Atrium Building** (*1914, Holabird & Roche*), 401 S. LaSalle Street. Formerly the Traders Building and originally the **Fort Dearborn Hotel,** it was built strategically close to the LaSalle Street Station (across the street), and in its day had a lively patronage from arriving long-distance train passengers. Converted to commercial use in 1985 by Booth/Hansen & Associates, it still retains much of its bygone grandeur. Enter the lobby to see the elegant Circassian walnut paneling and the lovely russet tiles from the kilns of the famous Rookwood Company, and on the mezzanine are murals showing scenes of early Chicago, including a mural at the lobby's rear of Fort Dearborn with Native Americans and early settlers. The quality renovation included the creation of a skylit atrium filling in the open center section of the building, the installation of elevators, and the placement of skylights above the second floor and roof.

Across LaSalle Street is the **site of the LaSalle Street Station,** demolished in the early 1980s. While the original buildings and trainsheds are gone, there is still a relatively small Metra Rock Island Division commuter station located at the rear of the Chicago Stock Exchange, across Congress Parkway.

To see the "replacement" buildings to best advantage, return to Van Buren Street, turn left, walk past LaSalle Street to S. Financial Place, turn left into the landscaped plaza to the west of the Board of Trade Options Exchange Building.

To the left, as you enter the park-like plaza, is a row of three interconnected buildings which comprise the **Exchange Center.** From left to right, the 7-story **Chicago Board Options Exchange,** a 40-story tower called **One Financial Place,** and the 5-story **Chicago Stock Exchange.** Built into the rear of the Stock Exchange, on the second level, is Metra's **LaSalle Street Station.** The station, one of two formerly on the site, was razed and reconstructed as part of the financial complex. Not a vestige remains, however, of the once teeming terminal that served such long-distance railroads as the Rock Island, Nickel Plate, and New York Central.

Occupying the site of the former railroad station's headhouse, which had once extended all the way to Van Buren Street, is the **Chicago Board Options Exchange** (*1985, Skidmore, Owings & Merrill*), 141 W. Van Buren Street, with few windows to distract the traders on the 44,000-square-foot floor from their task of buying and selling options on various commodities such as agricultural products and financial instruments. Known as the CBOE, and pronounced "See-Bo" in the trade, it is connected to the Board of Trade Building to the north by a skybridge on the fourth floor, and can be visited on weekdays from the Visitors' Center at the Board of Trade. The three buildings share the same red-granite cladding, except that the CBOE's surface is matte, whereas its neighbors to the south have polished surfaces.

The adjacent and towering **One Financial Place** (*1985, Skidmore, Owings & Merrill*), 440 S. LaSalle Street, was built at the same time and by the same architects as its neighbor to the north and is also situated over the former station's trainshed and tracks. It, in turn, is joined to the south to the six-story **Chicago Stock Exchange** (also by SOM, in 1985), formerly known as the Midwest Stock Exchange. A simple no-nonsense five-story structure clad in the same red granite with marble trim, it is distinguished by a pair of huge arched windows set above the bustling Congress Parkway–Eisenhower Expressway. The arches are intended to recall Adler & Sullivan's original Stock Exchange at 30 N. LaSalle Street, sadly lost in 1972 before the landmarks law could save it from the wreckers' ball. (*See* the reconstruction of the Stock Exchange Trading Room in the Chicago Art Institute, and the restored Stock Exchange Arch just behind the Institute building; pages 193–195.)

The Chicago Stock Exchange (1985) straddles W. Congress Parkway–Eisenhower Expressway. The twin arches are intended to recall Adler & Sullivan's original Stock Exchange (demolished 1972) that stood at 30 N. LaSalle Street. On the left is One Financial Place, and on the right, Metra's LaSalle Street commuter station, both connected to the Stock Exchange Building. (Photo by author)

At the south end of the plaza, officially called **Financial Plaza,** and decorated with "antique" lampposts, is the bronze horse, *San Marco II,* by Ludovico de Luigi, a replica of one of the four famous horses atop the Cathedral of San Marco in Venice. If you would like to see how the Metra station was incorporated into the complex, take the escalator in the open arcade leading to the Stock Exchange and walk south to the unobtrusive eight-track platform of the line that serves commuters as far away as Joliet.

The plaza affords excellent views of the Loop and the Chicago Board of Trade Annex. It also is a good vantage point to examine Daniel Burnham's Insurance Exchange Building which stands to the left of the Board of Trade, with an impressive cornice with acroteria. On returning to Van Buren Street, note the single-story building on the west side of the plaza, constructed as part of the complex, which houses a retail women's clothing shop.

Return to Van Buren Street and continue north on S. Financial Place (formerly called Sherman Street), noting the fifth-floor skybridge and its tubular steel T-support, connecting the CBOE with the Board of Trade Annex across Van Buren Street above the El.

Before arriving at the Board of Trade Building, take a moment to note the **Board of Trade Annex** (*1980, Murphy/Jahn, with Shaw & Associates, and Swanke, Hayden, Connell*), situated directly behind the Board of Trade and connected to it (entrance on Van Buren Street). While the 24-story structure

Financial Plaza's centerpiece is a modern replica of one of the bronze horses atop the Cathedral of San Marco in Venice. The pleasant plaza was created by the closing of S. Financial Place (formerly Sherman Street) between W. Van Buren Street and W. Congress Parkway. To the right is One Financial Place, an office tower connected by a pedestrian bridge to the Chicago Board Options Exchange. At the rear is the distinctive triangular gable atop Philip Johnson's 190 S. LaSalle Street Building. (Photo by author)

The powerful bronze equine sculpture by Ludovico de Luigi, San Marco II, is set on a fountain in front of One Financial Place. (Photo by author)

reflects the profile of the main building, including its pyramidal roof (visible only at a distance), the Annex's postmodern facade of black, green, and silver is in sharp contrast. Take a peek into the lobby and atrium, which as you will presently see, is a harmonious extension of the main lobby of the Board of Trade and complements the Art Deco motifs most gracefully. A highlight of the building is the second lobby and atrium on the 12th floor, itself 12 stories high under a 4-story pyramidal skylight. Take the elevator up to see the huge mural, *Ceres,* by John W. Norton, which was moved from its original location in the main building's trading room.

A *new* **Board of Trade Annex Building** is rising just east of the present Annex Building, between LaSalle and Clark streets and north of Van Buren Street, and will be connected to it by a bridge over LaSalle Street, with the entrance at 335 S. LaSalle Street. Designed by Fujikawa, Johnson & Associates, the new building is scheduled to be completed in early 1997.

Turn right on leaving the Board of Trade Annex, and look briefly across LaSalle Street at the **Insurance Exchange Building** (*1912, D. H. Burnham & Company; south section: 1928, Graham, Anderson, Probst & White*), 175 W. Jackson Boulevard. An impressive example of the work of Burnham's firm, its facade is sheathed in enameled brick, with ornate terra-cotta adornments. Graham, Anderson, Probst & White became the successor firm to D. H. Burnham & Company; according to the *AIA Guide to Chicago,* architect Ernest R. Graham was part owner of the building, and its success enabled him to endow the Graham Foundation for Advanced Studies in the Fine Arts. (GAP&W were also the architects of more than 40 major Chicago buildings, including the Merchandise Mart, the Wrigley Building, Union Station, Chicago Historical Society, and the Field Museum of Natural History.)

Turn right on exiting the Annex and continue north on S. Financial Place as it zigzags around the corner of Jackson Boulevard, to the main entrance of the Chicago Board of Trade.

For 45 years, the imposing 45-story **Chicago Board of Trade Building** (*1930, Holabird & Root; addition 1980, Murphy/Jahn, with Shaw & Associates and Swanke, Hayden, Connell*), 141 W. Jackson Boulevard, reigned as the tallest building in Chicago, until it was dethroned by the Prudential Building in 1955 (*see* page 169). The building replaced an earlier Board of Trade, erected in 1885 and razed in 1929. Since the exterior can be appreciated only at a distance, a description will be given later. In the meantime, enter the building and enjoy the superb abstract sculptural quality of the Art Deco ornament—the craftsmanship of Gilbert Hall, chief designer of Holabird & Root. Note the effect of passing through the low entrance corridor into this three-story-high lobby with its striking dark and light color marbles and soft, diffused light reflected from the translucent glass fixtures. Take the escalator or elevator to the fifth floor Visitors' Center. The enormous Grain Exchange room, once the largest in the world, was unfortunately divided in half horizontally to provide for a separate financial-instruments trading facility. The Chicago Board of Trade, founded in

(Left) Once the tallest building in the city, the Chicago Board of Trade presents a dramatic backdrop to the LaSalle Street "Canyon of Commerce." The 45-story building is a textbook example of fine Art Deco styling. Perched atop the peaked roof is a statue of Ceres. (Photo by author)

1848 to facilitate the buying and selling of grain, is the nation's oldest futures and options exchange, dealing mainly in wheat, corn, oats, soybeans, and long-term financial instruments such as U.S. treasury bonds, municipal bonds, and even air-pollution allowance credits!

A visit to the trading floor is one of the most popular features of Chicago city tours. The best time for a visit is 15 minutes prior to the opening of the Exchange, at 9:15 A.M., when a lecture and short film are presented, followed by the opening of microphones from the floor, permitting visitors not only to see but hear the wondrous cacaphony from the trading floor below. The tempo of trading is most frenetic at the opening, and again just before the close at 1:30 P.M. Shorter presentations are offered every half hour in between, but the mikes are turned on only at the first and at the last presentation at 12:30 P.M. (For further information, call 435-3590 before 1:15 P.M.) While on the fifth floor, it is possible to walk across the skybridge to the Board of Trade Options Exchange, the CBOE. Inquire at the Visitors' Center.

Before exploring Chicago's great "Canyon of Commerce," take a few steps north until the entire facade of the Chicago Board of Trade Building comes into view. As a striking backdrop to the towering walls of LaSalle Street's unbroken row of financial institutions, the 45-story structure presents a text-book example of the finest in Art Deco styling. The nine-story base is graced

The 32-foot-tall aluminum statue of Ceres, Roman goddess of grain—appropriate to the Board of Trade's role as the major American grain exchange—is faceless. Sculptor John Storrs must have assumed that the facial features of a statue 309 feet above the street would not be discernable from below. At the top of the building are high-relief sculptures and interesting low-relief details that are not easily seen from the street. (Photo by author)

by two carved figures that represent trade, set above an elegant clock, with the name of the institution in bold letters below. On each side are projections which rise 13 stories with twin vertical rows of windows in the center, marked by dark-colored spandrels which augment the impression of height. Above this setback rises a wide tower whose verticality is emphasized by continuous piers and unbroken rows of windows. Tight massing occurs toward the top, leading the eye to the pyramidal cap which is graced by a 32-foot aluminum statue of Ceres, the Roman goddess of grain, harvest, and plenty. Standing 309 feet above the ground, the sculpture, by John Storrs, is an appropriate symbol for the world's busiest grain exchange. An amusing sidelight to the design of the statue is its complete lack of facial details. The story goes that nobody would ever be high enough on any neighboring building to be able see its face—a strange conclusion, given the completion that year of many almost-as-tall buildings in Chicago. (And is it possible that the sculptor had forgotten that there were such things as binoculars?) Pick up a copy of Frank Norris's powerful novel, *The Pit* (1903), to learn about the fascinating machinations of the big-time Grain Exchange traders of a bygone era.

On the west side of the street is the **Federal Reserve Bank of Chicago** (*1922, Graham, Anderson, Probst & White*), 230 S. LaSalle Street. The 25-story headquarters of the Seventh Federal Reserve District is graced by six large Corinthian columns which support a simple pediment. Not visible are the three below-ground levels which contain the secure vaults. An addition to the huge limestone structure on the southwest was erected in 1957, by Naess & Murphy, and in 1989, a northwest section was added by Holabird & Root, as well as a major renovation of the building itself. All paper currency issued by the Federal Reserve Bank of Chicago can be identified by the letter *G* on the face.

Directly opposite is the **Continental Illinois National Bank & Trust Company Building** (*1924, Graham, Anderson, Probst & White*), a harmonious, 19-story white limestone Classical match to the architects' Federal Reserve Bank, except for the six columns in the Ionic order. Formerly known as the Illinois Merchants Bank, it was Chicago's oldest bank until its demise in 1984. A visit to the interior (on a weekday) is a must. Take the escalator to the second level, and see the Glory that was Rome! Like the Temple of Zeus, minus only the great god himself, the bank was designed, according to Louis Sullivan, with "no extravagance unturned." The Classic opulence of the two-story-high grand banking room flanked by 28 Ionic columns also prompted Sullivan's oft-quoted comment that "here bankers wear togas and speak Latin." Note, too, the murals in the frieze by Jules Guerin, depicting themes of world populations and the buildings of the 1893 World's Columbian Exposition. (It was Guerin who drew the architectural renderings for Burhham's 1909 Plan of Chicago.) When completed, this building and the Federal Reserve Bank across the street together provided a new and memorable Classic gateway to Chicago's financial center. A former Board of Trade Building, designed by William W. Boyington (the architect of the Old Chicago Water Tower), stood on the same site from 1885 to 1928, and added its own dramatic presence to the end of LaSalle Street.

Before continuing up LaSalle Street, peek around the corner of the Continental Illinois Bank, on the Jackson Boulevard side, to see the interesting plaque commemorating **the adoption of the standard time system in the United States,** October 11, 1883. The ceremony which established the four time zones, resolving what had become an impossibly chaotic situation nationwide, took place in the elegant Grand Pacific Hotel, which occupied the entire block from Jackson Boulevard to Adams Street, between Clark and Dearborn streets. A predecessor Grand Pacific Hotel on the site was about to open its doors when it was consumed in the Great Fire of 1871.

(If you are on tour at the moment, you may want to skip the following brief account of the Great Fire and read it at leisure.)

About the Great Chicago Fire.   During a particularly stifling and dry summer and fall of 1871, Chicago had been plagued by a series of fires. On Sunday, October 8, a warm southwest wind began to blow. During the previous 24 hours exhausted firemen had been fighting a major fire that destroyed four blocks along the Chicago River, at the site of the present Central Post Office. Meanwhile, in a stable behind the Patrick and Catherine O'Leary house, at 558 S. De Koven Street, about a quarter-mile west, a fire broke out at about 8:45 P.M. and

The Victorian-style Grand Pacific Hotel rose from the ashes of the Great Fire of 1871 after the original hotel was burned to the ground just days after its grand opening. Designed by Wiliam W. Boyington, the new hotel was the site of the adoption of the standard time system in the United States. The western half of the Grand Pacific was razed ca. 1895 to make way for the Illinois Trust & Savings Bank Building. The eastern half was remodeled by Jenney & Mundie and continued in operation until torn down for the construction in 1924 of the present Continental Illinois National Bank & Trust Company. (Chicago Historical Society)

(Above and below) The devastation of the Great Fire of 1871 is apparent in these two views of the ruins of the original Grand Pacific Hotel. (Chicago Historical Society)

spread rapidly. There is no evidence to prove that Mrs. O'Leary's cow kicked over a kerosene lantern, but it *was* the overturned lamp that ignited the hay.

The increasingly strong wind blew the ensuing flames in a northeast direction away from the O'Leary House (which never even caught fire), and within an hour the spreading blaze had reached the river, setting mills and furniture factories ablaze, and overwhelming the valiant fire companies that fought in vain to contain what had become a major conflagration. At midnight the fire leaped the river, racing inexorably forward, both eastward toward the lakefront and northward through the financial heart of the city. Thousands of poor workers abandoned their homes before the onslaught and fled in panic ahead of the growing wall of flames, joined by wealthier residents whose town houses and mansions on the East Side were also threatened.

The inferno then raged quickly into the heart of the city, consuming the banks, the Board of Trade, the many grand hotels (including the "fireproof" Palmer House), stores, theatres, opera houses, newspaper offices, churches, and even the courthouse, whose bell could be heard tolling above the roar of the fire. The fire also surged up along S. Water Street (now S. Wacker Drive), devouring all the riverfront warehouses, docks, and ships. The fleeing populace, both rich and poor, pushed north toward the main branch of the Chicago River, seeking to escape to safety on the north side, as they clogged streets and bridges, lugging whatever possessions they could save, either on their backs, or if lucky, in a cart. Looting was rampant; drunks, sotted with liquor stolen from abandoned taverns, staggered about; lost children screamed for their parents. The scene was complete chaos.

The holocaust had by now become a fire storm, feeding on itself as it engulfed block after block in rapid succession. The fire's churning whirlwind then began blowing sparks and flaming debris across the river, setting fire to more buildings and forcing the refugees again to flee onward. By midnight the next day, it started to rain, and the fire, which had spread as far north as the Water Tower, just over two miles from its starting point, slowly began to burn itself out. Within hours it was over, leaving one-third of the city a vast smoldering wasteland. Three and a quarter square miles of downtown Chicago were destroyed, 300 citizens lost their lives, 100,000 were left homeless, 18,000 buildings vanished, almost $200 million of property, or 30 percent of the total city property value was wiped out, and many irreplaceable art objects, historical documents, and financial and real estate records were lost forever.

At the next block north (Quincy Street), look west to the elevated **Quincy CTA Station.** In refurbishing the Loop El lines in 1988, the Chicago Transit Authority decided to restore this station to its original 1897 appearance. Under the direction of the city's Bureau of Architecture of the Department of Public Works, the original pressed sheet metal and wood framing and paneling was restored or replicated. If time permits, climb the two flights of stairs to see the shiny woodwork and ornamental metalwork. Another flight will bring you to the train platform, but it will cost you a fare. Unfortunately, none of the original 1897 trains has survived. A trip around the Loop by train is a pleasant way to

The recently restored Quincy CTA El Station was made to appear as it did when opened in 1897. Constructed of pressed sheet metal and wood framing and paneling, it displays low-relief Georgian-style pilasters, wreaths, and windows. (Photo by author)

see the city from another perspective. (Take the Orange Line; or from June through September, take one of the new Loop Tour Trains, co-sponsored by the City's Department of Cultural Affairs. Buy tickets at the Cultural Center, 78 E. Washington Street [$5.00 adult, $2.50 under 12]. Board at Randolph/Wabash station. Trains every 40 minutes; call 836-7000 for schedule.)

At the northwest corner of Quincy and LaSalle streets is the 20-story **208 S. LaSalle Street Building** (*1914, Graham, Burnham & Company*). Formerly the City National Bank & Trust Building, and originally the Continental & Commercial Bank, it is an even earlier Classic Revival–style monolith than the pair of buildings to the south, and one of the first financial skyscrapers on the street. The street-level arcade of eight fluted Doric columns is of granite, decorated with ornate rosettes in the spandrels, while a similar colonnade above serves as a support for the now missing cornice. The base is of limestone, with terra-cotta cladding on the walls.

It is interesting to note that in these two blocks of the LaSalle Street "financial canyon," the three main Classic orders are represented: Federal Reserve Bank (Corinthian), Continental Illinois National Bank (Ionic), and 208 S. LaSalle (Doric).

One of the most extraordinary and noteworthy buildings in the nation is **The Rookery Building** (*1885–1888, Daniel H. Burnham and John Wellborn Root; renovation of light court by Frank Lloyd Wright, 1907; remodeling of* *lobby and elevators by William Drummond, 1931; remodeling of ground floor by Graham, Anderson, Probst & White, 1972; renovations by Booth/Hansen &*

Associates, 1987; comprehensive restoration and rehabilitation by McClier Cor-poration, with T. Gunny Harboe, preservation architect, 1988–1992), 209 S. LaSalle Street. Many Chicagoans consider the Rookery their favorite building, and small wonder, for it epitomizes the work of some of its greatest architects and in many ways captures the spirit of the city. The construction of the build-ing presented serious challenges for co-architect John Wellborn Root, since the soft clay subsurface could not support a heavy masonry structure. To solve the problem he devised a crisscross system of rails imbedded in cement, forming a sort of floating foundation, reminiscent of Adler's foundation for the Audito-rium Building. Except for the side facing Quincy Court, in which he designed a somewhat primitive wrought-iron frame, the entire building is load-bearing.

The exterior of the 11-story bold Richardsonian Romanesque–style build-ing, which had been commissioned by the Central Safety Deposit Company, rests on a two-story rusticated granite base, with alternating stone columns and windows. The dark-red facade is adorned with sculptured terra cotta, with an imposing arched entry and slender tourelles above the central bay and at the four corners. The entire facade is divided into four horizontal bays, with the LaSalle Street side divided into two 4-window sections, with a prominent cen-tral bay rising to the full height of the building. Among the decorative design motifs are a pair of rooks carved into the granite columns bracketing the LaSalle Street entrance. The rook is a European cousin to the crow, but the ori-gin of the name actually hearkens back to the predecessor building on the site, a temporary City Hall, built in 1872, a year after the Great Fire. That somewhat seedy building, built around an old water tank, became a popular haunt for politicians, as well as a favorite roosting place for pigeons, and with the reputa-tion of officeholders for "rooking" the public, the name was a natural and was inherited by the present building.

The interior is an absolute delight! The square central light court is illumi-nated by a skylight above the second story, which not only creates an airy and cheerful courtyard, but also provides light for the interior office spaces. An exquisite cantilevered cast-iron oriel staircase climbs from the second level to the top, and leading up from the ground level is a grand staircase whose wrought iron balustrade is duplicated in the mezzanine. Among its innovations, the Rookery utilized the new hydraulic passenger elevator and employed extensive plate glass and fireproof materials throughout. In its early years it was considered the most modern of office buildings, and it became one of the coun-try's first retail arcades. The great achievements of partners Burnham and Root soon led to their being appointed the architectural directors for the 1893 World's Columbian Exposition.

The first remodeling took place in 1905 when Frank Lloyd Wright, who had briefly maintained an office in the building in 1888–1889, redesigned the lobby and atrium, replaced the light fixtures, and exchanged some of the ironwork and terra-cotta ornament with gold and white marble, using designs of his own. He also redid the mezzanine's iron staircase, substituting one of marble and adding huge marble planters at the base. Through the years there were other renovations, including one in 1931 by William Drummond, in which a double

Many Chicagoans consider the Rookery Building their favorite. The landmark 11-story bold Richardsonian Romanesque structure was designed by Daniel H. Burnham and John Wellborn Root, and completed in 1888. In 1907 Frank Lloyd Wright remodeled the light court. The dark red facade is adorned with sculptural terra cotta, with an imposing arched entry and slender tourelles mounted above the central bay and on the four corners. (Commission on Chicago Landmarks)

The interior of the Rookery is a surprising delight. The square central light court is lit from a skylight above. A unique feature is the exquisite cast-iron oriel staircase that climbs from the second floor to the top. (Photo by author)

lobby level was created and the mechanical systems were upgraded; but gradually the building began to deteriorate, and its future became problematic. By 1982 the original lease of the Central Safety Deposit Company expired, and the Rookery Building reverted to the City of Chicago.

In 1989, developer Thomas Baldwin, a dedicated preservationist, whose company had acquired the building the year before, recognized the architectural merit and historical significance of the Rookery; and despite a soft real estate market and the "burden" of landmark status in rehabilitating a property, he commited himself to a multimillion-dollar renovation to return the building to its turn-of-the-century appearance. The ambitious project required restoring all of the Rookery's historic features, including returning the exterior to its original reddish tone, even the investment of a million dollars to replicate the mosaic floor from 1888 photographs. On May 6, 1992, with the completion of cleaning and restoration by the McClier Corporation, the Rookery was once again opened to commercial tenants, and the City of Chicago regained a splendid architectural treasure as well as a unique "window on the past." Confirmation of Chicagoans love for the old building came in a recent *Chicago Tribune* Real Estate Section contest to pick the city's favorite historic property and favorite lobby. The Rookery won first place in both categories.

On the northeast corner of LaSalle and Adams streets looms the 43-story **135 S. LaSalle Street Building** (*1934, Graham, Anderson, Probst & White*). Originally built as a commercial venture by the Marshall Field Estate, it was first called the **Field Building,** and later the LaSalle Bank Building. The limestone structure was designed by GAP&W's Alfred P. Shaw. It is laid out in the traditional "H" form, with four 22-story corner sections framing a 43-story tower and a decorative band course around the building above the first floor unifying the base. The central shaft's strong verticality is emphasized by alternating limestone piers and window tiers with recessed spandrels, plus lofty setbacks. Its two-story lobby contains one of the city's first and fairly uncommon block-through arcades, and is decorated with attractive Art Moderne motifs set in polished black granite. Note, too, the nickel silver fixtures and the bronze mail chute with its low relief of the original Field Building. The balconies on the north and south are connected by shiny Art Deco bridges.

Perhaps more important than the building itself, is the fact that it occupies **the site of William LeBaron Jenney's Home Insurance Company Building,** considered the world's first steel-framework skyscraper, erected in 1884 and demolished in 1931. The 10-story building was framed entirely in steel, sheathed with a "curtain wall" of brick or masonry, as opposed to the former thick, load-bearing masonry walls which severely limited a structure's height. Cast-iron skeletons had been used for a number of years before the advent of structural steel, but iron had too many limiting characteristics. The steel frame, which permitted thinner walls and larger windows, resulted in a building of but one-fifth the weight of its load-bearing counterpart, and its steel columns enclosed in brick greatly improved its fireproof quality. The Home Insurance Company Building was also the first skyscraper with an elevator. With Jenney's new building technology firmly established, the skyscraper was born, and from then on, the "sky" was the limit.

Before continuing northward on LaSalle Street, take a short detour left (west) on Adams Street to:

The Midland Hotel (*1926, Vitzthum & Burns*), 172 W. Adams Street. One of only three major hotels remaining in the Loop (the Palmer House Hilton and the Bismark are the others), the Midland still exudes Old-World charm. The facade is completely rusticated to the top of its 22 stories, with a four-story base and matching pavilion above. The lobby is noteworthy for its barrel-vaulted ceiling and particularly the vaults over the mezzanine which are covered with low-relief plaster ornament. In the lobby to the left is a glass display case exhibiting ornamental artifacts from buildings by Louis H. Sullivan, Frank Lloyd Wright, and others. Peek into the mirrored Presidential Ballroom with its elaborate crystal chandeliers.

Return to LaSalle Street, and stand on the east side (or even back up a bit further east down Adams Street) for a good view of:

The 40-story, postmodern **190 S. LaSalle Street Building** (*1987, John Burgee Architects and Philip Johnson, with Shaw Associates*) makes a bold statement. Huge granite arches in the base lead the eye upward to the copper-clad roof topped by six crested free-standing gables. The novel design, according to the architects, is sensitive to its environment and contextual with its

William LeBaron Jenney's Home Insurance Company Building is considered the world's first steel-frame skyscraper. (Two floors were added to the original 10-story building prior to this ca. 1920 photo.) Erected in 1884 on the northeast corner of LaSalle and Adams streets, it survived until 1931 when it was replaced by the Field Building. (Courtesy of the Art Institute of Chicago)

The Home Insurance Company Building was the first skyscraper equipped with elevators. In this ca. 1930 photo, a trio of visitors examines the highly ornate elevator bank. (Courtesy of the Art Institute of Chicago)

The S. LaSalle Street skyline presents a study in contrasting architectural styles: In the foreground, D. H. Burnham & Company's Classic Revival Insurance Exchange Building (1912); on the right, Holabird & Root's Art Deco Chicago Board of Trade (1930); in the center, the top of Perkins & Will and C. F. Murphy Associates' modern First National Bank Building (1969); and on the left, Philip Johnson's graceful postmodern 190 S. LaSalle Street (1986). (Photo by author)

older, more traditional neighbors, as well as with the history of Chicago. The "Richardsonian" arches and red granite reflect the facade of the Rookery Building, the vertical rows of punched-out windows recall those in the shafts of the earlier limestone skyscrapers on the street, and the pointed gables are a direct reference to Burnham and Root's fancifully gabled Masonic Temple (1892), which stood, not on this site, but at the southwest corner of State and Randolph streets until 1939 (*see* photo on page 91). The Johnson/Burgee partnership is credited with creating the first new designs to break with the tradition of the ubiquitous "glass box," the style popularized by Mies van der Rohe in the 1950s (although it was Philip Johnson, together with architectural historian Henry-Russell Hitchcock, who first introduced the International style in the United States in 1932, at the famous "International Style Show" at the Museum of Modern Art in New York). The 190 S. LaSalle Street building is Johnson's only structure in Chicago.

Cross the street and enter the sumptuous marble-clad vaulted lobby, with its light and dark Botticino marble floor and red Alicante marble highlighting the walls. The gold leaf on the ceiling is set off by a rich wraparound marble molding which conceals soft indirect lighting. Don't miss the huge wall tapestry by Helena Hernmarck, which represents the famous 1909 Burnham Plan of Chicago.

Just to the north is **120 S. LaSalle Street** (*1928, Graham, Anderson, Probst & White*), once the Bank of Chicago Building, now occupied by the LaSalle Bank as a major tenant. A typical Classic Revival–style building in the

GAP&W tradition, it boasts four fluted Ionic columns on the LaSalle Street facade.

Across the street, on the southeast corner of LaSalle and Monroe streets, is the **Harris Trust & Savings Bank** (*East Tower: 1911, Shepley, Rutan & Coolidge; renovation 1960, Skidmore, Owings & Merrill; West Tower: 1974, Skidmore, Owings & Merrill*), 115 S. LaSalle Street and 111 W. Monroe Street. Here is a dramatic contrast between the traditional "bank style" and the International style, with both parts neatly intertwined. The older, red granite building's 20 stories are almost dwarfed by the two newer stainless-steel additions which rise 23 and 38 stories, respectively. Note how three stories of the five-story base are recessed behind Ionic columns. Interesting is the treatment of the windows of the East Tower with thin stainless-steel mullions that enliven the otherwise bland glass panels, while on the West Tower, the windows are wider, with large spandrels that emphasize horizontality.

On the plaza, a tiered-bronze fountain by Russell Secrest (1975) pours its waters over pedestals in the shape of flower petals. Take a few steps further to where the 111 W. Monroe Street building projects out a few feet onto the sidewalk, and notice the huge bronze plaque—a kind of elegant "cornerstone"—with a low-relief sculpture of a lion, together with the original date of construction, 1910. Then return to LaSalle Street.

Across Monroe Street, on the northeast corner, is one of the oldest buildings in the "canyon," **39 S. LaSalle Street** (*1894, eastern half 1898 Jenney & Mundie; additional story 1903, architect unknown*). One of the earliest steel-frame structures, it is said that during construction, sections of the "curtain wall" were attached to the frame at different levels at the same time, instead of systematically from below—a "first" in skyscraper construction.

One of Chicago's most imposing "cornerstones" is this bronze plaque with low-relief lion marking the 1910 date of construction of the Harris Trust & Savings Bank Building. The plaque is set to the right of the 111 W. Monroe Street entrance. (Photo by author)

Across LaSalle Street, on the northwest corner is **The Northern Trust Company Building** (*1905, Frost & Granger; two-story roof addition 1928, Frost & Henderson*), 50 S. LaSalle Street. A rather attractive Classic-style building, its solid granite facade is topped by a colonnade. To the west, on the Monroe Street side, a more modern addition was designed in overall harmony with the main bank building. Look for the little plaque on the Monroe Street side indicating that this is the "Number One City Datum," from which all heights in the city are measured.

At **19 S. LaSalle Street** (*1893, Jenney & Mundie*), the Association Building, also known as the Central YMCA Building, is another early design by the partnership which designed 39 S. LaSalle Street a year earlier, and whose guiding spirit was William LeBaron Jenney. It shows clearly his characteristic horizontal-band treatment. To the right, little Arcade Place has been repaved with cobblestones, with an archway above, and illuminated by antique-style lamps.

Adjacent to the north is **11 S. LaSalle Street** (*1915, Holabird & Roche*), originally built as the Roanoke Building and later renamed the Lumber Exchange Building, hearkening back to the time when lumber was a major commodity shipped through Chicago. The very attractive commercial building began its life as a 16-story structure, and in 1922 the same architects added another five floors, duplicating the original roof cornice. The attractive arches at the fourth floor were once repeated at the top, but disappeared in the renovation. A tower with setbacks was added four years later by the combined efforts of additional architects, primarily Andrew M. Rebori, and duplicated the vertical rows of paired windows on the main elevation. In 1984 another renovation, by Hammond, Beeby & Babka (designers of the Harold Washington Library Center) restored some of the original details which had been destroyed in a 1950 "remuddling," but now with a postmodern look.

Chemical Plaza (*1989, Moriyama & Teshima*), 10 S. LaSalle Street, displays a rather interesting feature. To conform to the LaSalle Street "wall," the architects chose to preserve the four-story ornate granite base of the former Otis Building (1912, Holabird & Roche) and place a modern office tower on top of it. The upper 35-story facade of blue-painted aluminum and glass, highlighted in light green, boasts a striking seven-story semicircular entranceway; and from the 19th story upward, a single row of bay windows.

Madison Street is the dividing line between north and south addresses. (State Street to the east divides east and west addresses.)

On the northeast corner of LaSalle and Madison streets, **1 N. LaSalle Street** (*1930, Vitzthum & Sons*) displays the typical planar qualities of the Art Deco style, with vertical strips of windows emphasizing the verticality of this 49-story limestone skyscraper. At the fifth floor are relief panels commemorating **Robert Cavalier, Sieur de LaSalle,** the early explorer who visited this site in 1679, and for whom the street is named. The building replaced the 13-story Tacoma Building (1889–1929), one of Chicago's tallest iron-frame buildings, and an early commission by Holabird & Roche.

On the northwest corner, **2 N. LaSalle Street** (*1979, Perkins & Will*) was erected on the foundations of the old Hotel LaSalle (not visible from the exterior). The sleek facade displays alternating bands of flush windows and aluminum panels, with rounded corners that carry the design smoothly around to the Madison Street side. At the second-floor level are windowless corners that indicate the location of the transfer beams that tie the new structure to the old foundation. The old Hotel LaSalle was the site of the worst hotel fire in Chicago history, when early on the morning of June 6, 1946, 61 guests perished in a blaze whose cause was never determined.

Turn right (east) for a brief detour to the church in the middle of the block, on the north side of Madison Street.

St. Peter's Roman Catholic Church "in the Loop" (*1953, Vitzthum & Burns*), 110 W. Madison Street, occupying the site of the old LaSalle Theatre, was built to serve Catholic workers in the Loop and visitors to the city. The building, nestled between tall commercial office towers, is a strong presence on the block. Dominating the five-story marble facade and set in front of a Gothic-arch stained-glass window, is what may be the largest stone crucifix in the Midwest, *Christ of the Loop.* Eighteen feet tall and weighing 26 tons, it is the work of sculptor Arvid Strauss. The interior, which is open to the public, contains a large open sanctuary, designed in basilica style, sheathed in marble, with a huge baptismal font at the entrance. On the walls are artistic represen-

The once luxurious 22-story Hotel LaSalle (1909, Holabird & Roche) stood on the northeast corner of S. LaSalle and W. Madison streets. The LaSalle was the site of one of the worst hotel fires in Chicago history, when on the morning of June 6, 1946, 61 guests perished in a mysterious blaze that began in the cocktail lounge near the LaSalle Street entrance. Oddly, the hotel's public garage still functions at 219 W. Washington Street. (Chicago Historical Society)

tations of Moses, Jesus, the archangels Michael, Gabriel, and Raphael, as well as the oft-forgotten Uriel.

Return to LaSalle Street and continue west.

On the south side of Madison Street, just beyond Chemical Plaza, rises the 50-story postmodern **Paine Webber Tower** (*1990, Cesar Pelli and Associates*), 181 W. Madison Street. Expressing bold verticality, truncated setbacks on the white granite tower add to the effect. An unusual touch is the use of reflective metal mullions projecting from the windows with nickel-plated finials above. Enter the building under the steel-frame "marqee," into the cavernous five-story vaulted lobby and gaze at the coffered ceiling and the huge low-relief sculptures by Frank Stella that dominate each end, *Loomings* and *Knights and Squires.* The developers of the building, Miglin and Beitler, asked architect Pelli to design the 100-foot-long marble-clad lobby to serve as a public exhibition space for Stella's pair of sculptures. The sleek building's exterior design is somewhat reminiscent of the one submitted by Eliel Saarinen in the Chicago Tribune Tower Competition in 1922, which took second prize. (*See* 333 N. Michigan Avenue, pages 165–166; and Tribune Tower, pages 221–222.)

The same developers have also filed plans to build what would be the world's tallest skyscraper, the Miglin-Beitler Tower, just to the east, at Wells and Madison streets. If they ever go ahead with it, the proposed tower would be 1,950 feet high, about 500 feet taller than the Sears Tower! Although approval has been granted by the Federal Aviation Administration, and there would be no danger to planes using O'Hare and Midway airports, it remains to be seen if the softening real estate market and current state of the economy will allow Miglin and Beitler to obtain the necessary financing for such a behemoth. Given the occupancy problems of the Sears tower, the project at this writing seems rather unlikely.

Continue west on Madison Street. Cross Wells Street (under the El) to the northwest corner.

Madison Plaza (*1982, Skidmore, Owings & Merrill*), 200 W. Madison Street, with its bold, serrated front, offers a distinctive and exciting treatment of the curtain wall. The steel-frame building was partially prefabricated to expedite construction. Its exterior is essentially a steel tube clad with alternating bands of gray granite and silver reflective glass. (The energy efficiency of its glazing was recognized with an award.) The roof slopes backward at an angle at the 39th floor, rising to the 50th-story top floor. The site plan with its recessed plaza provides an ideal setting for Louise Nevelson's *Dawn Shadows* (1983), a 30-foot-tall steel sculpture painted in her favorite color, black. It represents her impression of the elevated train as it curves around the Loop, and can be appreciated from many angles, *en face,* in the reflections of the faceted glass wall, or from above on the elevated train platform.

The serrated facade of Skidmore, Owings & Merrill's Madison Plaza, at 200 W. Madison Street, presents an attractive backdrop for Louise Nevelson's 30-foot-tall steel sculpture Dawn Shadows *(1983), painted in her favorite matte-black color. (Photo by author)*

Walk to the southeast corner of Franklin Street.

On the north facade of the corner building (1 S. Franklin Street), the **Jewish Federation Building,** is a bronze relief, *The Spirit of Jewish Philanthropy,* by Milton Horn, (1958).

On the northeast corner looms **1 N. Franklin Street** (*1991, Skidmore, Owings & Merrill*). These tower elements have been compared to giant bookends. Step back a short distance to gain a better perspective of the building and its neighbor to the north. The most interesting aspect of this 38-story cast-stone structure is the vertical window arrangement—ranks of paired windows on each side, with a "column" of single windows, drawing the eye to the circular towers at the top, framing the central dark-glass section. The base is clad in Rainbow granite, with glassed-in corners cantilevered over the pedestrian walk.

Turn right (north), and immediately to the north is the slightly older **225 N. Washington Street** (*1987, Skidmore, Owings & Merrill*). Here again the windows are particularly significant. As a tripartite building (with base, shaft, and capital), the 28-story tower stands on a polished red-granite "base" enclosing a pedestrian arcade. Its windows, reminiscent of the Chicago school, are set in the "shaft," surrounded by concrete aggregate trimmed in red granite which express the building's steel grid. At the top, a recessed three-bay-wide arcade forms the "capital." (The traditional Chicago window has a wide central pane bracketed by narrower double-hung windows.) Vaulted arches mark the Franklin and Washington Street entrances, although the Washington Street arch is a fake! In comparing the two buildings, note the polychromatic contrasts between the windows, stone surfaces, and bases of each.

Turn right (east) on Washington Street, to the middle of the block.

The **Hotel LaSalle Public Garage** (*1919, Holabird & Roche*), 219 W. Washington Street, is an interesting holdover from the early age of the automobile. Although the Hotel is long since gone (its site was noted at 2 N. LaSalle Street), the building still serves its original purpose. Five stories high and 15 bays wide (five were added in 1923 by the same architects), it preserves many pleasant details: the dark-purple brick highlighted by black Roman brick striping, sharply detailed spandrel panels, a stringcourse, and cornice. Ignore the latter-day accretion on the roof.

At the corner, the **Washington Block** (*1874, Frederick & Edward Baumann*), 40 N. Wells Street, is a charming anachronism. Built three years after the Great Fire, the five-story structure is characteristic of the more fire-resistant commercial masonry buildings that replaced the earlier wood structures consumed in the holocaust. Note the ornate corner cornice, Italianate lintels, and other "Victoriana" typical of the so-called neo-Grec style which was so popular in the 1870s.

Turn right at Wells Street and walk south to the parking lot.

Assuming that progress has not yet destroyed a few vestiges of the past, look through the parking lot at the wall of the garage. Barely visible is a hundred-year-old sign advertising "Hides, Pelts, and Tallow." On the roof are old wooden water tanks, and also on the wall are the ghost outlines of former attached buildings.

Return to Washington Street, and turn right (east).

The 12-story **180 W. Washington Street Building** (*1929, Hyland & Corse*), once known as the Equitable Building, has an attractive terra-cotta facade with ornamental columns and colonnettes that rise to decorative pediments.

Just to the east, at No. 176, is the former Elks Club Headquarters Building, now the **"I Am Temple,"** (*1916, Ottenheimer, Stern & Reichert*). Both buildings are best seen from across the street. The facade and window treatment is particularly interesting, and is the work of the Viennese design architect Rudolph Schindler. The "I Am" Religious Activity of the Saint Germain Foundation was founded in the early 1930s by Mr. & Mrs. Guy W. Ballard, who according to the organization, were chosen by Saint Germain "to serve as the 'Open Door' through which the 'I AM' *Ascended Master Instruction* could be given to mankind." The building was purchased from the Elks Club in 1948. Visitors are welcome.

Across the street, **175 W. Washington Street** (*1933, N. Max Dunning*) is a pleasant addition to the streetscape. The Bedford limestone building is the headquarters of the Chicago Federation of Musicians. Although not immediately detectable, a third story was added in 1949, appropriately in complete harmony with the original structure.

Continue east to the corner of LaSalle Street.

On the southeast corner, the 38-story **American National Bank Building** (*1930, Graham, Anderson, Probst & White*), 33 N. LaSalle Street, presents a rather eclectic facade. Designed originally in Art Deco style for the now-defunct Foreman State National Bank, it is built on a rose granite base upon which rests a limestone shaft that tapers slightly at the top. Note the clock (a duplicate of the one on 1 N. LaSalle Street), the sculpturing on the base, and the hints of pediments at the fourth-floor level. In a 1971 "modernization," all the Art Deco details on the limestone shaft up to the 18th floor were stripped off in favor of a Colonial Revival treatment. (Surely there must be a place in purgatory reserved for the perpetrators of such architectural travesties.)

Just south of Washington Street, at 30 N. LaSalle Street, the 43-story blue-paneled and glass office building marks the **site of the old Chicago Stock Exchange,** designed by Dankmar Adler and Louis H. Sullivan in 1894 and demolished amid great protest in 1972. The Stock Exchange was the city's first building constructed on "Chicago" caissons, cylindrical concrete piles driven down to either hardpan or bedrock. The Trading Room is now restored and preserved in the Chicago Art Institute, and one of the Exchange's great entrance arches can be seen mounted behind the Institute, in Grant Park.

Walk north on LaSalle Street to No. 120, the astonishing **Savings of America Tower** (*Murphy/Jahn, 1992*). On a relatively narrow mid-block plot, Helmut Jahn has used stone and glass elegantly to create an atmosphere both of solidity and of lightness. The 39-story structure projects a gently curved bay of gray-tinted butt-glazed windows beginning at the sixth floor over La Salle Street, surmounting a granite-paneled trellis above the entrance loggia. The off-center design of the tower was deliberately chosen to hide the mechanical service areas behind the vertical granite-clad panels, while an abundance of light is admitted through the long horizontal bands of the window wall to the right. Crowning the summit is a four-story-high, half-vaulted curved-glass penthouse. Enter the polished-granite lobby, sheathed in alternating bands of light- and dark-gray flame-cut granite. The centerpiece is the colorful 20- by 50-foot mosaic by artist Roger Brown, *Flight of Daedalus and Icarus*. In Greek mythology, Daedalus was a skilled inventor, who when refused permission to leave Crete by King Minos, built wax and feather wings for himself and his son, and they flew off together. However, when Icarus soared too close to the sun, his wings melted and he fell to his death. His father then escaped to Sicily. In the rear of the lobby is another work, John Buck's *LaSalle Corridor and Holding Pattern,* a fanciful and stylized impression of the "Wall Street" of Chicago.

No. 160 N. LaSalle Street, the **State of Illinois Building** (*1924, Burnham Bros.; renovation and addition 1992, Holabird & Root*), was known as the Burnham Building, after its builders (the sons of Daniel H. Burnham), until the state of Illinois purchased it in 1946. The 20-story structure underwent a major renovation which filled in its former U-shaped light court and replaced it with a reflective glass curtain wall, providing more space for courtrooms and state offices. The exterior is the customary tripartite design. A "penthouse" was

(Left) The old Chicago Stock Exchange, designed by Adler & Sullivan in 1894, stood on the southwest corner of LaSalle and Washington streets. Its demolition in 1972 provoked a loud but futile public outcry, but did give impetus to the growing preservation movement. Only the entrance arch and grand iron staircase were saved. The arch now sits behind the Art Institute of Chicago in Grant Park, and the staircase is displayed in the American Wing of the Metropolitan Museum of Art in New York. A more poignant tragedy was the death of photographer/preservationist Richard Nickel, who was crushed when a floor collapsed while he was documenting the demolition. (Courtesy of the Art Institute of Chicago)

added, sheathed in matching limestone and fitted with a "proper" cornice, to accommodate new mechanical systems. The arched entry was remodeled to provide access to the renovated "Mediterranean style" skylit lobby.

Across LaSalle Street is the massive **County Building/Chicago City Hall,** built during the era when public architecture proclaimed progress and pride. Designed in 1911 from plans by Holabird & Roche, it occupies the entire block, LaSalle Street to Clark Street, and Washington Street to Randolph Street, with the entrance to City Hall at 121 N. LaSalle Street, and the County Building at 118 N. Clark Street. Accommodating the city administration in the west half and Cook County in the east, it is a splendid Classic monolith, encircled on all sides by what are arguably Chicago's largest Corinthian columns. A 24-foot-high entablature is supported by massive piers and a majestic colonnade that stands 75 feet tall, with capitals the height of a full story. The walls and ceilings of the lobby are sheathed in Botticino marble and extend the full

From the top of the Chicago Temple, the Savings of America Tower (1992, Murphy/Jahn) presents an iconoclastic but fascinating profile, adding unique punctuation to the Chicago skyline. To the right is the old Steuben Club Building at 188 W. Randolph Street (1929, Vitzhum & Burns), with its ornate telescoping buttresses, set against the dark facade of 333 W. Wacker Drive (1983), and at the extreme right, the postmodern cupola-topped 225 W. Wacker Drive (1989), the latter two by Kohn Pederson Fox with Perkins & Will. (Photo by author)

Above the lobby entrance to the Savings of America Tower is the striking 20- by 50-foot mosaic by Roger Brown, entitled Flight of Daedalus and Icarus. *(Photo by author)*

Chicago's second courthouse, designed in 1853 by the city's first architect (actually a carpenter by trade), John Mills Van Osdel, stood in the center of the block bounded by LaSalle, Clark, Randolph, and Washington streets. (The first courthouse was erected in 1835 at the corner of N. Clark and W. Randolph streets.) Renovated in 1858, the "new" courthouse was consumed 13 years later in the Great Fire. This excellent photo was made by William Shaw soon after the renovation when a new Classic-style cupola was added, as well as a small bell tower. The bell, clearly visible, was severely damaged in the fire, but was rescued by the U.S. Mint, which then melted it down to make commemorative medals of the Chicago Fire to be sold to the public the following year. (Chicago Historical Society)

Fourteen years after the second Cook County Courthouse and City Hall was destroyed in the Great Fire of 1871, a third structure, designed by Chicago city architect James J. Egan, was erected on the site. A massive and somber pile of masonry with rows of polished granite columns, it cost the taxpayers $5 million. It was torn down in 1906–1908 to be replaced by the present County Building/City Hall in 1911. Note the open trolley cars used during the city's hot summer months. (Chicago Historical Society)

width of the building, with a "crossing" at the center whose intersecting corridor runs the full length. At each end are four low-relief sculptures and along the vaulted passageways, elegant bronze lamp standards cast a warm glow.

The County Building/City Hall replaced several predecessors on the site. The first, designed by John Mills Van Osdel, was built in 1853 and was where Abraham Lincoln lay in state on May 12, 1865, on his way to ultimate burial in Springfield. Six years later it was consumed in the Great Fire. (Van Osdel, who arrived from New York in 1837, is considered Chicago's first architect.) A second, by James Egan, the Cook County architect, was begun right after the fire, but was not completed until 1885. It survived only 20 years until it was razed for Holabird & Roche's present building. The mayor's office and county board offices are located on the fifth floor, and the city council chamber on the second. (Tours of the building are available. For the schedule, inquire at the desk in the lobby.)

End of tour.

Merchandise Mart

Chicago River

E. Wacker Pl.

Haddock Pl.

Haddock Pl.

El Loop

Dearborn St. Subway

Lake St.

James R. Thompson Center

Benton Pl.

Start

ndolph St.

County Building-City Hall

Daley Plaza

Marshall Field's

Court Pl.

shington St.

Wacker Dr.

Calhoun Pl.

Wells St.

La Salle St.

Dearborn St.

Wabash Ave.

Michigan Ave.

Gra
Pa

dison St.

Franklin

Arcade Pl.

First National Plaza

Carson Pirie Scott

nroe St.

Marble Pl.

Clark St.

ams St.

Sears Tower

Quincy St

Rookery

Federal Plaza

State St. Subway

El Loop

A
Ins
o
Chic

Federal Reserve Bank

kson Blvd.

0   250   500 Ft.

Chicago Board of Trade

Monadnock Block

State St.

n Buren St.

Harold Washington Library Center

Auditorium Building

ngress Pky.

Chicago Board Options Exchange

Financial Pl.

Stock Exchange

Dearborn St. Subway

Federal Pl.

Plymouth Ct.

rrison St.

2. The Loop II: The James R. Thompson Center to State Street

The tour begins at the northwest corner of N. Clark and W. Randolph streets.

Many adjectives have been used to describe the **James R. Thompson Center,** formerly the State of Illinois Center (*1985, Murphy/Jahn with Lester B. Knight & Associates*), 100 W. Randolph Street, but "astonishing" is perhaps the most appropriate. When completed in the mid-1980s, the sentiment at the time was, "You will either love it or hate it," but in the decade or so since, people have recovered from their initial shock, and more have come to like it than dislike it. No one, however, can be neutral about it, and it remains controversial. Whether the aesthetics of its design will withstand the judgment of time remains to be seen.

Monumental in scale, the massive building, which is basically rectangular, but with a broad curved entrance, is former Governor Thompson's ambitious legacy and his proclamation of the dignity and authority of state government. The sloping and stepped-back glass and steel curvilinear facade topped by a truncated cylinder is perhaps Helmut Jahn's concept of a new-age domed government building, its tricolor scheme a patriotic reference, and the open 17-story atrium a suggestion of accessibility by the public. The Center occupies an

The astonishing James R. Thompson Center, formerly known as the State of Illinois Center, was designed by Helmut Jahn in 1985 for the offices of over 50 state agencies. Although the design has been very controversial, Chicagoans have come to accept it (and even like it), but whatever one's opinion, the building certainly cannot be ignored. Its unconventional sloping and stepped-back glass-and-steel curvilinear facade, topped by a truncated cylinder is a radical departure from any previous architectural tradition. The 160-foot-diameter circular rotunda is skylit, while free-standing elevators whisk riders to the top, offering a breathtaking view of the atrium. On the southeast corner of the plaza, and visible in front of the building, is Jean Dubuffet's 39-foot-high fiberglass sculpture Monument with Standing Beast, *with four components that suggest a standing animal, tree, portal, and architectural element. (Photo by author)*

entire block, including a broad plaza, with a conspicuous slant on the southeast side. The facade is divided into three setbacks, with a colorful interplay of opaque and clear glass, in silver, blue, and salmon. Its siting makes it the center of attraction from a great distance, and an essential component of a cityscape that includes the City Hall/County Building to the west, the Daley Civic Center to the south, and the Clark-Dearborn corridor to the east.

On the southeast corner of the plaza, a row of gradually receding granite pillars that continue outward from the building's pedestrian arcade become free-standing and pull the eye toward Jean Dubuffet's *Monument with Standing Beast*. A 29-foot-high fiberglass sculpture, it suggests a combination of an upright animal, tree, portal, and architectural component, each observed from a different viewpoint. Some visitors, unfamiliar with the style of Dubuffet, have referred irreverently to the work as "Snoopy in a Blender"; others have asked, "Which is the monument and which is the beast?"

Enter the broad rotunda with its spiral-designed marble and granite floor that continues the curving motif of the interior, and observe how the two elevator banks and escalators, which lead to the offices of over 50 state agencies, extend into the 160-foot diameter circular space. Take a dizzying ride up in one of the free-standing elevators to appreciate the wide expanse of the atrium; then go down to the lower level, where there is a food court and retail establishments. Placed about the skylit glass rotunda are 19 specially commissioned artworks funded by the State of Illinois Art-in-Architecture Program. The building has not been without some problems, however. The wide expanses of glass have created heating and ventilation problems, and the noise level and accumulation of dust have been a source of annoyance to workers in offices facing the atrium.

As you cross Clark Street, look south for a view of an unusual "Gothic skyscraper" that rises one block away: the unique Chicago Temple, which will be seen at close hand later in the tour.

On the northeast corner of Randolph and Clark streets rises the 50-story **Chicago Title & Trust Center** (*1992, Kohn Pederson Fox*), 161–171 N. Clark Street. The tall tower, with a 13-story companion annex to the left, is the first half of a planned twin-tower project to be built to the north. The annex, which will actually be part of the base, is scaled to harmonize with the City Hall/County Building, while the soaring granite and white-painted aluminum and glass shaft presents a bold, sleeker appearance. At the entrances, the "awnings" have different designs, while the top of the tower displays unique latticework rows of projecting finials, which make the building a particularly distinctive addition to the skyline. This was the last skyscraper completed in the Loop before the bubble burst in the building boom that had been going on

The 17-story Schiller Building at 64 W. Randolph Street, a splendid work by Adler and Sullivan, was erected in 1892, and once housed the Schiller Theatre, whose marquee is visible below. Both the building and the theatre were later renamed the Garrick, after the greatest English actor and stage manager of the 18th century. This fine example of the architects' genius was torn down in 1960, to be ignominiously replaced by a parking garage. (Chicago Historical Society)

since the 1920s. As with all such tall buildings crowded together in a small area, it is necessary to step back some distance to appreciate their characteristics and scale.

Adjacent to the east is the **Garrick Garage** (*1961, William M. Horowitz*), 60–64 W. Randolph Street. In a vacuous gesture to the former occupant on the site, the Schiller Building and Theatre, a splendid 1892 Adler & Sullivan masterpiece, the designer of the replacement saved and duplicated a few of the ornamental terra-cotta panels and mounted them on the concrete grill of the present parking structure. The garage is named for the successor theatre to the Schiller, the Garrick.

Continue east to the northwest corner of Dearborn Street.

Dearborn Street is named for Gen. Henry Dearborn, who was Secretary of War under President Thomas Jefferson and a congressman from Massachusetts. He fought at the Battle of Bunker Hill, helped plan the removal of the Indians west of the Mississippi, and had the famous fort here named for him. During the War of 1812 he led an ill-fated expeditionary force to invade Canada, but failed before he could even cross the border, and in the action lost the fort at Detroit. (And after that the name of Chicago's fort was still kept?)

The Garrick Garage (1961), 60–64 W. Randolph Street, is named for the building and theatre that occupied the site. Architect William W. Horowitz managed to save a few of the original building's Sullivan-designed ornamental terra-cotta plaques, and he had 232 copies made to form the screen of the front wall. An original plaque is visible in the photo projecting from the center of the second row from the bottom in the second group from the right, just above the two "Enter" signs. (Photo by author)

Across Dearborn Street stands the charming **Delaware Building** (*1874, Wheelock & Thomas; two-story addition 1888, Julius H. Huber; renovation 1982, Wilbert R. Hasbrouck*), 36 W. Randolph Street. A rare and fortunate survivor from the post-Great Fire of 1871 reconstruction era, it is possibly the oldest building in the Loop, and has been restored to its turn-of-the-century appearance. Built as the Bryant Building, and later called the Real Estate Building, its ornate facade presents a wide variety of High Victorian details, with recessed bays in Italianate style, deep moldings, fluted pilasters, piers of quoins, a rather elaborate roof cornice, and lesser cornices at the fifth and sixth floors. A chamfered corner is surmounted by a rounded cornice at the sixth floor, above which the building maintains the curve of the 1888 addition. The first two floors are of cast iron, and the upper floors of cast stone. The use of cast iron permitted larger windows for the building's retail establishments, whereas the upper load-bearing floors, used for offices, required more masonry support, hence narrower windows. Peek into the lobby on the Randolph Street side to see the skylighted atrium, also a feature of the 1888 renovation.

Just to the north of the Delaware Building is the **Oliver Building** (*1908, Holabird & Roche, with a 1920 addition by the same firm*), 159 N. Dearborn Street. The advantages of cast iron are eminently clear in the excellent decorative spandrels and ground-floor treatment which depict the old Oliver typewriter—one of the most popular brands in the early 20th century—as well as the company emblem. Chicago windows above the second floor, framed by decorative cast-iron spandrels, add to the interesting facade. (The Chicago window, a unique feature of the Chicago school of architecture, consists of a wide window pane bracketed by narrower double-hung windows.)

Continue north on Dearborn Street.

The **Theatre District Self Park** garage (*1987, Hammond, Beeby & Babka*), 181 N. Dearborn Street, celebrates its location in the theatre district with several unusual features. The neo-Classical exterior boasts no fewer than two brightly lit "theatre marquees," and each of the 12 parking levels is dedicated to a particular Broadway musical hit. Go inside, take the elevator up, and see for yourself. Not only are there posters advertising the show, but recorded musical excerpts are played as well, from such hits as *Oklahoma!, Fiddler on the Roof, Cabaret, Brigadoon, Hello, Dolly!,* and others. With the particular show in mind, drivers will likely remember where they parked.

If you do go upstairs, walk outside *above* the fourth level and look down across Dearborn Street. Two historic theatres, long dark and recently slated for demolition, have been granted a last-minute reprieve. The Goodman Theatre Group has announced plans to rehabilitate them for major stage shows and discontinue theatre productions at the Goodman Theatre in Grant Park. The **Harris Theatre,** 186 N. Dearborn Street (to the left), and the **Selwyn Theatre,** 170 N. Dearborn Street, were built in 1922 from plans by Crane & Franzheim, and although the two structures are similar in scale and plan, they differ in style. The Selwyn displays a restrained English facade; the Harris, a rococo

(Left) The pristine Delaware Building on the northeast corner of W. Randolph and N. Dearborn streets, built in 1872 just after the Great Fire of 1871, may be the oldest building in the Loop. The first two floors of this High Victorian Italianate–style building are sheathed in cast iron, and the six above are of masonry. Note how the floors are successively smaller toward the top to reduce the load, and incidentally to create an appearance of greater height. (Photo by author)

design with Italian motifs. Both are designated Chicago landmarks and are listed on the National Register of Historic Places. Also, the construction of an 800-seat auditorium just to the south of the theatres is underway, from plans by Kuwabara, Payne, McKenna & Blumberg, with completion scheduled for early 1999. As you leave the garage, look up at the facade and note how the design picks up the classic motifs of the two theatres across the street.

Return to the southwest corner of Dearborn and Randolph streets.

The **Richard J. Daley Center** (*1965, C. F. Murphy Associates; with Skidmore, Owings & Merrill, and Loebl, Schlossman and Bennett*) was built as the Chicago Civic Center, but was renamed in honor of the late mayor of Chicago, Richard J. Daley. The Center is a forceful and dramatic presence, sited diagonally opposite the Thompson Center and in strong contrast to the immense

The Oliver Building, just to the north of the Delaware Building, demonstrates several of the advantages of cast-iron construction, particularly in the decorative enframements of its Chicago windows and intervening spandrels. Built for the Oliver Typewriter Company, the spandrel panels of the building display low-relief typewriters and the company name. (Photo by author)

The landmark Harris (left) and Selwyn theatres were slated for demolition, but a last-minute decision by the Goodman Theatre Group to relocate here from Grant Park saved the pair from the wrecker's ball. (Photo by author)

The Loop has always suffered from the glut of heavy traffic, but this 1909 scene at the corner of W. Randolph and N. Dearborn streets must certainly call for a new definition of gridlock. No fewer than 30 streetcars are backed up on just one of the streets converging on the intersection. The mounted policemen (in white hats) seem in no hurry to help untangle the apparently hopeless congestion. (Chicago Historical Society)

neo-Classic City Hall/County Building, to the west. The elegant Miesian-inspired tower which reaches 648 feet, seems taller than its 31 stories, due not only to the high ceilings of its offices and court rooms, but to the monumental proportions of the facade and the arrangement of the bays. Each bay measures an incredible 87 feet wide and about 48 feet deep, with six-foot-high spandrels that reach across the facade like solid bridge girders, separating rows of twelve-foot-high bronze-tinted windows. Adding to the sense of strength and height are great perimeter columns that project outward from the base of the exterior walls and taper gently as they soar upward. The spandrels, columns, and window mullions are clad in Cor-Ten, a self-weathering steel that ultimately "rusts" to a rich, dark brown. Cor-Ten had its origin in the construction of railroad coal cars in the 1930s, but was later adapted to building technology as well as to metal sculpture. The Daley Center is reputed to be the first skyscraper to employ the Cor-Ten technology. The imposing tower, designed by Jacques Brownson, of C. F. Murphy Associates, represents possibly the finest example of the International style in America.

Daley Plaza is, in many ways, the heart of Chicago—a great forum and place of civic function, public gathering, and outdoor entertainment, with such goings-on as concerts, farmers' markets, art exhibits, political rallies, and anti-war demonstrations. It is named for Richard J. Daley, Chicago's longest-term mayor, who served from 1955 to 1976. At the southern end of the festive plaza, facing Washington Street, is the astonishing 50-foot-tall Cor-Ten steel sculpture, *Untitled,* by Pablo Picasso (1967). Donated by the artist to the city, it has emerged from initial public consternation and disdain to acceptance and acclaim, and has become a proud symbol of the city. The sculpture was the first major piece to be placed in the Loop and became the forerunner for a host of followers. According to the Department of Cultural Affairs, "The Picasso," as it is often called, is described as "a three-dimensional planar design abstracted from the head of a woman . . . as a series of simplified geometric details . . . and a work that combines frontal and profile views into one." The viewer is thus forced to examine the sculpture in a new way. When first unveiled, the front of the enigmatic statue was thought to resemble Picasso's pet afghan hound (he had two), although when viewed from the rear, the profile was said to represent the artist's wife. Today it is one of the favorite subjects for visitors' cameras. (At the Daley Civic Center, 50 W. Washington Street, free cultural programs are presented weekdays at noon by the Chicago Department of Cultural Affairs. Dial 346-3278 for information.)

To the east across Dearborn Street is the **Dearborn Street Substation of Commonwealth Edison Company** (*1931, Holabird & Root*), 117–121 N. Dearborn Street. The much-altered Art Deco–style powerhouse furnishes electricity for the Dearborn Street Subway which runs underneath. Note the low-relief panel above the window, which according to "Com Ed," is by sculptor Sylvia Shaw Judson.

On the southeast corner of Washington Street, **33 N. Dearborn Street** (*1967, Skidmore, Owings & Merrill*), the Connecticut Mutual Life Insurance Company Building, is another variation on the Miesian theme, with thin

(Left) "The Picasso," as everyone calls the 58-foot-tall Cor-Ten steel sculpture, was the first major piece to be placed in the Loop and the forerunner of many to come. It sits prominently on Daley Plaza in the center of Chicago's "great gathering place" and has become a proud symbol of the city. Donated by the artist to the city, it is named Untitled, *but Chicagoans have their own interpretation of what it represents, from one of Picasso's Afghan hounds to a profile of his wife. (Photo by author)*

masonry sheathing on its steel frame. A popular pedestrian arcade on the first floor was later filled in to accommodate more shops.

Across Dearborn Street, on the southwest corner, the 38-story **Brunswick Building** *(1965, Skidmore, Owings & Merrill),* 69 W. Washington Street, presents a strong contrast to its neighbor across the street. Although designed by the same architectural firm, the differences are quite apparent. Here we have completely different technology: a concrete central core (for the elevators) and a concrete exterior wall, providing a column-free interior. Go into the lobby and see how this "tube in a tube" functions. The collaborative reinforced-concrete tube design by SOM's Myron Goldsmith, Bruce Graham, and Fazlur Khan was chosen to preserve Daley Plaza's material and structural identity, and the following year it received a Citation of Merit from the American Institute of Architects. When completed it was the Loop's tallest building to be erected since the 1930s. Interestingly, the building envelope occupies only 50 percent of the site.

From outside, look up at the second floor, which is without windows, because behind this broad panelled-concrete "blind" level is a huge ring girder that serves to transfer the enormous weight of the many vertical members to the ten columns on the first floor—a neat trick which resulted in a relatively open ground floor area. Particularly significant is the gently curving facade of the tower above the transfer girder which immediately brings to mind the sloping profile of the historic Monadnock Block (*see* page 17).

Walk west past the Brunswick Building.

Standing in the Brunswick Building Plaza to the west is Joan Miró's *Miss Chicago,* a 39-foot-tall sculpture made of steel, wire-mesh, concrete, bronze, and ceramic tiles, placed here in 1979. Following earlier designs, Miró created the ceramic portions of this huge earth-mother in his Majorca studio, had the bronze element cast in Barcelona, and the rest of the components, including the steel armature, fabricated and assembled in Chicago. The giant figure has been described as having "a simplicity that is both child-like and spell-binding."

The adjacent **Chicago Temple** *(1923, Holabird & Roche),* 77 W. Washington Street, which was seen at a distance earlier on the tour, is a 21-story Indiana limestone commercial building, surmounted by an eight-story elaborate Gothic-style steeple. Actually, as the home of the First United Methodist Church in Chicago, it boasts the only church spire in the Loop; and because of its placement atop the office tower, it has the unique distinction, according to the *Guinness Book of Records,* of being the world's tallest church (568 feet). A carillon tolls the hours and quarter hours in pleasant contrast to the cacaphony of the traffic. Take a moment to study the ten attractive stained-glass windows arranged in the east wall of the building (facing the Miró), which depict the history of the church. This is the fifth Methodist church to be built on this site since the first structure in 1845. The Methodists' first building, a log structure and the first church building in Chicago, was built in 1831 at Wolf Point, on the Chicago River adjacent to what is now the Merchandise Mart, and was later floated downstream, then pulled on log rollers to the present site. There are two separate entrances to the building, the one on Washington Street serves the commercial tenants, while the Clark Street entrance provides access to the ground-floor sanctuary and the church offices. The attractive T-shaped lobby is richly adorned with Gothic motifs.

Within the spire itself are the parsonage and the diminutive 400-foot-high **Chapel in the Sky** and parsonage, accessible by a small elevator from the 22nd floor. The 30-foot-diameter octagonal chapel is adorned with 16 colorful stained-glass windows by Giannini & Hilgart depicting "The Story of Faith since Creation" and the history of Methodism. The room is completely oak panelled, with massive cross-braces in the shape of St. Andrew's crosses. The two-story chamber was dedicated in 1952 as a memorial to drugstore magnate, Charles Walgreen, and was donated by his widow, who also contributed the oak trees from the family estate in Dixon, Illinois, to create the interior furnishings. The communion table has an unusual sculpture of Jesus brooding over the city of Chicago, carved by Jerome Walters, on which all the nearby skyscrapers of the 1950s are depicted in bold relief. When the building was

The Chicago Temple, at 77 W. Washington Street, is a 21-story commercial skyscraper, that also houses the sanctuary and offices of the First United Methodist Church in Chicago. The structure is surmounted by an eight-story Gothic-style spire—the only church spire in the Loop. According to the Guinness Book of Records, *it is the world's tallest church, 568 feet high! Just below the steeple is the Chapel in the Sky, accessible by a small elevator from the 22nd floor. (Photo by author)*

originally planned, the maximum permissible height for a skyscraper in Chicago was 260 feet, but a variance was obtained from the city fathers to add the extra height to the building, which then permitted congregants to worship a bit closer to Heaven. (Public tours are given weekdays at 2:00 P.M.; special tours by private arrangement, phone 236-4548.)

Continue west to Clark Street.

Across Clark Street on the southwest corner, is the **Chicago Title and Trust Building** (*1913, D. H. Burnham & Company, and Graham, Burnham & Company; renovation 1947, Holabird and Roche; 1986, Jack Train Associates*), 111 W. Washington Street. The 21-story building was built as the Conway Building by the Estate of Marshall Field, and named for Field's birthplace, Conway, Massachusetts. When Daniel H. Burnham died in 1912 before the completion of the building, his company was reorganized as Graham, Burnham & Company, and the work carried on by the successor firm. The gleaming white terra-cotta cladding of the building reflects Burnham's predilection for the Beaux Arts style, which was popularized by the World's Columbian Exposition of 1893 and later in his Plan of Chicago of 1909, is apparent. In a 1947 renovation, the building's interior light court was filled in to the sixth-floor level, for the addition of office space. A later renovation in 1986 restored the atrium and added bay windows. Fortunately, little has been done through the years to damage the integrity of the Classic facade, and the venerable structure still displays its original rounded corners, a three-story-high rooftop colonnade, ornate balustrade, and columned entrance.

Turn left (south) on Clark Street, to just below Madison Street, on the west side of the street.

The **Chicago Loop Synagogue** (*1957, Loebl, Schlossman & Bennett*), 16 S. Clark Street, uses its narrow lot to good advantage. Above the entrance, and set in front of a wall of stained glass, is a bronze and brass sculpture, *Hands of Peace,* by Israeli artist Henri Aziz (1963), depicting priestly hands raised in benediction, against a background of the text of the ancient threefold blessing, in Hebrew and in English.

The building is divided into a ground-floor meditation chapel and a sanctuary above. If the building is open, go up the ramp to the visitors' gallery and note the right-angle arrangement of the sanctuary and the stunning stained-glass eastern wall, by Abraham Rattner, entitled *Let There Be Light!* from the theme of Creation in Genesis 1:3. It was commissioned by the building's architects in 1957 and took three years to complete. The window was fabricated by Barrillet's, the leading stained-glass studio of Paris.

The construction of the synagogue was the culmination of efforts to replace a former hotel room where daily services were conducted for workers in the Loop as well as for visitors from out of town. It has grown to become the city's central synagogue and, in a sense, the symbol of the Jewish religious presence in Chicago.

Under a triple-gable roof, the Chicago Loop Synagogue (1957), at 16 S. Clark Street, presents an unusual facade consisting entirely of stained-glass wall panels. To the right, above the entrance, is a bronze and glass sculpture, Hands of Peace, *by Israeli artist Henry Aziz, depicting priestly hands raised in benediction. (Photo by author)*

The stained-glass wall of the Loop Synagogue dominates the sanctuary. The attractive and colorful panels by Abraham Rattner represent the command inspired by the Book of Genesis, Let There Be Light! *(Reproduced with permission of the publisher, Loyola University Press, from the book* Chicago Churches and Synagogues, *by George A. Lane)*

Return to Madison Street.

On the north side of Madison Street, occupying the entire blockfront to Dearborn Street and set on an irregular site, is **Three First National Plaza** (*1981, Skidmore, Owings & Merrill*). The building is actually a complex of three, with a 57-story tower connected by a nine-story atrium-lobby to an 11-story structure, all clad in carnelian granite with bronze reflective glass in the bays. Interesting are the exposed steel trusses in the atrium and the sawtooth-angled setback configuration on the southeast side, providing additional "corner" offices on each floor. Trapezoidal windows recall the Chicago school style, and above, six setbacks are equipped with greenhouses. It is said that the tower was built lower than the neighboring First National Bank Building so that panoramic views from the bank's top-floor boardrooms would not be obstructed. In the sloped glass-enclosed atrium is a 22-foot-tall bronze Henry Moore sculpture, *Large Upright Internal/External Form* (1983). A skybridge across Madison Street connects with the First National Bank, the next site on the tour.

Turn right (east) on Madison Street.

On the south side of the street, looms the **First National Bank Building** (*1969, C. F. Murphy Associates, with Perkins & Will Partnership*), One First National Plaza, with its unmistakable inward-curving, or "skirt-bottom," pro-file. The design is not only graceful, but functional as well. The bank required broad, open public spaces at ground level, with conventional office space above. At the time, no branch banking was permitted under state law; hence the need to handle a large volume of patrons under one roof. To further accom-modate the needs of such a spacious lobby, the elevator banks were placed at each end of the building. The inward-sweeping curve was therefore the solu-tion—providing space, structural integrity, wind-bracing, and aesthetics. The 60-story steel-frame structure, the tallest bank building in the world, is clad in gray-speckled Texas granite, which contrasts well with the bronze-tinted glass windows and is carried out to the plaza, as well as into the broad ground-level area. The facade consists of six vertical bays divided into three horizontal sec-tions, rising to a top-floor row of penthouses surmounted by "notches" which hide the mechanical systems. Because of its sloping north and south sides, the top floor is only half the size of the ground floor.

Take some time to walk around the building and explore the plaza.

The multilevel sunken **First National Plaza,** one of several dictated by the demand for open space in the then densely packed Loop, is one of the most popular in the city, with various services situated around a fountain. Its center-piece is Marc Chagall's monolithic 1974 mosaic mural, *The Four Seasons* (*Les Quatre Saisons*). Made of hand-chipped stone and glass fragments, it measures 70 × 14 × 10 feet, and according to the *Loop Sculpture Guide,* Russian-born Chagall observed that "the seasons represent human life, both physical and spiritual, at its different ages." Depicted in Chagall's inimitable way are his familiar images of fish, birds, suns, flowers, and lovers, plus six fanciful scenes from Chicago, in soft pastel hues, created in over 250 colors and thousands of tiny inlaid chips. The design was realized in the artist's studio in France with the assistance of a mosaicist, then transported to Chicago, where Chagall added bits of Chicago brick and brought the mural "up to date" with the inclusion in the design of many buildings that had been built since his last visit 30 years before.

On the Monroe Street side, the bronze clock mounted on a granite pedestal was rescued from the former First National Bank Building on the site. Note the eagles on the upper corners and the Greek-inspired acanthus lead motif in the center.

(*Note:* The State-Madison Building, at the northeast corner of Dearborn and Madison streets, is discussed later in the tour.)

At Dearborn Street, turn right (south) to the northwest corner of Dearborn and Monroe streets.

This is a good vantage point to view the noteworthy **Inland Steel Building** (*1954–1958, Skidmore, Owings & Merrill*), 30 W. Monroe Street, across Dearborn Street. Enjoying a number of significant firsts, the building was the first skyscraper erected in the Loop since the Depression, the first downtown project for Skidmore, Owings & Merrill, and the first major project by the firm's designer, Bruce Graham. It was also the first skyscraper to be built with external supports, together with a flat, unadorned thin steel-and-glass curtain wall; the first to be constructed with an attached structure to house the service and mechanical systems; the first major structure erected on steel pilings (driven 85 feet through mud and clay to bedrock), rather than on the customary concrete caissons; the first to use a combination of steel-beam bracing and soldier-beam piling to sustain excavation walls and support the weight of adjacent streets and neighboring buildings until permanent walls and floor could take the pressures. Still more "firsts" include: the first completely air-conditioned building, the first with dual glazing, and the first major high-rise with indoor underground parking facilities.

On both the west and east sides of the 19-story stainless-steel and blue-green glass structure are seven columns encased in stainless steel that are connected to 60-foot girders that support the entire building, providing broad expanses of column-free open space throughout—the largest building ever erected employing the clear-span construction principle. Occupying only 66 percent of its site, the building demonstrates an excellent site plan, in harmony with its neighbors. The adjoining unobtrusive 27-story steel-clad windowless service tower contains such service features as the elevators, fire tower, electric and telephone lines, loading dock, garage entrance, and mechanical systems.

The Inland Steel Company, founded in 1901 in Chicago Heights, Illinois, is the only steel company based in Chicago and the eighth largest in the United States. It was a pioneer in the use of stainless steel as a cladding material, the result of which is evident in the structure's facade of graceful proportion and elegant detailing. In the lobby is an attractive wire sculpture by Richard Lippold, commissioned for the site.

From the same vantage point, looking toward the southeast and southwest corners are:

No. 33 W. Monroe Street (*1980, Skidmore, Owings & Merrill*), one of the first multi-atrium office towers, is sheathed in gray-painted insulated aluminum panels and reflective glass. Three atriums of from 7 to 12 stories in height are stacked one above the other within the building, providing interior as well as exterior windows. The north wall was kept to a height of 19 stories to maintain harmony with the Inland Steel Building and to lighten the foundation load, while the succeeding stories step upward in pairs to the 28th floor.

The Xerox Center (*1980, C. F. Murphy Associates*), 55 W. Monroe Street, is easily identifiable at a distance by its smooth wraparound facade of alternating enameled-white aluminum and silver reflective glass. A sleek 40-story reinforced concrete structure, its prominent rounded corner recalls some of the old buildings of the Chicago school, such as the Old Colony or Carson Pirie Scott. The break with the conventional in this Helmut Jahn plan extends not only to the facade, but to the inward curves of the entrances and to the diagonal sidewalk paving, whose motif is carried into the lobby and its ceiling lighting. From a distance the sharp curvilinear shape of the penthouse has been compared to a grand piano. The building design also took into account the occasionally harsh Chicago weather, by the proportion of double-glazing on each wall. The north side, from which it is best observed, receives virtually no direct sunlight, and consists of 75 percent glass, whereas the east, facing the morning sun, is reduced to 50 percent.

Continue south on Dearborn Street, just past Marble Place.

At the northwest corner of Dearborn and Adams Street, the **Marquette Building** (*1893–1895, Holabird & Roche; west bay addition 1896; renovation 1980, Holabird & Root*), 140 S. Dearborn Street, is one of Chicago's most remarkable early commercial high-rise structures. It is designed with the traditional "tripartite" facade—a 2-story ornamented base, a 12-story midsection, and a once-ornate cornice (now replaced by an ugly and inappropriate top floor) represent the three main sections. The 17-story structure, in the true early skyscraper tradition so prolifically expounded by Holabird & Roche, clearly reveals its rectangular steel-frame skeleton in the details of its brick and terra-cotta cladding. A feeling of height is augmented by strong piers in contrast to the recessed spandrels which embrace rows of "Chicago windows." The bays at the four corners project slightly outward, creating a "frame" for the entire structure, and are highlighted by stringcourses at the 3rd, 4th, 16th, and 17th floors.

Both the exterior and interior of the Marquette Building are remarkable. Above the Dearborn Street entrance are bronze bas reliefs by New York sculptor, Hermon Atkins MacNeil, which depict events from the 1673–1674 expedition of Father Jacques Marquette. The Jesuit missionary priest, accompanied by Louis Joliet and others from French Canada, were the first Europeans to visit the region. The building was named for Marquette by Owen

(Left) The Inland Steel Building (1954–1958, Skidmore, Owings & Merrill), looking north up N. Dearborn Street from W. Monroe Street, was the first skyscraper built in the Loop since the Depression and the first to be built with external supports, with an unadorned steel-and-glass curtain wall. It was also the first building constructed with an attached structure (on the right) to house the service and mechanical systems, the first major structure erected on steel pilings, plus a host of other "firsts," including the first completely air-conditioned building, the first with dual glazing, and the first with indoor underground parking. (Courtesy Richard M. Penner and Inland Steel Industries Photographic Services)

Aldis, the agent for the building's developers, who translated the priest's journal. Aldis's enduring passion for the history of the Northwest Territory is even more evident in the lobby.

Enter the beautifully restored two-story rotunda-like lobby, and spend a few minutes examining the splendid balcony frieze which depicts the discovery of the Northwest in mother-of-pearl and favrile-glass panels, by J. A. Holzer, the chief mosaicist of Tiffany & Company; and the 16 bronze reliefs of Native American chiefs and French missionaries and explorers above each of the elevator doors, designed by Edward Kemeys, the sculptor best remembered for his pair of lions guarding the entrance to the Art Institute of Chicago. The Marquette Building has just undergone a multimillion-dollar renovation by its owners and largest tenant, the John D. and Catherine T. MacArthur Foundation.

In the block to the south, bounded by Dearborn, Clark, and Adams streets and Jackson Boulevard, as well as the blockfront on the east side of Dearborn

The Xerox Center is easily recognized by its smooth wraparound surface. Helmut Jahn's curvilinear plan (1980) also extends from the inward curves of the entrance to the penthouse. The First National Bank Building, across the street, is mirrored in the silver reflective glass that sheathes the exterior. (Photo by author)

One of several relief sculptures by Hermon Atkins MacNeill over the portal of the Marquette Building portrays the Jesuit missionary priest, Father Jacques Marquette, on his journey down Lake Michigan to the Illini Indians, passing through what is now Chicago. In this sculpture, Father Marquette and a group of Indians are about to embark by canoe into "strange lands." (Photo by author)

Street, stands the monumental complex of buildings comprising the **Chicago Federal Center,** commissioned by the U.S. General Services Administration as a federal administrative and judicial center. The 15-year-long project was designed by Ludwig Mies van der Rohe in 1959, and was his first urban mixed-use land plan; but it was not completed until after his death in 1969, and after a long string of budgetary delays when the project direction was taken over by the firms of Schmidt, Garden & Erikson, and C. F. Murphy Associates, with A. Epstein & Sons, who completed the work in 1974. A more recent addition to the federal group came in 1991 with the completion of the Ralph H. Metcalfe Building, at 77 W. Jackson Boulevard, by Mies's successor firm, Fujikawa, Johnson & Associates.

Federal Plaza was the site of two previous federal buildings, the U.S. Custom House and Post Office Building, built in 1879 and demolished in 1896, and the Federal Building, erected in 1905, and razed in 1965–1966. An interesting sidelight to the demolition of the earlier 1879 government building is that the structure *still* exists, but in another incarnation! The stones of the razed building were obtained by a pastor from the Archdiocese of Milwaukee, who had them transported 85 miles north on 500 railroad flatcars to the city of Milwaukee, to be used in the construction of St. Josaphat's Basilica, an enormous domed Baroque-style edifice which stands today as one of only four Roman Catholic basilicas in the United States. Using volunteer labor, the basilica, whose style was inspired by St. Peter's in Rome, took five years to complete, and was dedicated in 1901.

The heart of what is now the Loop, ca. 1880, shows the rapid rise of the city after the Great Fire. Few buildings then exceeded six stories, as structural steel was yet to be perfected. In the right rear is the French Renaissance–style U.S. Custom House and Post Office (1879), with peaked roof and dormers. Not one building in this view survives today. (Chicago Historical Society)

The 1879 U.S. Custom House and Post Office stood on the northwest corner of N. Clark and W. Adams streets, the site of the present Chicago Federal Center. In the left rear is the Owings Building (1888). The Custom House and Post Office was demolished in 1896, and the masonry and fixtures were sent to Milwaukee to build St. Josaphat's Basilica. (Chicago Historical Society)

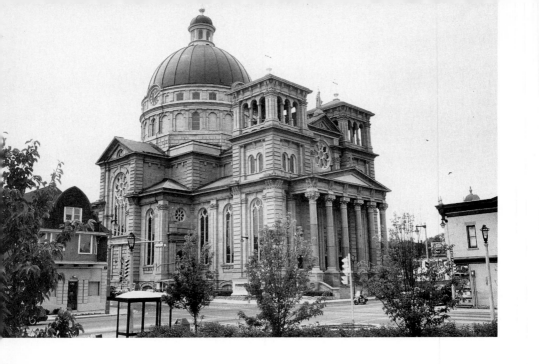

(Left, above) St. Josaphat's Basilica in Milwaukee, designed by Erhard Brielmaier, was completed in 1901, mostly by volunteer labor, five years after the pastor of Milwaukee Archdiocese arranged to obtain the salvaged masonry from the demolished 1879 Chicago Custom House and Post Office. Five hundred railroad flatcars were required to transport the 200,000 tons of masonry, plus six huge polished granite columns, doors, hardware, and light fixtures. The design of the structure—America's first Polish Roman Catholic basilica, and one of only 16 basilicas in the United States—was inspired by St. Peter's in Rome. Its dome is larger than the Taj Mahal's. (Photo by author)

(Left, below) Following the razing of the old Custom House and Post Office, a new Federal Building took its place. Designed by Henry Ives Cobb and completed in 1905, this bold neo-Classic domed structure served until 1965. It had a 300-foot-high octagonal rotunda surmounted by a 100-foot-diameter dome that was larger than on the Capitol in Washington. A splendid civic structure that should have been preserved, its courtrooms witnessed 60 years of Chicago's turbulent legal history, including such events as the fining of Standard Oil by Judge Kenesaw Mountain Landis and the conviction of Al Capone for income tax evasion. (Chicago Historical Society)

The walking tour of the Federal Center Plaza consists of a "clockwise loop" beginning at the northeast corner of the plaza, at Dearborn and Adams streets, swinging completely around, but staying within the plaza, and ending back at the northeast corner.

Although the visitor to the Center may at first feel somewhat over-whelmed by the massing of International-style skyscrapers, one should try to get a full perspective of the Plaza and its repeating grid pattern, from the lines that "enter" the buildings to the repeating grid pattern throughout. The Plaza has been described as a study in geometric perfection, and the buildings that comprise Federal Plaza have often been referred to as the ultimate expression of "the Second Chicago school of architecture."

The main attraction for visitors to the Plaza, however, seems to be the spectacular 53-foot-tall vermilion-colored abstract stabile, *Flamingo,* by Alexander Calder. It stands in brilliant and vital contrast to the somber glass-and-steel curtain walls of the adjacent buildings, but also as a wholly integrated element of the plaza environment. The "stabile" (a word invented by French artist, Jean Arp, to differentiate a stationary free-form sculpture from the "mobile," the name given by Marcel Duchamp to describe a suspended sculpture that can be set in motion by currents of air), was commissioned by the U.S. General Services Administration, and set on the Plaza in 1974. Calder, whose stabiles are purely abstract designs, called this work "Flamingo," simply because "it was sort of pink and has a long neck." This is the southernmost of the three major plazas that boast large and outstanding pieces of sculpture.

Facing the Plaza on the east side of S. Dearborn Street is the **Everett McKinley Dirksen Building** (*1964*), 219 S. Dearborn Street, a 30-story structure that serves as an office and federal courthouse building. It was the first completed and is one of the finest examples of the influential Miesian style, and was named for the late long-term U.S. senator from Illinois. Note how the

(Left) The centerpiece of Federal Center Plaza and its main tourist attraction, is Alexander Calder's monumental abstract stabile, Flamingo *(1974). Standing 53 feet tall, the vermilion-colored steel sculpture is a pleasing counterpoint to the somber glass and steel of the surrounding Federal Center buildings. (Photo by author)*

projecting I-beam mullions set off the uninterrupted walls of glass and steel, which give the steel-frame building a feeling of proportion and symmetry.

At the southeast corner of the plaza rises the **John C. Kluczynski Federal Building** (*1974, Office of Mies van der Rohe, with Garden & Erikson, A. Epstein & Sons, and C. F. Murphy Associates; also the Dirksen Building and Loop Post Office*), 230 S. Dearborn Street. The 43-story office tower shares a facade similar in style to the Dirksen Building, as well as a common lobby design and sidewalk paving pattern. The building honors the former Illinois state representative and congressman who before his death in 1975 fought for federal support for a national highway system.

(Across W. Jackson Boulevard, at the southwest corner of S. Dearborn Street, is the landmark Monadnock Block, described in Tour 1; *see* pages 17–18.)

Standing on the southeast corner of W. Jackson Boulevard and S. Clark Street is the **Ralph H. Metcalfe Federal Building** (*1991, Fujikawa, Johnson & Associates*), 77 W. Jackson Boulevard. This more recent 27-story government building, while constructed of concrete and faced with granite, is respectful of its Miesian neighbors; and with credit to its architects, does not detract from the plaza complex with unharmonious postmodern detailing. Like its neighbors on the plaza, it, too, retains open lobbies of similar height and sidewalk

The Great Northern Hotel, originally called the Northern Hotel, by Burnham & Root (1892), stood on the northeast corner of W. Jackson and S. Dearborn streets. Like so many of the grand hotels built at the turn of the century, the cost of modernization was too great for them to survive, and the 16-story Great Northern fell victim to the wreckers' ball in 1940. The design of the circular corners may have influenced Holabird & Roche's plan for the Old Colony Building, built two years afterward, in 1894. (Chicago Historical Society)

paving design. The building is named for the noted track star from the 1936 Olympics, who died in 1978 and who had also served as a city alderman, congressman, founding member of the Congressional Black Caucus, and vigorous civil rights advocate.

Enter the Metcalfe Building and note the enormous sculpture in the northwest corner of the lobby. The first impression is one of a pile of scrap metal piled helter-skelter. On closer examination it is an intricate arrangement of shaped castings, honeycombed aluminum, and carved and twisted fragments of salvaged metal. Frank Stella's *The Town-Ho's Story: With Postscript & the Gam* (1993), commissioned by the General Services Administration's Art-in-Architecture Program, stands 22 feet high on a 12×15 foot base. According to the descriptive plaque, "the materials reflect Chicago's industrial origins, and the title is taken from Herman Melville's allegorical novel *Moby Dick*. The work relates to the story of Steelkit, an audacious sailor who uses both mind and fist to resist maltreatment." The description goes on to say that "the sculpture embodies similar energies in aluminum and steel using the power of abstraction to compress into one expansive piece the gleaming, combative essence of literary work and an American city." (The building is open weekdays only, but the sculpture can easily be seen through the glass windows.)

Across the street from the Metcalfe Building (at the corner of Jackson and Clark) is the unusual sculpture group, *Ruins III,* by Nita K. Sunderland (1978) depicting three dark-bronze figures examining three "columns from antiquity."

At the northwest corner of the plaza is the single-story **U.S. Post Office— Loop Station** (*1974*), 219 S. Clark Street, connected to the Kluczynski Building by a common basement. Although a low-rise structure, it is a harmonious partner on the plaza.

Across Clark Street from the Post Office, and in rather sharp contrast, is the **Bankers Building** (*1927, Burnham Bros.*), 105 W. Adams Street. The 41-story building, whose style is a mixture of Classical and Art Deco, is faced in a rough-grained concrete that extends up to the fourth-floor level. Peek into the lush lobby, and note the red marble walls and carved oak columns.

Diagonally across, at the northeast corner of Adams and Clark Street, is the massive **Commonwealth Edison Building** (*1907, D. H. Burnham and Company*), 72 West Adams Street. Designed in Renaissance Revival style by the successor firm after the death of Daniel H. Burnham, this richly ornate 18-story structure is the home of "Com Ed," Chicago's electric company. While its main offices are located in the First National Bank Building, its control center and consumer service offices are located here. Do not miss the historical ground-floor window displays of early lighting fixtures and equipment. An interior pedestrian arcade with retail and food shops connects with the Marquette Building, to the east.

Turn right (east) along Adams Street, past Dearborn (crossing your former route), and continue east to the middle of the block.

On the south side of Adams Street, in midblock, are a trio of unusual survivors tied together as **The Berghoff Restaurant,** and sharing the same address,

17 W. Adams Street. They were built the year after the Great Fire of 1871; the architect of the former No. 15, then known as the Stone Building, is unknown; but former No. 27, once the Palmer Building, was designed by and named for Charles M. Palmer. The **Stone Building,** coincidentally built of stone (sandstone), displays typical round-arch Italianate windows, and on the second floor, the sixth bay from the left contains an unusual dual-arched window within an arched frame. The third floor, whose windows are noticeably larger, once served as a public meeting hall, a ubiquitous 19th-century building usage, and now the last vestige of such a hall in Chicago.

The **Palmer Building** (No. 27) is one of only two remaining cast-iron-front buildings in the city (the other, the Page Brothers Building, at 171–191 N. State Street, will be seen later on the tour). The building was built for Potter Palmer, a major Chicago real estate tycoon, member of Chicago high society, State Street merchant prince, and builder of the famed Palmer House. It was Palmer who set off the Gold Coast land rush north of the Chicago River, when he abandoned his South Side residence in 1882 and built himself a million-dollar "castle" on North Lake Shore Drive. The Berghoff, a highly popular German-style restaurant and Loop landmark, began as a beer hall at the 1893 World's Columbian Exposition, and is Chicago's oldest restaurant.

Cast-Iron Architecture. The use of cast iron dates from late 18th-century England, but it did not achieve popularity as a building material until after the

A trio of buildings at 17 W. Adams Street, erected the year after the Great Fire, somehow survived in the middle of the Loop, with most of their original features intact. The group is now occupied by Berghoff's, one of the city's most popular German-style restaurants. (Photo by author)

middle of the 19th century. With the success of Joseph Paxton's enormous London Crystal Palace Exhibition Building of 1851, and a similar iron-and-glass exhibition building in New York two years later, the popularity of cast iron became widespread, particularly in the United States. Its success as a structural and architectural medium is credited to two New York engineers, Daniel D. Badger and James Bogardus. Badger's Architectural Iron Works mass-produced the first complete iron-front building, and Bogardus, whose early iron-front warehouse still survives, was also the inventor of the I-beam.

The advantages of cast iron were obvious. In masonry buildings, the load is borne by the interior and exterior walls whose thickness depends on the height of the structure. On the other hand, in pure iron construction the load is borne by a skeleton of vertical and horizontal rolled iron beams, with the exterior brick walls attached to the framework and serving only as a skin. Cast-iron parts making up the facade are then attached to the brick walls. The use of cast iron, in effect, anticipated the principle of the modern skyscraper, where similar "curtain walls" surround a structural steel frame. Cast iron was also fire-resistant and the iron skeleton of a building made it a lightning-proof "Faraday's Cage." It was lighter and cheaper than stone, and much quicker and less expensive to erect. Cast iron could be mass-produced from standardized molds—the iron parts being interchangeable and easily replaced from the foundry's catalog. Cast iron could be molded into many different shapes and styles, and could be painted and repainted in any color, and was often painted to resemble stone. Its coefficient of expansion was similar to the brickwork to which it was attached, obviating the danger of separation under extremes of weather, and it had greater structural integrity than any other building material at the time (steel had not yet been developed).

A major benefit from the elimination of massive bearing walls was the ability to insert large windows—a boon to factories and offices which then could enjoy light and ventilation hitherto unavailable. There were some disadvantages, however. Cast iron could not prevent fires when flooring, joists, and beams were of wood. Iron was brittle and lacked the tensile strength of steel, and it could crack on severe impact or under sudden temperature changes. Rusting, too, was always a problem when moisture could seep into interior sections. Until displaced by structural steel, cast iron remained a highly popular building material until the first decade of the 20th century.

Walk east to State Street.

State Street for many years was both the retail shopping center and "Great White Way" of Chicago. In the eight blocks between Congress Parkway and Lake Street were all the famous department stores, many of the great legitimate theatres, and the largest of the hotels. Centrally located, "The Great Street," as it was called, was easily accessible by trolley car or El train, and later by subway and buses. Chicago's first street cars, drawn by horses, began operation in 1858 on State Street, south from Randolph Street. Through the years the street boasted one of the greatest concentrations of department stores in America, with such notable emporiums as Sears Roebuck, Montgomery Ward, Goldblatt's, Siegel-Cooper, Schlesinger and Mayer, Carson Pirie Scott, Wieboldt's, the Boston Store, Stevens Store, the Fair Store, and Marshall Field. Today, only Carson Pirie Scott, Marshall Field's, and a few smaller stores survive on the street. The north end of State Street was also Chicago's Rialto, but of the many playhouses in that lively theatre district, only the great Chicago Theatre, the Schubert, and a scant handful of others remain; and only one last hotel, the "grande dame" of them all, the Palmer House, still holds forth, as luxurious as ever. While much of the fashionable retail trade has moved up to North Michigan Avenue, and most of the old department stores have closed their doors forever, they have left behind on State Street a rich architectural heritage in the form of huge and sprawling buildings, now used for other purposes, but still highly visible and in many cases, very ornate, and in an excellent state of preservation.

In 1979, in an effort to stem the rapid deterioration of State Street, the city developed a plan to revitalize the retail shopping district by closing it to vehicular traffic, widening the sidewalks, and converting it into a pedestrian mall. However, the traffic snarls that occurred in an already congested and compressed surrounding area forced the city fathers to compromise by opening two lanes to buses and taxis. Still, various amenities were added, including new bus shelters and subway entrances, some lively signage, and public sculpture. But the effort was a dismal failure and shoppers continued to stay away in droves, ignoring the colorful banners that proclaimed "Welcome to State Street where the Shopping is Great!"

In 1996 the city came up with a brand-new plan to save the retailing district. The plan was coordinated by the **State Street Renovation Project,** with the architectural firm of Skidmore, Owings & Merrill providing urban design, architecture, and engineering services that included new lighting, and a landscaping and signage plan. Consoer Townsend Envirodyne Engineers, Inc., created the design for the widening of the roadway, which would open State Street to public vehicles for the first time since 1979. Among the new street amenities designed by SOM to create an historic aura to celebrate the street's great past are light poles whose fixtures are replicas of the ones President Coolidge switched on when he opened the street in 1926. SOM also was responsible for the design of the sidewalks, graphics, luminaires, CTA escalator, and stair and escalator enclosures, as well as the granite planters for shade trees and ornamental ground cover; the street furniture was specifically designed to complement the turn-of-the-century architecture of the street's building facades. It is the city's fond expectation that the newly revitalized State Street will attract many more people to the area and bring back the shoppers who had abandoned the street for North Michigan Avenue.

Note: In Tour 1, the itinerary passed along the lower two blocks of State Street between Congress Parkway and Jackson Boulevard. (*See* page 12 for details of the department store buildings in those blocks.) The following is just a brief

summary, as the two blocks can be visited at another time, or by taking that part of Tour 1:

On the east side of State Street, occupying the complete block between Congress Parkway and Van Buren Street, is **One Congress Center** (*1891, William Le Baron Jenney*), originally the **Siegel-Cooper Store,** and until 1983, the flagship store of **Sears, Roebuck & Company.** It is now a multiple-use building for a number of establishments. Built for developer Levi Z. Leiter, it was known also as the Second Leiter Building.

One block north, also on the east side of the street, is the block-long **DePaul Center** (*1912, Holabird & Roche; 1993 renovation, Daniel P. Coffey & Associates*), originally the **A. M. Rothschild & Company Store** (until 1923), then the **Davis Store,** owned by Marshall Field's (until 1936), and later the **Goldblatt Store** until 1981. Ten years later DePaul University converted the building into a downtown campus, with commercial rental space, retail stores, and a food court. The adaptive reuse plan by Daniel P. Coffey & Associates included two 2-story atriums, a rooftop deck, and an activities center for students, plus four floors for city offices. At the northwest corner of Adams Street, and extending to Dearborn, was the **Fair Store,** another of Chicago's great emporiums.

Continue north on State Street, one-half block.

Dominating the east side of the block is the massive **Palmer House** (*1927, Holabird & Roche*), 17 E. Monroe Street. Now the Palmer House Hilton, it is one of Chicago's oldest and most distinguished hotels. Unfortunately, three 5-story-high ugly panels obstruct the view of the facade. The street floor is an upscale commercial arcade lined with a variety of retail shops. Enter the building at 119 N. State Street, go through the arcade which leads to Wabash Avenue, but turn left at the escalator bank leading up to the lobby, and continue up to the mezzanine. From there one can appreciate the dazzling restoration of the *fin de siècle* hall. It is a splendid space, whose ornate ceiling with 21 paintings by Louis Rigal was meticulously restored by the Florentine artist noted for his work on the Sistine Chapel. The entire lobby is tastefully furnished with authentically reproduced fabrics and carpeting, and illuminated by elaborate candelabra and crystal chandeliers, the pleasing result of a 10-year-long renovation. Note the plaster work on the ceiling above decorative pilasters, and a lovely marble clock. After relaxing a while in one of the soft lounge chairs, take the elevator to the fourth floor to see the State Ballroom and the Red Lacquer Room, then walk around the corridor corner to the Grand Ballroom, with its faux marbre and crystal chandeliers.

This is the third Palmer House on the site, and is named for tycoon/developer Potter Palmer, who more than anyone else, was responsible for the development of State Street as a great retail center. The first hotel opened in 1871, just in time to be consumed by the Great Fire. Four years later the second, designed from John Mills Van Osdel's plans for the earlier hotel, opened its doors to much fanfare, claiming to be the first fireproof hotel with elevators in

A computer-generated picture of the State Street renovation, with real people superimposed, shows the new 1920s-era lampposts, landscaping, repaved sidewalk, and subway entrance as they would appear upon completion of the project in 1996, looking north from Washington Street in front of Marshall Field's. (Courtesy of Skidmore, Owings & Merrill and McCartney & Company)

An 1870 advertisement for the Palmer House depicts the "Palace Hotel of the World," and optimistically predicts its completion three years later. The "Only Thoroughly Fire-Proof Hotel in the United States" actually opened ahead of schedule in 1871, just in time to be consumed in the Great Fire. The present Palmer House Hilton is the third on the site. (Chicago Historical Society)

Chicago. Some years later, it boasted the first to be equipped with the "new-fangled" telephone.

Take a short detour left (west) to No. 22 E. Monroe Street, the **Shubert Theatre** (*1906, Edmund R. Krause, with George L. and Cornelius W. Rapp*), a textbook example of terra-cotta artistry at its best. When it opened as the Majestic Theatre on New Year's Day 1906, it was described as the largest theatre in town presenting "first class vaudeville." Among some of the early performers were Harry Houdini, Lily Langtry, and Mabel McKinley. The adjacent 20-story Majestic Building, where the Shubert's executive offices are located, still keeps the theatre's former name. In 1945 the theatre was purchased by Lee and J. J. Shubert, who renamed it the Sam Shubert, just as they did a large number of other theatres acquired by the Shubert Organization across the country, in memory of their older brother who was killed in a train wreck in 1903. Since 1991 the theatre has been owned by the Nederlander Organization. Although Randolph Street, three blocks north, was Chicago's main theatre thoroughfare, the Shubert is one of only a scant few survivors of what was once a thriving theatre district in the Loop.

Architectural Terra Cotta.   In the 1870s the first architectural terra-cotta factory in America, the Chicago Terra Cotta Company, was established, and within a few years the city became the center of the industry. *Terra cotta* ("cooked earth" in Italian) had the dual advantage of being a durable and fireproof building material, as well as a medium that lent itself easily to ornamental carving and inexpensive design reproduction. Its use became widespread after the Great Fire of 1871 with the demand for safer building materials. Technological progress and architectural innovations stimulated experimentation, and with the development of steam-powered machinery, the close accessibility of clay deposits, and the superb transportation system, it was only natural that Chicago should find itself at the forefront of a thriving industry. With the birth of the Chicago school in the 1880s and for the following half century, architects used terra cotta extensively to sheath their steel-frame buildings. But by the early 1930s, the elaborate terra-cotta facades gave way to smooth fronts of terra-cotta ashlars and the manufacture of ceramic tiles. Today, with the popularity and economy of other building materials, there is no longer a large demand for terra cotta, and the Chicago factories have all vanished.

Return to State Street.

Across State Street, just south of Monroe Street, at No. 120 S. State, stands the 10-story **Singer Building** (*1926, Mundie & Jensen*). Built for the Singer Sewing Machine Company on a very narrow 25-foot lot, it makes up for its width with a facade of attractive neo-Gothic ornament in white-glazed terra cotta. A polygonal top crowns the building. The Singer Company was originally located diagonally across the street in an 1879 building they erected where the Marshall Field store stands today. Singer, a long-time devotee of architectural elegance, built its world headquarters tower in New York in 1908, which was for a time the tallest in the world and an imposing landmark on the famous Manhattan skyline.

On the northeast corner of State and Monroe streets is the **Mentor Building** (*1906, Howard Van Doren Shaw*), 39 S. State Street. Look above the "modernized" ground floor at the towering facade that displays a variety of architectural styles. Recessed horizontal bands of windows rise to a Classic-style cornice. This is Shaw's only high-rise design.

Occupying the rest of the block north to Madison Street (and best seen from across the street) is the landmark **Carson Pirie Scott & Company** department store (*1899, 1903, 1906, Louis H. Sullivan; five-bay addition 1906, D. H. Burnham & Company; State Street addition 1960, Holabird & Root; restoration 1980, John Vinci*), 1 S. State Street. The firm was founded by Samuel Carson and John T. Pirie, immigrants from Belfast, Ireland, who set up a small wholesale business first in Amboy, Illinois. They then sold out and moved to Chicago in 1864. Although their building was consumed in the Great Fire of 1871, the story goes that as the wall of flame approached the store, manager Andrew MacLeish (father of poet Archibald MacLeish) offered 50 dollars to anyone who would take a wagonload of merchandise and carry it to safety—a clever ploy that purportedly saved 40 percent of their stock. In the meantime, Pirie had married Carson's sister, and Carson had married Pirie's, and in 1890 the two now-related partners were joined by John E. Scott.

Sullivan designed the steel-frame building for the predecessor store of Schlesinger & Mayer as one of his last large commercial commissions. In 1903, when the nine-story three-bay-wide structure facing Madison Street was purchased by Carson Pirie Scott, a 12-story section with a curved corner added seven more bays. Through the years the building was extended with two major additions (in 1906 by D. H. Burnham & Co., and in 1960 with five more bays by Holabird & Root), but the stylistic integrity of Sullivan's design was faithfully maintained. The Carson Pirie Scott building has always been admired for the bold expression of its structural frame, which included the broad expanse of recessed Chicago windows, the continuous bands of stringcourses and the strong vertical piers. It still stands as a pioneer model for the adaptation of skyscraper technology and fireproof construction to the needs of the modern department store—an ideal example of Louis Sullivan's philosophy that *form should follow function*. From a purely practical point of view, the wide windows were planned to admit as much light as possible into the showrooms and selling floors. The lower floors were reserved for the retail business and the upper floors for wholesale.

Cross the street to the main entrance at the Madison Street corner.

Sullivan's passion for ornament on commercial buildings achieved its highest level in his treatment of the first and second floors, the huge canopy that covered the original main entrance for the "carriage trade," as well as the spectacular "grand entrance" corner. He felt that a store's show window should be a decorative "frame" for the merchandise displayed within, and he designed

The ornate entrance corner of the landmark Carson Pirie Scott department store, on the southeast corner of State and Madison streets, displays the artistic genius of Louis H. Sullivan in the intricate variety of intertwining cast-iron forms. (Photo by author)

The detail of the filigree cast-ironwork above the first floor entrance corner of Carson Pirie Scott shows Sullivan's artistry to good advantage. The architect even worked his LHS initials into the complicated designs (to the right and left, part way up the arch). The entire building was renovated in 1979–1980 by John Vinci, who also restored the delicate decorative cast iron to its original dark-green patina over a red undercoat. (Photo by author)

rich and delicate patterns in cast iron to highlight the effect. The semicircular entranceway with its riot of filigree scrollwork on ornamental panels, displays a variety of intricate intertwining forms, ranging from floral motifs to geometric patterns, with the architect's initials "LHS" worked unobtrusively into the design. Two key players in the execution of his ornament were George Grant Elmslie, Louis Sullivan's chief draftsman, and Kristian Schneider, a skilled modeler who prepared the molds for the ornate designs. Among John Vinci's building renovations in 1979–1980 was the restoration of the cast-iron decorative forms along the first and second floors and at the corner to their original appearance. By re-creating the dark-green patina over a red undercoat, the desired impression of aging bronze was successfully effected.

Walk into the vestibule, and observe the mahogany paneling and the leafy capitals on the columns which welcome you into a magical Sullivanian "forest" inside. Once within, note the seemingly endless rows of support columns, all adorned with those leafy capitals. In 1978 Carson Pirie Scott finally acquired title to the land it had occupied for so long, which was originally the property of Marshall Field, and later of the Field Museum from whom CPS purchased it. The company, which now owns 53 department stores in the upper Midwest, was recently purchased by P. A. Bergner, a retail chain based in Milwaukee, that also owns the Boston Store. Carson's prides itself on being the official retail outlet for merchandise promoting the Chicago Bulls, and team memorabilia is sold on the main floor. The Chicago flagship store's Christmas store-window displays are one of downtown's major attractions.

 Across the street, on the southwest corner of State and Madison streets, rises the 15-story **Chicago Building** (*1904, Holabird & Roche*), 7 W. Madison Street, built for the Chicago Savings Bank; it is a fine example of the Chicago school of architecture style. On a prominent site, the typically dark-red brick building displays strong verticality with its alternate rows of Chicago windows, narrow piers, and projecting bays. The strong corner piers as columns of quoins recall the architects' Marquette Building, seen earlier on the tour. Happily, the building's cornice and ornate entablature have survived intact.

The corner of State and Madison has been called "the busiest intersection in the world." Whether or not typical Chicago hyperbole, the corner does mark the geographic center, or "baseline" of the Chicago street-numbering system, from which all north-south and east-west addresses are measured. Note that the building lines on all four corners are not quite aligned—the result of several surveying crews working at different times who apparently did not compare notes.

The **State-Madison Building** on the northwest corner (*1905, Holabird & Roche, renovation 1917*), 22 W. Madison Street, designed a year after the architects' Chicago Building, is another Chicago school design, although not as effective as their earlier building. The very conspicuous Corinthian colonnade at the top detracts from the overall plan. The building was once occupied by the Boston Store, a chain of department stores based in Milwaukee.

On the northeast corner of the intersection, **1 N. State Street** (*1912, Holabird & Roche*), the third of the trio of Holabird & Roche buildings on the "busiest corner," was originally built for the Mandel Bros. Store, and later became Wieboldt's Department Store. After Wieboldt's demise, the 15-story building was subdivided for retail businesses, including Filene's Basement, T. J. Maxx, and The Body Shop. A 12-story annex of the Mandel Store, by the same architects, still stands on the corner of Wabash Avenue to the east, bridging little Holden Court, a narrow street which is swallowed up on the other side by Carson Pirie Scott.

Further north on State Street, in the middle of the same block, stands **17 N. State Street** (*1912, D. H. Burnham & Company*). Built for the Charles A. Stevens Store, which used only the first seven floors; the rest of the 18-story building was rented to smaller, noncompeting merchants. The present tenant is Lerner New York, a women's specialty store.

Continue north one block to the northeast corner of Washington Street, and look to the southwest corner.

The 15-story **Reliance Building** (*1891, Burnham & Root, foundations and base; 1895, D. H. Burnham & Company*), 32 N. State Street, perhaps more than any other, symbolizes the Chicago school. At first glance its curtain-wall design gives it the appearance of a much more recent building; in fact, its system of wind bracing through use of steel columns firmly tied to deep girders is very similar to the technique used in the construction of the 1974 Amoco Building. Rejecting the customary heavy portal bracing, the architects' use of prefabricated trusswork columns allowed for lighter weight and greater height, making

Burnham & Root's 1891 Reliance Building, like no other, symbolizes the Chicago school of architecture. Prefabricated trusswork columns permitted greater height (15 stories), while steel columns tied to deep girders provide wind bracing, and as one of the first glass towers, it became a true precursor of the modern skyscraper. Note the skillful use of white-glazed terra cotta and glass in a vigorous horizontality free of conspicuous piers. The city of Chicago conducted a complete restoration of the landmark building in 1995–1996. (Commission on Chicago Landmarks)

the Reliance Building a true precursor of the modern skyscraper and one of the world's first glass towers. In the original construction project, the foundations and base were built from plans by John Wellborn Root, but he died unexpectedly of pneumonia in 1891, and the rest of his plans disappeared. Four years later, Burnham continued the work on the original base, but with a new and innovative plan by his new designer, Charles B. Atwood.

One of the most significant features of the building is the skillful use of white-glazed terra cotta and glass in a vigorous horizontality free of conspicuous piers, and in strong contrast to the dark-red-brick building style of the past. Wide Chicago windows in projecting bays between alternating rows of decorative spandrels with Gothic quatrefoil motifs hide the vertical columns; and at the corners, where the supporting structural uprights cannot be masked, the designer placed pairs of bundled colonnettes in front, to disguise them. One of the building's early tenants was Carson Pirie Scott, prior to the remodeling by Daniel Burnham of the Schlesinger & Mayer Building.

At this writing, the once seriously endangered landmark Reliance Building is being rehabilitated under a recently approved $6.5 million appropriation by the city of Chicago.

Marshall Field & Company occupies the entire block from Washington to Randolph streets, and State Street to Wabash Avenue. The flagship store of this famous department store chain has been on the site since before the Great Fire, occupying successively larger buildings as the firm grew. One of its original buildings, on the southeast corner of Washington Street and Wabash Avenue, still stands, and is perhaps the architectural gem of the complex. Take a short detour east to see this Renaissance Revival–style building, designed in 1892 by Charles B. Atwood of D. H. Burnham. Displaying thick load-bearing walls and heavy arched windows, it was built as the annex to an 1879 building at the southwest corner (the former Singer Sewing Machine offices) which it had acquired earlier and later demolished. In 1900 the Central Music Hall was demolished on the Randolph Street corner to make way for a north section, which was designed by Burnham and completed two years later. It was the 1879 Central Music Hall which launched the careers of Adler and Sullivan, who soon afterward received the commission for the Auditorium Building. After the death of Daniel H. Burnham, his successor firm, D. H. Burnham & Company completed the south section in 1907, after the demolition of the other 1879 building. On the Wabash Avenue side, a middle section was completed by Burnham in 1906, and the final piece, the north section, was added in 1914 by the D. H. Burnham successor, Graham, Burnham & Company.

Burnham's early success with Marshall Field's led to other department store commissions: John Wanamaker in New York (1902), Selfridge's in London (1906), Gimbel Brothers in New York (1909), John Wanamaker in Philadelphia (1909), the May Company in Cleveland (1912), and Filene's in Boston (1912). In 1992 a $110 million renovation of the entire store was completed by HTI/Space International, and the chain was purchased by the Dayton-Hudson Corporation of Minneapolis, which has promised to maintain the respected Marshall Field traditions.

The 14-story Columbus Memorial Building, which stood at the southeast corner of N. State and E. Washington streets, was erected in 1892 and took its name from the World's Columbian Exposition, which opened the following year. Designed by William W. Boyington, it displayed a statue of Columbus over the Washington Street entrance as well as other "Columbiana" in the interior fixtures. The roofline is a radical departure from other Chicago high-rise buildings with its ornate corner cupola, exaggerated dormers, and large stone eagles. The building was razed in 1959. (Photo by John Taylor. Chicago Historical Society)

The northeast corner of State and Washington streets in 1902, with Marshall Field's store occupying the entire block north to E. Randolph Street, has changed considerably through the years. The more modern north section has just replaced the Central Music Hall. In 1907 the south section was completed. The clock, however, still remains (with another at the Randolph Street corner). Note the rather uniform attire of the pedestrians of that era—hoop skirts for the women and derby hats for men. A horse-drawn omnibus in the foreground is about to turn north as soon as the State Street cable car moves on. (Chicago Historical Society)

Through the years the store pioneered many firsts: the first buying office of any store, the first customer orders shipped directly from the country of origin, the first restaurant within a store, the first bridal registry, the first "bargain basement," the first elaborate display windows, and the first personal shopping service.

Founder Marshall Field began in business with a partnership with Levi Z. Leiter in a large retail store which they opened at the northeast corner of State and Washington streets, but it was destroyed in the Great Fire of 1871. However, Field's lavish mansion on elegant S. Prairie Avenue, built the same year, was not in the path of the fire. The partners then opened another retail establishment at the corner of Lake Street which lasted until 1882. In the meantime Marshall Field commissioned noted architect Henry Hobson Richardson to build his Wholesale Store, a splendid Romanesque Revival–style structure on the block bounded by Adams, Quincy, Wells, and Franklin streets, to accommodate his burgeoning wholesale business. In 1883 Field bought out Leiter for a reputed $3 million in cash, which confirmed him as Chicago's wealthiest citizen.

Marshall Field's career began with a partnership with Levi Z. Leiter in this large retail store that stood on the northeast corner of State and Washington streets. The building, erected in 1868, lasted only three years, when it was devoured in the Great Fire. The partnership survived a little longer, until 1882, when Field set off on his own to build a great merchandising empire. The photo, complete with horse and buggy, was made by a nearby commercial studio in 1870. (Chicago Historical Society)

By 1900 Marshall Field had become the largest wholesaler in the country. Sadly, Richardson's only commercial building in Chicago fell victim to the Depression, and was razed in 1930. (His only other building in Chicago is the Glessner House; *see* pages 329–331.)

Field's lavish emporium on State Street, built in sections from 1892 to 1914 on the block between Washington and Randolph streets, became the trendsetter for the development of the State Street retail center. Marshall Field, a rare entrepreneur who really understood human nature, is still remembered for his highly successful slogan, "Give the lady what she wants!" and to this day, the salespeople are known as "associates." Marshall Field's is no longer the same corporate entity, having been acquired by the Dayton-Hudson chain, but the management strives to maintain the image.

The facade of the store, which is listed on the National Register of Historic Places, is typical of the Chicago school, with its strong horizontality, solid piers,

Marshall Field commissioned noted Boston architect Henry Hobson Richardson to design a wholesale store as part of his burgeoning enterprise. The solid Romanesque Revival–style structure, completed in 1885, filled the entire block bounded by Adams, Quincy, Wells, and Franklin streets. This outstanding example of Richardson's talents was demolished in 1930 during the Depression, ostensibly to save on taxes. (Courtesy of the Art Institute of Chicago)

broad expanse of Chicago windows, and tripartite division of the elevations—two-story base, eight-story shaft, and two-story top capped with an entablature and an ugly replacement cornice, plus prominent stringcourses above the 2nd, 3rd, and 10th floors. Four Ionic columns supporting an entablature mark the State Street entrance. Most noticeable as one approaches the massive structure are the charming seven-and-three-quarter-ton bronze clocks suspended over the Washington and Randolph street corners, which were handed down from the earlier Field building on the site. "Meet me under the clock" has been a tradition for generations of shoppers . . . but *only* under the Randolph Street clock. Carl Condit, in his seminal study, *The Chicago School of Architecture,* called the building "the ultimate achievement of the Chicago School and one of the great works of modern commercial architecture."

On the sidewalk in front of the store is the stainless-steel sculpture, *Being Born,* by Virginio Ferarri. Celebrating both art and technology, it pays tribute to the tool and die industry that commissioned and fabricated the work. According to the *Loop Sculpture Guide,* the Italian sculptor explained that "the circular element symbolizes the precision and skill of this industry. The two stainless steel elements fit exactly into each other, symbolizing the process

(Left) A pair of Marshall Field bronze clocks, handed down from earlier Field Buildings, adorn both the Randolph and Washington street corners. For generations of shoppers, "Meet me under the Clock" has been a tradition—but only at the Randolph Street corner, illustrated here. (Photo by author)

of die making." That the industry continues to grow is suggested by the open outer ring. The sculpture rests on a round granite base that conceals a mechanism that releases a continuous flow of water over a central surface that acts as a reflecting pool.

Take the time to explore the store and see the accomplishments of the sweeping renovation. Several atriums are a unique and very attractive feature. In the southwest building, rising above the fifth floor is their "jewel in the crown," the **Tiffany Dome.** Designed in 1907 by Louis Comfort Tiffany, the 6,000-square-foot irridescent blue and gold mosaic is composed of 1,600,000 pieces of Favrile glass, laid by hand by more than 50 artisans and supervised by Mr. Tiffany himself, and took two years to complete. Take the escalator to the fourth or fifth floor for a closeup view. Continue north to the northwest building where another atrium rises the full 12 stories, surrounded by columned balconies on each level, to a clear glass ceiling. A third atrium is new, and connects the South State area to South Wabash. In tying the two buildings together, a former light well was remodeled into an 11-story courtyard with soaring glass elevators and crossing banks of escalators. Antique replica lampposts and grillwork recall the State Street of an earlier era, echoed by the splashing of the

The famous Masonic Temple, erected 1890–1892, from plans by Burnham & Root, stood on the northeast corner of State and Randolph streets, across from Marshall Field's. The structure was designed as a commercial skyscraper, with the upper floors reserved for various Masonic organizations and offices. Its twin pyramidal gables are said to have been the inspiration for Philip Johnson's 190 S. LaSalle Street Building. The impressive structure, which was the tallest building in the world when completed, was razed in 1939 for the same reason as the Marshall Field Wholesale Store, to save on taxes. (Chicago Historical Society)

spectacular fountain, inspired by the original 1901 design. Still another atrium can be found on the seventh floor, rising four stories to the roof, next to the elegant Walnut Room restaurant. (There is a large food court in the basement, plus several restaurants, if refreshment is needed.)

Across State Street from Marshall Field's is (at this writing) a vacant lot known as "Block 37" awaiting development under Chicago's North Loop Redevelopment. At present Sears, Roebuck & Company is seriously considering opening a new store in the space. Sears has not had a presence on the "Great Street" since it closed its landmark 403 State Street store in 1983. Temporarily located on the site is the Hot Tix theatre ticket booth which sells day-of-performance discounted tickets for live theatre, dance, and music events (telephone 977-1755), and the Sears-sponsored Skate-on-State winter ice-skating rink. At the western end is Com Ed's electric substation, seen earlier, on the back wall of which is the colorful and amusing *Plug Boy* mural.

At the corner of Randolph Street, look briefly to the west.

Just down the block, at 32 W. Randolph Street (formerly No. 24–28), in the heart of what was the center of the theatre district from the turn of the century until after World War II, stood the lavish **Iroquois Theatre.** On December 30, 1903, a month after opening night and during a sellout Christmas-season performance of *Bluebeard,* with Eddie Foy, Sr., fire broke out above the stage, caused by an overloaded electrical circuit. Although touted as a fireproof structure, the curtain, props, and furnishings were not; and in minutes, flames and smoke filled the house. Of the 22 exits, few could be used or even found, and most doors opened inward. In the ensuing panic 602 people perished; about half were either suffocated near their seats or trampled to death in the darkness as they piled up at the doors. Among a number of children attending that fateful matinee were the two sons of Frank Lloyd Wright, John and Lloyd, who were pulled to safety. The Iroquois Theatre disaster is still remembered as the worst theatre fire in the history of the United States. The Iroquois was rebuilt and renamed the Colonial, and became a vaudeville house for a number of years. Chicago's Rialto, whose many theatres offered legitimate stage productions and vaudeville, later became popular with the big bands, and finally declined into 24-hour movie houses, most disappearing altogether by the 1970s.

 Occupying the present site is the **New United Masonic Temple and Oriental Theatre Building** (*1926, Cornelius W. and George L. Rapp*), 32 W. Randolph Street. The 22-story building was designed by the country's most eminent theatre architects to house not only the 3,200-seat auditorium, but halls and offices of the Masonic Order. The Masons moved out long ago, and the theatre has been dark for years. In the interim the building was renamed the Chicago Real Estate Board Building, but in recent years it has been vacant. At this writing it was announced that a Toronto-based producer, Garth Drabinsky's Livent, Inc., has obtained an option on the Oriental Theatre, and is planning to revive and expand it—a move that is certain to inject new life into the once-vibrant theatre district.

A charred page from the program of the "absolutely fireproof" Iroquois Theatre announcing the beginning of the sixth week of the performance of "Mr. Blue Beard," on December 28, 1903. Two days later the Iroquois was the victim of the worst theatre fire in American history, with the loss of 602 lives! The theatre, at 24–28 W. Randoph Street, in what was the heart of Chicago's theatre district, was subsequently rebuilt and renamed the Colonial. (Chicago Historical Society)

The rebuilt Colonial Theatre, formerly the Iroquois, never achieved the popularity of its predecessor, no doubt owing to the grim disaster. In this 1913 photo, the once-proud theatre has been reduced to a cheap vaudeville house. (Chicago Historical Society)

Continue north on State Street to the Chicago Theatre.

   The Chicago Theatre (*1921, Cornelius W. & George L. Rapp*), 125 N. State Street, was designed for the theatre-developer chain of Balaban & Katz by the same firm that designed the New United Masonic Temple and Oriental Theatre. The work of the brothers Rapp could be seen across the country, from such palatial houses as the two Paramount theatres in New York City, to the still extant small-town Al Ringling, in Baraboo, Wisconsin. Built as opulent vaudeville or legitimate theatres, they were able to survive by converting in the 1920s to movie houses, and a surprising number are still in existence. The Chicago Theatre, which Balaban & Katz called the "Wonder Theatre of the World," was built at a cost of $4 million, specifically for the showing of films during the era when the great movie palaces were the main source of public entertainment. The State Street side is dominated by the enormous six-story "Chicago" sign suspended in front of an ornate facade whose triumphal arch was patterned after the Arc de Triomphe, in Paris. Although the present marquee is the third (installed in 1949), the vertical sign is original and one of only a scant few in existence. For years it has been a Loop landmark and an unofficial symbol of the city.

   The entire 60-foot-wide front is clad in off-white terra cotta embellished with fanciful neo-Baroque designs. This is but a hint of the elaborate interior, (but to get in to see it you will have to purchase a ticket to a show). The lofty grand lobby was patterned after Francois Mansart's Chapelle Royale, at Versailles, and the original draperies, carpeting, and fine furnishings were supplied by Marshall Field and Company. The 3,800-seat theatre is built in an L-shape, with the auditorium facing Lake Street. Because of the noise and vibration anticipated from the overhead Lake Street Elevated, that side of the building was erected with a double wall. The first of three renovations of the theatre was completed in time for the opening of the 1933 Century of Progress Exposition. The second took place in the early 1950s when much of the interior was "modernized," with panels and false ceilings covering much of the original ornate design.

   With declining revenue in the 1970s and early 1980s, the Chicago Theatre was slated for demolition. It was saved at the last minute partly because of its historic landmark status, but primarily through the intervention of a new partnership, the Chicago Theatre Restoration Associates, which assumed ownership of the theatre and the adjacent Page Brothers Building, incorporating it into the theatre building, with retail establishments, restaurant, and office space. The plan, developed with the architectural staff of the Illinois Historic Preservation Agency, was implemented, and restoration of the two buildings began in 1985, with the theatre to be restored to its 1933 appearance. While some critics would have preferred restoration to the original 1921 plan, and others lamented the sale of the "mighty Wurlitzer" organ, all Chicagoans were delighted to have the Chicago Theatre back for an "encore performance." In a recent development, the Walt Disney Company has agreed to take over the operations of the theatre, presumably to present a variety of extravagant family stage shows.

The landmark Chicago Theatre was designed by the nationally famous pair of theatre architects, Cornelius W. and George L. Rapp, and is one of the city's major entertainment spots. Called the "Wonder Theatre of the World" when it opened, it remains one of the country's most notable theatre palaces. Set in front of a huge arch on the front facade inspired by the Arc de Triomphe, is the enormous six-story-tall "Chicago" theatre sign. The prominent sign, among the largest in the world, has been adopted as one of the unofficial symbols of the city. (Photo by author)

Across State Street is the 13-story **ABC (American Broadcasting Company) Building** (*1917, Cornelius W. and George L. Rapp*), 190 N. State Street. Another Rapp & Rapp theatre building, but in a style that broke with the Chicago school tradition, being designed for mixed use as the State-Lake Theatre and an office tower. A major renovation was undertaken in 1984 by Skidmore, Owings & Merrill, which included the installation of an atrium, new windows, a storefront, and the restoration of the terra-cotta facade, ornate cornice, and acroteria. The name of the former movie palace, which was built as part of the Orpheum Circuit, is emblazoned over what was the theatre entrance, but is now the main entry to the building. The old auditorium is used for television productions of WLS-TV Channel 7, and radio station WLS. (When WLS received its original broadcasting license, its call letters stood for "World's Largest Store," Sears, Roebuck & Company, where the radio station's studios were then situated.) WLS-TV, whose antennas are located atop the Sears Tower, was the first television station in Chicago and the third in the nation.

Back across the street again, at the corner of Lake Street, is the **Page Brothers Building,** also called The Loop End Building (*1872, John Mills Van Osdel*), 171–191 N. State Street. Architect Van Osdel is considered Chicago's first practicing architect, and he designed this building as a tannery and warehouse. Completed the year after the Great Fire, on the site of the burned-out City Hotel, it is one of the oldest surviving structures in the Loop area. The entrance was originally on Lake Street, but when State Street replaced Lake as the prime retail

The Page Brothers Building, designed by John Mills Van Osdel in 1872 on the southeast corner of State and Lake streets, was built for a tannery and warehouse. Originally a full cast-iron-front building, a "modernization" in 1902 left only the Lake Street facade intact. It is one of two remaining cast-iron-front buildings in the Loop (the other is the four-story building, No. 27 W. Adams Street, of the Berghoff restaurant complex). The photo was taken from the platform of the State/Lake El station—the only good vantage point to observe the cast-iron facade. (Photo by Bob Thall for the Commission on Chicago Landmarks)

district, a sixth floor was added, and the State Street facade, which was of cast iron, was cemented over. The original cast-iron sections were ordered from Daniel D. Badger's Architectural Iron Works, in New York (*see* page 76). The "modernization," by Hill & Woltersdorf in 1902, fortunately left the Lake Street side's cast-iron front and ornate cornice intact. In 1986, as part of the renovation of the adjoining Chicago Theatre which wraps around the Page Brothers Building, the two buildings were joined, as described above; however, before the connection could be made, the wood-frame structure of the Page Brothers Building had to be upgraded. The very difficult project of preserving the delicate cast-iron facade and exterior walls was conducted by Daniel P. Coffey & Associates, who gradually replaced the old framework with reinforced concrete, thus saving the only one of two cast-iron-front buildings in the Loop, at the same time assuring that the Chicago Theatre would also survive.

Turn right on Lake Street one block to Wabash Avenue.

On the northeast corner is **203 N. Wabash Avenue** (*1928, Cornelius W. & George L. Rapp*). Still another Rapp & Rapp building (the firm was known for its commercial office buildings as well as for its theatres), it was the former Old Dearborn Bank Building, and is distinguished only for the ornate terra-cotta spandrels on the lower three floors and the terra-cotta designs along the parapet of this 24-story structure.

Immediately to the right is a rather unusual place to end the tour. The **Self Park** (*1986, Stanley Tigerman & Associates*), 60 E. Lake Street. To appreciate what Tigerman created for the owner of this parking garage, who wanted something "different" but unmistakably associated with the automobile, it will be necessary to stand across the street. You are now looking head-on at an approaching automobile! And without much imagination, one can identify the baked enamel "fenders" as awnings over the two side entrances, the Self Park "license plate" in between, above which is the shiny "chromium grille," "radiator," and "headlights" surmounted by a "hood ornament." The entrance and exit ramps are between the "wheels."

End of tour. Michigan Avenue is just ahead.

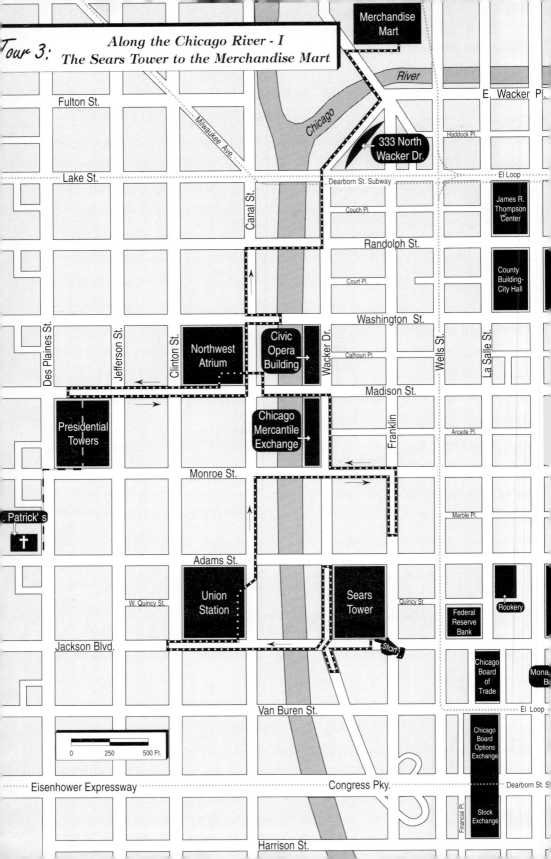

Tour 3:

**Along the Chicago River - I
The Sears Tower to the Merchandise Mart**

Merchandise Mart

Chicago River

E. Wacker Pl.

Haddock Pl.

333 North Wacker Dr.

Fulton St.

Milwaukee Ave.

Lake St.

Dearborn St. Subway

El Loop

Canal St.

Couch Pl.

James R. Thompson Center

Randolph St.

County Building-City Hall

Court Pl.

Washington St.

Des Plaines St.

Jefferson St.

Clinton St.

Northwest Atrium

Civic Opera Building

Wacker Dr.

Calhoun Pl.

Wells St.

La Salle St.

Madison St.

Presidential Towers

Chicago Mercantile Exchange

Franklin

Arcade Pl.

Monroe St.

Marble Pl.

Patrick's

Adams St.

Union Station

Sears Tower

Quincy St.

Rookery

W. Quincy St.

Federal Reserve Bank

Jackson Blvd.

Start

Chicago Board of Trade

Mona B

Van Buren St.

El Loop

0   250   500 Ft.

Chicago Board Options Exchange

Dearborn St. S

Eisenhower Expressway

Congress Pky.

Financial Pl.

Stock Exchange

Harrison St.

3. Along the Chicago River, I: The Sears Tower to the Merchandise Mart

There is no better way to begin this tour than with a visit to the 103rd-floor Sky-deck of the Sears Tower. Visibility on a clear day extends for almost 35 miles, with an unsurpassed panorama of virtually every major Chicago skyscraper, the web-like network of expressways and railroads that radiate from the central part of the city, the broad shoreline of Lake Michigan, and the narrow Chicago River with its many lift bridges, winding its way southward and extending a branch to the lake.

The tour will take you back and forth across the river several times, ending at the monumental Merchandise Mart building on the river's north bank. Much of the walk will be along Wacker Drive, which parallels the river as far as the lake. In his famous 1909 Plan of Chicago, Daniel H. Burnham envisaged Wacker Drive as an essential element in a ring of roadways around the Loop. It is named for Charles Wacker, first chairman of the Chicago Plan Commission, and was opened in 1925, replacing the South Water Street Produce Market. The area along the river and South Wacker Drive, sometimes called the Gateway because of its access by water and rail to the West, has changed dramatically in the past 25 years. Rows of undistinguished warehouses of Chicago's garment district suddenly yielded to a building boom of mammoth proportions, with the soaring dark silhouette of the Sears Tower among the first to dominate the skyline. And, as you will soon see, high-rise construction continues unabated.

The **Sears Tower** (*completed 1973, Skidmore, Owings & Merrill; Bruce Graham, chief architect; renovations and remodeling, 1985, 1992*), 233 S. Wacker Drive: Although the formal entrance to the building is through a four-story glass-enclosed entrance on Wacker Drive (the product of a major 1984 renovation by the original architects), the Skydeck has its own new south plaza entrance on Jackson Boulevard. But do return later to enjoy Alexander Calder's humorous rotating and swinging sculpture called *Universe,* set against the lobby's rear wall.

The 100-story bold stepped-back tower sheathed in black aluminum and bronze-tinted glass rises 1,454 feet (443 meters), and, at this writing, is the world's tallest office building. Construction is now underway in Kuala Lumpur, the capital of Malaysia, on a pair of mega-skyscrapers, designed by architect Cesar Pelli, that when completed in 1997 will be 22 feet taller than the Sears Tower. Not to be outdone in the race to the sky, China has *two* new blockbusters on the drawing board: one in Chongqing that will be 46 feet higher than the Sears Tower, and another in Shanghai, to be called the International Financial Center Tower, that would reach a record height of 1,509 feet! Closer to home, developers have filed plans to build what would be the world's tallest building right here in the Loop. (*See* page 40.) With the twin antenna towers, the Sears Tower's total height reaches 1,707 feet, exceeding the former record height of the New York World Trade Center's twin towers by 100 feet. Construction took three years, with 1,600 workers employed on the project.

The structure is imbedded into an enormous concrete slab set on 114 rock caissons securely socketed into bedrock. Anchored into the slab is a tough steel frame which consists of a bundled "tube" of nine 75-foot squares made of I-beams spaced 15 feet apart, the entire framework weighing 76,000 tons. The nine tubes rise to the 50th floor, above which seven continue to the 66th floor, five to the 90th, and the last two to the top, with the final steel girders for the tower section delivered by a Sikorsky Skycrane helicopter. The ingenious design of this single rigid structure, by the late Fazlur R. Khan, provides lateral strength which can withstand Chicago's frequent stiff winds while allowing for more interior and cosmetic space. The Tower has more than 16,000 bronze-tinted windows and 28 acres of duranodic aluminum skin. A frequently asked question: How do they wash the windows? Answer: There are six automatic window-washing machines that clean the building exterior eight times a year.

Take the time to visit the **Skydeck,** but perhaps not just now. The lines are often long, especially during the summer and on holiday weekends (the best time is early morning before the usual onslaught of visitors); skip the multimedia show, but before zooming up to the 103rd floor in one of the two nonstop elevators that make the ascent in just over a minute, do spend a few minutes at the interesting ground-floor exhibit which displays the American Institute of Architect's selection of Chicago's ten most architecturally significant buildings. The view from the top is, of course, breathtaking, with a broad panoramic view of the entire city and many of its suburbs, as well as a view far out into Lake Michigan. Recorded narrations are continuous on all four sides, with descriptions of many of the significant landmarks of downtown Chicago. There is also an observation deck on the 100th floor, used for overflow crowds, but one can't go from one to the other. Once down, you can save more time for the tour by bypassing the profusion of souvenir shops on the way out.

The history of Sears, Roebuck & Company dates back to the 1887 partnership of watchmaker Richard Warren Sears and businessman Alvah Roebuck, whose mail-order general merchandise enterprise flourished and became an American institution. Within a few years business was so good that they erected their first "Sears Tower," a 12-story "skyscraper" on the corner of Honan and Arthington streets, on Chicago's west side, and the story of Sears Roebuck went on to become an American legend. Recently most of the company's operations were moved to Hoffman Estates, Illinois, about 30 miles to the west; however, the corporate headquarters will still remain in the Sears Tower. In 1994 an agreement was reached to restructure the building's troublesome financing, and ownership of the Sears Tower was transferred to a pension fund partnership. The name, however, will be retained, and the Sears Tower will continue to symbolize Chicago's dynamic growth and development.

(The Skydeck is open daily from 9:00 A.M. to 9:00 P.M., and to 10:00 P.M. in summer. Admission: adults $6.50, seniors $4.75, youths 5–17 $3.25, no charge for children or military in uniform. Information: 875-9696.)

On leaving the Sears Tower, turn right to the corner of S. Wacker Drive, turn left and cross Jackson Boulevard.

Set on a plaza just 390 feet away from the Sears Tower and covering the entire block, is the imposing vertical shaft of **311 S. Wacker Drive** (*1990, Kohn Pederson Fox, in association with HKS*). The 65-story building enjoys the distinction of being the tallest reinforced concrete structure in the United States, soaring 970 feet (the world's tallest is the Central Plaza, in Hong Kong), exceeding by 100 feet the former tallest concrete building in Chicago, Water Tower Place. It is also the fourth tallest structure in Chicago (after the Sears Tower, Amoco Building, and John Hancock Center). The building, whose octagonal configuration above the 14th floor provides eight corner offices at each level, is sheathed in several shades of granite plus five different tones of marble, and displays a variety of window styles. The 14-story base is essentially a rectangle with two corners cut diagonally. Above the 65th floor, a Gothic framework of columns and beams breaks free from the mass of the tower. Terminating the building is a circular crown 105 feet tall and 65 feet in diameter surrounded by four 25-foot-diameter cylinders, all internally illuminated at night by 2,000 fluorescent lamps.

As it now stands, flanked by tight 51-story wings, it is a graceful addition to the skyline as it tapers upward; however, the builder is said to be planning two identical towers to be placed alongside. With the severe massing that would result, one can't help wondering whether "more is better," especially in view of so much unrented space in the Sears Tower. The 200-foot-long projecting extension, of the same building design, encloses a barrel-vaulted glass arcade

(Left) The Sears Tower glistens in the late afternoon sun, its towering profile dwarfing its neighbors. At 1,454 feet, it is still the tallest building in the world (but for how long?). The view from the Skydeck is breathtaking and well worth the usual wait. (Photo by author)

leading to the entrance. It appears somewhat overscaled for just one building entrance, and lends credence to the developers' worrisome plan to insert the two additional buildings on that relatively small plot. Nevertheless, it is a pleasant, airy space designed as a wintergarden, and a nice spot for a moment's relaxation. Eight 40-foot-tall simulated palm trees rise almost to the 100-foot-high glass ceiling that is supported by steel trusses, while pairs of white-painted steel columns flank the interior. Just beyond the entrance, at the head of a long sunken atrium, is a huge bronze fountain with a cascading wall of water dominated by Raymond Kaskey's sculpture of Neptune on a clamshell, entitled *Gem of the Lakes*. At this writing the developers are planning an underground pedestrian passageway, incorporating an old freight tunnel under the Chicago River, to provide weather-protected access to Union Station.

Turn right (north) on S. Wacker Drive one block.

A sharply angular plot requires its building envelope to accommodate it, and **200 S. Wacker Drive** does just that. Designed by Harry Weese & Associates in 1981, its triangular geometry is reminiscent of Weese's Metropolitan Correctional Center and the Swissôtel. To observe the unusual placement of the northeast 7-story addition atop the 38-story white-painted aluminum and tinted-glass polygonal-shaped building may require stepping back across the drive. (Watch out for the traffic!) The 45-degree angles are even carried to the base, where the exterior support columns are rotated. The three-story lobby is contained within an angled glass wall which forms an arcade around the building, particularly attractive along the river.

Return to Jackson Boulevard, turn right and cross the Chicago River.

Pause for a moment in the middle of the **Jackson Boulevard Bridge** (*1915, Edward H. Bennett, consulting architect of the Chicago Plan Commission*). There are 50 city-owned movable bridges and several owned by railroads, of which 43 cross the 100-foot-wide **Chicago River**—20 in the downtown area alone—more than in any other city in the world. Most are of the double-leaf trunnion bascule type, spans which lift from each end on a horizontal axle or trunnion, and are counterbalanced from underneath. (The word *bascule* derives from the French word for "seesaw," which describes how the bridges operate.) All Chicago River lift bridges downtown are double-leaf, except the railroad bridge at the entrance to the North Branch and the Kinzie Street Bridge, which are single-leaf, and will be seen later. Some of the highways, however, cross on fixed, immovable bridges. Most of the modern lift bridges, which are so characteristic of Chicago, were built after the river course was altered early in the 20th century. Chicago boasts more movable river bridges per mile than in any other city. (In second place is Milwaukee, with 13.)

(Left) No. 311 S. Wacker Drive, cheek-by-jowl and competing with the Sears Tower for lebensraum, *presents another idiom in skyscraper technology. The 65-story behemoth is the tallest reinforced concrete structure in the country and the fourth tallest building in Chicago. Above the 14th floor the shaft becomes octagonal in shape. The 105-foot-tall circular crown is surrounded by four 25-foot-diameter cylinders—all illuminated after dark by fluorescent lighting. (Photo by author)*

A Brief History of Chicago's Bridges. The first bridge across the Chicago River, for pedestrians only, was built in 1832 at Kinzie Street. Until then the only way to get across was by boat or canoe, although a ferry service had begun three years earlier at approximately the site of the present Lake Street Bridge. In 1834 the first bridge designed to carry vehicles was constructed at Dearborn Street. It was a drawbridge 300 feet long, but was a hazard to vessels passing underneath, and in 1839 so many ships had collided with it that a group of irate citizens tore it down.

With the growth of the city, more practical bridges were built, all of timber, largely through funds obtained by subscription from adjacent property owners and businesses. In 1857 the first municipally owned and financed bridge was opened at Madison Street. From then on, all bridges built until the turn of the century were of the swing type, made of iron and timber and supported on a

The Chicago River is spanned by 43 bridges, 20 in the downtown area alone. In this view looking south toward the confluence of the north and main branches, the Kinzie Street Bridge is being raised to permit river traffic to pass. Just behind is the Chicago & Northwestern Railway (now Union Pacific) Bridge, also a single-leaf bascule bridge, but counterbalanced by a huge concrete block, rather than by a trunnion. The railway bridge is usually kept in the open position except when an occasional freight train makes a delivery to the Merchandise Mart or the Sun-Times. (Photo by author)

cluster of piers in the center of the river. Although these steam-operated swing bridges were quite efficient, rotating fairly quickly in a 90-degree arc on their central pivot, their position in the center of the river channel made them a nuisance to navigation, and collisions were frequent. For a number of years other types of movable bridges were experimented with, including a "folding bridge," which turned out to be impractical; then a vertical lift bridge, whose tall steel towers were deemed unsightly, found favor with the railroads. Finally in 1895 the first bascule-type bridge was opened at Van Buren Street. Powered by electricity, it was immediately successful and led the way for all swing bridges to be replaced. The first of these bascule bridges were of the "rolling" type that projected outward before lifting. They were soon replaced by the more practical trunnion type which is still widely used throughout the world.

Reversing the River.   In 1900 Chicago pulled a spectacular engineering trick by literally reversing the flow of the river. After 10 years and the expenditure of $40 million, the south branch of the Chicago River was dredged to a depth significantly lower than the main and north branches, and with the installation of locks and dams, the river's waters were forced by gravity to flow southward, *out* of Lake Michigan where formerly they had emptied *into* the lake. The south branch, which before had ended in an odorous swamp, was then tied to the newly dug Sanitary and Ship Canal to connect the Chicago River with the Desplaines River, which flowed into the Illinois River and then into the Mississippi. The new river project also replaced the earlier Illinois and Michigan Canal, a shallow waterway opened in 1848 that ran between Chicago and La Salle, where it connected with the Illinois River. It was finally abandoned in 1914, and the Stevenson Expressway was built on the old canal bed.

The success of the project became a model for the construction of the Panama Canal, and interestingly, more earth was removed during the Chicago River excavation than in Panama. A continuous deep-draft navigable waterway was thus created that extended from the Great Lakes to the Gulf of Mexico; and as a vital benefit, the polluted waters of the Chicago River would no longer flow into Lake Michigan to contaminate the city's water supply. With the opening of the St. Lawrence Seaway in 1959, ocean-going vessels could pass through all the Great Lakes, and Chicago became the largest inland port in the world, with the Chicago River an integral part of the city's harbor. The reversal of the Chicago River has been designated a National Historic Engineering Landmark.

Much of the success of the development of the Chicago River as "core" of the central city, rather than its "back door," is due not only to the gradual carrying out of the famous 1909 Burnham Plan of Chicago, but to the recently adopted "Chicago River Urban Design Guidelines," which were prepared by a citizen's group, Friends of the Chicago River, in collaboration with the City of Chicago's Department of Planning. The guidelines establish "a continuous riverside walkway throughout the downtown river corridor, easily accessible oases of green space for workers and visitors in the central area, and the transformation of the downtown river section into a high-profile tourist attraction and recreational amenity to enhance Chicago's image as a desirable place to

The Chicago River has always been a busy waterway, especially since the completion of the St. Lawrence Seaway. The river is a vital connecting link between the Great Lakes and the Gulf of Mexico. Here a tugboat shepherds a huge barge loaded with fuel oil on its way from New York City to some southern destination. (Photo by author)

live, work, and visit." The success of the downtown River Walk in San Antonio, Texas, is a model of riverfront urban design that Chicago is working hard to emulate. Chicago's somewhat similar plan, which is well underway, includes landscaped promenades, dock-level shops and cafes, and more marinas, and will cover the entire main branch of the Chicago River from Lake Michigan to Wolf Point, as well as the North Branch to Chicago Avenue and the South Branch as far as Cermak Road. In many ways, the Chicago River, no longer considered the city's "back door" or "ugly cousin," is fast becoming the city's second lakefront.

To the southwest, and occupying two full blocks, is the gargantuan Art Deco–style **U.S. Post Office—Central Station,** which Chicagoans refer to simply as the Main Post Office (*1931, Graham, Anderson, Probst & White*), with a new addition rising to the south. The Eisenhower Expressway passes underneath. To the south, and overhanging the east bank of the river are the dramatic white circular towers of **River City** (*1986, Bertrand Goldberg Associates*), a residential complex described in Tour 8.

Closer by, along the west bank of the river and imitating its S-curved course is the 22-story **Gateway Center IV** (*1984, Skidmore, Owings & Merrill*), 300 S. Riverside Plaza. The dark, reflective green glass skin which looks almost black, conceals two individual buildings. This is the most recent of four Gateway projects designed by SOM beginning in 1965, using the air rights of Union Station and its railroad yards.

After crossing the river, the building on the right (best seen from across Jackson Boulevard) is the former **MidAmerica Commodity Exchange** (*1971, Skidmore, Owings & Merrill*), 444 W. Jackson Boulevard. The huge black aluminum crisscross trusses were required to support the broad interior trading room, which now is no longer used, since the Exchange has moved to a new facility several blocks east, and can be visited on Tour 1. The odd proportions of the building have led some to comment that it resembles a skyscraper lying on its side. The structure is built over the tracks of Union Station, and there are passenger entrances to the station on Jackson Boulevard, on Canal Street, and on the river side. While on the south side of the street, look behind you at the curved-glass **train sheds** below. Since the station was built during the "age of steam" before dieselization, slits run along the length of the sheds to allow the smoke from locomotives to escape.

Immediately north of the MidAmerica Commodity Exchange is **Gateway Center III** (*Skidmore, Owings & Merrill, 1972*), the third of SOM's Gateway Center office buildings. The address is officially 222 S. Riverside Plaza, but don't look for any Riverside Plaza street signs; there aren't any! (Apparently Canal Street was not an elegant enough name for the developers of the Gateway Center project.) The 35-story tower is sheathed in a cream-color concrete, and includes most of the Union Station passenger concourse on the lower level and a pedestrian and vehicular entrance to the station.

Return to the corner of Jackson Boulevard and cross Canal Street, and continue west along Union Station to Clinton Street.

At the southwest corner is **547 W. Jackson Boulevard,** the Burlington Building (*1911, Marshall & Fox*). The ornate Gothic Revival–style structure, sheathed in bright white terra cotta, is characterized by an arcade at the ground floor which is repeated at the top. This was once the headquarters of the Chicago, Burlington & Quincy Railroad, a major Chicago-based line whose motto was "Everywhere West," until its merger with the Great Northern Railroad into the giant Burlington Northern system.

Return to the middle of the block and enter Union Station. Turn right and descend the stairs to the main waiting room.

Union Station (*1913–1925 Graham, Anderson, Probst & White; renovations 1992–1995*) is one of the last remaining great railway terminals in America and one of only four left in the Loop area, where once there were seven. Union Station, erected on the site of the earlier Union Passenger Station, built in 1881, figured in the 1909 Burnham Plan of Chicago for West Loop development. The name "Union" referred to the union of four railroads that originally shared the depot's facilities: the Pennsylvania Railroad, the Chicago, Burlington & Quincy, the Chicago & Alton, and the Chicago, Milwaukee & St. Paul. The recently restored travertine-clad waiting room is once again a magnificent interior space. Fluted Corinthian columns mark the various exits, each bracketed by a pair of bronze lamp standards. Framing the vaulted entrance passage to the trains are two large allegorical statues of *Day* (with a rooster) and *Night* (with an owl). The two goddesses symbolize what was once the railroads' motto, "Service around the Clock."

Union Station (1913–1925, Graham, Anderson, Probst & White) occupies the entire block bounded by W. Jackson Boulevard and W. Adams, S. Canal, and S. Clinton streets, and is one of the last of the great passenger terminals, as well as the only one in Chicago serving transcontinental passenger trains. It is also the only terminal with two opposing sets of tracks for northbound and southbound long-distance and commuter lines. (Photo by author)

After the first union depot was demolished, the present Union Station complex included another structure across Canal Street, a Classic-style concourse building that was razed in 1969 to make way for the rather bland pair of SOM buildings now on the site. Underneath the new building are the Metra and AMTRAK train platforms. A unique feature of Union Station is the track layout. It is the only terminal with two opposing sets of stub tracks, with lines entering from the north and south. The station has an active commuter service with Metra lines radiating to many suburban communities. AMTRAK also uses Union Station, although its reduced schedules are a mere ghost of yesteryear's glamorous, frequent, and dependable trains. Yet today, despite the decline of passenger service, Chicago still remains the heart of the nation's railroad network. There were seven great railroad terminals in Chicago, which during the heyday of the passenger train, served 21 major railroads. Union Station is the last historic survivor. From this station luxury trains of the Milwaukee Road, Pennsylvania Railroad, Burlington, and Gulf, Mobile & Ohio departed many times daily for such far-flung destinations as Seattle, New York, Washington, Denver, and New Orleans.

Exit the station from the northern stairway to Canal Street, turn left to Adams Street, and cross Canal Street to the northeast corner.

Look back at the facade of Union Station. Note the eight-story office tower above, set back from the lower section so as not to detract from it. Union Sta-

tion, with its 22 massive columns, stands as a grand monument to Chicago's role as railroad transportation center of the nation.

In the next block, at No. 130 S. Canal Street, is the **Florsheim Shoe Company Building** (*1949, Shaw, Metz & Dolio; addition 1977*), with the company name emblazoned on the tower. The *AIA Guide to Chicago* describes it as "the first major Chicago structure to emphatically embrace the design elements of European modernism." Sheathed in a light-colored glazed brick and "banded" horizontally with continuous rows of ribbon windows, it represents the new trend in building style that became so prevalent after World War II. The center infill addition in 1977 changed the original building shape from a "U" to a solid block.

Its neighbor to the north, **525 W. Monroe Street** (*1983, Skidmore, Owings & Merrill*), is a Z-shaped office tower whose 24 stories set on a red granite base are highlighted with bands of two tones of glass windows—blue-black opaque and nonreflective green—with thin strips of aluminum accenting the window frames. The shape of the sloped top is repeated in the large glass entrance atrium.

Across Monroe Street, the **Heller International Tower** (*1992, Skidmore, Owings & Merrill*), 500 W. Monroe Street, is a bold statement in sharp contrast to the previous SOM buildings on the street. Its imposing 45-story corner tower marks it as the tallest skyscraper west of the river. The narrow windows of the tower, highlighted with aluminum bands, contrast sharply with the rest of the windows which are set flush in the walls. The light-colored granite building appears to descend westward in a series of setbacks, while the eastern facade displays an interesting assymetry. Along the Monroe Street side is an arcaded pedestrian sidewalk. The unconventional design can best be appreciated at a distance.

Turn right (east) on Monroe Street.

Before crossing the Chicago river on the Monroe Street Bridge (*1919, John Ericson, engineer*), note the pair of 20-story office buildings bracketing Monroe Street, **Gateway Center I** (to the north), 10 S. Riverside Plaza, and **Gateway Center II,** 120 S. Riverside Plaza, both by Skidmore, Owings & Merrill. The former, the first in the "Gateway" quartet, was erected in 1965, and the latter in 1968. Both reflect the influence of the then-popular "glass box" style, popularized by Mies van der Rohe. Wide landscaped pedestrian areas along the river add a pleasant touch to these otherwise undistinguished buildings.

As you reach the east side of the river, look back and note how both buildings rest on columns over the busy rail yards. From this point the Heller International Tower can be seen to best advantage.

On the southwest corner of Monroe Street and S. Wacker Drive is the **Hartford Building** (*1961, Skidmore, Owings & Merrill*), 150 S. Wacker Drive, formerly Chicago headquarters of the Hartford Fire Insurance Company. (The Hartford Group is now located at 200 W. Madison Street.) This 21-story "exoskeletal" structure offers floor upon floor of shady office space while showing off its concrete framework. The Hartford Building has been likened to the style of the Chicago school of architecture in which the skeletal structure of a building is visible in its facade. Sharing the blocklong plot on what is called Hartford Plaza, is **No. 100,** a polished black-granite high-rise rectangular structure whose only distinguishing feature is the way the piers extend outward at the base, giving it a skirt-like effect. Both buildings provide pedestrian walkways overlooking the river.

The vacant lot across S. Wacker Drive (which may no longer be vacant when you read this) was the site of the 1963 **U.S. Gypsum Building** (*Perkins & Will*), 101 S. Wacker Drive. A novel cruciform-shaped 19-story structure set at a 45-degree angle to the street line, it had to be razed in 1994–1995 because of the need for extensive renovation and an irretrievable amount of asbestos in its structural members. Also, taxes on an empty building would be higher than on a vacant lot, so demolition seemed the only recourse. The unusual "pre-Postmodern" building was vacated in 1990, and the company moved to new offices at 125 S. Franklin Street. Preservationists are now pondering the question of how to protect an architecturally significant building younger than the minimum 50 years required for landmark designation when it has outlived its economic viability.

The former U.S. Gypsum Building (1963, Perkins & Will) stood on the west side of S. Wacker Drive at the southeast corner of W. Monroe Street, but had to be demolished in 1994–1995. Prohibitive remodeling costs, an irretrievable amount of asbestos in its structural members, and high taxes on an unused building led to the decision. Its unusual design and 45-degree rotation from the street wall attracted considerable attention, and many lamented its loss. The U.S. Gypsum Company, now USG Corporation, moved into a spanking new building a block away. (Courtesy USG Corporation)

Stand on the northwest corner of W. Monroe Street and S. Wacker Drive and look past the vacant lot to the southeast to the striking pair of buildings occupying the entire blockfront on S. Franklin Street between W. Monroe and W. Adams streets, the **AT&T Corporate Center** and the **USG Building,** completed in 1989 and 1992, respectively, and designed by Adrian Smith of Skidmore, Owings & Merrill, (227 W. Monroe Street and 125 S. Franklin Street). Take a brief detour to get a close-up look at how the pair of buildings—one 60 stories tall and the other 35—have similar but distinguishing characteristics, and how the buildings and their elegant lobbies are interconnected. The AT&T building recalls the Art Moderne period with its strong verticality in a style introduced by Eliel Saarinen in the *Chicago Tribune* competition of 1922. The facade is divided into three sections with setbacks at the 30th, 45th, and 59th floors that relate to neighboring buildings and are sheathed in a light rose-beige granite, with a polished red-granite base that also encircles the USG Building. An interesting touch is the silkscreened dark-green pattern around each of the window spandrels. Crowning the tower are four tall pinnacles and several shorter ones that create distinctive punctuation to the city's skyline.

The shorter USG Building boasts a metal-hipped roof, reminiscent of the Board of Trade Building, and a somewhat different treatment of the facade, with a wider central bay. Enter the AT&T Building first, at the Monroe Street side, into the 44-foot-high main lobby, illuminated by three chandeliers. Rich Italian marble in a range of colors and shapes adorns the floors and walls which are highlighted with gold leaf, satin bronze, and oak wood trim. The design of the three banks of 36 elevators includes bronze doors and ceilings. As you pass through the two ground-floor elevator lobbies, note the very attractive wall sconces, the etched bronze doors, and the marble floors and walls. The adjoining Franklin Street lobby features a dramatic 16-story atrium. On exiting the USG Building, turn around and compare the twin skyscrapers, then note USG's "neo–Art Deco" entrance. At this writing it was announced that the AT&T and USG building complex has been purchased by a Singaporean pension fund.

Return to Wacker Drive and Monroe Street.

In the block to the north, on the west side of the Drive, is the prominent **Chicago Mercantile Exchange** (*1983, 1988, Fujikawa, Johnson & Associates*), 30 and 10 S. Wacker Drive. The complex consists of twin 40-story towers, the south tower completed in 1983, the north in 1988, embracing a center section. To permit the very broad space required for the trading floors, the towers had to be cantilevered over the trading rooms in the base section, requiring enormous trusses, thicker bearing walls, and heavy columns. As an added attraction for tenants in a building closely confined to a relatively narrow site, the corners of the towers are serrated, thus providing 16 additional "corner" offices on each floor.

The "Merc" evolved from the Chicago Produce Exchange (1874) and the Chicago Butter & Egg Board (1898) into the world's largest marketplace for futures and options trading in currencies and short-term financial instru-

Rising above the entire blockfront on S. Franklin Street, between W. Monroe and W. Adams streets, are the stunning AT&T Corporate Center (1989) and the USG Building (1992), both designed by Adrian Smith of Skidmore, Owings & Merrill. The AT&T building is 60 stories tall and the USG, 35. Although sharing many similarities, the AT&T building recalls the Art Moderne era with its strong verticality, but both are sheathed in rose-beige granite and share a common red-granite base. Crowning the taller structure are four prominent pinnacles surrounded by a host of smaller ones. The USG Building is topped by a metal hipped roof and has a wider central bay. (Photo by Jon Miller, copyright © Hedrich Blessing)

ments, such as U.S. Treasury bills and Eurodollars, as well as in agricultural futures contracts for cattle, hogs, and pork bellies. The vast electronic trading system is conducted on two trading floors, with a 40,000-square-foot main floor measuring 215 feet by 90 feet and an additional 30,000-square-foot floor directly above it. Although the Exchange turns its back on the river, it does offer a very pleasant amenity in the shady riverwalk and cafe in the rear, similar to the one behind Hartford Plaza. Enter the lobby and see the 100-foot-high escalator well.

One South Wacker Drive (*1983, Murphy/Jahn*), at the southeast corner of S. Wacker Drive and Madison Street, is an example of architect Helmut Jahn's application of the skyscraper-setback style of the 1920s and 1930s to the emerging postmodern style of the early 1980s. Two broad setbacks characterize the building's three main sections, each with three-story angled atriums above and below. A five-foot modular grid in each section adds to the sense of verticality, particularly with the gray, coral, and silver reflective glass set in somewhat abstract patterns. Visit the ground floor atrium which boasts a multilevel galleria replete with retail shops on a passageway connecting the Wacker Drive and Madison Street entrances.

Diagonally across the Drive is the famous **Civic Opera Building** (*1929, Graham, Anderson, Probst & White*), 20 N. Wacker Drive, which occupies the entire block to Washington Street on the site of the old Market Square Warehouse. The enormous 45-story structure, said to be "shaped like a throne," is essentially an office building with a 3,500-seat opera house and a 900-seat the-

The lavish main lobby of the AT&T Corporate Center is 44 feet high, illuminated by three chandeliers, with walls and floors adorned with rich Italian marble in a range of colors and shapes, highlighted with gold leaf, satin bronze, and oak wood trim. The lobbies of both buildings are interconnected. (Photo by Jon Miller, copyright © Hedrich Blessing)

The twin 40-story towers of the Chicago Mercantile Exchange (1983, 1988 Fujikawa, Johnson & Associates) rise majestically over the Chicago River and S. Wacker Drive, between W. Monroe and W. Madison streets. The serrated design allows for 16 additional "corner" offices on each floor. (Photo by author)

The "glitzy" One South Wacker Drive, a concrete structure sheathed in gray, coral, and silver reflective glass, displays Helmut Jahn's application of the skyscraper-setback style of the 1920s and 1930s. The vertical rows of black glass define the window pattern. (Photo by author)

atre. (For a time the building was renamed for a tenant, the Kemper Insurance Company.) A covered pedestrian arcade extends along the entire front, with the entrance to the opera house at the south end and the theatre entrance at the north. Over each entrance is an oversized pediment with two allegorical figures and a pair of persona masks. The style of the building is a curious mixture of French Renaissance and Art Deco, perhaps reflecting the strange combination of the aesthetic taste of builder Samuel Insull, himself a dedicated opera buff, with the popular building trend of the times. Insull, a public utilities tycoon and director of Commonwealth Edison, also controlled a number of traction companies, including the three major suburban-interurban railroads that served Chicago from points as distant as Aurora, Elgin, South Bend, and Milwaukee (only the Chicago, South Shore & South Bend RR survives). Insull did not endear himself to the citizens of Chicago when he opened his new opera house, as it forced their beloved Auditorium Theatre to close, and adding insult to injury, audiences soon discovered that the acoustics and sight lines were not nearly as good. Few Chicagoans mourned when his enormous financial empire collapsed during the Depression. Nevertheless, the Opera House is home to the Chicago Lyric Opera, one of the most distinguished companies in the world. Try to visit the 40-foot-high Grand Foyer, which, unfortunately, is only open just before and during performances.

The northeast corner is the **site of the Marshall Field & Company Whole-sale Store,** designed by Henry Hobson Richardson in 1885 and demolished in 1930. Only one Richardson-designed building survives in Chicago, the Glessner House. (*See* pages 87–89 and 329–331.)

Turn west on Madison Street to the bridge across the river.

The Madison Street Bridge was reconstructed in 1994 and renamed the Lyric Opera Bridge. From the center of the bridge there is a superb view of **Riverside Plaza,** the former Chicago Daily News Building (*1929, Holabird & Root*), 2 Riverside Plaza. In the background are the modern **Morton International Building** with the exposed trusses on the roof, and to its left, the castellated red-brick 1911 **River Center** (both to be seen later). Riverside Plaza is a fine example of the Art Deco style—its broad, symmetrical sculptured limestone facade adding an impressive touch to the riverscape. Two entranceways open up to a broad formal plaza, the nearer of which provides access to the Metra suburban trains of the Northwestern Station, one block west. Spend a moment to examine the low-relief sculptured panels, some of which bear the names of noteworthy newspaper publishers in American history (Franklin, Greeley, Pulitzer, etc.). The now defunct *Chicago Daily News* was founded in 1875. One of the great buildings of the 1920s, it was the first to be constructed on railroad air rights and the first on air rights to have a public plaza. And perhaps in anticipation of the realization of Burnham's 1909 Plan of Chicago, which foresaw the transformation of the river's edge in the European tradition, the building faces the river, while on the other hand, the Civic Opera House, with its huge blank rear wall, snubs it. Riverside Plaza appears decep-

(Left) The gargantuan Civic Opera Building, designed in 1929 by Graham, Anderson, Probst & White, has been described as resembling an enormous throne. Essentially a 45-story office building with a 3,500-seat opera house and a 900-seat theatre, the building has been the site of Chicagos' major operatic and theatrical events for years. The opening of the Opera House in 1929 sounded the death knell for the Auditorium Theatre, even though the acoustics were not as good. Today it is the home of the world-renowned Chicago Lyric Opera. Unlike most of the buildings built along the Chicago River in recent times, the Civic Opera Building "turns its back" on the river with a broad blank wall. (Photo by author)

tively large, but it was built on a relatively narrow plot, and the building's east-west elevation is many times broader than its width.

Enter No. 2 Riverside Plaza and walk up the incline past the row of retail shops (note the ceiling murals in the lobby concourse by John W. Norton, illustrating the daily activities of a large newspaper), then cross Canal Street via the glass-enclosed skywalk that leads to the Northwestern Atrium Center and the Chicago & Northwestern Railway Station.

   The Northwestern Atrium Center (*1987, Murphy/Jahn*), 500 W. Madison Street, replaced the 1911 Chicago & Northwestern Railway terminal, a distinguished Beaux Arts–style structure and west-of-the-Loop landmark for three-quarters of a century. The C&NW was Chicago's first railroad, and coincidentally, was founded by Chicago's first mayor, William B. Ogden. Chartered

The open Madison Street Bridge (also called the Civic Opera Bridge) permits an uninterrupted view of the lofty Morton International Building (1990, Perkins & Will) with its unusual exposed roof trusses that support the south end of the building while adding a decorative touch intended to reflect the architecture of the river bridges. To its left is River Center, an adaptively reused former factory, and at the extreme left, the massive Riverside Plaza, formerly the Chicago Daily News Building (1929, Holabird & Root). (Photo by author)

(Left) The Northwestern Atrium Center, at 500 W. Madison Street, is another unmistakable Murphy/Jahn dazzling confection. The design of blue-enameled aluminum and silver-and-blue glass, with prominent setbacks in distinctive smooth curves, produces a striking visual effect. The building replaced the 1911 Chicago & Northwestern Railway Terminal, although the building still serves as the depot for the C&NW Metra commuter trains. Primarily a commercial skyscraper, the interior is cleverly designed with a broad atrium whose exposed girders create the atmosphere of one of the great old-time railroad terminals. (Photo by author)

in 1836 as the Galena & Chicago Union, it ran its first train to Oak Park with a secondhand locomotive called the "Pioneer" 12 years later. (The old locomotive is on display at the Chicago Historical Society.) The C&NW, Chicago's oldest surviving public corporation, grew to become the nation's eighth largest railroad; but in 1995 it was purchased by the Union Pacific. The acquisition now gives the UP direct access to Chicago, which is still the nation's largest railroad hub. Some years earlier, the local commuter lines of the Northwestern were absorbed into Chicago's extensive Metra (Metropolitan Rail) commuter

The former Beaux Arts–style Chicago & Northwestern Railway Terminal, designed in 1911 by Frost & Granger, stood at N. Canal and W. Madison streets. When this photo was taken in 1961, the C&NW was still running commuter and transcontinental trains. The attractive depot was demolished to make way for the Northwestern Atrium Center. (Photo by Ed Kall, Chicago Historical Society)

system. Chicago's history as a major railroad center dates back to 1852 when the first train from the East arrived over the newly built Michigan Southern and Northern Indiana Railroad.

You will now be on the so-called sky lobby, which to the right, leads to the Metra tracks. Above the entrance to Track 8 is a three-sided clock, rescued from the former station. All is glass and steel, with the structural steel girders exposed in dramatic fashion. This is particularly evident as you turn around and walk north toward Madison Street, where the crisscross steel beams and soaring multilevel galleries create a fanciful high-tech interplay. Then take the escalator down to the street level (there is a food court to the rear, should you need a pit stop), and leave from the 500 W. Madison Street exit (marked Citicorp Center). Cross the street (carefully!) and take in the immense and almost overwhelming facade of this unique addition to the cityscape. Inspired perhaps by the streamlined trains of the 1930s, Helmut Jahn's dazzling design of blue enameled aluminum and silver and blue glass, with prominent setbacks in smooth curves, plus a telescoping glass entranceway, produces a striking visual effect. The architect appears to have followed Louis Sullivan's famous adage that "form should follow function" by tailoring the size of the floors to fit the needs of his building's clients.

Walk west a block to see one of Chicago's most unusual sculptures.

Claes Oldenburg's **Batcolumn** (1977), a 100-foot high latticework Cor-Ten steel column rises in front of the **Harold Washington Social Security Admin-**

Claes Oldenburg's 100-foot-tall Cor-Ten steel latticework sculpture, Batcolumn *(1977), on W. Madison Street, just beyond the Northwestern Atrium Center, is intended to recall the crisscross trusses of Chicago's bridges, and in its verticality, the city's former profusion of tall smokestacks. Most locals, however, swear that it's the sculptor's tribute to the Cubs and White Sox. In the right rear, the tower with the flattened corners is one of the Presidential Towers, a group of four 49-story apartment buildings, designed in 1986 by Solomon Cordwell Buenz & Associates. (Photo by author)*

istration–Great Lakes Program Service Center (*1976, Lester B. Knight & Associates*), 600 W. Madison Street. The baseball bat–shaped sculpture was commissioned by the federal General Services Administration's Art-in-Architecture Program, and according to Swedish-born Oldenburg who grew up in Chicago, the sculpture is reminiscent of the crisscross trusses on Chicago's bridges and elevated structures, and repeats the motif of many of the city's former tall smokestacks against a more horizontal city panorama. Some locals swear, however, that it's a tribute to the Windy City's two baseball teams, the Cubs and White Sox. Anyway, nobody will argue that this isn't the largest baseball bat in the world. Look back (east) down Madison Street for a sweeping view of the glitzy, smooth-stepped facade of the Northwestern Atrium Center.

Across the street from the sculpture is the quartet of the 49-story high-rise **Presidential Towers** (*1986, Solomon Cordwell Buenz & Associates*), 555, 575, 605, and 625 W. Madison Street, staggered in their positioning to provide maximum visibility for tenants. The buildings, designed with flattened corners and concrete-and-tinted-glass facade, are interconnected and include a wintergarden and shopping mall, with recreational facilities on the third level. The construction of the high-rise complex and the nearby Social Security Administration Center has contributed substantially to the rebirth of a formerly seriously blighted area. The complex is built on a raised two-square-block brick podium, under which are retail stores at the bottom of a slight slope at the corner of Clinton and Monroe streets. Jefferson Street slices through the center below grade on the south side, and is bridged by a pair of overpasses.

Although a bit of a digression from the tour, you can take an optional detour to see Chicago's oldest church by following the directions below; otherwise return to Canal Street and turn left (north), walking on the east side.

Walk diagonally through the Presidential Towers complex over Jefferson Street to Desplaines and Monroe streets, then turn left (south) one block to:

 St. Patrick's Roman Catholic Church (*1852–1856, Carter & Bauer*), 140 S. Desplaines Street, is Chicago's oldest surviving church building, and one of only a handful of structures that escaped the ravages of the Great Fire of 1871. Before entering, examine the unusual facade which displays two different style towers, the taller south tower with a conventional spire, although with replacement red bricks; and the north tower with an onion dome—the former symbolizing the Western (Roman) Church, and the latter, the Eastern (Byzantine) Church. The structure is clad in Cream City brick made from a yellow clay which was formerly found along the shores of Lake Michigan, in and around Milwaukee; the base is of Joliet (Illinois) limestone. Below the gable is a pyramidal row of corbels typical of the *rundbogenstil,* or round-arch early Romanesque Revival style.

St. Patrick's Roman Catholic Church is not only the oldest Catholic church in Chicago, but the oldest surviving church building. Built 1852–1856, it has two distinctly different towers. The taller south tower has a rather conventional spire, while the shorter north tower is topped by an onion dome. The structure is clad in Cream City, or Milwaukee brick made from clay once found in great supply along the southwest shores of Lake Michigan. The church originally ministered to waves of Irish immigrants who fled the "Great Hunger" of 1845–1846 caused by the potato blight which destroyed Ireland's one-crop economy. (Reproduced with permission of the publisher, Loyola University Press, from the book Chicago Churches and Synagogues, *by George A. Lane)*

The interior is exceptionally wide, with an attractive painted ceiling supported by unusually broad trusses that carry the round-arch design. The church, which replaced an earlier one built in 1846 on the site, was built to minister to the waves of Irish immigrants who settled in Chicago after escaping the "Great Hunger" caused by the potato crop failure. Appropriately, the stained-glass windows on the side walls all represent different Irish saints, with their names inscribed below in Gaelic (St. Patrick is the front left window), and were done by Thomas A. O'Shaughnessy. The church was restored in 1912, with many incongruous Gothic-style replacements. Unusual is the skylit barrel-vaulted window over the chancel.

Return past the Presidential Towers to Madison Street and walk east to Canal Street, then turn left (north), walking on the east side of Canal Street.

When you reach Washington Street notice how the architecture of the railroad viaduct changes. The Beaux Arts style of the *former* C&NW Railway station is very much in evidence, as no "modernization" has taken place from this point north.

Turn right (east) on Randolph Street, past the huge red-brick former **Butler Brothers Warehouse,** (*1913, D. H. Burnham & Co.*), 111 N. Canal Street, whose name is prominently emblazoned over the entrance. The building was gutted in 1982 and completely renovated for commercial purposes and renamed **River Center**—a fine example of adaptive reuse by the Balsamo/Olson Group.

Adjacent to the east is the imposing **Morton International Center** (*1990, Perkins & Will*), 100 N. Riverside Plaza, which can best be appreciated from across the Washington Street bridge. Built on an air-rights site over the tracks leading to Union Station, the headquarters building of the world-famous salt company is divided into a 36-story main section with clock tower and a 12-story south end. The lobby extends for the full length of the building with considerable spaces dedicated to computer operations. Above the south section an exposed rooftop truss (visible before from 2 Riverside Plaza, but obscured by the tower here) serves the dual function of helping to provide support for that end of the building and adding a decorative element supposedly reflecting the architecture of the river bridges.

A Metra commuter train northbound out of Union Station offers riders a brief but spectacular view of the Chicago riverfront, especially the convex-shape of the 38-story 333 W. Wacker Drive (1985, Kohn Pederson Fox with Perkins & Will). Reflected in the building's dark-green glass facade are the distorted images of the Merchandise Mart (left) and the Chicago Apparel Center. (Photo by author)

(Left) Passing south under the open C&NW Railway Bridge, a stunning panorama of riverfront skyscrapers comes into view, dominated in the background by the Sears Tower. Partially open is the Lake Street Bridge during reconstruction of the double-deck bridge and the Lake Street El in 1995–1996. (Photo by author)

To the right rear, in the distance, is the cream-colored brick industrial Romanesque Revival–style former warehouse building of the C&NW Railway (*1922, Graham, Anderson, Probst & White*), 165 N. Canal Street, renovated in 1992 by Graham-Thomas Architects, and renamed **One Northwestern Center.**

After crossing the Randolph Street Bridge (*1984, Chicago Department of Public Works*), continue to the southwest corner of N. Wacker Drive.

South of Randolph Street on the east side of N. Wacker Drive are a pair of buildings by the same architectural firm, Perkins & Will: **123 N. Wacker Drive** (*1986*) and to the south, **101 N. Wacker Drive** (*1990*). No. 101 (to the right) is a 24-story modernistic block with alternating bands of light and dark gray glass covering the spandrels between windows of reflective glass. The glass was chosen for its energy efficiency, with heat-absorbing glass on the east and north faces, and silver reflective insulated glass on the sunny south and west faces. Hidden monitors adjust to the amount of sunlight, and reflect light or absorb heat as required. No. 123 is quite different, with a strong feeling of verticality and a pronounced division between the two side bays and the center section. The granite skin of the side elevations with its punched out windows contrasts starkly with the glass curtain wall and vertical window treatment of the center bay. The arcade on the ground floor and the setbacks above recall those of the Civic Opera House, one block south. The prominent and unique pyramidal structure at the top, which hides some of the building's mechanical functions, is somewhat reminiscent of the soon-to-be-seen Merchandise Mart.

Turn left (north) on N. Wacker Drive, staying on the west side.

Across Wacker Drive at the corner of Lake Street is a rather large nine-story red-brick commercial structure whose Romanesque Revival–style corbel table (below the cornice) is typical of the type of industrial buildings built during the period of the 1880s and 1890s, and as a lone survivor on the street, gives some idea of the scale and type of architecture in this area prior to its redevelopment.

At Lake Street, the El crosses the river on the Lake Street Bridge (*1916, John Ericson, city engineer and Thomas G. Pihlfeldt, engineer of bridges; renovated 1995*). Plaques on the stone monument to the left of the roadway recount the history of the area, with two low reliefs showing the neighborhood in 1864 and the teeming **South Water Street Market** in 1920. Wacker Drive below the bend in the river was built from 1949 to 1958 following the route of the former Market Street, while the north section, which replaced the congested South Water Street Market, was begun in 1924 and completed two years later.

The southwest corner of W. Lake Street and Market Street, now Wacker Drive, was **the site of the Sauganash Hotel** in the 1830s, where owner and innkeeper, Mark Baubien, a tempestuous French-Canadian, was Chicago's first ferryman, and for that matter, Chicago's first hotelier. At that time, Chicago, which had just become an official townsite, had a population of 350. In 1833 a group of citizens got together in the log-cabin structure to vote for the town's incorporation, and a few months later the tavern witnessed Chicago's first municipal election.

Across the river are the exposed tracks used by Metra, AMTRAK, and CP Rail (formerly the SOO Line, and originally the Milwaukee Road). Further to the right, the Chicago River splits, with the main branch flowing in from Lake Michigan. Just visible to the north beyond the confluence of the two branches of the river at Wolf Point, is a steel railroad bridge for a spur that runs under the Merchandise Mart to the Chicago Sun-Times building—one of only two *single*-leaf bascule bridges downtown, and usually in the open position; however, the railroad bridge is not a trunnion, but a counterweighted bascule bridge. **Wolf Point,** according to Norman Mark in his *Chicago Tours* book, got its name from a wolf that was killed trying to get into the meat supply of a tavern. It then became the Wolf Tavern, with the adjoining spit of land named for it.

At the southwest corner of what is now Lake Street and Wacker Drive stood Chicago's first hotel, the Sauganash, named for a local Potawatomi chief. It was a simple wooden structure, and was run by the tempestuous Mark Baubien, a French Canadian, who also had the distinction of being the city's first ferryman. The hotel's tavern witnessed Chicago's first municipal election in 1833. (From A History of Chicago, *by Alfred T. Andreas, 1884. Chicago Historical Society)*

Just beyond is the **Kinzie Street Bridge** (*1908, John E. Ericson, city engineer and Thomas G. Pihlfeldt, city bridge engineer*). And thereby hangs a tale . . . for it was on the east side of the river, just beneath that bridge, that the **Great Chicago Flood of 1992** began. On April 13, a work crew of the Midwest Dredge & Dock Company, drilling a new piling, accidentally pierced the concrete wall of a tunnel that had been under the city for almost 90 years. Within minutes millions of gallons of Chicago River water surged into a network of almost 60 miles of underground railroad tunnels, flooding the basements of virtually every building downtown and bringing the city to a standstill. Electric power

For almost three-quarters of a century Chicago's downtown business establishments were served by an extensive network of underground narrow-gauge electric trains. The lines which brought in coal, mail, and other supplies, brought out ashes, and ran under almost every street in and around the Loop, crisscrossing under every major intersection. In this posed photo taken under the intersection of State and Madison streets (note the street names printed on the walls), an electric locomotive, drawing power from overhead wires, heads east along the Madison Street tunnel. The system was abandoned in 1959 and almost forgotten until the catastrophe of the Great Flood of 1992, when millions of gallons of water from the Chicago River flowed in through a break in the tunnel wall, flooding not only the abandoned tunnel system, but the basements of virtually every building in the Loop, bringing the business life of the central city to a halt for several weeks. (Chicago Historical Society)

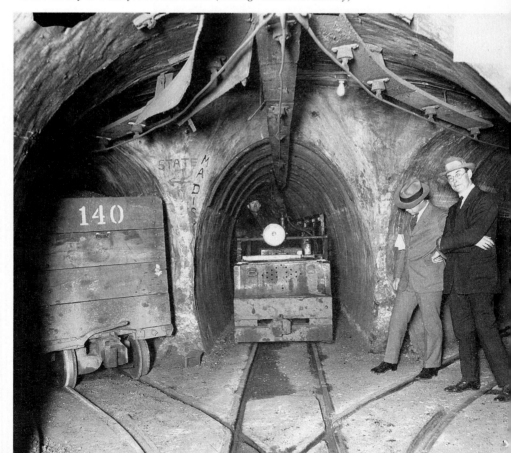

THE FAR SIDE

By GARY LARSON

ACETYL

In a tunnel under the Chicago River, a descendent of Mrs. O'Leary's cow follows her calling.

was cut off to most Loop buildings as well as to the two subway lines, and it took a week to stanch the flow. By that time the department stores and other nearby businesses had lost millions of dollars, and the cost to the city was astronomical. Those tunnels, built between 1898 and 1906, were originally planned to carry telephone lines, but were expanded to accommodate a narrow-gauge electric railroad whose tracks ran under almost every downtown street to provide freight service between business establishments and the many railroad lines around the city. The diminutive trains also carried coal and mail, and brought out the accumulated piles of ashes—a convenient and practical service, given the crowded, narrow streets of the Loop. The line, run by the Chicago Tunnel Company, ultimately fell into disuse and was abandoned in 1959, forgotten by most Chicagoans until the flood. (For a detailed account of the underground railroad and the flood, see *Forty Feet Below,* by Bruce Moffat, in the Recommended Readings.)

Just to the north, on the west side of the north branch of the river, is a red building, **Fulton House** (*1908, architect unknown*), 345 N. Canal Street, the former North American Cold Storage Company warehouse, which was converted to a condominium apartment building in 1981 by Harry Weese & Associates. The conversion required punching out all the windows and balconies in the solid brick walls of the former refrigerated warehouse and adding an additional floor. The ornate cornice and the circular windows in the entablature were, fortunately, preserved.

The confluence of the three branches of the Chicago River, which come together in the shape of a "Y," was the inspiration for the winning entry in a contest sponsored by a local newspaper in 1892 for the design of a logo for the City of Chicago. Look for it in various places throughout the city, on public buildings such as the Harold Washington Library, the Cultural Center, and the Chicago Theatre, on transit tokens, on traffic signal control boxes, and even on occasional manhole covers. The logo has been changed twice since.

Stay on the left side of Wacker Drive as it curves to the east.

To the right, on a wedge-shaped plot and conforming to the bend in the river, is the gleaming facade of **333 W. Wacker Drive** (*1983, Kohn Pederson Fox; with Perkins & Will*). Walk ahead to the Franklin Street Bridge for a panoramic view of one of Chicago's most exciting buildings! The 365-foot-wide energy-efficient green-glass curtain-wall arc, reflecting the river, the sky, and the surrounding buildings, is one of the city's most visible and photographed sites, and ideally designed for the location. The granite and steel office tower, hidden for the most part behind the mirrored facade, was recognized in 1984 by the National American Institute of Architects with their Design Honor Award. And in a recent *Chicago Tribune* Real Estate Section "My Favorite Building" contest, readers awarded No. 333 first place.

The dramatic facade of the award-winning 333 W. Wacker Drive was designed to have its curved side conform to the bend of the river, while the flat front side parallels the street grid. (Photo by author)

To the rear, the geometry of the Loop side of the building follows the street grid, and forms a kind of truncated triangle, with an interesting vertical "notch" in the glass facade above the Franklin Street entrance. The building's huge three-story base, which hides the mechanical functions, is of Vermont marble and polished granite, with louvered medallions covering ventilation ports set on columns placed at a 45-degree angle to the building. The completion of this 36-story tower established New York–based Kohn Pederson Fox as a major player in the Chicago architecture scene.

Directly south of No. 333 stood the famous **Wigwam,** a temporary building erected in just five weeks in 1860 for the Republican National Convention, which nominated Abraham Lincoln for the presidency.

From the vantage point of the Franklin-Orleans Street Bridge, the adjacent tower to the left, **225 W. Wacker Drive,** by the same architectural firm and completed six years later in 1989, presents a striking contrast. The granite and glass cladding was selected as a more appropriate medium to conform to the city grid, rather than to the river, although both buildings fit side by side harmoniously with their common three-story base and circular louvered vents. The four corner lanterns atop the structure which rise gently from the side bays, add variety and unobtrusive punctuation to the skyline, while relating to the corner towers of the Merchandise Mart, across the river.

Cross the Franklin-Orleans Bridge (*1920, Edward H. Bennett, consulting engineer***). At this point Franklin Street becomes Orleans Street. Turn right to the plaza in front of the Merchandise Mart.**

The Merchandise Mart (*1930, Graham, Anderson, Probst & White; renovations 1986–1992, by the same firm; remodeling of the first two floors in 1992 by Beyer Blinder Belle*): The massive 25-story Mart, with its 4.2 million square feet of floor space, spans two entire city blocks, and is the world's largest commercial building, second only to the Pentagon in floor space. Its modified Art Deco styling is typical of the period, with a large central tower, smaller corner towers, and restrained geometric ornament. Perhaps no other building expresses more vividly Carl Sandburg's description of Chicago as the "City of Big Shoulders." The Merchandise Mart was built by renowned retailer Marshall Field on the site of a former Chicago & Northwestern Railway depot (at Orleans and Kinzie streets, demolished in 1911) as a central marketplace for retailers to buy wholesale merchandise for their stores, and today it is the world's largest wholesale buying center. In addition to two floors with more than 50 retail shops, it is home to more than 1,200 designer showrooms. In 1946, it was purchased by Ambassador Joseph P. Kennedy, the father of JFK, and is still owned and managed by the Kennedy family. The Merchandise Mart complex is so large that the post office has assigned it its own zip code (60654). In an interesting anachronism, the Mart is cooled during the summer through the production of two million pounds of ice each night when energy rates are lower; during the day the melting ice cools the building—not an inconsiderable feat considering the building's 4,000 windows.

The immense Merchandise Mart sits majestically at Wolf Point, where the three branches of the Chicago River meet. Erected in 1930 from plans by Graham, Anderson, Probst & White, the 25-story Mart spans two city blocks and is the world's largest commercial building. (The Pentagon is larger, but hardly "commercial.") Built by Marshall Field on the site of a former Chicago & Northwestern Railway depot, it was planned as a central marketplace for retailers to buy wholesale merchandise for their stores—a function it still performs today as the world's largest wholesale buying center. In the foreground is the graceful Franklin-Orleans Bridge. (Photo by author)

The Mart complex also includes the World Trade Center Chicago, an ExpoCenter, and the building to the west, the **Chicago Apparel Center** (*1977, Skidmore, Owings & Merrill*), whose upper floors include the Holiday Inn Mart Plaza. The Mart also houses a number of industry associations such as the American Institute of Architects (AIA), the Illinois Chapter of the American Society of Interior Designers (ASID), the Illinois Chapter of the International Society of Interior Designers (ISID/CID), and others. Only the lobby, the retail mall on the first two levels, and the 13th floor (specializing in kitchen and bath products showrooms) are accessible to the general public, unless accompanied by an interior designer, architect, or other design professional. It is said that the Sultan of Brunei furnished his new 60-room palace in a one-week $1.6 million shopping spree at the Mart. The murals in the lobby by Jules Guerin portray world commerce. The Apparel Center is connected by a pedestrian bridge, designed in 1991 by Murphy/Jahn in a style respectful of the Art Deco motifs of the Mart. At night the Merchandise Mart is illuminated, and the sight from across the river is breathtaking. (The Mart offers 90-minute professionally guided public tours Monday through Friday at noon, departing from the south lobby. Adults $7.00, seniors and students $6.00; no children. Call 644-4664.)

In front of the Mart is the **Merchandise Mart Hall of Fame** displaying eight 4-times lifesize busts of famous American merchandisers, mounted on tall marble pillars. Seven were unveiled in 1953 by President John F. Kennedy, who represented the Kennedy family, with the eighth added in 1972. From right to left

The Merchandise Hall of Fame, in front of the Mart, displays the larger-than-life busts of eight famous American merchandisers, with Aaron Montgomery Ward at the right (see text for the names of the other merchant princes). (Photo by author)

Looking west beyond the Wells Street Bridge at dusk, the brightly illuminated facade of the Merchandise Mart, reflected in the Chicago River, is one of the city's most dramatic sights. (Photo by author)

(with sculptors' names): *Aaron Montgomery Ward* (Milton Horn), *Edward A. Filene* (Henry Rox), *George Huntington Hartford,* of A&P (Charles Umlauf), *John Wanamaker* (Lewis Iselin), *Marshall Field* (Henry Rox), *Frank Winfield Woolworth* (Milton Horn), *Julius Rosenwald,* of Sears Roebuck (Charles Umlauf), and *Gen. Robert E. Wood,* also of Sears Roebuck (Minna Harkavy).

End of tour. To return to the center of the Loop or Michigan Avenue, either walk back across the Franklin Street Bridge and take any of several bus lines, or walk to the second floor of the Mart, turn right to the east end of the floor where there is a direct connection to the Brown Line of the El, which makes a complete circuit of the Loop, offering an excitingly different perspective of the city (fare $1.50, $1.25 on weekends).

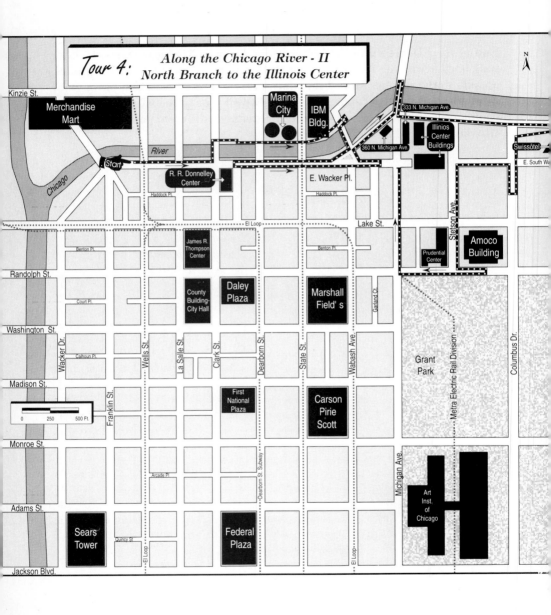

Tour 4: *Along the Chicago River - II*
North Branch to the Illinois Center

Kinzie St.

Merchandise Mart

Marina City

IBM Bldg.

333 N. Michigan Ave

River

Illinios Center Buildings

Start

360 N. Michigan Ave.

Swissôtel

Chicago

R. R. Donnelley Center

E. Wacker Pl.

E. South Wa

Haddock Pl.

Haddock Pl.

El Loop

Lake St.

James R. Thompson Center

Benton Pl.

Benton Pl.

Prudential Center

Amoco Building

Randolph St.

Court Pl.

County Building-City Hall

Daley Plaza

Marshall Field's

Garland Ct.

Stetson Ave.

Washington St.

Calhoun Pl.

Wacker Dr.

Wells St.

La Salle St.

Clark St.

Dearborn St.

State St.

Wabash Ave.

Grant Park

Madison St.

First National Plaza

Carson Pirie Scott

Michigan Ave.

Metra Electric Rail Division

Columbus Dr.

0   250   500 Ft.

Franklin St.

Monroe St.

Arcade Pl.

Dearborn St. Subway

Adams St.

Sears Tower

Quincy St.

Federal Plaza

Art Inst. of Chicago

El Loop

El Loop

Jackson Blvd.

N

4. Along the Chicago River, II: The North Branch to the Illinois Center

The tour begins at the northwest corner of W. Wacker Drive and Wells Street, at the point where the Wells Street Bridge (1922) crosses the river. This bridge, like the Lake Street Bridge, is doubled-decked, carrying both the roadway and the El.

The pedestrian walkway along the river offers an unsurpassed panorama of Chicago's architectural treasures. From buildings erected during the second decade of the 20th century to contemporary skyscrapers designed by the world's foremost architects, all can be seen in a dramatic setting along the river. As in Tour 3, the itinerary will require crossing and recrossing the river to view the buildings to best advantage.

Looking across the river, a variety of interesting and unusual structures can be seen. From left to right: the **Merchandise Mart** (described in the previous tour); the **Helene Curtis Building** (*1912, L. Gustav Hallberg*), 325 N. Wells Street, the company's corporate headquarters, in an adaptively reused former riverfront coffee warehouse, whose complete renovation in 1984 by Booth/Hansen & Associates included the addition of a green-glass roof pavilion that serves as the board room; and in the distance, **900 N. Michigan**

The old double-deck Wells Street Bridge, looking north across the Chicago River, carries two levels of transportation, the Ravenswood El line above, and the vehicular roadway beneath. In this ca. 1905 photo, a southbound El train has just stopped at the Kinzie/Wells Station in front of the ornate former Chicago & Northwestern Railway Wells Street terminal. The station, built in 1882, was demolished in 1927, and promptly replaced by the mammoth Merchandise Mart. The El station was then renamed for the Mart. At the right, the laker Alaska of the Anchor Line—one of the Great Lakes' largest fleets—rests in the turgid waters of the river, awaiting another cargo. Note the Quaker Oats sign; the company's headquarters today is just two blocks east. (Photo by Barnes-Crosby. Chicago Historical Society)

Avenue (*1989, Kohn Pederson Fox, with Perkins and Will*), with four prominent pyramidal lanterns (described in Chapter 6); the dark, tapering tower of the **John Hancock Center** (*1969, Skidmore, Owings & Merrill*), 875 N. Michigan Avenue, Chicago's third-tallest building (after the Sears Tower and Amoco Building), surmounted by twin communication antennas (also in Chapter 6); and:

    The City of Chicago Central Office Building (*1914, George C. Nimmons*), 320 N. Clark Street and 321 N. LaSalle Street. An imposing contrast to the row of modern riverside behemoths, the eight-story steel and concrete structure displays a rectilinear red-brick facade trimmed with dark-red terra cotta, replete with a broad expanse of windows. The prominent three-story clocktower over the central bay is a fairly typical feature of large industrial buildings erected around the turn of the century. Built as a warehouse for Reid, Murdoch Company, its location facing the river made it one of the first major structures to conform to the Burnham Plan of 1909. Just before LaSalle Street was widened in 1930, the western 20-foot bay of the building had to be razed, thus destroying its original symmetry. The city adaptively renewed the building in 1955 for a vari-

The new Wells Street Bridge today still performs the same function as in the previous photo. A Brown Line (Ravenswood) El train gives riders a quick, but dramatic panoramic view of the riverfront skyscrapers along the Main Branch of the Chicago River. Whenever river traffic demands the opening of the bridge, all trains, vehicular traffic, and pedestrians must wait. (Photo by author)

ety of administrative functions, including a municipal court. A pedestrian walkway in front of the building connects LaSalle and Clark streets.

To the right (east) of the Central Office Building, and soon to be seen close at hand, are the glassy blue-green **Quaker Tower,** the gray granite and tinted glass **Hotel Nikko Chicago,** and the extraordinary towering twin "corncobs" of **Marina City.**

Continue east along the pedestrian walkway following the river.

The walkway along Wacker Drive that parallels the south side of the Chicago River from Franklin Street to the Michigan Avenue Bridge is dedicated to the late Ira J. Bach, who, among many municipal positions, served as first Commissioner of Planning of the City of Chicago and, most recently, as Director of City Development. He was the author of many books on Chicago architecture including *Chicago on Foot* (*see* Recommended Readings), and in 1984 the city designated the **Ira J. Bach Walkway** as a "permanent acknowledgment" of his contributions to the city.

Wacker Drive is named for Charles Wacker, civic leader, brewery owner, and first chairman of the Chicago Plan Commission. The plans for the Drive were drawn by Edward H. Bennett, Wacker's consulting architect and former assistant to Daniel H. Burnham. It was built between 1926 and 1928, and is a bilevel roadway. The upper level, built on slabs supported by reinforced concrete columns, is designated for local traffic and a pedestrian walkway, while the

(Left) In this view from the pedestrian walkway of the Wells Street Bridge, is 222 N. LaSalle Street, a building that was constructed in two sections at widely different times. On the left, the older (1927) Graham, Anderson, Probst & White structure, and on the right, the narrower (1986) Skidmore, Owings & Merrill addition. A glass-enclosed mansard roof was added to tie the two sections together, and the design of the newer half is very sympathetic to the original facade, with the inclusion of four rows of projecting bays to enliven the front. (Photo by author)

lower level has four lanes for through and truck traffic. The Drive is **the world's first double-deck roadway,** and, in effect, "marries" the city to the riverfront in much the same way as Paris embraces the Seine. All along the Drive are Parisian touches—limestone balustrades bordering a riverside promenade, lampposts in the shape of obelisks, public sculpture, grand staircases leading down to the river's edge, boat landings, space for open-air cafes, and in every direction magnificent architectural panoramas. Bennett also provided for a railroad line that has never been built. He also served as consulting architect on the Chicago Plan Commission during the teens and twenties and was responsible for the design of a number of Chicago River bridges. The design for Wacker Drive follows the original 1909 Burnham Plan of Chicago which envisioned a

The City of Chicago Central Office Building, designed by George C. Nimmons in 1914, stands in sharp contrast to the neighboring modern behemoths along the river. Its red-brick facade is typical of the Industrial Romanesque Revival style of the late 19th and early 20th centuries. The prominent three-story clocktower was also fairly typical of the era. Built as a warehouse for Reid, Murdoch Company, it was one of the first buildings in Chicago to conform to the 1909 Burnham Plan of Chicago. The structure was adaptively remodeled in 1955 for a number of city administrative functions, and to many Chicagoans it is the most hated building in town, where traffic fines must be paid. (Photo by author)

The busy South Water Street Market was the main produce center of the city until it was removed in the early 1920s and replaced with Wacker Drive. Looking west from N. Dearborn Street in this ca. 1900 photo, the only vehicles in the teeming market are horse-drawn. (Chicago Historical Society)

circumferential beltway around the Loop following the European tradition of using the river as the central core of a city. This section of the roadway replaced the congested South Water Street Market, the central wholesale grocery market which was located conveniently alongside the river to allow transshipment of provisions between the lake and the land. Unfortunately, this part of the Drive was the only one to adhere closely to the Burnham Plan. Wacker Drive below the bend in the river moves inland following the route of former Market Street as far south as Congress Parkway. The originally proposed southern east-west section, which would have connected the river to Grant Park and the lakefront, is yet to be built . . . but don't hold your breath.

Continue east along the river to just beyond the LaSalle Street Bridge. Notice the plaque attached to the fence.

The small historic plaque commemorates the location of "Hubbard's Folly," the site of Chicago's first warehouse, built by Gordon Hubbard in the early 19th century.

A few yards farther is a setback in the fence with a larger plaque. This is **the site of the *Eastland* disaster,** a particularly grim event in the history of Chicago, and one that still lingers in the memory of many old-timers here. On the dark and drizzly morning of July 25, 1915, at a dock just west of the Clark Street Bridge, the excursion steamer *Eastland*—the fastest on the Great Lakes—had just boarded over 2,000 Western Electric Company employees and their families for an outing to Michigan City, Indiana. Suddenly the ship began to list slightly to port, possibly because so many passengers had rushed to that side to watch another ship passing alongside. The crew was immediately ordered to pump water into the ballast tanks to adjust the ship's trim, and the *Eastland* slowly began to level off, but not completely. As the ship prepared to cast off from the dock, it developed a much more severe list to port, and passengers were ordered to move quickly to starboard. But the frantic push to the right side came too late. Torrents of water began pouring into openings on the port side, chairs and tables cascaded overboard, and the huge ship slowly rolled completely over. Hundreds of passengers were hurled into the river, while many were trapped below decks, and still others crushed in a stampede to the staircases. Rescuers on shore and in nearby river craft struggled desperately to save as many as they could, but when the final death toll was taken, 812 souls had perished, including 22 entire families, making this the worst Great Lakes maritime disaster. The number of lives lost was higher even than in the Great Chicago Fire of 1871. After a lengthy investigation and series of lawsuits which dragged on until 1936, no precise cause for the tragedy could be determined, except that naval architects felt that the ship was somewhat unstable, and its ballast tanks had been improperly filled at dockside. The *Eastland* was subsequently righted, and a year later purchased by the U.S. Naval Reserve and converted into a gunboat training ship. Renamed the *U.S.S. Willmette*, it served for many years, and was finally scrapped in 1948 at a ship-wrecking yard on the south branch of the Chicago River.

The Clark Street Dock was the site of another tragedy three years before, when just before Christmas, throngs had gathered to await the arrival of a

Survivors and rescuers gather on the overturned hull of the excursion steamer Eastland, *which had just capsized at its Chicago River pier as it was about to set sail to Michigan City, Indiana, with 2,500 passengers on a Western Electric Company family outing. The tragedy on June 25, 1915, claimed 812 lives and was the worst Great Lakes maritime disaster. In the background is the old Clark Street Bridge, then an iron swing span. (Great Lakes Marine Historical Collection, Milwaukee Public Library)*

three-masted schooner, the *Rouse Simmons,* which every year brought a shipload of Christmas trees for sale from the Upper Michigan forests. The traditional arrival of the schooner, familiarly called "The Christmas Tree Ship," was a much anticipated event for Chicagoans, and the 1912 holiday season was no exception. However, the crowds that gathered at dockside waited in vain, for the ship had been caught in a fierce December gale, and disappeared with all hands off the Wisconsin shore. For years afterward, fishermen hauled up Christmas trees in their nets, but the wreck site was not located until recently.

Should you be taking this walk around mid-March, don't be astonished if the Chicago River seems to have turned a bright kelly-green. It has been the custom around the St. Patrick's Day holiday for the city to dump a nontoxic dye into the river to add a little "local color." The ducks that frequent the river don't seem to mind, and they too, turn a shade of green for a time.

The LaSalle Street Bridge is considered the river's second most beautiful bridge (after the soon-to-be-seen Michigan Avenue Bridge). The bridge was completed in 1928 from plans by Edward H. Bennett, with Donald H. Becker, engineer, and like several Chicago River bridges designed by Bennett, it displays a long, sweeping profile created by the broad pony trusses which support it. Like the Michigan Avenue Bridge, it also boasts four large ornamental limestone bridge houses. Take a moment to examine the decorations, but do not cross the bridge; turn around and look south down LaSalle Street, Chicago's great "Canyon of Commerce," toward the Board of Trade Building, a dramatic backdrop which rises in the distance. Notice how the street narrows slightly as it approaches the Board of Trade, adding to the effect. (*See* Tour 1, and watch out for traffic on the bridge!)

At the southwest corner of LaSalle Street, and extending the entire block-front back to Wells Street in two sections, is **222 N. LaSalle Street** (*1927, Graham, Anderson, Probst & White; additions and renovation 1986, Skidmore, Owings & Merrill*). Known earlier as the Builders' Building, it is a solid structure, typical of the late 1920s, but with the addition of a glassed-enclosed mansard roof that covers both the eastern as well as the newer western section (best seen from a distance). On the LaSalle Street side is a covered pedestrian arcade with a recessed three-bay center section. Enter the building to see the strikingly attractive atrium with its stencilled vaulted arches and grand staircase. At one time it was the exhibition space for the building trades which constructed the building. Classic columns above the 17th floor on the older western section are reflected in the substitute piers in the newer section, which are set above 12 floors of dark-tinted projecting bay windows.

Across LaSalle Street, at Number 221, is the **LaSalle-Wacker Building** (*1930, Holabird & Root*). This towering 39-story H-shaped building owes its strong appearance of height to the vertical rows of windows set off by dark metal spandrels. The setbacks were dictated by the zoning ordinance of 1917 which established the ratio of building height to floor area above a certain height. From the top of the "H," a tower rises straight up for an additional 16 stories.

Continue ahead to the Clark Street Bridge (1929–1931), cross the river and turn right in front of the Quaker Tower, on the plaza facing the river. (But before crossing the bridge, note the little plaque on the fence just east of the bridge, marking the original site of the founding of the Chicago Board of Trade, **on April 3, 1848.)**

The **Quaker Tower** (*1987, Skidmore, Owings & Merrill*), 321 N. Clark Street, is a 35-story typical steel-frame and glass curtain-wall "box" of the post-World War II International style espoused by Ludwig Mies van der Rohe, and widely popular until the mid-1980s. One of the last of this style to be built (the Miesian trend has been in decline for over a decade), it is no longer the building of choice for a corporate headquarters. A close look reveals a grid of shiny, semicircular, stainless-steel mullions behind the glass which enhances the feeling of height. Enter the glassed-in lobby to see what may be the world's largest oatmeal box—the symbol of the company. (If the building is closed for the weekend, walk around to the right side and turn right through the glass doors of the Hotel Nikko Chicago.) In the lobby of the Quaker Tower, take a brief look at the attractive green marble arches leading to the elevator banks, then turn right through the glass doors which lead directly into the lobby of the **Hotel Nikko Chicago** (*1987, Hellmuth, Obata & Kassabaum*), 320 N. Dearborn Street. The hotel lobby is designed in typical Japanese decor with a number of art works: screens, urns, bowls, and even a Samurai battle vest. Turn right and approach the riverside windows which open on a miniature Japanese Garden (to be seen momentarily at close hand). Then return to the doors through

Looking past the Clark Street Bridge are: the Quaker Tower (1987, Skidmore, Owings & Merrill), the Hotel Nikko Chicago (1987, Hellmuth, Obata & Kassabaum, with Takayama & Associates), and the twin "corn cob" towers (only one visible here) of Marina City (1959–1967, Bertrand Goldberg Associates). In the foreground is the Dearborn Street Bridge. (Photo by author)

(Left) The striking 50-story R. R. Donnelley Center, designed in 1992 by Spanish architect Ricardo Bonfil, with De Stefano/Goettsch, makes a bold, if somewhat controversial statement. Its broad silver-tinted curtain walls and triangular pediments, together with the building's unusual horizontal and vertical divisions are still quite avant-garde, even for the postmodern idiom. But Chicagoans have come to like this building that adds so much pizzazz to the skyline. To the left are 55 W. Wacker Drive and the Leo Burnett Building. (Photo by author)

which you entered, but instead of exiting, go down the stone staircase one level and outside to see a pleasant series of multilevel landscaped promenades and terraces. Turn left to the lovely *ryoan-ji* Zen garden, inspired by Kyoto's Zen temple's stone garden, where the sand traditionally represents the sea, and the rocks, the earth.

This is an excellent vantage point to examine three prominent buildings across the river which will be viewed close-by, later. From right to left (from N. Clark Street eastward):

The R. R. Donnelley Center (*1992, Ricardo Bofill Arquitectura/Taller USA with De Stefano/Goettsch*), 77 W. Wacker Drive. For the country's largest commercial printer, Spanish architect Bofill, in his first American commission, has produced what some have called "an exaggerated modern classic." Sheathed in silver-tinted curtain walls and surmounted by four triangular pediments, this 50-story skyscraper presents a striking, if somewhat unconventional appearance. With its 42-foot high white-granite base, its thinly detailed glassy shaft, and pedimented "capital" set on a rather pronounced entablature, the effect is that of a modern classic column. Nonetheless, the architect's handling of the horizontal and vertical divisions is unique, and with the wide expanse of window glass, the views from within must be splendid. The Donnelley Center Building was the last skyscraper to be built in the recent rapid development of the Loop. It is tastefully illuminated at night. Later, when the tour itinerary returns to 77 W. Wacker Drive, take a few minutes to go inside and view the glistening marble-clad lobby.

55 W. Wacker Drive (*1968, C. F. Murphy Associates*), formerly the Blue Cross/Blue Shield Building, is presently owned by the P. M. Realty Group. It is a massive beige-colored concrete-aggregate building whose upper sections are cantilevered, with duct enclosures counterbalanced by heavy spandrels and cornices. The vertical members appear as huge pylons, and when seen close up, reveal bush-hammered striations which create a feeling of verticality. The horizontal members, however, are smooth.

The Leo Burnett Building (*1989, Kevin Roche—John Dinkeloo & Associates, with Shaw & Associates*), 35 W. Wacker Drive. Another skyscraper "column" marks the world headquarters of Chicago's largest advertising agency, the Leo Burnett Company, Inc. Its 50 stories, emphasized by projecting corners (which provide additional desirable office space), deeply recessed reflective glass windows with stainless-steel circular mullions, a gray-green granite five-story columned arcade below, and a pronounced cornice above each corner, suggests a postmodern "pillar," and creates a rather unique impression—some have even said controversial. The building's facade of alternating blocks of light and dark gray granite add to the overall cubist effect.

Return to the top of Hotel Nikko's stone staircase, turn right and walk ahead to the iron gate opening into the charming Japanese Zen garden. Tiptoe in and enjoy a tranquil little piece of Japan, complete with miniature temple and stone lantern, and 40 tons of hand-picked boulders strategically strewn about, designed by David Engel. The 20-story Hotel Nikko Chicago, with its polished light-gray granite facade and trapezoidal-shaped dark-tinted glass vertical bays, was built as a joint venture by Japan Airlines and Tishman Realty & Construction Company, and is popular with visitors from the Far East. Note how the low-level lobby is tied to its three riverside terraces.

Continue east, and on N. Dearborn Street observe the historical plaque on the Dearborn Street Bridge house (*1963, Dick Van Gorp, chief engineer, Stephen J. Michuda, chief bridge engineer*) that depicts **Chicago's first movable bridge.** The bridge, the fourth on the site, received "The Most Beautiful Steel Bridge Award" in 1963 from the American Institute of Steel Construction. Then continue ahead to:

Marina City (*1959–1967, Bertrand Goldberg Associates*), 300 N. State Street. Considered the first building to address the river neighborhood, it is actually a "city within a city" with its 900 apartments, plus retail and convenience shops, bowling alley, theatre, bank, marina, television studio, health center, swimming pool, skating rink, exhibition space, and convenient open parking on the first 18 stories. As a mixed-use building it also includes a number of floors of offices. Marina City was designed to provide the amenities of suburban living in the heart of the big city at an affordable rent for young, middle-class workers. Architect Goldberg, briefly a student of the influential Ludwig Mies van der Rohe (Director of the Bauhaus School in Germany in 1930), soon rejected the master's theories of rectilinear and somber steel and glass building grids. Instead, with the design of these twin 60-story "corncobs," he successfully created a complex which provided a sense of a real community.

So distinctive is the design of Marina City, that Goldberg unhesitatingly called it "the most photographed building in the world." Whether or not worthy of the claim, it is arguably still one of the most striking, and certainly one of the most dramatic features of the Chicago skyline. It was built at the behest of William McFetridge, head of the Building Service Employees International Union, who saw the threat of middle-class flight to the suburbs and the consequent damage to the economic vitality of the central city—a pattern that had already begun in the 1950s; he hired Goldberg to come up with a viable solution. The result was the pair of reinforced concrete-core towers—the tallest in the world when completed—with each floor attached to the central stem like a succession of petals on a flower; and as for the curvilinear shapes, Goldberg points out that "there are no right angles in Nature." The apartments, in a repetitive pattern of pie-shaped slabs with semicircular cantilevered balconies, create a bright and airy atmosphere, and are set above the office floors, high

Marina City's twin circular towers—a "city within a city"—is a self-contained mixed-use complex and the first to address the river as its "front door." One of the most striking sights along the Chicago River, its circular reinforced concrete-core towers, the tallest in the world when completed, cantilever their floors outward with each level attached to the central stem, like a succession of petals on a flower. The first 18 floors are reserved for parking, with the apartment and office floors above, providing unobstructed views for the tenants. In the foreground of this ca. 1970 photo is the recently widened State Street Bridge. (Chicago Historical Society)

enough to provide broad panoramic vistas of the city. Goldberg was quoted as selecting the circular shape rather than the conventional grid as his personal rebellion against the "century of static space . . . the straight line . . . and the idea of man made in the image of a machine." (*See* also Goldberg's Prentice Women's Hospital–Northwestern University Institute of Psychiatry Building, pages 257–259, and River City, pages 291–292.)

Walk east beyond Marina City to State Street.

Before crossing, note the plaque designating the replacement for the former State Street Bridge as the **Bataan-Corregidor Memorial Bridge.** It was completely rebuilt as a six-lane span in 1949, replacing an earlier iron rolling-lift span opened in 1903. It also eliminated the traffic bottleneck that had been created when State Street was widened in 1930. In 1979 State Street south of the bridge underwent a major transformation, this time to a pedestrian mall and two-lane thoroughfare. The construction of the bridge was particularly difficult because of the location of the State Street Subway tubes directly beneath. It required the insertion of special horizontal trusses to support the bridge and prevent structural members from coming in contact with the subway. The bridge was dedicated in honor of the 600 residents of Chicago who were members of the U.S. Army garrison on Bataan and Corregidor in the Philippines, of whom more than half died when it was beseiged by the Japanese at the outbreak of World War II. Note the Art Deco-style sculptures on the wall of the bridge house showing a ship passing under the raised bridge leafs.

Looming high above a broad plaza, and set somewhat back, is the **IBM Building** (*1971, Office of Mies van der Rohe, with C. F. Murphy Associates*), 330 N. Wabash Avenue. Mies, one of the most distinguished members of the Bauhaus School in Germany, was invited to Chicago in 1938 to assume the directorship of the Armour Institute of Technology, which in a later merger became the noted Illinois Institute of Technology. As teacher and architect he developed the plans for its new campus, including the College of Architecture's S. R. Crown Hall (1956). It was at IIT that he popularized the so-called International style that became the exemplar for the steel-frame/glass curtain-wall building and the enduring expression of his philosophy that "less is more." (The International style had actually been introduced for the first time in the United States in 1932 by architect Philip Johnson and architectural historian Henry-Russell Hitchcock at the big "International Style Show" at the Museum of Modern Art in New York.)

After his retirement Mies remained in Chicago, and designed a number of noteworthy buildings, including the soon-to-be seen Illinois Center. Mies died in 1969. It is therefore rather ironic to note that his last and tallest office building, the IBM Building, should stand so close to and in such sharp contrast to Marina City, the project that was designed by the pupil who rejected him. In its day, the style of this solid, harmoniously proportioned "box," whose exposed steel frame and tinted-glass curtain wall was a direct expression of its form and function, became the prototypical no-nonsense format for the corporate office tower. The 52-story dark-bronze-tinted structure was deliberately sited some-what back from the river to accommodate a below-street-level Chicago & Northwestern (now Union Pacific) railroad spur, which leads to storage space reserved by the Sun-Times, as well as to take advantage of the views presented by the S-curve of the Chicago River, and also to avoid obstructing the sight lines of Marina City. In the spacious travertine-sheathed lobby is a bust of Mies van der Rohe, by Marino Marini.

During the blustery winter months ropes are strung in the plaza to keep pedestrians from being blown into the river. Popular myth to the contrary, Chicago's appellation as the Windy City derives *not* from the strong and fre-quent gusts that blow in from the lake or the western prairie, but from the rep-utation of its congressional delegation which became notorious for long and "windy" promotional efforts to secure Chicago as the site for the World's Columbian Exposition. The disdain held by Easterners for the braggadocio of those Chicago politicos was embodied in a comment by Charles A. Dana, edi-tor of the New York *Sun,* who said "Don't pay any attention to the claims of that Windy City."

Continue along the riverfront, but before crossing N. Wabash Avenue, note that the bridge was renamed in 1985 for Irv Kupcinet, popular late columnist of the *Chicago Sun-Times.* A plaque reveals that the former Wabash Avenue Bridge received the American Institute of Steel Construction annual award when it was built in 1930.

The **Sun-Times Building** (*1957, Naess & Murphy*), 401 N. Wabash Avenue, the six-story building housing one of the two major Chicago dailies, is, alas, dreary and undistinguished, with an almost "temporary pre-fab" look about its gray facade. The trapezoidal shape of the building was dictated by the irregu-lar street geometry. See the presses in action which can be viewed from out-side. The plaza is one of the oldest on the river, dating from 1958. (The *Sun-Times* offers free one-hour tours on Tuesdays, Wednesdays, and Thursdays at 10:30 A.M., by advance reservation. The tours are for groups only, but indi-viduals may phone in advance to inquire whether there is room on any of the tours. Call 321-3251 after 9:00 A.M.)

The area along the north side of the Chicago River from here to where the Michigan Avenue Bridge is now was, in the middle of the 19th century, a noto-rious sailors' red-light district known as The Sands.

Return to the Wabash Avenue Bridge and cross to the south side of the Chicago River.

★ **Heald Square** (pronounced "Heeld") is named for Nathan Heald, com-mandant of Fort Dearborn, Chicago's first settlement, which was located just to the east. More a triangle than a square, it boasts two distinctly different pub-lic sculptures. To the east is the cast-iron *Children's Fountain* (*1983*), said to be a modern evocation of the spirit of Burnham's 1909 Plan of Chicago. Directly

The unique George Washington–Robert Morris–Haym Salomon Memorial (1941) in Heald Square, is Chicago's monument to religious tolerance. The sculpture group is by Chicago artist Lorado Taft. (Photo by Robert Nickel for the Commission on Chicago Historical and Architectural Landmarks)

opposite is the unique *George Washington–Robert Morris–Haym Salomon Memorial (1941)*, Chicago's monument to religious tolerance. The idea for the statue came from Chicago lawyer, Barnet Hodes, who felt that the contributions of Jewish Americans to the American Revolution had not been publicly acknowledged, so a private foundation was established to commission the statue. Washington is portrayed clasping hands with two patriots who were important supporters during the Revolution. Morris, a successful merchant and a signer of the Declaration of Independence, helped raise funds to support Washington's army during the war, earning the title of "financier of the Revolution." Salomon, also a wealthy merchant and member of the small but loyal Jewish community, loaned Washington great sums of money to finance the revolution, and is credited with keeping the wartime economy afloat. The loans were never repaid, and both Salomon and Morris died in poverty. Two sculptors are responsible for this "triumvirate of patriots"—Chicago sculptor Lorado Taft, who designed the monument and modeled the head of Washington after a bust by the French sculptor, Jean-Antoine Houdon, but who died before its completion; and Leonard Crunelle, a student and associate of his, who finished the work based on Taft's original maquette.

Now spend a few moments to admire one of Chicago's great architectural gems from the 1920s, the ornate **former Jewelers Building** (*1926, Giaver & Dinkelberg, with Thielbar & Fugard*), officially known by its street address, **35 East Wacker Drive.** Sheathed in cream-colored terra cotta, the neo-Baroque plus Renaissance Revival–style 24-story building is surmounted by domed neo-Classical tempietti at each corner which conceal water tanks, with an enormous 17-story center tower built around a large chimney and crowned by an even larger tempietto. To reach the 40th floor in the dome, it is necessary to take a small circular elevator on the 35th floor. Look closely at the detailing, and note the initials JB (*Jewelers Building*) and the huge decorative three-faced clock mounted on the northeast corner. The clock, which weighs six tons, is itself a real "jewel," with a gilded-bronze "Father Time" perched watchfully above, adding much to the charm of the structure. Through the years the ornate edifice has gone through several name changes; in more recent times it was known as the Pure Oil Building, then the North American Life Insurance Building. An interesting aspect of the building's early history was the private parking facility built in on each of the first 22 floors. Tenants could drive directly into the building from the lower level of Wacker Drive, and the car (minus the driver) would then be whisked up by elevator to the desired floor. By 1940, as cars grew larger and elevator breakdowns became more frequent, this classy parking system was discontinued and the space remodeled for offices. Among a variety of tenants are the offices of architects Murphy/Jahn. Helmut Jahn, who is very fond of the building, but has reservations about its architectural attributes, calls it "eccentric, idiosyncratic, and romantic."

An optional detour may be made to examine at close range the three buildings seen earlier from across the river: The Leo Burnett Building (35 W. Wacker Drive), 55 W. Wacker Drive, and the R. R. Donnelley Center (77 W. Wacker Drive), as well as a few others. This is also a good place to look across the river to admire Marina City and the IBM Building from another vantage point.

At the corner of State Street is the **United of America Building** (*1962, Shaw, Metz and Associates*), 1 E. Wacker Drive. This 41-story monolithic skyscraper creates a strong feeling of verticality, and is reputed to be the tallest marble-clad building in the world.

Across State Street is the **Stouffer Riviere Hotel** (*1991, William B. Tabler Architects, with Mann, Gin, Ebel & Frazier Ltd.*), 1 W. Wacker Drive. The hotel's wide-bay staggered 24-story tower is a great improvement over the rather tacky two-story section facing Wacker Drive.

Walk west and take a closer look at the fronts and lobbies of the Leo Burnett Building, 35 W. Wacker Drive; cross Dearborn Street to No. 55, then to No. 77:

The R. R. Donnelley Center, described earlier from a vantage point across the river, is one of the most recent additions to the Loop and certainly one of the most unusual in design, and is almost as exciting inside as it is controversial outside. The dazzling cream-white marble lobby is highlighted with clumps of towering bamboo, broad windows flooding the large space with light, and contrasting light-gray marble floor and wall panels. Triangular pediments over all doorways repeat the exterior motif of the building. In the center is a grouping of four, tall free-standing impressionistic stone figures, painted black, entitled *Three Lawyers and a Judge,* by Spanish sculptor Xavier Corbero. (Note the

(Left) One of Chicago's architectural gems is 35 East Wacker Drive. The building, designed in 1926 by Giaver & Dinkelberg with Thielbar & Fugard, has gone through several name changes (Jewelers Building, Pure Oil Building, among others), but now is known only by its street address. The 24-story highly ornate neo-Baroque/Renaissance Revival–style structure is sheathed in cream-colored terra cotta and surmounted by a domed neo-Classic tempietto at each corner (which conceal water tanks). The huge center tower is built around a large chimney and is crowned by an even larger tempietto. (Photo by author)

realistic woman's foot at the bottom of one of them.) At the east end of the lobby is *Twisted Columns,* by the building's design architect, Ricardo Bofill, set on a black marble platform over which flows a thin sheet of water. The sound of the bubbling water adds a quieting touch. Before leaving, peek into the Caffè Bacci with its multicolored stone floor, suspended ceiling ornaments, central fountain, and modern paintings. After exiting the building walk around on the Wacker Drive side and look into the charming alley that separates the Donnelley Center from 55 W. Wacker Drive. The passageway, lined with seven urns, leads to a rear double-staircase and pedimented doorway, beyond which is no "secret garden," but a summer outdoor patio.

Return to Heald Square.

Just beyond Heald Square is the unmistakable white curved facade of the **Seventeeth Church of Christ Scientist** (*1968, Harry Weese & Associates*), 55 E. Wacker Drive, the 17th Christian Science Church to be founded in Chicago. The seven-sided lot for the building was chosen after the church had moved

The decorative three-faced wall-mounted clock on the northeast corner of 35 East Wacker Drive is a real treasure. Perched atop the decorative timepiece is a gilded "Father Time" holding an hourglass—a charming addition to an already splendid building. (Photo by author)

(Left) Looking west over the Lake Street El, an Orange Line train has just left the newly renovated Clark/Lake Station and Transportation Center. Barely visible on the left is the James R. Thompson Center, and to the right, the massive 203 N. LaSalle Street Building. Designed by Skidmore, Owings & Merrill in 1985, the unusual structure is really a garage with an office tower above. The parking garage section can be distinguished by its narrow horizontal slits, whereas the commercial space above has wider glazing, creating an interesting overall harmony. A glass tower in the center of the Clark Street facade contains the garage elevator, while the sloping glass enclosure on the roof covers two interior atriums. (Photo by author)

from several previous sites since its organization in 1924. The architect's concept was to build a house of worship that would be "modern in design, individualistic and strong, so as not to be dwarfed by the surrounding 'high-rises' of brick and mortar." The exterior is of reinforced concrete sheathed in travertine brought from Tivoli, Italy. The unusual semicircular building which rests on exposed reinforced concrete columns, according to church officials, is designed in the shape of a smile, accommodating a 1,000-seat auditorium, with travertine inside walls trimmed with walnut, in the center of which is an Aeolian Skinner organ with 3,316 pipes. Light is admitted through long, narrow win-

Looking beyond Heald Square's fountain and the Washington-Morris-Salomon monument is the distinctive white-curved facade of the Seventeenth Church of Christ Scientist (1968, Harry Weese & Associates). Built of reinforced concrete and clad in Italian travertine, it is the visual focus of the intersection. The architect created a plan for the church that would be "modern in design, individualistic and strong, so as not to be dwarfed by the surrounding 'high rises' of brick and mortar." Within the circular section is a 1,000-seat auditorium. The small round dome above the pyramidal lead-coated roof is illuminated every evening until 10:30 P.M. (Photo by author)

dows above. The building has seven floors, two of which are below ground level, with the recessed Reading Room and lobby on the street-level third floor. Outside, a bituminous-block sidewalk defines the property line. The pyramidal, lead-coated roof is supported by girders sheathed in travertine, above which is a prominent circular dome, illuminated by indirect lighting every evening until 10:30 P.M. (Tours may be arranged.)

On leaving the church, walk to the left into E. Wacker Place.

A few yards down, on the same side of the street (but best seen from across the street) is **Wacker Tower** (*1928, Holabird & Root*), 68 E. Wacker Place. A sleek, restrained Art Deco–style building, almost lost among its taller neighbors, its 16 stories display a slightly bowed center bay, with ornamental Art Deco designs in the spandrels, and an entrance festooned with decorative cast-iron Art Deco motifs. Enter the surprisingly spacious lobby, which is illuminated by a number of layered-dish light fixtures, and on the balconies at each end see the Art Deco metalwork designs. As the headquarters of the Chicago Motor Club of the AAA, a roadmap is an appropriate accouterment, and on the 50-foot-long United States wall map, painted by John W. Norton, are depicted the major U.S. highways and national parks in the year 1928.

Retrace your steps to the Church and turn right, walking east on E. Wacker Drive. For best views, cross the Drive (with caution).

At 71 E. Wacker Drive is the 35-story **Clarion Executive Plaza Hotel** (*1960, Milton M. Schwartz & Associates*). Unfortunately, the building's facade of alternating bands of dark-blue tinted glass and aluminum do little to enhance the cityscape, although the recessed roof pavilion must offer excellent views for the guests.

75 East Wacker Drive (*1928, Herbert Hugh Riddle; renovated 1983, Harry Weese & Associates*). Originally called the Mather Tower, later the Lincoln Tower, it boasts the questionable distinction of being the skinniest skyscraper in the city, with the least amount of floor space per story. Designed in a somewhat neo-Gothic style, the office tower is divided into a 24-story rectangular lower section surmounted by an 18-story octagonal shaft.

Rounding the bend in the river, the last building in the block is the imposing **360 North Michigan Avenue Building,** formerly known as the London Guarantee & Accident Building (*1923, Alfred S. Alschuler*). A delightful building, typical of the neo-Classical conventions of the early 20th century, it is a good example of the tripartite skyscraper, where the design of the facade is divided like the columns of antiquity, into a base, shaft, and capital. The building's somewhat trapezoidal shape was dictated by the street geometry and the curve in the river. Best appreciated from a distance, the front elevation is concave in shape, presenting an attractive introduction to the 21-story building. An elaborate five-story base includes a tall triumphal-arched entranceway flanked

On the east end of Heald Square is a charming cast-iron fountain whose 19th-century design is in sharp, but pleasing, contrast to the River Plaza Condominium, the Wrigley Building, and the Tribune Tower, across the river. (Photo by author)

by four huge Corinthian columns with allegorical figures in the spandrels and topped by a classic entablature. (Unfortunately, the polished-stone panel which was subsequently inserted above the entrance does not enhance the appearance of the "grand entrance.") The sixth floor is bracketed by two cornices which embrace the structure, and on top of a 12-story "shaft" of vertical rows of windows is another cornice, above which are eight three-story-high columns surmounted by the main entablature and a balustrade. Crowning the structure is a columned belvedere or tempietto. The building is strikingly similar to New York City's Classic-style Municipal Building, designed by McKim, Mead & White in 1914. At this writing, the front facade gives a somewhat dingy, "down at the heels" impression; and considering the building's prominent location and the recognition it has received for architectural merit from so many organizations (see plaque), a bit of steam cleaning would be greatly appreciated.

Directly across Wacker Drive, just before the entrance to the Michigan Avenue Bridge, and on the west side of Michigan Avenue also, look for several brass strips imbedded in the roadway which mark the **site of Fort Dearborn.** Although what is now Chicago had been visited earlier by Marquette and Joliet in 1673, by Canadian fur traders in subsequent years, and by Jean Baptiste Point du Sable, an African-American fur trader from the island of Hispaniola who built a homestead across the river around 1779, the first real settlement was not built until 1803. Fort Dearborn, a log structure to serve as an outpost of the U.S. government, was erected to defend the western frontier, but it survived only nine years, until the War of 1812. The inhabitants, fearing

On the south side of the Chicago River, west of the Michigan Avenue Bridge, is Chicago's skinniest skyscraper, 75 East Wacker Drive (1928, Herbert Hugh Riddle). Formerly called the Mather Tower, then the Lincoln Tower, it "boasts" the least amount of floor space per story of any skyscraper. The 42-story building, designed in a vaguely Gothic style, is divided into a rectangular section below and an octagonal shaft above. To the right is the Clarion Executive Plaza Hotel and the picturesque 35 East Wacker Drive. Chicago's First Lady, one of a number of river excursion vessels, awaits the next load of sightseers. (Photo by author)

attack by the British from the north, decided to abandon the fort, and led by Nathan Heald and Captain William Wells (for whom Wells Street is named), moved south to join the less isolated community at Fort Wayne, Indiana. When they had marched about two miles down the lakeshore near the present site of Prairie Avenue, the group of about 100 men, women, and children, who had been assured safe passage by the Indians, was instead ambushed, and 53 of the settlers were savagely butchered, with the survivors taken captive, in an event that has come to be known as the **Fort Dearborn Massacre.** The fort was then burned by the Indians, and the site lay abandoned until 1816 when the government built a new fort. Later, still another fort was built on the site, and logs from this third fort were ultimately salvaged, and may be seen today as part of a blockhouse reconstruction of Fort Dearborn at the Chicago Historical Society (N. Clark Street at North Avenue).

Because of its historical significance, the area surrounding Wacker Drive and Michigan Avenue has been placed on the National Register of Historic Places and designated the **Michigan-Wacker Historic District.**

From a good vantage point in River Plaza, on the north side of the Chicago River, is the 360 North Michigan Avenue Building (formerly the London Guarantee & Accident Building). Designed by Alfred S. Alschuler in 1923, it is typical of many of the neo-Classic skyscrapers of the period, except this one has a concave front and a trapezoidal building envelope, dictated by the shape of the lot. Near the top is a three-story-high row of columns, above which is a prominent belvedere, or tempietto. In the right rear is the "skinny" skyscraper, 75 East Wacker Drive. (Photo by author)

One of the many imaginative portrayals of Fort Dearborn, built in 1803 by Captain John Whistler (grandfather of painter James McNeill Whistler). The fort was attacked and burned by Potawatomi Indians on August 15, 1812. A few hours earlier the fort had been abandoned by the settlers, who sensing danger, set off for Fort Wayne. The group of 100 men, women, and children got only about two miles south when they were ambushed by the Indians and 53 were brutally massacred. (Commission on Chicago Landmarks)

A commemorative plaque affixed to the wall of the 360 North Michigan Avenue Building marks the site of Fort Dearborn. The fort's parade ground was located where the south end of the Michigan Avenue Bridge is today. (Photo by author)

Before continuing eastward along the Chicago River, take a short detour across the Michigan Avenue Bridge. Begin by examining the bridge house at the southwest corner, then cross on the west pedestrian sidewalk to see the pair of houses at the north end. Return via the sidewalk on the east side of the bridge to the southeast bridge house. Be extremely wary of the traffic, and cross only at the crosswalks!

✦   **The Michigan Avenue Bridge** is the world's first and one of Chicago's four double-deck, double-leaf trunnion bascule bridges; the others are the Outer Drive Bridge, and the Wells and Lake street bridges—the latter two carrying El trains on the upper level. Designed in Beaux Arts style by Edward H. Bennett, with Hugh Young as engineer, the 255-foot-long flag-decked bridge was modeled after Paris's Pont Alexandre III which was built in 1900 and considered the most beautiful bridge on the Seine. When the Michigan Avenue Bridge was completed in 1920 after two years' construction, it was acclaimed as the most beautiful bridge on the Chicago River; but more than that, it solved a major traffic congestion problem. Until that time, Michigan Avenue dead-ended at the Chicago River, with north-south traffic compelled to use the old 1856 Rush Street Bridge, the first iron bridge in the Midwest, located one block to the west (now demolished). Ships entering and leaving the river had to do some fancy navigation to avoid the center stanchion of the old iron swing bridge, and collisions were frequent. The new bridge, which could be opened or closed in barely a minute, not only opened the river to greater maritime trade, but opened the area to the north for rapid commercial development. The lower roadway of Wacker Drive also had a direct connection to the north side of the river. The plan was, in fact, an essential element in Daniel H. Burnham's 1909 Plan of Chicago, which Bennett, in his role as consultant to the Chicago Plan Commission, was able to carry out most successfully.

    The graceful and highly functional limestone bridge displays 40-foot pylons at each corner that serve as bridge control houses (only the house at the northwest corner is used). On each bridge house is a heroic sculptural relief. Beginning at the southwest bridge house, the dramatic high relief entitled *Defense,* by Henry Hering, portrays the tragic Fort Dearborn Massacre. (Now cross the bridge.) On the north end's houses are *The Pioneers,* showing early settler and fur trader, John Kinzie, who purchased du Sable's log cabin in 1804; *The Discoverers,* which illustrates 17th-century French explorers Marquette, Joliet, LaSalle, and Tonti. Both reliefs are by the celebrated sculptor, James Earle Fraser. Fraser also designed some of our nation's coinage, including the famous "buffalo" nickel. Returning along the east side of the bridge, there are plaques commemorating its construction, plus a small plaque recognizing the designation of the Reversal of the Chicago River, a National Historic Engineering Landmark (*see* page 106). On the southeast bridge house is *Regeneration,* also by Henry Hering, which commemorates the disastrous Great Chicago Fire of 1871 and the city's rise from the ashes.

    Among the many colorful flags that decorate the bridge is the **flag of the city of Chicago:** two horizontal blue stripes on a field of white with four red

(Left) The high-relief sculpture on the southeast bridge house of the Michigan Avenue Bridge, executed by Henry Hering, memorializes the Great Fire of 1871 and honors the city's phoenix-like rise from the ashes. (Photo by author)

stars. The blue stripes represent the two branches of the Chicago River; the intervening white stripes from top to bottom are the North, West, and South sides; and the four stars recall the four major events in the history of the city: Fort Dearborn, the Great Chicago Fire of 1871, the World's Columbian Exposition of 1893, and the Century of Progress Exposition of 1933–1934.

If you look back across the river, you will see a spectacular pair of skyscrapers, the Wrigley Building (with the clocktower, on the west side of Michigan Avenue) and the Tribune Tower, directly across Michigan Avenue. These are but a few of the interesting buildings to be visited in Tour 6, The Magnificent Mile and Streeterville.

Before crossing to the southeast corner of Wacker Drive and Michigan Avenue, note the building on that corner:

333 N. Michigan Avenue (*1928, Holabird & Root*). Although bearing a Michigan Avenue address, this attractive Art Deco–style skyscraper faces north and looks out across the river, standing as a symbolic gateway to the canyon of skyscrapers to the south. The smooth limestone structure, erected on a rela-

The Michigan Avenue Bridge is the most beautiful and one of the busiest on the Chicago River. It connects lower Michigan Avenue with the "Magnificent Mile" to the north. In the center background and topped by a round gilt dome, is the Hotel Inter-Continental, formerly the Medinah Athletic Club; and to the right, the lovely Gothic-style Tribune Tower. (Photo by author)

tively narrow lot, rises 24 stories along the east-west elevation and 35 stories in a soaring tower marked by strong piers and vertical rows of windows at the north end. The successive clearly defined setbacks are the result of Chicago's zoning ordinance of the early 1920s which dictated the ratio of a building's height to its horizontality and drastically influenced future skyscraper construction. A four-story polished-marble base and a band of stylized incised reliefs bracketing the windows around the fifth floor are the building's major ornament. These reliefs, by sculptor Fred M. Torrey, portray figures from the history of Fort Dearborn: hunters, traders, pioneers, and Native Americans. The plan for the building was influenced by Eliel Saarinen's entry in the 1922 *Chicago Tribune* Tower Design Competition, where he was awarded second prize (*see* Tribune Tower, in Tour 6).

Cross Michigan Avenue.

This final part of the tour will examine the group of buildings which comprise **Illinois Center,** as well as a group of skyscrapers along the north edge of Grant Park. The plan for the development of the Illinois Center project dates to the 1920s when the Illinois Central Railroad began abandoning many of its freight yard and warehouse facilities that extended as far north as the river. Several architectural firms, including Holabird & Root, who had designed the adjacent 333 N. Michigan Avenue, presented plans for development of the 83-acre site, but little happened until 1967 when Ludwig Mies van der Rohe came up with a master plan which would use the air rights over the former railroad yard. The plan for this "New East Side" called for a mixed-use development as a "city within a city," encompassing 7,500 residential units, 16 million square feet of office space, 3,500 hotel rooms, plus retail stores, interconnecting underground passageways, pedestrian amenities, landscaping, and three below-ground parking levels.

Walk past 333 N. Michigan Avenue to the Illinois Center complex.

The first building finished was **One Illinois Center** (*1970, Office of Mies van der Rohe*), 111 E. Wacker Drive, a 30-story steel frame, bronze-painted, and tinted-glass office tower. Mies died in 1969 and did not live to see the completion of the project. Just beyond the building is a stairway leading up to the central plaza of the development. Unfortunately, the dense massing of so many tall buildings on such a relatively small site obscures most of the sunlight and creates an oppressive, confining atmosphere.

At the rear of the plaza is **Two Illinois Center,** 223 N. Michigan Avenue, completed in 1973 by the Office of Mies van der Rohe, and identical in size and style to the first structure.

To the left (east) is one of the two buildings which comprise the 36-story, twin-tower **Hyatt Regency Chicago** hotel, 151 E. Wacker Drive (*1974, A. Epstein & Sons*). The dark-red-brick fortresslike structure offers only slight relief from the architectural monotony of the plaza.

The tightly massed Illinois Center complex along the south side of the Chicago River was constructed in the early 1970s and planned as a self-contained city within a city. It comprises a number of high-rise office towers, apartment buildings, and hotels; even an athletic club and firehouse. From right to left are the 36-story fortress-like Hyatt Regency Chicago; the 48-story Columbus Plaza rental apartment building; the 28-story Miesian-style Three Illinois Center; and the triangular-shaped 42-story Swissôtel Chicago. (Photo by author)

Cross Stetson Avenue.

Connecting the west tower of the Hyatt Regency Chicago to the east tower (*1980, A. Epstein & Sons*) is a glass-enclosed skywalk which includes part of the lobby and a restaurant. The glitzy front section of the tower, an enormous two-story glass wintergarden, is the main entrance to the hotel. Go in and take a look around. In the center is a changing seasonal display. The escalator leads to the registration desk and restaurant. There is also a below-ground level (which you can skip) that connects with a pedestrian concourse leading to other buildings in the complex.

Further to the east is the 48-story concrete high-rise, **Columbus Plaza** (*1980, Fujikawa, Conterato, Lohan & Associates*), 233 E. Wacker Drive, a rental apartment tower. The architectural firm is the successor to Mies's office, and has continued the development of the Illinois Center complex, although breaking with the steel-and-glass-box tradition in this structure, with its narrow vertical concrete strips embracing tinted, wide glass windows.

Cross Columbus Drive.

With the adjacent **Three Illinois Center** (*1980, Fujikawa, Conterato, Lohan & Associates*), 303 E. Wacker Drive, the firm continued the Miesian tradition with a 28-story steel frame office tower with dark aluminum and tinted-glass curtain walls.

A few steps further is the surprising **Swissôtel Chicago** (*1989, Harry Weese & Associates*), 323 E. Wacker Drive. A member of the international chain of Swissair-owned hotels, the unconventional design of this luxury hostelry is a startling (and welcome) change from most of the other Illinois Center structures. Planned in the familiar triangular shape of two other Harry Weese buildings in Chicago (the Metropolitan Correctional Center and 200 S. Wacker Drive), the 42-story facade differs considerably, however, in its walls of alternating bands of reflective and opaque glass. Wags have referred to the shape as resembling a large wedge of Swiss cheese. The cheerful, triangular glass-enclosed lobby displays a large clock (also glass-enclosed) that functions by the changes in the atmosphere.

At this point, if you look across the river toward the north side, a dramatic panorama of architecture presents itself. From west to east (left to right): Wrigley Building, Tribune Tower, NBC Tower, Sheraton Chicago Hotel, Chicago Tribune Freedom Center, Centennial Fountain, North Pier Apartments, the undulating Lake Point Tower, and to the extreme right, Navy Pier. (*See* Tour 6.)

Return to Columbus Drive and turn left to E. South Water Street.

Alongside Three Illinois Center, and in a similar aluminum and glass style, is the diminutive two-story **Fire Station CF-21** (259 N. Columbus Drive), erected in 1982 from plans by Fujikawa, Johnson and Associates.

Cross to E. South Water Street and note the three underground levels and their connections with adjoining streets. Although the railroad tracks are long since gone, one can see the extent of the Illinois Central yard on the grassy lot below.

At the next corner south is the 37-story **Fairmont Hotel** (*1987, Hellmuth, Obata & Kassabaum, with Fujikawa, Johnson and Associates*), 200 N. Columbus Drive. Its light-gray granite facade adds a bit of warmth to the otherwise austere agglomeration of buildings. The entrance is catercorner to the intersection, a convenience for vehicles depositing guests right at the door to the hotel. The lobby is rather small, but luxuriously appointed and cozy.

Turn right (west) on E. South Water Street to Stetson Avenue, then left again one short block to Lake Street.

On the left is the eye-catching **Athletic Club–Illinois Center** (*1990, Kisho Kurokawa*), 211 N. Stetson Avenue. Erected in what the club calls Japanese Industrial style, this delightful exposed-steel framework building is the "jewel in the crown" of Illinois Center. Its human-scale structure is the first in the nation to be designed by the Japanese architect, Kurokawa. It boasts an interior that is four stories high, with two below-ground levels, and contains a wide array of sport facilities and physical health services, even a daunting seven-

At 211 N. Stetson Avenue, just behind the Hyatt Regency Chicago, is the most interesting building in the complex, the Athletic Club–Illinois Center. The structure is constructed on an exposed steel framework, above which are free-swinging wind sculptures attached to 17-foot-high steel-frame towers. (Photo by author)

story rock-climbing wall set within a six-story atrium. On the roof, four 17-foot steel frame towers support free-swinging wind sculptures that resemble box kites, entitled *Children of the Sun,* by Osamu Shingu.

Diagonally across Stetson Avenue is **Two Prudential Plaza** (*1990, Loebl, Schlossman & Hackl*), 180 N. Stetson Avenue. One of Chicago's most conspicuous buildings, "Two Pru" is a daring step forward from Prudential's earlier 1955 skyscraper, adjacent to the southwest. Designed in a postmodern style by principal architect Steve Wright, its soaring 40-foot spire and chevron-like setbacks on the north and south facades are strongly reminiscent of Helmut Jahn's One Liberty Place, in Philadelphia (1987), and suggestive of Robert Van Alen's Chrysler Building in New York City (1930). These setbacks also provide additional corner offices, while the tapered pyramidal top section conceals water-cooling tanks, and mechanical and elevator systems. The hollow spire, 12 feet wide at the base, consists of two 20-foot sections that were snapped together like a child's toy. "Two Pru" was designed as an integrated part of the larger Prudential Plaza complex and shares mechanical systems with One Prudential Plaza for operational efficiency. The exterior of the 64-story tower features Mondariz and Caledonia granite with gray reflective glass, and is designed to be compatible with the limestone and aluminum facade of One Prudential Plaza while maintaining its own distinctive appearance. "Two Pru" is illuminated at night, and is a prominent visual landmark on the downtown skyline. A landscaped one-acre plaza to the west leads to an atrium connecting with One Prudential Plaza.

The 80-story Amoco Building soars 1,136 feet above Grant Park, and is Chicago's second-tallest skyscraper and the fourth tallest in the United States. Designed in 1973 as the Standard Oil Building, by Edward Durrell Stone, with Perkins & Will, the building was originally sheathed in Carrara marble. It had to be reclad in speckled North Carolina granite in 1990–1992, because the marble did not stand up under the extremes of Chicago weather and began buckling, threatening pedestrians beneath. The sheer verticality of this monolithic shaft makes it a dominant feature of the Chicago skyline. To the left are the twin towers of the Prudential Center, and to the right, the Fairmont Hotel to which the Amoco Building is connected by the Pedway, and in the distance, the 48-story Columbus Plaza and Three Illinois Center. (Courtesy of the Amoco Corporation)

Before visiting the first Prudential Building, turn left at E. Randolph Drive to the towering Amoco Building.

The 82-story **Amoco Building** (*1973, Edward Durell Stone, with Perkins & Will*), 200 E. Randolph Drive, is the second tallest building in Chicago, and the fourth tallest in the United States. The 1,136-foot-tall Amoco Oil corporate headquarters rises in one sheer swoop overlooking Grant Park, and is visible for miles. The tower, with its unbroken vertical rows of windows, is designed as a long, hollow tube whose exterior walls incorporate V-shaped columns which contain most of the building's mechanical services, such as steam, air-conditioning, and electric utility lines, which then allows for interiors free of columns as well as flush inside walls.

When completed, the structure was known as the Standard Oil Building and was the world's tallest marble-sheathed building . . . but not for long, as numbers of thin chunks along the southeast corner began to buckle, creating a massive hazard, not only endangering the lives of those below, but also threatening the integrity of the building. The marble, cut in sheets that were far too thin, could not endure Chicago's extremes in temperature. This design disaster did little for the reputation of Edward Durell Stone, and forced Amoco to engage Perkins & Will to reclad the building completely with speckled North Carolina granite, a task which required two years, from 1990 to 1992. According to the *AIA Guide to Chicago*, the architect and client completely depleted the Carrara marble quarry that Michelangelo had used, and the debacle that later ensued, according to folklore, was perhaps retribution for their hubris. The building's main entrance and plaza facing E. Randolph

Drive was added in 1985, after the closing of the former Lake Street entrance. The sunken plaza, built of gray granite and red polished marble with a reflecting pool, is a most attractive addition. A circular "island" is surrounded by a pleasant seating area, and the whole can be viewed from a mini-pavilion on the street level above.

On the adjacent plaza to the east, beyond the row of flagpoles representing all the states, and facing Grant Park, is one of Chicago's most unusual sculptures, Henry Bertoia's *Untitled Sounding Sculpture (1975)*. (Although officially "untitled," a small plaque on the base calls it *Offering to the Winds*.) Constructed of copper-beryllium alloy, brass, and granite, it consists of eleven units of flexible rods set at right angles to each other and positioned in a square reflecting pool. Blowing winds make the rods vibrate and collide with each other, and depending on their length, make sounds of corresponding frequencies, creating pleasant musical tones. According to the sculptor, as quoted in the Chicago Department of Cultural Affairs' *Loop Sculpture Guide,* "his inspiration came from nature—the memory of wheat fields swaying in the breeze, and the sound of the mythological Aeolian harp activated by the winds."

Take a quick walk around the grounds of the Amoco Building and find two more unusual pieces of sculpture: *Reflections (1986)*, a work in bronze by Joseph Burlini, and three *Deer (1986)*, made of chrome-plated automobile bumpers, by John Kearney. (You may have noticed the "deer" as you walked along Stetson Avenue.)

The circular fountain on the plaza in front of the Amoco Building, 200 E. Randolph Drive, offers a colorful and attractive entrée to Chicago's second-tallest building. The 16 jets of water create an eye-catching interplay with the marble tile pattern beneath. (Photo by author)

A walk around the Amoco Building reveals some interesting "wildlife." Grazing in the rear garden are three Deer *(1986) by John Kearney, fabricated of chrome-plated automobile bumpers! (Photo by author)*

Walk west on E. Randolph Drive to:

One Prudential Plaza, also called The Prudential Building (*1955, Naess & Murphy*), 130 E. Randolph Drive, was Chicago's first skyscraper to be erected after the Depression and World War II, and the first to use the air rights over the Illinois Central Railroad yards. The 40-story structure also had the distinction, albeit briefly, of being Chicago's tallest office tower. Clad in limestone trimmed with aluminum, it is reminiscent of the 1920s building style, and once sported a top-floor observation deck. The lobby is quite attractive and worth a visit. Look for Alfonso Ianelli's west wall low-relief sculpture in the east wing depicting the Rock of Gibraltar, the logo of the Prudential Insurance Company.

Continue west on E. Randolph Drive past Baubien Place, to Michigan Avenue, and turn right one block to the northeast corner of Lake Street.

Boulevard Towers South (*1985, Fujikawa, Johnson & Associates*), 205 N. Michigan Avenue, the newer of the pair of Miesian towers and 44 stories high, is an integral part of the Illinois Center development, and typical of the style of One, Two, and Three Illinois Center.

Boulevard Towers North (*1981*), by the same architects, 225 N. Michigan Avenue, is 24 stories high, and is connected by a 19-story addition to the south tower. For a dizzying view of the pair of towers, enter the building and take the escalator to the lobby level, walk to the rear of the concierge's desk, and look straight up through the glass roof for the stunning visual effect of the three towers looming overhead!

Under the south building is the busy **Randolph Street Station,** the terminal of the Metra Electric Division (formerly an Illinois Central commuter line) as well as the Chicago, South Shore & South Bend R.R., whose interurban trains serve northwest Indiana; these lines carry thousands of daily commuters. The South Shore Line is America's last surviving electric interurban railroad, where once there were hundreds all over the country. There is also an entrance to the **Pedway,** the Loop's extensive underground pedestrian walkway network (*see* pages 429–431).

On the corner plaza is another of Chicago's dazzling sculptures, *Splash,* a 21-foot curvaceous aluminum construction, by Jerry Pearl. Created in 1986, its flowing multicolor forms are designed to present a pleasing juxtaposition to the dark, rectilinear grid of Boulevard Towers and a bit of bright punctuation to the Michigan Avenue skyscraper wall. From the plaza are excellent views of the superb row of buildings along Michigan Avenue, including the unique Carbon & Carbide Building, across Michigan Avenue at E. Wacker Place, which is described in Tour 5.

End of tour.

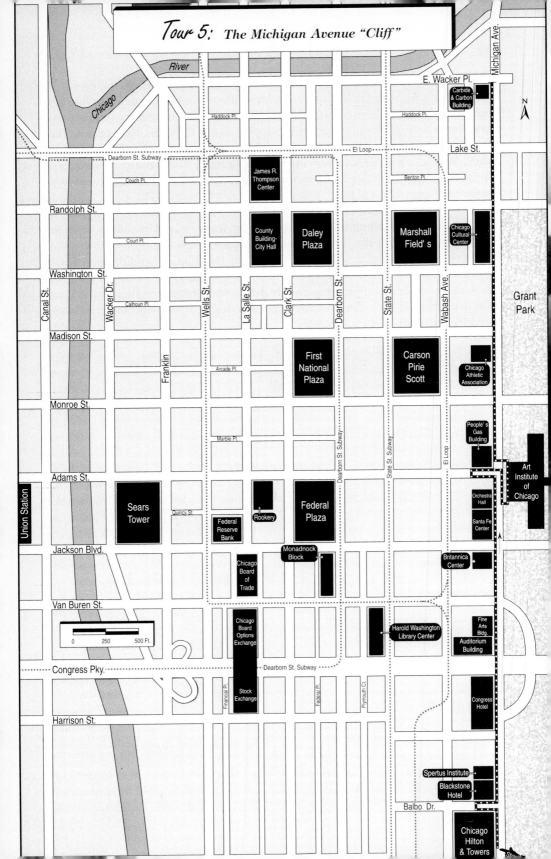

Tour 5: The Michigan Avenue "Cliff"

5. The Michigan Avenue "Cliff"

The tour begins on Michigan Avenue, at the block between 8th Street and E. Balbo Drive, and continues north along Michigan Avenue for about a mile, with only a few minor detours. The tour follows the western edge of Grant Park to afford the best views of the variety of buildings which comprise the "Cliff" (or "Wall," as it's sometimes called), but it will be necessary to cross Michigan Avenue from time to time to get a closer look at details, enter building lobbies, and explore some of the side streets. (To avoid that "run-down feeling," please be sure to use the pedestrian crosswalks and obey the traffic signals.)

The **Chicago Hilton and Towers Hotel** (*1927, Holabird and Roche; 1986 renovation, Solomon Cordwell Buenz & Associates*), 720 S. Michigan Avenue, was built by James W. Stevens to be the largest hotel in the world. When it opened with great fanfare in May 1927, it boasted 3,000 rooms and many hitherto novel amenities, such as a rooftop 18-hole miniature golf course, its own hospital, a 1,200-seat theatre with "talking motion picture" equipment, and a three-story laundry. Stevens named the luxurious hotel after himself, and through the years it attracted celebrity guests from around the world, including eight presidents, and such foreign dignitaries as Emperor Hirohito of Japan, Queen Elizabeth, and Prince Philip of England. The Depression era, however, took its toll, and by the mid-1930s the Stevens was bankrupt. In 1942, during World War II, the hotel was taken over by the Army Air Corps as a technical training facility and barracks, with the opulent grand ballroom converted to a mess hall. After only one year "in the Army" the Stevens was returned to civilian life and reopened under new management.

In 1945 Conrad N. Hilton purchased the hotel for $7.5 million, and six years later, renamed it The Conrad Hilton, as the flagship hotel for his chain. The enormous establishment even made the *Guinness Book of World Records,* when one evening 480 waiters served 7,200 dinners—the largest number of people ever served at one meal. A series of renovations took place between

1956 and 1970, culminating in a $150 million project in 1986. Prefabricated Imperial Suites were placed on top of the hotel by helicopters, and it is the only Chicago hotel approved by the Secret Service for presidential visits because of the complete privacy of a separate floor. The number of rooms was reduced to 1,600 to provide larger guest accommodations, and the world's largest hotel exhibition hall was created.

Although the main entrance—a modern porte-cochère—has been added to the Balbo Drive side, enter on the Michigan Avenue side, pass through the lobby and continue ahead to the tall four-sided *faux-marbre* clock, watched over by a bust of Conrad Hilton. Enter the Grand Stair Hall and walk up one flight leading to the Grand Ballroom; but before entering, take a few minutes to examine the sumptuous furnishings: fluted columns on the east side, fluted pilasters on the west side, ceiling and wall frescoes, bronze and crystal chandeliers, and steps of Belgian marble. Then walk into the columned front room, known as the Normandy Lounge. The paneling and chairs were salvaged from the French luxury liner *Normandie,* which caught fire and capsized in 1943 while being refitted as a troopship at a Manhattan pier. The furnishings were purchased two years later for the hotel. A plaque at the head of the north staircase tells the story. The Grand Ballroom, decorated in French Renaissance style, easily recalls the Palace of Versailles, with its mirrored doors and walls, 26 elaborately adorned arched windows with romantic paintings between, and suspended from the lofty ceiling, huge crystal chandeliers. The size of the ballroom is so immense that it could accommodate ten 2-story houses in two rows of five each. To create such an unobstructed open space was a daunting challenge, which the architects met by constructing four huge horizontal steel trusses to substitute for 55 structural pillars; these trusses had to be strong enough to support the 22 stories above. On leaving the hotel, note the initial S, for Stevens, on the second-floor balconies.

 At the northwest corner of E. Balbo Drive is the venerable **Blackstone Hotel** (*1909, Marshall & Fox*), 636 S. Michigan Avenue. Designed in a French Second Empire style, it has recently been renovated, and once again exudes Old-World charm, from its ornate mansard roof to its luxurious lobby. Note the three-story limestone base containing an arched window arcade, and particularly the row of pedimented windows on the third floor. The hotel is named for a close friend of the developers, Timothy Blackstone, president of the Chicago & Alton Railroad, whose mansion was formerly on the site. His home and all the elegant Michigan Avenue row houses of Chicago's elite that were built after the Great Fire of 1871 were ultimately demolished as the area became commercial. The Blackstone gained fame through the years as the site of selection of presidential candidates, the most notable being Warren G. Harding, who was chosen by the Republicans in the original "smoke-filled room" (Suite 804–805). For a time in the 1960s it was known as the Sheraton-Blackstone. On the Michigan Avenue side of the 20-story hotel, which was the first high-rise hotel on Michigan Avenue, are four antique lamp standards. Ignore the unattractive marquee, and go inside and look around the cozy wood-paneled lobby. Within the hotel is the **Mayfair Theatre,** which has had the distinction of

playing host to Chicago's longest-running play, *Sheer Madness,* by Paul Port-
ner, a whodunit-comedy with audience participation that opened September
22, 1982. Exit on the Balbo Drive side, walk a few steps to the right, and cross
the street.

From here you can get a good view of the **Blackstone Theatre** (*1910, Marshall & Fox*), 60 E. Balbo Drive. Now renamed the Merle Reskin Theatre, of
DePaul University, it still bears its original name above the entrance and
retains its neo-Classic facade intact, from the row of Ionic columns to the roof
balustrade.

For the curious story of how Balbo Drive got its name, *see* page 319.

Return to Michigan Avenue and turn left (north).

Adjacent to the hotel is one of two buildings occupied by **Columbia College Chicago** on the block. No. 624 (*1908, Christian A. Eckstorm*), is a 14-story
building designed in the Renaissance eclectic style that was very popular for
hotels and commercial buildings at the turn of the 20th century. It was known
originally as the Musical College Building, later the Blum Building, then the
Barnheisel Building, later the Grant Park Building, and still later, the Torco
Building. Although acquired by Columbia College in 1990 as part of its four-
building South Loop Campus, it is still referred to as the Torco Building. The
walls of dark-red brick display the typical window treatment of the time, with
limestone trim and exaggerated lintels; those in the center bay are splayed,
while the outer windows have block, or panel lintels. In 1922, seven additional
stories were added from plans by Alfred S. Alschuler. The Torco sign at the top
recalls the previous owner, the Torco Oil Company, which still retains the right
to display its sign. (One might wish that it were the college's name instead.)
Look into the lobby and note the ornate coffered ceiling, the chandeliers, and
the elaborate bronzework above the elevator doors.

The neighboring building to the north is the home of the **Spertus Institute
of Jewish Studies,** No. 618 N. Michigan Avenue. The Institute was founded in
1924 by Maurice and Herman Spertus, immigrants from Ukraine, and is dedicated to "continuing the legacy of Jewish thought and culture." The Institute
purchased this building in 1974 from the previous owner, International Business Machines, Inc. The structure's original 1911 facade had been stripped by
IBM in the late 1950s and replaced by the then-fashionable International-style
aluminum and glass curtain wall. Spertus Institute consists of Spertus College,
a graduate institution; the Asher Library, the largest public Jewish library in
the central United States, which includes the Targ Center for Jewish Music and
the Chicago Jewish Archives; the Joseph Cardinal Bernardin Center, which
strives to promote Catholic-Jewish and Polish-Jewish interfaith dialogue in
Poland and Chicago in cooperation with the Archdiocese of Chicago; and the
Spertus Museum. The museum houses one of the largest permanent collections
of Judaic art in America, and sponsors changing exhibits throughout the year.
(Museum hours: Sunday–Thursday, 10:00 A.M.–5:00 P.M.; Friday, 10:00 A.M.–
3:00 P.M.; closed Saturday. $4.00 adults; $2.00 seniors, students, children.)

In the Julian and Doris Weinberg Sculpture Garden (to the right), the centerpiece is the stainless steel sculpture, *The Flame,* by Leonardo Nierman.

Columbia College's building at **No. 600** (and 79 E. Harrison Street) was erected for an earlier client in 1907 by the same architect as its No. 624 building, Christian A. Eckstorm, and is easily recognized by its enormous cornice. The 25-story structure, purchased by the college in 1978, was formerly known as the Fairbanks Morse Building, and contains the college's visual and communication arts programs, the Ferguson Theatre, plus the ground-floor **Museum of Contemporary Photography,** open to the public Monday–Friday 10 A.M.–5 P.M., Thursday till 8 P.M., and Saturday 12–5 P.M. (free).

Occupying most of the next block is the **Congress Hotel** (*1893, Clinton J. Warren; additions 1902, 1907, Holabird & Roche*), 520 S. Michigan Avenue. It was planned as an annex to the Auditorium Building to the north, and the two buildings appear to form a massive "entrance gate" to Congress Parkway. Although the building, then known as the Pick-Congress Hotel, is a steel-framework structure and the Auditorium Building is load-bearing, there are many similarities that renovations through the years have not erased, particularly the window arcade above the seventh floor in the north section, the rough granite base (now somewhat obliterated by recent modernizations), and the appearance of the paired windows in the upper three stories. When Congress Parkway was widened some years ago, it required a section of the ground floor to be opened and arcaded on both the Congress Hotel and the Auditorium Building. The Michigan Avenue facade of both hotel sections reveals row upon row of projecting bay windows, which provide superb views of Grant Park and Lake Michigan, and were a special boon to guests before the advent of air-conditioning.

The lobby gives only a hint of former grandeur, particularly in the mosaic frieze. The hotel opened in time for the World's Columbian Exposition in 1893, which celebrated (a year late) the 400th anniversary of Columbus's arrival in the New World. Like the neighboring Blackstone Hotel, the Congress also figured importantly in political history. Here in 1912 Theodore Roosevelt opened his Bull Moose Convention, and in 1932 Franklin D. Roosevelt accepted the Democratic presidential nomination. Among the famous names on the hotel register have been Thomas Edison, Enrico Caruso, Jack Dempsey, and Sophie Tucker. Go up to the second floor and take a peek at the very impressive "Gold Room," the hotel's grand ballroom, which will reveal a bit of the hotel's former elegance. The Auditorium Theatre across the street now maintains offices in the hotel, which recalls the Congress's original purpose as an annex. For the last few years the hotel has been affiliated with the Ramada Inn chain.

Note: **The Auditorium Building in the next block marks the beginning of Tour 1 (The Loop I: Old Chicago and the Financial District); however, because of its dominant position on Michigan Avenue and its vital role in the history of modern architecture, the description of the Auditorium Building is repeated here for consistency and to obviate the need for turning pages.**

On a summer afternoon, ca. 1912, homeward-bound commuters descend the staircase from the old Van Buren Street Viaduct over Grant Park to board Illinois Central trains to suburbs south of Chicago. Clothing fashions were rather rigid, demanding dark suits and straw hats for men and tight-waisted skirts and brimmed hats for women. In the background along Michigan Avenue are (left to right) the Congress Hotel, the Auditorium Building, and the Studebaker (now Fine Arts) Building. The row of town houses at the extreme left are still occupied by the city's elite. (Photo by Copelin. Chicago Historical Society)

Before approaching the Auditorium Building, cross Michigan Avenue and step back a short distance into Grant Park to get a broad perspective of the structure and to appreciate its scale.

The construction of the **Auditorium Building,** 430 S. Michigan Avenue, came at the time when Chicago was emerging from the incredible devastation of the Great Fire, only 15 years before. It was commissioned by Ferdinand Wythe Peck, a prominent Chicago businessman, lover of the arts, and president of the 1885 Opera Festival. His intent was for the construction of a hotel, an office building, a much-needed opera house and concert hall, convention hall, and place for public events, all to be built under one roof. To carry out the grandiose project, he selected Dankmar Adler, an engineering genius, and his partner, Louis Sullivan, a master of design, who together had planned a number of successful music halls, including the highly praised Central Music Hall on State Street (*see* page 85). Although it was their first major commission, its subsequent success rocketed them to international fame and contributed immeasurably to their reputation. With Adler's talent in engineering and acoustics and Sullivan's consummate skill as an architectural ornamentalist, they were an unrivaled design team.

A two-horse team (with a dog in the back of the buggy) waits in front of one of the elegant town houses on Michigan Avenue, between Congress Parkway and E. Harrison Street. The houses in this ca. 1885 photo are the same as in the previous photo. (Chicago Historical Society)

The cornerstone was laid on October 5, 1887, and when the building was completed two years later, it set a number of records in the city: With its $3,200,000 price tag, it was the most costly; its 17-story tower made it the tallest; it was also the largest, most massive, and most spacious; and its 110,000-ton weight also made it the heaviest building in the world. The design of the facade was influenced by the then-popular Romanesque Revival style, made famous by Boston architect Henry Hobson Richardson, who in 1887 designed Marshall Field's Wholesale Store. Although the style of the Auditorium Building was somewhat similar to the Wholesale Store, the tower was a unique element. The structure is of load-bearing construction, with a base of rusticated granite above which the arched walls are of smooth Bedford limestone.

The 4,200-seat Auditorium Theatre was completely surrounded by the hotel and office sections, and set within a fireproof brick enclosure. It was lavishly adorned with stenciling, stained glass, decorative rows of electric lights, and ornate plaster reliefs. Six huge trusses support the elliptical vault over the theatre, with four successively larger elliptical arches adorned with light bulbs dividing the ceiling and acting as sound reflectors. The acoustics of the theatre are superb and the sight lines uninterrupted, a crowning achievement of Adler's talent. Adler also designed a clever system of iron frames and trusses that "hung" the kitchen and banquet hall above the auditorium. To support the weight of the immense building, Adler sunk a thick support "raft" made of wooden beams, rails, and I-beams; and to compensate for the structure's settling into the soft clay, he devised the unusual plan of dumping pig iron and bricks into the lower levels to increase the load on the foundation. The construction of the Auditorium Building has been described as the most important achievement in the history of modern architecture.

Opening night came on December 9, 1889, attended by President Benjamin Harrison and Vice President Levi Morton, who had received the Republican nomination at the site just 18 months before. The Auditorium Theatre immediately became Chicago's cultural center, with both the Chicago Opera and the Chicago Symphony Orchestra taking up residence. The Chicago Symphony presented its inaugural concert on October 16, 1891. In addition to musical events, there were circuses, conventions, sports events, and charity balls with thousands of people dancing on the huge stage. The hotel section opened in January 1890, together with a business section for offices and shops.

In 1929, both the onset of the Depression and the opening of the rival Civic Opera House (*see* pages 115 and 117) rang the death knell of the hotel and theatre. With the opera and symphony gone, the corporation went bankrupt, and later during World War II, the only tenant was the U.S.O., which used the auditorium stage as a bowling alley. In 1946 Roosevelt University purchased the Auditorium Building and adapted the facilities for classroom and office facilities. A major restoration project was undertaken by Harry Weese & Associates in the 1960s, and on October 31, 1967, the Auditorium Theatre reopened to a packed house for a gala performance by the New York City Ballet. Additional renovations were conducted in more recent times by Skidmore, Owings & Merrill, and the Office of John Vinci; and the theatre, now restored to its former opulence, is again one of Chicago's most popular sites for concerts and dramatic performances. The former hotel's banquet hall/ballroom is now the Rudolph Ganz Memorial Recital Hall, the ornate barrel-vaulted dining room serves as the University's library, and the grand staircase once more leads up to the magnificently restored Ladies' Parlor.

Some years ago, when the city widened Congress Parkway, the sidewalk along the Auditorium Building had to be removed. To provide for pedestrians, a passageway was gouged through the building, creating a covered arcade, but destroying part of the lobby entrance and much of the street side of the ground floor. The work was carried out with some care, however, and to the casual observer today, the passageway and lobby entrance appear to be part of the original design.

Enter the Michigan Avenue lobby and see the fruits of the years of painstaking rehabilitation. (Tours are available of the theatre complex. For information, call in advance 431-2354; $4.00, $3.00 students and seniors.)

Along the west sidewalk of Michigan Avenue are ornate **cast-iron kiosks,** providing access to passages under the avenue leading to the Metra Van Buren Street Station of the Electric District and South Shore line trains, located in an open cut in Grant Park. Two of these kiosks are also located on the previous block. The decorative iron work and glass of these little structures add a bit of old-fashioned charm to the streetscape.

Adjacent to the Auditorium Building is the **Fine Arts Building** (*1885, Solon S. Beman; renovation and addition 1898, Solon S. Beman*), 410 S. Michigan Avenue. The building bears a fairly strong resemblance to its neighbor, with its multistory Romanesque arches, rough-cut stone base, and horizontal courses. The window treatment differs, and one wonders at the placement of two isolated center columns rising from the third floor. The building, originally eight stories high, was designed for the Studebaker Company, builders of horse-drawn wagons and carriages, which used the first five floors for showrooms and the rooms above for assembly. The company then shifted to the exclusive manufacture of horseless carriages, in their former wagon and blacksmith shop in South Bend, Indiana. Studebaker continued to make automobiles until hard times forced a merger with the Packard Motor Car Company in 1954—an unhappy marriage that ended with the demise of both partners in 1963.

In 1898, at the behest of a group of investors, the building was renovated by architect Beman into studio space for artists and musicians. The upper floor was removed and three additional stories were added, topped by a prominent cornice. The remodeled building soon became a center for innovation in the arts, including fine and commercial art, theatre, literary publishing, and music. In 1917 the Studebaker Theatre was installed in the building, and its name remains emblazoned on the facade and on several doors. Four separate Fine Arts cinemas were built in 1982 to show foreign and avant-garde films. Within the confines of the building is a skylit atrium surrounded by balconies called the Venetian Court. The upper floors today are occupied mostly by professional musicians and musical instrument sales and repair shops. Through the years the studios of the Fine Arts Building have attracted a wide variety of creative minds. The list of tenants from the past and present reads like a Who's Who of American design talent, and includes such greats as Frank Lloyd Wright, Lorado Taft, and L. Frank Baum.

At the corner, with its entrance at 81 E. Van Buren Street, is the exclusive **Chicago Club** (*1930, Granger & Bollenbacher*). Designed in a modified Romanesque Revival style, it is a harmonious partner to its two southern neighbors. Although the nine-story building is of brownstone and has a rather smooth facade, it is divided in similar fashion, with a two-story arcaded base balanced at the top with a top-floor loggia and colonnade, surmounted by a corbel table and simple cornice. On the site previously was a building designed in 1887 by Daniel Burnham and John Wellborn Root for the Art Institute of Chicago. When the Institute moved to its present location across Michigan Avenue at the turn of the century, the building was acquired by the prestigious Chicago Club, founded in 1869. In 1929, as the structure was being renovated, it suffered a partial collapse and had to be demolished. The triple-arched Van Buren Street entrance was not destroyed however, and was incorporated into the present Granger & Bollenbacher building. Note the bronze eagle above the pair of flagpoles.

The 20-story **McCormick Building** (*1910, Holabird & Roche*), 332 S. Michigan Avenue, is a simple straightforward design with a smooth and unadorned facade punctuated with deeply recessed windows. It still retains its ornate cornice, but the ground floor has been "modernized" out of recognition. Look into the lobby to see its very attractive bronze coffered ceiling, about all that's left after a series of renovations. An extension of the building in 1912 added a few bays to the north.

The adjacent **318 S. Michigan Avenue** (*1885, architect unknown*) began its existence as the Hotel Richelieu, but by 1911 it was converted to an office

The view south on Michigan Avenue from E. Jackson Boulevard in 1887 reveals a still-undeveloped Lake Park (Grant Park was not established until 1901) and a continuous row of modest hotels. Among them are (right to left) the Leland, the Richelieu (with the square cupola and empty flagpole), and at the corner of E. Van Buren Street, the Victoria. (Chicago Historical Society)

building and many of the details were removed from the facade. A 1982 major renovation by Nagle Hartray & Associates brought limestone cladding to the two lower floors, creating a more distinguishable "base" to the building. Note the ornate spandrels and the 10 arched windows at the top (seventh) floor.

The Britannica Center (*1924, Graham, Anderson, Probst & White*), 310 S. Michigan Avenue, is the home of the famed *Encyclopaedia Britannica.* To appreciate the scale and details of the structure, formerly called the Straus Building, walk back into Grant Park at least 100 yards, until the rooftop adornments are visible. Capping the 28-story edifice, above a tall central bay, is a stepped pyramid, which Schulze & Harrington, authors of *Chicago's Famous Buildings,* compare with the Tomb of Mausolus at Halicarnassus. Not satisfied with reproducing one of the seven wonders of the ancient world atop their building, the architects placed four bison heads on their "ziggurat," which represent thrift, industry, strength, and city, and support an enormous beehive-shaped blue-glass lantern. Before blaming the encyclopedia publishers for this architectural extravaganza, it should be remembered that the building was constructed for a former client, the investment banking firm of S. W. Straus & Company. The larger lower-floor windows once admitted light into the broad banking floor, the beehive was a traditional symbol for thrift, and a beacon which once shone from the lantern represented the firm's "global reach."

The view north from E. Van Buren Street at the same block four years earlier shows a predecessor to the Victoria Hotel, a "French Flats," or luxury apartment building, soon to be torn down. To its right is the same Richelieu Hotel, and on the extreme left, on the southwest corner, the first home of the Art Institute of Chicago. (Chicago Historical Society)

Until the passage of the 1923 zoning ordinance, no Chicago building could be built higher than 260 feet. The new regulation required setbacks if a structure of greater height was to be built, and the receded columned center bay was the architects' solution. Just below the beehive is a belfry that contains four bells, ranging in size from 1,500 pounds to three-and-a-half tons. After hanging silent for years, the bells, which strike the hours and quarter hours and provide a pleasant contrast to the traffic din on Michigan Avenue, were reactivated in 1979 in honor of the visit of Pope John Paul II. However, the bells operate by computer, rather than by the original Seth Thomas clockwork. At night, the bright lantern, lit by six 1,000-watt bulbs in a blue-glass box, and its

(Right) Only a handful of commuters still use the Van Buren Street Station of the Metra Electric Division (formerly the Illinois Central Railroad's commuter line) in Grant Park. In a photo taken in 1995 close to the same spot as in the first photo in the chapter, a northbound suburban train of the Chicago, South Shore & South Bend Railroad, America's last electric interurban railroad, which uses Metra's tracks in downtown Chicago, heads north to its final stop at the Randolph Street terminal. Looming in the rear on Michigan Avenue is the 28-story Britannica Center, which is capped by a ziggurat and beehive-shaped blue-glass lantern. Built for a banking firm in 1924 from plans by Graham, Anderson, Probst & White, the building has been home to the noted encyclopedia publisher for many years. (Photo by author)

supporting pyramid are a colorful landmark on the "Cliff's" panorama, but the color and intensity of the blue light atop the building has been likened by wags to a giant "bug-zapper."

The corner of S. Michigan Avenue and E. Jackson Boulevard, at Grant Park, marks the site of the starting point of the nation's first cross-country highway, the famous **Route 66.** Inaugurated in 1926, the 2,000-mile highway, now mostly replaced by the Interstate system, headed west on Jackson Boulevard, crossed seven states and ultimately linked Chicago with Santa Monica, California.

 At the northwest corner of Jackson Boulevard is the glistening **Santa Fe Center,** formerly the Railway Exchange Building (*1904, D. H. Burnham & Company; renovation 1985, Metz, Train & Youngren, with Frye, Gillan & Molinaro*), 224 S. Michigan Avenue and 80 E. Jackson Boulevard, which represents one of Burnham's finest building designs. The solid 17-story structure is sheathed in shiny white-glazed terra cotta, and is planned around a central light court. The most characteristic elements of the gracefully ornamented facade are the undulating oriel bays that rise between the fourth and twelfth floors, with an unusual row of decorative bull's-eye windows beneath the cornice. The design of the building recalls the rather similar facade of his celebrated Flatiron Building in New York, which was completed at the same time. Burnham felt that this was an appropriate structure to showcase his architectural design prowess, and he established an office on the 14th floor. It was here that he and his associate, Edward H. Bennett, worked together on the famous 1909 Plan of Chicago. The sparkling cream-color facade is also a reminder of Burnham's "White City," the 1893 World's Columbian Exposition.

The building served for years as offices of the more than a dozen major railroads that served Chicago, and for a long time was the division headquarters of the Atchison, Topeka & Santa Fe Railway, which was recently merged with the Burlington Northern Railroad. The distinctive Santa Fe sign still graces the top of the building, and hopefully will remain there, even though the railroad's offices were moved to Schaumburg, Illinois. Take a few minutes to explore the elegantly restored lobby, which is somewhat reminiscent of the plan of Burnham's Rookery Building (*see* pages 30–33), and is the site of frequent exhibits in the Chicago Architecture Foundation's Atrium Gallery. Note the gleaming terra-cotta reliefs in the vestibule as you enter.

In the 1985 renovation, the spacious lightwell was covered with a glass roof, and a second glass skylight placed above the lobby. The building's main entrance was then shifted to the Jackson Boulevard side. The entire lobby was restored with cream-white marble for the flooring and wall paneling, as well as on the balustraded balcony and grand staircase.

The building is also the headquarters and storefront bookshop of the **Chicago Architecture Foundation.** The CAF is dedicated to advancing public interest and education in architecture and design, and pursues this mission through a comprehensive, year-round program of walking tours, bus and boat tours, exhibitions, lectures, and special events—all designed to enhance the

One of Daniel H. Burnham's finest designs is the glistening white-glazed terra-cotta Santa Fe Center, built in 1904 as the Railway Exchange Building. The Santa Fe Railway has moved its offices, as have all the other railroad companies that had offices in the building. On the ground floor of the recently restored Center are the offices, bookshop, and Tour Center of the Chicago Architecture Foundation. (Photo by author)

The elegant lobby and atrium of the Santa Fe Center are lined with marble, and the vestibules with glazed terra cotta. This fine relief of "Progress" adorns the Jackson Boulevard entrance. (Photo by author)

public's awareness and appreciation of Chicago's outstanding architectural legacy. Browse through the **Shop and Tour Center,** which offers an extensive collection of books, gifts, and architectural memorabilia, and pick up a schedule of daily tours and events as well as membership information. (Recorded tour information: 922-8687.) The CAF also maintains a Shop and Tour Center on the concourse level of the John Hancock Center.

On the sidewalk in front of the Santa Fe Center are bronze and glass kiosks covering stairways that lead to underground parking facilities under Grant Park. (Compare them with the ornate cast-iron kiosks near the Auditorium Building.)

☆ **Orchestra Hall,** immediately to the north (*1905, D. H. Burnham & Company; renovations: 1967, Harry Weese & Associates; 1981, Skidmore, Owings & Merrill*), 220 S. Michigan Avenue, known officially as The Theodore Thomas Orchestra Hall, illustrates another facet of Burnham's versatility with styles. From the Romanesque Revival, which was so popular until the World's Columbian Exposition, he moved with facility to the Georgian Revival. The eight-story red-brick facade is divided harmoniously into three sections: three arched windows on the second and third floors, flanked by pedimented windows denoting the lofty ballroom; four floors of windows topped by splayed limestone lintels; an eighth floor enframed with limestone and bordered by a pair of swags at each end; and vertical rows of limestone quoins bracketing the building. Surmounting a classic cornice is a typical Georgian balustrade. On the entablature above the third floor are emblazoned the names of Bach, Mozart, Beethoven, Schubert, and Wagner. The 1981 renovation—actually a complete rehabilitation of the space—increased the size of the stage, brought new seating, and improved the hall's acoustics. The concert hall now seats 2,590.

Daniel Burnham's interest in the hall was more than just commission-related. He was a trustee of the Orchestral Association, and had supported the repeated demands for a new hall, under threats of resignation, by Theodore Thomas, conductor of the Chicago Symphony Orchestra. The orchestra, founded by Thomas in 1891, had been performing in the Auditorium, but he objected to its enormous size and acres of empty seats, insisting on a more intimate space. Burnham then donated his services, and in December 1904 Thomas conducted the first Chicago Symphony concert at Orchestra Hall. Unfortunately, he died three weeks later, unable to enjoy another season in the hall he fought so hard to obtain. The Association then named the building in his honor. A commemorative monument to Thomas stands in Grant Park, near the corner of Michigan Avenue and Balbo Drive, and is described in Tour 9 (*see* pages 298–299). The present conductor of this world-class symphony orchestra is the renowned Daniel Barenboim, appointed in 1994.

In 1908, a ninth-floor penthouse, virtually hidden from view, was added by Howard Van Doren Shaw to house the **Cliff Dwellers' Club,** which still occupies the space. Through the years the club has been a noted gathering place for Midwestern authors, architects, artists, and musicians, whose membership once included Louis Sullivan, Frank Lloyd Wright, and Carl Sandburg. It was founded by Pulitzer Prize–winning writer Hamlin Garland as "a home for all workers in the fine arts." Today the club counts among its members Saul Bellow, Studs Terkel, and Roger Ebert. At this writing the 400-member club is involved in a dispute with the Orchestral Association, which would like to take over the space with its vaulted ceiling and Lake Michigan views for its own purposes, and since the tenure of the club is based on an original handshake agreement with the Association, the future of this "oasis of gentility" atop Orchestra Hall remains uncertain.

At the corner of Adams Street is a typical International-style "glass box"—the style that took the world by storm in the early 1950s. The **Borg-Warner Building** (*1958, A. Epstein and Sons, with William E. Lascaze*), a steel-framework structure sheathed in alternating rows of blue-glass windows with a grid of aluminum mullions, was the first so-called modern building erected on Michigan Avenue, and fortunately did not become a trendsetter. The building replaced the former **Pullman Building** (*1884, Solon S. Beman*) that housed the headquarters of George Pullman's famous Palace Car Company, whose factory and planned company-town was located 15 miles south of Chicago in the suburb of Pullman. On the entrance lobby wall is a stainless-steel sculpture, *Silver Blade,* by Barry Tinsley.

Take a brief detour west on Adams Street to see two greatly contrasting buildings.

No. 63 E. Adams Street (on the south side), the former Chapin & Gore Building (*1904, Richard E. Schmidt and Hugh M. G. Garden*), displays a rather unusual facade. The dark-red-brick structure is divided into three sections, each with its own window arrangement corresponding with the building's original function. As a wholesale and retail liquor distributor, the company's ground floor required good light to show the merchandise; the second and third floors demanded more solid storage space, and the upper five floors with their Chicago windows reveal the location of the company's offices. Note how the windows on the second and third floors are paired together with terra-cotta "frames" and separated by ornate spandrels, which together with the decorative band course above, seem to indicate the influence of Louis Sullivan. Above the three central brick piers is just blank brickwork—the result of a later "remuddling" which, unfortunately, destroyed the once-ornate capitals and large cornice.

Across the street, at the corner of Wabash Avenue, is the towering **55 E. Monroe Street** (also 125 N. Wabash Avenue), which has a similar entrance on Adams Street (*1972, Alfred Shaw & Associates*). This 50-story behemoth, in a more recent and much more sophisticated version of the International style than the Borg-Warner Building, rises straight up in one sweep, its uninterrupted shiny stainless-steel piers adding to the strong and unremitting sense of verticality. In the lobby are two modernistic paintings by the Zhou brothers, Shan Zuo and Da Huang, entitled *Life Symphony* and *Dream of Chicago.* The building is clearly distinguishable after dark with its bright horizontal bands of light punctuating the night sky.

(Left) The brick-and-granite Pullman Building, designed in 1884 by Solon S. Beman for the offices of the sleeping-car magnate George M. Pullman, stood on the southwest corner of Michigan Avenue and E. Adams Street until the early 1950s, when it was razed for the construction of the Borg Warner Building. The building's early Romanesque Revival style influenced many of the later designs of the Chicago school. (Chicago Historical Society)

Return to Michigan Avenue and cross over to:

The Art Institute of Chicago (*1893, Shepley, Rutan & Coolidge; additions and renovations as noted below*), Michigan Avenue at Adams Street, in Grant Park. The Institute, arguably Chicago's most popular tourist attraction and its cultural "jewel in the crown," was built at the same time as the World's Columbian Exposition. The influence of the "White City" is immediately apparent in the dignified Beaux Arts style of its architecture and the light color of its masonry. The complex of buildings grew through the years, with wings and galleries added as recently as 1988. After the tracks of the Illinois Central

No. 63 E. Adams Street, formerly known as the Chapin & Gore Building, was designed in 1904 by Richard E. Schmidt and Hugh M. G. Garden. It displays a rather unusual facade divided into three horizontal sections, each with its own window arrangement. A later "modernization" destroyed the once ornate capitals and cornice. (Commission on Chicago Landmarks)

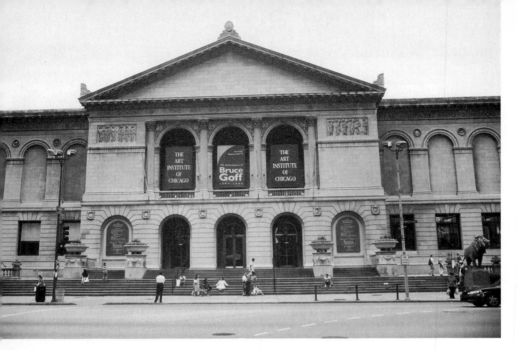

The world-class Art Institute of Chicago, on Michigan Avenue opposite E. Adams Street, is the city's most popular attraction. The influence of the World's Columbian Exposition "White City" is evident in the light-color masonry and its dignified Beaux Arts facade. Many wings have been added to the building through the years without disturbing the harmony or integrity of its original Shepley, Rutan & Coolidge 1893 design. Modern additions have been tastefully hidden in the rear. (Photo by author)

Railroad behind the Institute's main building were depressed, the Institute was able to expand eastward to Columbus Drive. As the only structure permitted on the Grant Park side of Michigan Avenue, the Classical facade of the original 1893 Allerton Building is a dramatic presence. It consists of a central three-story pedimented bay with a triple-arch arcade set above a ground floor of rusticated limestone, below which are three arched doorways flanked by blind arches to form the grand entrance. A low-relief frieze beneath the cornice at each end of the bay replicates the Panathenaic Procession on the Parthenon. Both north and south wings continue the smooth ashlar of the upper stories and the rustication of the lower, with seven blind arches above square windows on each wing. Guarding the approach to the Institute are the famous **pair of bronze standing lions,** the symbol of the Museum, by Edward L. Kemeys, considered the leading sculptor of animals in his lifetime. Kemeys first discovered his interest in portraying animals when he worked under Frederick Law Olmsted as an axeman clearing land for New York's Central Park.

The Institute was founded in 1879 as the Chicago Academy of Fine Arts. The name was changed three years later to the Art Institute of Chicago, and a building was purchased at the corner of Michigan Avenue and Van Buren Street. In 1887 a new building on the same site was designed for the Institute by Burnham & Root. By 1893 a major building at the present Institute location was planned in cooperation with the World's Columbian Exposition, and the former structure was sold to the Chicago Club. After a summer of use by the World's Congress Auxiliary of the Exposition, the new building was formally dedicated on December 8, 1893. The majestic lions, commissioned by Mrs. Henry Field, came the following year. Among the extensive holdings of the Art Institute are paintings, sculpture, bronzes, photography, miniature furnishings, even paperweights. The collection of Medieval and Renaissance paintings is outstanding, but the prize acquisitions are the Impressionist and post-Impressionist canvases, including Seurat's *Sunday Afternoon on the Island of La Grande Jatte,* Toulouse-Lautrec's *At the Moulin Rouge,* as well as priceless masterpieces by Cezanne, Renoir, Monet, Gauguin, and Van Gogh. One of the Institute's gems is the Burnham Library of Architecture, established from a bequest of Daniel H. Burnham himself, which boasts a wide-ranging collection of architecture books, drawings, manuscripts, archives, and documentary photographs and the most complete collection of material on Louis Sullivan.

Additions to the Institute's building began soon after it opened and have continued through the years: Fullerton Hall in 1898, Ryerson Library in 1901, Blackstone Hall in 1903, the Grand Staircase in 1910, Gunsaulus Hall, erected over the railroad tracks, in 1916 (all by the original architectural firm); the Burnham Library, by Howard Van Doren Shaw, in 1920; the Hutchison Wing and McKinlock Memorial Court, by Coolidge & Hodgdon, in 1924; the Goodman Memorial Theatre, by Howard Van Doren Shaw, in 1925; the Agnes W. Allerton Wing, by Coolidge & Hodgdon, in 1927; the Robert Allerton Wing, by Holabird & Root, in 1939; the B. F. Ferguson Memorial Building, by Holabird & Root and Burgee, in 1958; the Morton Wing, by Shaw, Metz & Associates, in 1962; Stanley McCormick Memorial Court and south garden, by landscape architect Dan Kiley, in 1965; new school and extension of the east wing, and east garden, by Skidmore, Owings & Merrill, in 1976–1977; reconstruction of the Trading Room and entrance arch from the demolished Chicago Stock Exchange Building (Adler & Sullivan, 1893–1894), by Vinci-Kenny Architects, in 1977; renovation of the Allerton Building, by Skidmore, Owings & Merrill, in 1985–1987; restoration of the Michigan Avenue entrance lobby, by the Office of John Vinci, in 1987; construction of the Daniel F. and Ada L. Rice Building, by Hammond, Beeby & Babka, in 1985–1988.

A visit to the Art Institute of Chicago is a must; however, that should be left for another day.

When you do go, pick up the floor plan and schedule of activities at the Information Desk. Don't miss the reconstruction of the **Trading Room** of the old Stock Exchange (1977), mentioned above. Walk straight back on the first floor, and through the McKinlock Court Gardens (a great spot for lunch!). The room was reconstructed from the salvaged parts of the original, with missing sections carefully replicated. Fortunately, the superb artistry of Louis Sullivan can again be seen in the fixtures, decorations, and incredible polychromed stenciling that embodies as many as 52 colors. The Stock Exchange Building fell victim to the wreckers' ball in 1972, to the shock and dismay of preserva-

The Trading Room of the Chicago Stock Exchange was reconstructed and installed in the Art Institute of Chicago's Arthur Rubloff Building by Vinci-Kenny architects in 1977, five years after the demolition of the Exchange. According to architect John Vinci, the Trading Room was hailed in its day as "unexcelled in the magnificence of its appointments and decoration by any room used for like purpose in the country." Sullivan's rich decoration, expressed in the more than two dozen colors employed in the stencilling, was considered remarkable for a commercial space. (Courtesy of the Art Institute of Chicago)

tionists and architectural historians worldwide who had waged a vigorous campaign to save it. Another tragic casualty was architectural photographer Richard Nickel, who had fought valiantly to preserve not only the Stock Exchange, but many other historic buildings in Chicago. On April 13, 1972, while attempting to recover some salvageable examples of Sullivan's work in the partially demolished building, a section of the Trading Room floor collapsed, burying him under tons of crushed masonry. His body was found four weeks later. Except for the restored Trading Room, the huge **LaSalle Street entrance arch** (mounted in the East Garden at the rear of the Institute near the Columbus Drive entrance), and the ornate iron staircase (on display in the American Wing of the Metropolitan Museum of Art, in New York), the Stock Exchange Building is but a sad memory—"the Wailing Wall of Chicago's Preservation Movement," as the *AIA Guide to Chicago* puts it.

Before continuing along Michigan Avenue's "cliff," spend a few minutes to explore the fascinating collection of sculpture in the front gardens of the Institute.

Behind the Art Institute, in the East Garden, is the preserved LaSalle Street entrance arch of the old Stock Exchange Building, demolished in 1972. (Photo by author)

To the right of the entrance, along the south wing of the Museum, at the rear of the formal gardens of Stanley McCormick Court, is the remarkable *Fountain of the Great Lakes* (1913) by native Illinoisan, Lorado Taft. Each of the classical female figures holding conch shells on this 22-foot-tall bronze statue represents one of the five Great Lakes, positioned in such a way that running water pours from from one shell to another, just as the waters flow eastward from one lake to another, until they reach the St. Lawrence River. In the sculptor's words, "Superior on high and Michigan on the side both empty into the basin of Huron who sends the stream to Erie whence Ontario receives it and looks wistfully after." The statue was originally set on the south side, but was moved in 1936 to its present, more visible site.

Then walk to the north court to see three works: Alexander Calder's stabile, *Flying Dragon* (1975), a steel-plate assemblage painted in his favorite bright vermilion, the same color as his *Flamingo,* at the Chicago Federal Plaza (*see* pages 71–72); David Smith's welded stainless-steel *Cubi VII* (1963); and Henry Moore's powerful *Large Interior Form* (1982). The Moore sculpture is cast from the inner element of a piece that can be seen in the atrium of Three First National Plaza (*see* page 63), and represents a human figure.

 Dominating the northwest corner of Michigan Avenue and Adams Street is the **People's Gas Building** (*1910, D. H. Burnham & Company; restoration 1987, Eckenhoff Saunders, Architects*), 122 S. Michigan Avenue. This 22-story steel-framework building, which replaced the 1883 Brunswick Hotel, is sheathed in ornate terra cotta and is typical of Burnham's late work (he died in 1912). Essentially a tripartite skyscraper, the base is significant for the iron-and-glass storefront bay windows, above which are ornate panels with light

(Left) One of the famous lions that grace the entrance to the Art Institute looks out across Michigan Avenue at the People's Gas Building (1910, D. H. Burnham & Company). The entire facade of this 22-story steel-framed building is covered with ornate terra cotta—most noticeably in the horizontal bands through the windows and as intervening courses. The building's 10 huge three-story polished-granite columns dominate the building's front. (Photo by author)

globes surrounded by rosettes; the shaft of the building is noted for the sculptural quality and horizontality of the design, with carved bands connecting the rows of windows; and the building's "capital," for its three-story colonnade and intricately worked cornice and supporting consoles. Ten huge gray polished-granite columns dominate the Michigan Avenue facade. An interesting feature is that these massive columns do *not* support the exterior wall. Above the second-floor level large concealed cantilever girders shift the load to the interior frame. The lobby, which has been remodeled, still preserves the original marble floor. A low skylight covers the atrium, but the former customer service center and public amenities are gone. Look inside, anyway.

The adjacent **Lake View Building** (*1906, Jenney, Mundie & Jensen; renovation 1912*), 116 S. Michigan Avenue, was formerly the Municipal Court Building, and served briefly as the Chicago City Hall until the new municipal offices were finished in 1911. Originally 12 stories high, four more were added in the renovation the following year. The three-bay-wide building is faced with white terra cotta. Of the trio of architects, William LeBaron Jenney is acknowledged as the father of the modern high-rise, having designed the first successful steel-frame skyscraper (*see page 34*).

The **School of the Art Institute of Chicago** (*1908, Barnett, Haynes & Barnett; addition 1985, Swann & Weiskopf*), 112 S. Michigan Avenue. Built originally for the Illinois Athletic Club, the limestone facade of the building displays an interesting variety of details. Best seen from across the avenue, are three heroic statues at the second-floor level, set in the broken pediments of arched stained-glass windows. At the 11th floor is an attractive sculptured frieze by Leon Harmant depicting Zeus overseeing athletic competitions. Surprisingly, the lobby is circular in shape. The 1985 six-story addition, employing similar building materials, increased the building height to 18 stories, but did not harmonize successfully with the original. The building was purchased from the Club in 1992 for the Art Institute's school, which moved from its earlier location at the Institute. A major project in the renovation of the building was the rehabilitation of the elegant 1927 ballroom.

The last building on the block, with its conspicuous pyramidal gable, is the **Monroe Building** (*1912, Holabird & Roche*), 104 S. Michigan Avenue and 76 E. Monroe Street. Built in the era when ornament was an essential element of the overall design, this Italian Gothic Revival–style building is a fine exemplar of the tradition. It was planned to equal in height its neighbor across Monroe Street, the University Club, also by the same architects, but the peaked gable turned out to be an afterthought to match the Club's. Step back to examine the gable's windows, triple bifora in style (*bifora,* meaning in pairs under a single

Looking north along the Michigan Avenue "Cliff" toward E. Monroe Street and beyond, are (left to right) the People's Gas Building, the Lake View Building, the former Illinois Athletic Club Building (now the School of the Art Institute of Chicago), and with the pyramidal gable, the Monroe Building. Across E. Monroe Street is the University Club, the Gage Group, and at the extreme right, the Stone Container Building with its strange truncated diamond-shaped top. (Photo by author)

arch), bracketing a two-story central window. The ground floor is reserved for retail establishments, and the pink-gray granite base contrasts with alternating bands of grey terra cotta above. Three dormers can barely be seen atop the east-west roof.

Enter the building to see the superb vaulted vestibules and lobby, decorated with Rookwood faience. The glazed tile of many shades produced by this company achieved widespread popularity at the turn of the century during the rise of the Arts and Crafts Movement. In the lobby, blue is the dominant color of the vaulting, whereas in the vestibules of the Michigan Avenue and Monroe Street entrances, the motif is checkered black and white. The Gothic-style vaults rise from sculptured capitals set on tile-faced columns. A variety of Gothic motifs are displayed throughout the building. Quatrefoils, for example, can be seen not only on the spandrels outside, but inside on the radiator grilles.

The design of the 12-story **University Club** (*1908, Holabird & Roche*), 26 Monroe Street, demonstrates how a delicate Tudor Gothic style can be adapted to a tall modern building. The University Club of Chicago was founded in 1887 by a group of college graduates whose stated goal was "the promotion of literature and art, by establishing and maintaining a library, reading room, and gallery of art." The building, which, unfortunately, is not open to the public, has splendid interior furnishings, including the three-story Cathedral Hall at the ninth floor, whose arched stained-glass windows by Frederic

Clay Bartlett can clearly be seen from the street. Architect Martin Roche also contributed the paneling and carvings in the second-floor Michigan Room, where the painted ceiling panels were also the work of Bartlett.

The adjoining trio of buildings form what is known as the **Gage Group** (*1899, Holabird & Roche*), 18, 24, and 30 S. Michigan Avenue. In stark contrast to the ornamented facades of the University Club and Monroe Building, these relatively simple structures express their steel-frame construction with plain red brick, broad terra-cotta spandrels, and strong vertical piers, all of which embrace wide Chicago windows in the first two (Edson Keith and Theodore Ascher Buildings), and tight groups of four and five windows in the third (Gage Building, now renamed the Stanmac Building). The original owners, Ascher, Keith, and Gage, were millinery wholesalers who moved to the brighter Michigan Avenue site from the more densely packed and darker Wabash Avenue.

The tan terra-cotta tile facade of the 12-story **Gage Building** (No. 18) was designed by Louis Sullivan. Rising above the strong twin center piers are two lively bursts of ornate terra-cotta floral forms, a typical Sullivanian touch. The

In this ca. 1900 view of the Gage Group, 18–30 S. Michigan Avenue, the original cornices of this Holabird & Roche–designed trio are still virtually intact. Although additions were built in 1902 and the ground floor "modernized," the buildings remain virtually unchanged. The terra-cotta tile facade with foliate ornamentation on No. 18 was designed by Louis Sullivan. (Chicago Historical Society)

(Left) Looking for all the world like a palace on Venice's Grand Canal, the Chicago Athletic Association Building (1893) shows the versatility of architect Henry Ives Cobb. The charming and intricate Venetian Gothic facade remains in pristine condition. One of the largest athletic clubs in Chicago when built, it is still an exclusive enclave. (Photo by author)

wide spandrels are also adorned with foliate designs. It is likely that the Gage Brothers felt that such a distinctive building front would attract more business, and the open expanse of Grant Park would provide more light. Although there have been many renovations through the years, including a 1953 "modernization" of the entire ground floor which eliminated the cast-iron display windows, and a 1970 additional floor on No. 30, the Commission on Chicago Landmarks, in one of its earliest designations (*see* landmark plaque), praises the Gage Group for "the fine relations between piers, windows, and wall surfaces, the excellence of proportions throughout, and the imaginative use of original ornament."

☆ The **Chicago Athletic Association Building** (*1893, Henry Ives Cobb*), 12 S. Michigan Avenue, would sit well next to the *Cà d'Oro* on Venice's Grand Canal. Like other highly ornate buildings along the avenue, a few steps backward are necessary to take in this riot of Venetian Gothic illusion. Architect Cobb was an extremely versatile designer who worked effectively in many styles, from the English Gothic of the buildings of the University of Chicago to the Romanesque of the Newberry Library. In cooperation with Charles Sumner Frost, he produced the Potter Palmer "castle" in 1882, on Lake Shore Drive. Looking upward from the carved owl above the arched entrance, each succeeding floor is a delightful surprise, with arcades of intersecting ogive arches above the fourth and eighth levels, and quoins along the four piers up to the entablature. The overall design is enlivened by the delicate brickwork, the narrow lancet windows and tracery, and an ornate frieze below the cornice. Above the cornice a relatively bland parapet is topped by nine "portholes," but the door at the right is a strange incongruity. One of the largest athletic clubs in Chicago when built, it still remains an exclusive enclave.

At the corner, stands the **Willoughby Tower** (*1929, Samuel L. Crowen*), 8 S. Michigan Avenue. Named for an earlier Willoughby Building on the site, the towering 36-story Indiana limestone structure is, despite its size, an unobtrusive addition to the Michigan Avenue "Cliff." Gothic motifs can be seen on the mock stone balconies above the entrance and the fifth floor, as well as at the cornice.

Take a brief detour west on Madison Street.

An **Annex Building** to the Chicago Athletic Association, at 71 E. Madison Street (*1907, Richard E. Schmidt, and Garden & Martin*), is a far less ornate structure, with a seven-story addition in 1926 by the same architects. Look up at the lions' heads on the 10th through 13th floors and at the unusual brickwork at the corners of those floors which is suggestive of the Prairie school.

Turning left (south) at the corner of Wabash Avenue about 100 feet, is one of those "hidden gems" buried on the less-traveled thoroughfares of the Loop, the **Jewelers' Building** (_1882, Adler & Sullivan_), 19 S. Wabash Avenue (not to be confused with 35 E. Wacker Drive, which for a time was also called the Jewelers Building; _see_ pages 152–153). Here, partially obscured by the El, is the oldest example of Adler & Sullivan's architectural designs. Alas, the ground floor has been "remuddled," but the upper four stories reflect Louis Sullivan's interest in the Ruskinian Gothic as well as the influence of a former mentor, Frank Furness of Philadelphia. Note the treatment of the central window section, the use of contrasting colors in the red brick and white masonry, and the early Sullivanian ornamentation, particularly above the fifth floor. (It is worth the fare to go up on the elevated platform to obtain a good view of the entire building.)

Return to Madison Street and cross to the park side of Michigan Avenue. Madison Street is the dividing line between north and south addresses in the city.

At the northwest corner of Madison Street and Michigan Avenue is the **Tower Building** (_1899, Richard E. Schmidt; addition 1923, Holabird & Roche; remodeled 1955, Loebl, Schlossman & Bennett_), also known simply by its address, 6 N. Michigan Avenue. Before crossing the avenue for a closer look at the building, turn around and read the recently installed plaque at the edge of the park, in the Aaron Montgomery Ward Gardens, that honors the founder of the renowned mail-order business. The huge structure that was the headquarters of the firm, is 17 stories high, with a central bay rising an additional three stories to form a tower. Although still an impressive building despite its grimy facade, it once sported a 10-story tower topped by a 3-story pyramid, tempietto, and a well-remembered electrically illuminated 22.5-foot-tall gilded weathervane in the form of a female figure called _Progress Lighting the Way for Commerce._ The building, which bore the sobriquet "The Busy Beehive," has undergone a number of renovations, including the addition of four floors and the "circumcision" of its picturesque tower in 1947, but some interesting details still survive beneath the accumulated pollution on the terra-cotta spandrels. Montgomery Ward and Company, always identified with the city of Chicago, was founded in 1872 and began in business at the next corner north. As the firm's active mail-order business grew, the present building was commissioned. The administrative, warehousing, and distribution functions remained here until 1908, when the company moved to the site of its present huge complex on West Chicago Avenue, on the Chicago River.

As the plaque indicates, Aaron Montgomery Ward was singularly responsible for the preservation of Chicago's lakeshore as an open space, and for twenty years fought tirelessly "to assure that the city's 'front yard' would remain free and clear, providing magnificent views and recreational opportunities to all of its citizens. Grant Park is his legacy to the city he loved . . . his gift to the future."

The headquarters of the Montgomery Ward enterprise was moved in 1908 from its earlier Michigan Avenue site to the present complex of buildings situated on the North Branch of the Chicago River, at W. Chicago Avenue. Designed by Schmidt, Garden & Martin in 1906–1908, it was the largest building of the Chicago school to be constructed on a concrete frame. Aaron Montgomery Ward was singularly responsible for the preservation of Chicago's lakeshore as a public open space. He fought indefatigably for the sanctity of Grant Park from his offices in the Tower Building, which still stands at 16 N. Michigan Avenue. (Photo by author)

Before continuing further, note that while the concrete benches spaced at intervals along the east side of Michigan Avenue are a considerate amenity for walkers, they serve another purpose. A glance behind them will reveal that they cleverly conceal ventilators for the parking garages under Grant Park.

The **Illinois State Medical Society** (*1885, Beers, Clay & Dutton; addition 1892; renovation 1985, Nagle, Hartray & Associates*), 20 N. Michigan Avenue, was formerly an operations center for Montgomery Ward's mail-order catalog business, and known for years as the Ward Building. This old red-brick and timber-frame structure was sympathetically renovated in 1985, preserving much of the original detail. A limestone base was added; six very wide bays, each with three windows, were enframed with metal; the rosettes in the spandrels were preserved, as were the five scallop-design motifs atop each pier. The medical society's name was then carved across the front.

The adjacent **30 N. Michigan Avenue Building** (*1914, Jarvis Hunt*) is easily recognizable, less from its architectural merit than for the enormous electric sign on the roof that proclaims the Michigan Avenue National Bank. Originally 15 stories high, 6 more were added in 1923. Note the Gothic motifs in the spandrels between the 2nd and 3rd floors, above the 12th floor, and again on the roof parapet. The main entrance of this U-shaped building is at 77 E. Washington Street.

Turn left (west) on Washington Street, and stay on the north sidewalk to just beyond Garland Court.

Across Washington Street looms the imposing 38-story **Pittsfield Building** (*1927, Graham, Anderson, Probst & White*), 55 E. Washington Street, for a short time the tallest building in Chicago, and still a conspicuous visual landmark. The building was erected in accordance with the zoning regulation of 1923 which dictated the height limit of 260 feet and required the arrangement of setbacks in a ratio with the building's height—more precisely that the height not exceed one-sixth of its volume, or one-quarter of the structure's footprint. The building conforms to the formula with its setbacks at the 22nd, 35th, and 38th floors. Each setback is emphasized with little turret-like Gothic features. The Pittsfield Building was developed by the Marshall Field estate, and was named for the city in Massachusetts where Marshall Field got his first job. In style it anticipated the Art Deco movement. Interesting are the four vertical masonry bars in each spandrel, creating the visual effect of an upward sweep in each line of windows, adding considerably to the almost overwhelming sensation of height. Note the polished black-granite base as you enter the lobby; then the coffered ceiling that is beautifully decorated with gilt hexagons. Look at the splendidly ornate polished-brass elevator doors, floor indicators, convector grilles, lobby mailbox, and decoration above every doorway on the ground floor. Continue into the surprisingly lovely central atrium with its fine marble and brass fittings, surrounded by four levels of balconies, with a sculpted corbel table above the third balcony; and suspended in the center, a huge ornate chandelier. Graham, Anderson, Probst & White was the successor firm to Graham, Burnham & Company, which in turn succeeded D. H. Burnham & Company.

Return to Michigan Avenue and turn left (north).

Look northeast across Grant Park for a dramatic panorama of three skyscrapers: From left to right, One Prudential Plaza, Two Prudential Plaza (with the soaring spire), and the towering Amoco Building (Chicago's second tallest). All are described in Tour 4.

Occupying the entire block from Washington to Randolph streets is the ★ **Chicago Cultural Center** (*1897, Shepley, Rutan & Coolidge; restoration 1977, 1993, Holabird & Root*). Until the completion of the spacious Harold Washington Library Center in 1991 (*see* Tour 1), this building served as the central operations center and main branch of the Chicago Public Library. The Center, a monumental Beaux Arts–style building, designed with both Classical Greek and Italian Renaissance motifs by the same architectural firm that was just completing the Chicago Art Institute, was erected on the site of Dearborn Park, part of the old Fort Dearborn military post. Securing the plot to erect the

The Chicago Cultural Center, a monumental Beaux Arts edifice, designed by the same architects as the Art Institute of Chicago, served as the city's main public library from its dedication in 1897 until the opening of the Harold Washington Library in 1991. The building now houses the nation's first free cultural center, designed to be a public venue for artistic expressions that reflect the city's rich multicultural heritage, while serving as a showcase for local talent. The building also houses the main Visitor Information Center and the Museum of Broadcast Communication. Among its interior treasures are two huge Tiffany domes and a great white Carrara marble staircase. (Photo by author)

library was not without problems. The Grand Army of the Republic, a Civil War Union Army veterans' organization, also laid claim to the parcel, but by 1891 the veterans (who were a political force to be reckoned with at the time), agreed to allow the library to be built, with the proviso that there be a memorial hall dedicated to their organization.

Oddly enough, the birth of Chicago's free public library was a consequence of the Great Fire of 1871. No books survived the devastating conflagration, and in response to the need, a group of generous contributors from England shipped more than 8,000 volumes to create the nucleus of what was called the "English book donation." According to the Library, the collection of works included autographed copies sent by such noted literary figures as Benjamin Disraeli, Thomas Carlyle, and Alfred Lord Tennyson. Even Queen Victoria made a contribution. The following year, the new Chicago Public Library opened . . . in an old water tank! But it would be another 25 years before it could move into this more permanent location. The plan was to open in time for the World's Columbian Exposition in 1893, but lack of funds and legal hassles caused a four-year delay, and to save money, the present priceless Tiffany mosaics were substituted for paintings that had originally been planned.

Before entering, spend a few moments examining the rich exterior. Huge arched windows line the second and third floors, and an Ionic colonnade encloses the upper two floors. The entablature is decorated with Adamesque swags topped by a classic cornice. Be sure to read the landmark plaque to the right of the Washington Street entrance which describes this "grand civic building," and gives just a hint of what is to be seen within. The building, affectionately dubbed the "People's Palace," was renovated in 1977 to be the nation's first free cultural center—"where the city could dispense arts and cultural services to everyone at no charge, just as a library lends books . . . an architectural showplace whose programs provide opportunities for artistic expressions that reflect the city's rich multicultural heritage, while serving as a showcase for local talent."

Enter on the Washington Street side through the arched Romanesque doorway into the splendid lobby, sheathed in white Carrara marble and reminiscent of a Renaissance palazzo. An imposing grand staircase dominates the three-story vaulted room, but before ascending to see the first of two magnificent Tiffany domes, walk ahead and visit the ground-floor **Museum of Broadcast Communications,** which through exhibits and live programs describes the many ways in which our culture has been shaped through the microphone and lens. Founded in 1987 the MBC is one of only two broadcast museums in America. Among its wide array of broadcasting memorabilia is an extensive public archives collection of more than 60,000 radio and television programs and commercials. Fans of old-time radio and TV will enjoy the Radio Hall of Fame, the Television Exhibit Gallery, the Kraft TeleCenter, the Advertising Hall of Fame, the Sportscaster Cafe, among other lively exhibits. (The Museum of Broadcast Communications is open 10:00 A.M. to 4:30 P.M., Monday through Saturday; noon to 5:00 P.M. on Sunday. Closed holidays. Admission is free. Information: 629-6000. For tour schedule: 629-6017.)

It is five stories to the top, but there is a nearby elevator for the faint of heart. At the third level is the building's major concert hall and showplace, Preston Bradley Hall. The shimmering mosaics in the staircase were designed by Prairie school architect Robert C. Spencer, Jr., and executed by J. A. Holzer of the Tiffany Studios. The staircase leads to the south dome, a splendid confection of stained glass and favrile glass, well worth the climb. Note the inlaid mosaics, the soaring arches, and, engraved overhead, the names of many of the great writers of the western world.

Walk through to the north section, and take the staircase to the second-floor G.A.R. Memorial Hall, also surmounted by a vast and lavish Tiffany dome. Both the south and north domes are lit from behind to show the superb stained glass to best advantage. Note the two separate Tiffany windows that were brought to the center from a church in Pennsylvania.

Space does not permit a description of all the halls and galleries, but do visit the newly restored 7,600-square-foot Italian Renaissance–style Sidney R. Yates Gallery, with its bronze doorways inlaid with verd antique marble, ornate gilded columns, and intricately detailed coffered ceiling. Pick up a guide and the descriptive flyer, "Discover the Chicago Cultural Center," at the Visitor Infor-

The splendid Tiffany dome above Preston Bradley Hall on the third floor of the Cultural Center is lit from behind, as is the slightly smaller Tiffany dome that graces the Grand Army of the Republic Memorial Hall, in the north section. (Photo by author)

The 16-story John Crerar Library Building, at the northwest corner of Michigan Avenue and E. Randolph Street, was designed in 1920 by Holabird & Roche to hold the huge collection of this large private library. The voluminous collection was ultimately transferred to the Chicago Public Library and moved to the Harold Washington Library. The photo was taken in 1964 before the demolition of the Crerar Library Building some 20 years later. The decorative recessed arched windows of the upper section are more typical of an earlier era. In its place today stands the controversial Stone Container Building. (Photo by Hedrich-Blessing. Chicago Historical Society)

mation Center in the Randolph Lobby, and stop at the adjacent Welcome Center desk, which provides orientation information on the city and a guide to Chicago's historic downtown. Also in the lobby is the pleasant Gallery/Cafe espresso bar—a popular meeting place and a good spot for a "refueling stop," where rotating exhibits of local talent are featured regularly. (The Center is open every day: Monday–Thursday, 10:00 A.M.–7:00 P.M.; Friday to 6:00 P.M.; Saturday to 5:00 P.M.; Sunday, noon–5:00 P.M.; closed holidays. Building tours are conducted by the Friends of the Chicago Cultural Center, Tuesdays and Wednesdays at 1:30 P.M.; free. Program information: 346-3278.)

Exit from the Randolph Street side, and observe the completely different facade with paired Doric columns and recessed entrance arcade. Around the corner on Michigan Avenue is another historic plaque, this one commemorating the site of the home of Jean Baptiste Beaubien, Chicago's second civilian settler. Note, too, the curbside kiosk with the map of the **Pedway,** Chicago's underground walkway system. (*See* Pedway map and description after Chapter 12.) The Pedway is a boon, especially in inclement weather, to pedestrians, who can dodge the heavy traffic of the Loop and reach many of the important buildings quickly.

Cross to the east side of Michigan Avenue, or use the Pedway. (The Pedway passage also leads to the Randolph Street Station of the Metra Electric Division and South Shore Line trains, on the site of the former commuter terminal of the Illinois Central Railroad.) Once on the other side, walk east on Randolph Street to the corner of Beaubien Street, for a better view of:

The **Stone Container Building** is also known by its street address, **150 N. Michigan Avenue** (*1984, A. Epstein & Sons*). Until 1994 it was called the Associates Center. A startling, and for many, a disconcerting structure, it rises arrogantly at the end of the Michigan Avenue "Cliff" to impose its out-of-scale proportions on the street wall, while belittling the splendid Cultural Center below. Particularly distracting is the horizontal aluminum banding that is totally out of harmony with the adjacent masonry buildings, contributing to its squat appearance—an effect magnified manyfold by the diagonal slice that lops off what aesthetically should have demanded at the very least another 10 stories of the 41-story building. It also lacks the customary "base" that maintains continuity with neighboring buildings along the street. Another jarring feature is the dark-colored downward-sloping roof that is split in the middle, creating two triangular building divisions that face Michigan Avenue and

(Right) A telephoto view of three prominent Chicago skyscrapers which presents a dynamic and contrasting vignette of modern skyscraper design. The trio, spanning a 20-year period, are (left to right) the 64-story Two Prudential Plaza built in 1990, with pyramidal top and soaring 40-foot-tall spire; the lofty 82-story Amoco Building (originally the Standard Oil Building) built in 1973; and the 41-story Stone Container Building (originally the Associates' Center) built in 1984, with white horizontal bands and downward-sloping split diamond-shaped roof. (Photo by author)

Grant Park at a 45-degree angle. Only after dark is the overwhelming effect mitigated somewhat when bright illumination of the roofline creates an interesting "diamond in the sky."

One redeeming feature of the Stone Container Building is the Yaacov Agam sculpture, *Communication X-9* (1983), an optical relief in painted aluminum, placed at the entrance. Observe the changes in color and pattern when viewed from different angles.

Continue north on Michigan Avenue past Lake Street.

On the east side of Michigan Avenue, for a block-and-a-half, almost to the Chicago River, is the western edge of the **Illinois Center** (described in detail in Tour 4). The first group of mixed-use buildings comprise **Boulevard Towers** (*1985, South Tower and 1981, North Tower, Fujikawa, Johnson & Associates*), a pair of Miesian 44-story skyscrapers connected by a 19-story addition. The architectural firm is the successor to Mies van der Rohe, who died in 1969. On the plaza is the dazzling sculpture, *Splash,* a 21-foot curvaceous aluminum construction by Jerry Pearl (1986). Its flowing multicolor forms are designed to present a pleasing juxtaposition to the dark, rectilinear grid of Boulevard Towers and a bit of bright punctuation to what is now the Michigan Avenue "canyon."

The plaza offers excellent views up and down Michigan Avenue, especially of the next point of interest, the **Carbide & Carbon Building,** 230 N. Michigan Avenue, at the southwest corner of Wacker Place. Designed in 1929 by Burnham Brothers, the sons of Daniel H. Burnham, it is one of Chicago's distinctive 1920s skyscrapers and an unusual (for Chicago) example of the Art Deco style. From this vantage point it is easy to distinguish the polished black-granite base, the dark-green terra-cotta tower, and the 50-foot, skinny upper tower trimmed with gold-colored terra cotta. The profile of the 40-story structure is illustrative of the 1923 zoning ordinance which required setbacks to allow for greater height and more light below.

Take a closer look, and note the typical stylized floral Art Deco designs set at the top of the base and the lacy grillework swirls at the entrance. As with many Art Deco buildings, the outside motifs are carried into the interior. Go into the relatively small lobby, whose floor of gray Tennessee marble is trimmed with black Belgian marble, while the entire travertine-lined interior—entranceway, elevators, lamps, and fixtures—is resplendent in ornate polished bronze and gilt trim. The building's dark polychromatic exterior treatment, while appropriate to its name, is not typical of Chicago's brighter Bedford limestone Art Deco facades, but rather reminiscent of New York's Art Deco buildings, particularly Raymond M. Hood's 1923 American Radiator Building, which presents a similar black-and-gold color scheme throughout, as well as decorative finials on the setbacks and top.

From in front of the Carbide & Carbon Building at the corner of E. Wacker Place (which changes its name to E. South Water Street on the east side of Michigan Avenue) look diagonally across Michigan Avenue; then cross over to see:

The 24-story **Old Republic Building** (*1925, Vitzhum & Burns*), 307 N. Michigan Avenue, originally named the Bell Building, is designed in Classic style, and is typical of the tripartite skyscrapers of the early 20th century. The three-story beige-granite base, embellished with fluted pilasters and surmounted by a cornice, supports a cream-color terra-cotta shaft with vertical rows of windows interspersed with low-relief spandrels. The "capital" displays eleven classic columns, above which a single top floor is capped by a more elaborate cornice. On each side of the entrance, under the flagpoles, are bronze medallions with "minuteman" reliefs, the emblem of the building's primary tenant, the Old Republic Life Insurance Company. The impressive three-story-high entrance arch, with the building's initials (added later) in the keystone, leads into a surprisingly small lobby, at the rear of which is a decorative bronze gate that displays decorative medallions with the same minuteman motif.

Across Michigan Avenue, and best seen from the east side, is **320 N. Michigan Avenue** (*1983, Booth/Hansen & Associates*). Originally planned as a residential building, this sliver of a structure towers 23 stories and has an additional 3-story glass-enclosed pedimented penthouse. The verticality of the building is emphasized even further by the four vertical piers that embrace three bays of Chicago windows which include protruding balconies at each floor. The ground floor is dull, and its twin unadorned columns add nothing to the aesthetics. The very visible side walls display the grid of the steel skeleton, with some windows punched out at the top. Apparently, the anticipated tall neighboring structures which were to hide the blank walls never materialized.

While this is the end of the Michigan Avenue "Cliff" Walk, you might want to walk north just a bit further to the end of the block where the avenue meets the Chicago River. *See* pages 158–159 and 163–165 of Tour 4 for a description of the twin buildings at both corners of Wacker Drive and the great Michigan Avenue drawbridge.

Lake Michigan

N

E.Lake Shore Dr.

One Magnificent Mile

The Drake

Iton St.

laware Pl.

Bloomingdales

E. Chestnut St.

John Hancock Center

W. Pearson St.

Water Tower

Water Tower Place

N. Mies van der Rohe Way

DeWitt Place

E. Chicago Ave.

Pumping Station

Museum of Contemporary Art

Chicago Place

E. Superior St.

City Place

Columbus Drive

E. Huron St.

Womens Athletic Club

E. Erie St.

E. Ontario St.

E. Ohio St.

N. State

N. Wabash Ave.

N. Rush St.

Hotel Inter-continental

N. St. Clair St.

E. Grand Ave.

N. McClurg Ct.

Peshtigo Ct.

E. Illinois St.

Tribune Tower

NBC

N. Fairbanks Ct.

E. Hubbard St.

Equitable Bldg.

N. Water St.

nzie Street

Sun-Times

Wrigley Building

Michigan Ave. Bridge

Chicago River

Sheraton Chicago

Centennial Fountain

arina wers

IBM

One Illinois Center

E. Wacker Drive

Hyatt Regency

Swissôtel

Lake Shore Drive

0   250   500 Ft.

6. The Magnificent Mile and Streeterville

The downtown Chicago area north of the river was one of the first to be settled, but the last to be developed. Around 1779 **Jean Baptiste Point du Sable,** a black immigrant from what is now Haiti, on the island of Hispaniola in the Caribbean, traveled up the Mississippi and built a cabin on the north bank of the Chicago River, and in so doing became Chicago's first permanent resident. He took a Potowatomi Indian bride and established a very active fur trading post. He remained until 1804 when he moved on to Missouri, selling his homestead to John Kinzie (for whom the nearby street is named). A silversmith by trade, Kinzie was among the group of settlers who were attacked in the Fort Dearborn Massacre eight years later, but he and his nine-year-old son survived. The fort, which was located across the river on the south side, was later rebuilt, but little further development occurred on the north side. The area along the river, which the Indians called *Che-Cau-Gou* (referring to the odoriferous wild onions that grew in profusion in nearby marshes), began to expand southward instead.

The residents of the settlement, realizing the importance of the river to trade and future development, constructed a breakwater into Lake Michigan in the 1830s, on the north side of the river's mouth, creating a small harbor and protecting the entrance to the river. As the years went by, the swift lake currents built up an extensive accumulation of sand behind the breakwater and for about a mile north of it, adding a significant amount of land to the shoreline.

Enter one of the more colorful characters in the history of Chicago. In 1885 a small ship arrived from nobody-knows-where, commanded by a Captain George Wellington ("Cap") Streeter, a disreputable character said to have been a gunrunner, whose ship promptly ran aground on those sandy shoals. A rather decrepit hulk, it settled slowly into the soft sand and became a permanent offshore fixture. Streeter, whose talents were more that of show promoter than a boat captain, constructed a rickety causeway from the stranded vessel to the shore. The crafty Streeter then persuaded developers who were clearing land for the construction of nearby "Gold Coast" mansions to dump the excavated debris into the water between his ship and the shore. As the landfill accumulated, he checked official Illinois maps, and finding that his newly developed "territory" was beyond the shoreline of the state, he staked out 186 lakefront acres and began selling lots for $1 apiece to his drinking pals and to naive investors, declaring the new properties to be an independent district of the United States. He also opened Chicago's first offshore tavern and built up a rather lucrative bootlegging enterprise for himself.

The State of Illinois was not amused, and moved to evict him, but without immediate success, and appeals dragged on for years. Law officers tried to evict him on several occasions. Finally, in 1918 when a policeman was shot and killed presumably by "Cap" Streeter, the state had enough, and the court resorted to a technique similar to one used by the federal government to convict the notorious Al Capone—not for his many murders, but for income tax evasion. In Streeter's case, he was undone for selling whiskey illegally on Sunday. In addition, the court ruled his land claim invalid. Two years later the city opened the Michigan Avenue Bridge, and legitimate development began in earnest. Today, the district to the east of Michigan Avenue as far north as Chicago Avenue still perpetuates the wily "Cap" Streeter's 20 years as "land developer," and the name still survives unofficially (even on CTA bus destination signs) as Streeterville. (Tour 7 also includes much of Streeterville in its itinerary along and near the Lake Michigan shoreline.)

The area along the north side of the river soon became heavily industrialized, with warehouses, dock facilities, and factories, but with little development beyond. By the 1920s this all changed. Northwestern University, in Evanston, acquired a large tract of land for its professional schools and hospital complex, and the new thoroughfare, built on the site of the old Green Bay Road to Wisconsin Territory, later the narrow Pine Street, was widened and became an extension of Michigan Avenue to the south. Major real estate development soon followed. The avenue actually became a realization of Burnham's 1909 Plan of Chicago, and his projected "Champs Elysees" witnessed the rise of a series of Art Deco and neo-Classical buildings, all clad in white limestone of more-or-less uniform eight-story height, much like their Parisian counterpart. While not exactly a Champs Elysees, the avenue is more akin to the Boulevard St. Michel, or "Boul' Mich" to Chicagoans who have come to love that 12-block stretch of upscale merchandising.

At the south end rose the magnificent Wrigley Building and Tribune Tower, but no similar anchor was constructed at the north end until 1969, when the completion of the 100-story John Hancock Tower encouraged a rash of high-rise construction that still characterizes the avenue today. The name "Magnificent Mile" was the prophetic idea of clever real estate developer Arthur Rubloff, who in 1947, proposed a major retailing center with low-rise buildings along the avenue, with taller ones placed behind, separated by a mini-green belt, in a plan to be developed by Holabird & Root. The plan, however, did not materialize; instead, upper Michigan Avenue has suffered the effects of an over-abundance of mixed-use behemoths. Nevertheless the avenue has become a lovely and popular promenade and the major fashionable shopping street of America, outpacing even New York's Fifth Avenue.

The tour begins at the north end of the Michigan Avenue Bridge. (For a detailed description of the bridge and its history, *see* pages 163–165.) Begin at the plaza on the east side of Michigan Avenue. Remain on the east side; the Wrigley Building may be seen close at hand a little later.

The broad plaza on the east side of Michigan Avenue, known as **Pioneer Court** (*1957, Louis R. Solomon and John D. Cordwell & Associates*), offers splendid views of the nearby skyscrapers, particularly the **Wrigley Building** (*1919–1924, Graham, Anderson, Probst & White*), across the avenue at 400 and 410 N. Michigan Avenue. Ask any Chicagoan what building symbolizes the city more than any other, and the answer unhesitatingly will be the Wrigley Building! (Only an out-of-towner might guess the Sears Tower.) The dazzling terra-cotta-clad cream-white structure was the first major high-rise building north of the bridge, the city's first air-conditioned building, and Chicago's principal standard-bearer in the development of the modern skyscraper.

The construction of the Wrigley Building also marked the transition of the neighborhood from one of dingy warehouses and docks to an elegant commercial district. Designed by Charles G. Beersman of GAP&W, it combines form, function, and elegance in a dramatic setting overlooking the Chicago River, at the entrance to the wide plaza that funnels into Michigan Avenue. The Wrigley Building draws its inspiration from the "White City" of the 1893 World's Columbian Exposition and from the Giralda in Seville, as well as from Cass Gilbert's 1913 Woolworth Building in New York, with adornments borrowed from the 16th-century Francis I style. As the ornate shaft rises, it displays six increasingly brighter shades of white terra-cotta tiles. The base is of conventional tripartite style and rises 16 stories to an ornate cornice. The center bay with its elaborate 3-story arched entrance and 10-story tower reaches a height of 398 feet, terminating in a square pavilion surmounted by a circular tempietto. The highly visible four-sided clocks have dials 20 feet in diameter whose hands are made of redwood, a material stiff and flexible enough to withstand the frequent strong winds; the hour hands are seven-and-one-half-feet long, the minute hands eleven-and-one-half-feet long.

When seen from its sharply angular right side, one can appreciate the problems involved in designing a building to conform to the street wall and an irregularly shaped plot. An interesting comparison may be drawn with Alfred S. Alschuler's London Guarantee & Accident Building, on the other side of the river (*see* pages 158–159 and 161–162), which was nearing completion at about the same time, and also displays the architects' predilection for Classic "temples" set atop their buildings. At night the Wrigley Building and the Michigan Avenue Bridge are bathed in brilliant illumination from over 100 high-intensity floodlights mounted on the south bank of the river on the east side of

(Left) Just beyond the lovely flag-bedecked Michigan Avenue Bridge, the world's first double-deck span and one of four in Chicago, are (left to right) the Wrigley Building, the Hotel Inter-Continental (formerly the Medinah Athletic Club), and the graceful neo-Gothic Tribune Tower. (Photo by author)

the bridge, a tradition that goes back to the building's opening. It is said that William K. Wrigley, Jr., chose this dramatic site for his office building so that it would be visible from the entire length of South Michigan Avenue.

The adjacent Annex, which is actually taller (excluding the tower of the main building), was completed in 1924 and is designed as a harmonious twin, but with many of its own characteristics, particularly in the small and delicate central tower. Connecting the pair of buildings is a two-story glassed-in "screen" through which one can enter a small courtyard with fountain and plantings.

In 1931 a stainless-steel-clad skybridge was erected at the 14th floor to connect the two buildings. According to legend, the purpose was to join two offices of Wrigley's National Boulevard Bank, and thus prevent Illinois state banking officials from accusing him of conducting illegal "branch banking." On the river side of the main building, a "grand staircase" leads down to a dock, from which excursion boats depart during the summer.

The pair of buildings (actually considered just one building with two street addresses) was erected by chewing-gum king William K. Wrigley, Jr., whose corporate headquarters are still located there. Wrigley began as a seller of soap, when he hit on the idea of including a piece of chewing gum in each soap package, much like the famous Cracker Jack toys. The little gifts of gum became so popular that he abandoned the soap business entirely, and the rest, as they say, is history. The family also owns the Chicago Cubs baseball team, which plays in (of course) Wrigley Field.

Here on the low wall to the right on Pioneer Court is a plaque noting the location of the homestead (the plaque says "mansion," which it wasn't) of Jean Baptiste Point du Sable (Chicago's first "businessman") and later, John Kinzie. On the next abutment is another plaque indicating the burial in 1965 of a time capsule by the Equitable Life Assurance Society, commemorating the dedication of its adjacent Midwestern Headquarters Building.

Set back on Pioneer Court is the towering Miesian-inspired **Equitable Building** (*1965, Skidmore, Owings & Merrill*), 401 N. Michigan Avenue. In purchasing the land from the Tribune Company for the construction of its building, Equitable agreed to erect its tower no taller than the Tribune Building, and sufficiently back from Michigan Avenue to allow for a spacious plaza, as well as for a setting which would not obstruct the Tribune Tower nor its occupants' view of the river. In 1992 the architects remodeled the plaza and the result provided a very pleasant public space which is used for summertime art exhibits and as a popular lunchtime gathering place for employees in the neighboring buildings. At the river's edge, a grand stone staircase sweeps down in a graceful curve to the lower level of Michigan Avenue.

The charming Wrigley Building and Annex (1910–1924, Graham, Anderson, Probst & White), more than any other building, has come to symbolize Chicago. The 398-foot-tall skyscraper, with its highly visible four-sided clock and ornate tempietto, is arguably the most recognizable structure in the city, if not the whole country. The nighttime illumination of the entire building and the Michigan Avenue Bridge by high-intensity floodlights is a sight not to be missed. (Courtesy Hedrich-Blessing)

Although the facade of the 35-story Equitable Building expresses the underlying steel frame in true Mies van der Rohe fashion, there are noticeable special touches which give the building special characteristics not generally found in the traditional "glass box." SOM's designer Bruce Graham organized the facade into five-bays of four windows, each marked by building-high mullions, with stone spandrels to indicate the floors, while thin fake hollow piers placed in front of structural piers carry the hot and cold air conduits for the offices. Bronze-tinted reflective glass windows are set off by light-tan aluminum sheathing, giving the building a unique airy quality. A wide pedestrian arcade surrounds the building, adding to the feeling of openness. The Equitable name in lights in front of the top-floor mechanical systems is a prominent nighttime sight.

The general area around Pioneer Court has been designated **Cityfront Plaza,** a 60-acre mixed-use private development of the Chicago Dock & Canal Trust, whose boundaries are the Chicago River, Michigan Avenue, Lake Shore Drive, and Grand Avenue.

Walk around the Equitable Building to the newest member on the Plaza, the **Downtown Center of the University of Chicago,** which includes the Graduate School of Business and School of Continuing Studies (*1994, Dirk Lohan Associates*), 450 N. Cityfront Plaza. The windowless west side is a series of protruding wedges; however, the east side's five-story main entrance is quite different. The six-story precast-stone-and-glass building material was selected to

A view from the Chicago River of the new Downtown Center of the University of Chicago (1994, Dirk Lohan Associates), showing to good advantage the unusual series of protruding wedges on the windowless west side of the Graduate School of Business and School of Continuing Studies. (Photo by author)

resemble the limestone of the adjacent NBC Tower. The structure boasts a broad, arched glass roof that covers the entire building, even a small pedestrian arcade on the south (river) side. Interestingly, the architect, Dirk Lohan, is the grandson of Mies van der Rohe.

Walk around the building and cross at the traffic circle.

The traffic circle in front of the building—the heart of blocklong Cityfront Plaza—surrounds a small elevated platform with benches that are popular study sites for students. This is also a good vantage point to observe the group of buildings on the south bank of the river which comprise Illinois Center (*see* pages 166–169), Chicago's "city within a city."

Across Cityfront Plaza is one of Chicago's most elegant buildings, the **NBC Tower** (*1989, Skidmore, Owings & Merrill*), 455 N. Cityfront Plaza and 454 N. Columbus Drive. Who said Art Deco was out of style? Here in this graceful 38-story postmodern limestone skyscraper, SOM has reincarnated the best of Art Deco detailing with a number of original touches. (The *AIA Guide to Chicago* calls it the city's favorite postmodern building.) The central bay sweeps upward in a statement of sheer verticality, while side sections in smooth limestone with rows of plain windows mitigate the dizzying feeling of height. Topping the setbacks are buttresses reminiscent of those on the skyscrapers of the 1920s, and at the 20th-floor setback the 12 squared-off buttresses really seem to "fly," adding beauty to the overall composition and texture. Just below the distinctive stone spire atop the building is the NBC peacock logo, which when illumi-

The graceful postmodern NBC Tower, designed by Skidmore, Owings & Merrill in 1989, combines the best of the still-popular Art Deco style with many original touches. The central bay rises upward in one uninterrupted sweep, ending in the NBC peacock logo, with distinctive stone spire above. Many Chicagoans have chosen it as their favorite postmodern building. (Photo by author)

nated at night adds another distinctive touch. The architecture is reminiscent of New York's Rockefeller Center complex, built in the early 1930s, especially the former RCA (now General Electric) Building. Within are the National Broadcasting Company studios of radio station WMAQ and TV Channel 5. Peek into the lobby. On the facing wall is Roger Brown's huge canvas *City of Big Shoulders* (1989), and at the north end, Judith Shea's bronze sculpture, *Endless Model* (1989).

Walk to the right around the NBC Tower, cross Columbus Drive, and continue toward the Sheraton Chicago Hotel.

To the left, facing little Park Street, across from the Sheraton, is the construction site of the new **Cityfront Center Music and Dance Theatre** (*Hammond, Beeby & Babka*), which when completed in the winter of 1997 will be one of Chicago's major cultural attractions. No fewer than 11 theatre and dance groups, presently scattered about the city, will perform in the new facility.

The **Sheraton Chicago Hotel & Towers–Cityfront Center** (*1992, Solomon Cordwell Buenz & Associates*), 301 E. North Water Street, occupies a highly desirable site overlooking the Chicago River and the Turning Basin. It has a pleasant riverwalk and sidewalk cafe offering excellent views of Lake Michigan and the downtown skyscrapers. Above the hotel's five-story base, the main section of the building rises an additional 26 floors to a circular "crown," while other sections rise to four similar features at different levels, all of which hide the structure's mechanical systems. The hotel's facade expresses the steel structure in a simple grid pattern, while sheer walls of windows provide maximum visibility for the 1,200 guest rooms. Unique are the curved tower sections at each end, vaguely reminiscent of the Loop's Old Colony Building, with the northwest tower the tallest. The Sheraton's 40,000-square-foot ballroom is the largest in the Midwest.

Return to Pioneer Court along the river and stop in the middle of the plaza.

The **Tribune Tower** (*1925, John Mead Howells and Raymond M. Hood; Holabird & Roche, engineers*), 435 N. Michigan Avenue, is another unmistakable and much-adored Chicago landmark, which together with the Wrigley Building create a grand entrance to the Magnificent Mile. Seventy-five years after the *Chicago Tribune*'s founding in 1847, publishers Robert R. McCormick and Joseph Patterson announced an international competition challenging architects from every nation to "design the most beautiful and distinctive building in the world." Entries poured in from far and wide—258 in all, from 23 nations—submitted by the most famous architects everywhere, resulting in one of the largest competitions in architectural history. The first prize of $50,000 went to New York architects John Mead Howells and Raymond Hood; the second-place prize of $20,000 went to Eliel Saarinen of Helsinki, Finland, and the third prize of $10,000 to Holabird & Roche of Chicago. Interestingly, while Saarinen's entry was only the runner-up, his design of solid verticality and graduated setbacks was to set the stage for the style of skyscrapers erected in the late 1920s. The success of the Howells and Hood design subsequently led to their New York commissions for the famous Daily News, McGraw-Hill, and American Radiator buildings, and for some of the Rockefeller Center buildings, but not another building in Chicago. The Tribune Tower's winning design was a neo-Gothic formula based on the Butter Tower of the Rouen Cathedral in France.

The 36-story tower is sheathed in Indiana limestone, giving the impression of a solid medieval masonry building, although it is a steel-framework structure. The essentially rectangular tower becomes octagonal at the 24th floor setback, with corner piers rising as flying buttresses. The Gothic details continue on a smaller tower above, reaching a total height of 456 feet. The beauty of the cathedral-like structure can be appreciated best at some distance, and especially at night when the illumination of the upper floors emphasizes the delicate and spidery traceries.

The site selected for the Tower was adjacent to the *Tribune*'s then-new printing plant (*1916, Jarvis Hunt*), which was conveniently located for the delivery of newsprint on the Chicago River. The plant, reclad in matching stone in 1965, can be seen to the east, with the newspaper's name emblazoned above in large Gothic letters. The despotic Colonel McCormick, nephew of Cyrus Hall McCormick, the inventor of the famous Reaper, embellished his new building with souvenir chunks of historical buildings and renowned monuments from around the world that were either gifts or were obtained one way or another by his correspondents. He had them embedded and duly labeled on the facade, and fragments are displayed from the Taj Mahal, Westminster Abbey, the Great Wall of China, the Cologne Cathedral, Hamlet's Castle, the Parthenon, the Alamo, Fort Sumter, and even a recent contribution from the Berlin Wall, among the more than 120 pieces collected through the years. The three-story arched entrance to the Tower is richly detailed with many characters from Aesop's Fables, plus a charming insertion by the architects of Robin Hood and a howling dog—visual and humorous allusions to their names. Their names appear in the corner block to the right front, opposite the 1925 cornerstone.

The *Chicago Tribune* also owns radio and TV stations whose call letters, WGN, doubtless requested by Col. McCormick, stand for "*W*orld's *G*reatest *N*ewspaper." Passersby can watch the operations of the ground-floor Studio D, although it does not broadcast from there continuously. Enter the handsome lobby, dominated by a huge relief map of North America set in a Gothic-style wooden frame. The wall is covered with aphorisms by Col. McCormick and other American historical and publishing figures, and in the center of the marble floor, a quote from John Ruskin. Above, a wood-paneled ceiling adds to the pleasant ambiance.

In the courtyard to the left of the Tower, adjacent to the *Tribune*'s Annex Building (*1935, Howells, Hood, and Fouilhoux*)—the original WGN radio and later television studios, which now houses the Hammacher-Schlemmer store—is a bronze **statue of Nathan Hale,** with hands and feet bound, awaiting his fate on the gallows for spying for the Revolutionary Army, with his purported "I

The runner-up and third place entries in the famous international competition "to design the most beautiful and distinctive building in the world," to serve as the new Chicago Tribune *office building: Eliel Saarinen's second-place design proposal (left), and Holabird & Roche's third-place entry. Although the winner was Howells and Hood, Saarinen's plan became greatly influential in setting the trend for solid verticality and graduated setbacks in future skyscraper construction. (From* The International Competition for a New Administration Building for the Chicago Tribune, MCMXXII*)*

only regret that I have but one life to lose for my country" engraved on the base. The statue, by B. L. Rall (1913), is an inferior copy of the famous 1893 sculpture by Frederick MacMonies, in New York's City Hall Park. To the right of the entrance is another souvenir, the amorphous stone "Swedish Viking Monument;" and just inside the ornate three-story Tudor Gothic entrance, behind a glass disk to the left, is a stone fragment from the "Cave of the Nativity where Christ was Born."

Now is a good time to cross Michigan Avenue for a better view of the Tribune Tower and a close-up look at the unusual shape of the Wrigley Building.

Walk through the glassy passageway between the two sections of the Wrigley Building to the plaza beyond. River Plaza, a pleasant mini-garden that leads to an excellent vantage point above the Chicago River, is named for the adjoining high-rise apartment building that helped create this pleasant oasis. It shares the space with the *Chicago Sun-Times,* and offers splendid views of the river and the lovely buildings on the south side, especially (from left to right): the London Guaranty Building, No. 75 E. Wacker Drive (Chicago's skinniest skyscraper), and the ornate former Jewelers Building (itself a real "jewel"), all described in Tour 4. The 697-unit **River Plaza Condominium** (*1977, Ezra Gordon and Jack Levin*), 405 N. Wabash Avenue, with its outstanding location, is one of the city's more successful condominium conversions. The 51-story brick-sheathed structure, which dwarfs the surrounding buildings, is set above three levels of commercial space. Its vertical rows of projecting bays permit residents to enjoy spectacular views of the heart of Chicago.

Return to Michigan Avenue and turn left.

Just to the north of the Wrigley Building, in a small plaza which covers Hubbard Street below, called the Plaza of the Americas (dedicated 1963), is a **bust of Benito Juárez** (1806–1872), the Mexican statesman who in 1864–1867 rebelled against and overthrew Maximilian, the French emperor of Mexico. The bust was presented to the City of Chicago in 1977 by José Luis Portillo, Mexico's president at the time.

Note how Michigan Avenue is built above ground level, so that local east-west streets can pass beneath, and vehicular traffic can reach the lower level of the Michigan Avenue Bridge without creating congestion on the main roadway above. A staircase leads down to Hubbard Street and the bustling **Billy Goat Tavern** underneath, a favorite lunchtime hangout for newspaper workers at the *Tribune* and the nearby *Sun-Times,* and a good place to get a "chizbugga." The "Goat" and its hectic atmosphere was the inspiration for John Belushi's *Saturday Night Live* sketch. A block to the north is Illinois Street, which also passes beneath, and connects to the west side of Michigan Avenue; and looking to the east, there is a fine view of the NBC Tower.

On the northeast corner of Illinois Street stands the **Hotel Inter-Continental Chicago** (*1929, Walter W. Ahlschlager*), 505 N. Michigan Avenue. Originally constructed as the Medinah Athletic Club, a luxury men's club for members of the Shrine organization, it was forced to close its doors during the Depression when a breakaway group of Shriners withdrew from the Club and formed another athletic association. Ten years later it reopened as a hotel, but after a series of owners failed to make a go of it, it closed again in 1986. The Inter-Continental Hotels Group, renowned for its portfolio of historic restorations, acquired the property in 1988 and began a $130 million two-year renovation. After discovering the original club's 1930 yearbook, the *Scimitar,* the architects (Harry Weese and Associates) were able to use the many illustrations to re-create the original Oriental furnishings and architectural details.

Before exploring the interior, note the interesting variety of details on this 45-story limestone-clad building: the shiny gold onion dome (also best seen from a distance), the three tall-framed windows topped by Egyptian figures at the fourth floor, a trio of similar figures looking down from the first central set-back, and the impressive Egyptian and Assyrian figures in the low-relief frieze that wraps around three sides of the building. The sculpture, by Leon Harmart, represents masons (a reference to the Freemasons' Guild in England, the forerunner of the Shriners' organization) on the south side; builders on the north side; and architects offering the building to the Egyptian pharaoh on the west.

Enter the dramatic lobby, which although relatively small, is impressive in the richness of its details. The visitor is greeted in Arabic with *Es Salamu Aleikhum* ("Peace be to Allah," a greeting still used by the Shriners) carved on the facing balcony. A curving double staircase climbs past a pair of ornate over-size columns decorated with huge sculptured capitals depicting medieval and hooded sleeping knights, while overhead, a splendid polychrome wood-beam ceiling painted in dark tones with Celtic and Mesopotamian motifs completes the composition. Several of the hotel's public spaces are worth seeing: the first-floor Biedermeier-style Salon and Bar (on both sides of the entrance lobby), the second-floor Hall of Lions, the King Arthur Foyer and Court on the fourth floor, and on the fifth floor, the Spanish Tea Court, the Renaissance Room Foyer, and Renaissance Room. (Guided group tours and individual audio tours are available; phone 321-8254 for information.) To quote from the *AIA Guide to Chicago,* "the interior spaces are modest in scale but grandiose in spirit, infused throughout with a romantic historicism."

Continue north one block to Grand Street, which passes underneath. Look to the east. In the far distance is the newly reconstructed Navy Pier, on the Lake Michigan shorefront.

On the southwest corner is the former McGraw-Hill Building, also at one time the Time-Life Building, but now known only by its street address, **520 N. Michigan Avenue** (*1929, Thielbar & Fugard*). A rather massive chunk of an Art Deco–style building, it has a smooth limestone facade which lends itself well to the fine sculptural details on the front facade. Note the tall fluted piers, the decorative bronze spandrels, and the incised figures of animals playing between the windows on the fourth floor; while above are three mythological sculptured figures: from left to right, Diana, Atlas, and Helios. (McGraw-Hill is now at 180 N. Stetson Street, in the Illinois Center.) At this writing the building has been recommended for landmark designation by the Commission on Chicago Landmarks, which hopefully will protect it from being razed for the construction of a proposed 500,000-square-foot mall to include a Nordstrom Galleria.

The Process of Landmark Designation.   After the Commission on Chicago Landmarks has determined that a building (or site) is worthy of designation, it must then seek the approval of the owner, who has 45 days to consent or request a 120-day extension. If the owner does want his or her property designated, the Commission then calls for a public hearing so that both sides of the issue can be heard. After receiving the report of the hearing, the Commission takes another vote on whether to make its recommendation to the Chicago City Council; and if affirmative, it goes to the Council's Historical Landmark Preservation Committee, then to the full Council for a vote. The final step is the signature by the mayor.

The **Michigan Terrace Condominium** (*1962, Richard A. Raggi and Guenter Malitz*), 535 N. Michigan Avenue, was one of the first residential towers to invade the upper Michigan Avenue retail district. The facade facing the avenue is narrow, but the broad north and south sides of the 33-story building with its 14 vertical ranks of tinted-glass bay windows makes up for the dull front. Note that the bay windows are arranged in the "Chicago Window" style, with a wide pane separated by a narrow one on each side.

The **Chicago Marriott Downtown** (*1978, Harry Weese & Associates*), 540 N. Michigan Avenue, does little to enhance the Michigan Avenue street wall. Although the 47-story hotel tower is set back to the rear, as is the custom with many of the skyscrapers along the avenue, the eight-story facade offers nothing but an ugly broad blank wall, which many feel is an insult to the "Mag" Mile. There are retail shops on the second floor, but the hotel, which occupies the entire building, has its main entrance on the Rush Street side. Its four-story atrium lounge is a pleasant place for a few moments' relaxation.

On the east side of the avenue, **543–545 N. Michigan Avenue** (*1929, Philip B. Maher*) presents an interesting contrast in style, proving that less is often more. This six-story retail shop, originally an exclusive women's clothing establishment, is basically Art Deco in style, but with a French accent; note the mansard roof. (Architect Maher had studied in France.) The low-relief sculptures must have added a touch of elegance when the shop first opened.

On the northeast corner of Michigan Avenue and Ohio Street is the former Lake Shore Trust Company Building, now simply the **Lake Shore Bank** (*1922, Marshall & Fox; remodeling and annex 1982, Perkins & Will*), 605 N. Michigan Avenue. A classic "temple," it is typical of bank architecture of the early 20th century. The Michigan Avenue facade has four large engaged Corinthian fluted columns, the Ohio Street side has five; while beyond is the 1982 addition, unobtrusively tucked away to preserve what little integrity is left after the "remuddling" of the original building. But why were the building's "eyes" poked out and replaced with huge tinted-glass panes?

Across the street, and occupying the entire blockfront from Ohio to Ontario streets, is **600 N. Michigan Avenue,** designed by Beyer Blinder Belle with Shaw & Associates (scheduled for completion in late 1996). The four-story retail and entertainment complex, including a nine-screen Cineplex Odeon theatre, replaced four separate buildings of some architectural merit: the 1925 Michigan-Ohio Building, by Alfred S. Alschuler; the 1927 Nelson Building, by Philip Maher; The De Frees Building, by Rapp & Rapp; and the 1949–1951 Arts Club Building, by Leichenko & Esser, with an interior by Mies van der Rohe. Preservationists fought hard to save the Arts Club Building, but the Landmarks Commission refused to designate it, and the building was demolished.

A *new* **Arts Club Building,** designed by John Vinci, at 201 E. St. Clair Place (one block east at the corner of Ontario Street), will open in early 1997. The new club, a two-story, unadorned taupe-brick and black-granite structure, displays a simple, free-flowing, open plan with a minimalist aesthetic. Although it is a private club, the public may attend the exhibitions, lectures, and performances. (Free admission.)

Not the aftermath of the Great Fire of 1871, but a scene of the destruction by developers in 1995 of the entire block on the west side of Michigan Avenue between E. Ohio and E. Ontario streets for the construction of a multiplex cinema and mall. Among the buildings razed were several worthy of landmark status, including the Mies van der Rohe–designed interior of the Arts Club Building. (Photo by author)

The ornate street-number plaque that had adorned No. 612 was saved by the wrecking crew from the former eight-story Michigan-Ohio Building, designed in 1925 by Alfred S. Alschuler for restaurant-chain owner John R. Thompson. (Photo by author)

★   On the northwest corner of E. Ontario Street stands the **Women's Athletic Club** (*1928, Philip B. Maher*), 626 N. Michigan Avenue. Again the elegant French touch is obvious in this fifth Maher-designed building on the avenue. Note the large second and seventh floor windows of the nine-story building, the sculptured panels on the Bedford limestone facade between the arches of the lower windows depicting rams and an urn, and the huge central pavilion above, topped by a mansard roof with four attic windows—all bespeak the influence of the Beaux Arts tradition. Even Cartier's adds to the ambiance.

    One block north, at the southwest corner of E. Erie Street (and best observed first from the northeast corner), is the incredible **Crate and Barrel** (*1990, Solomon Cordwell Buenz & Associates*), 646 N. Michigan Avenue. Architectural iconoclasm at its highest, but whatever one's opinion, the building can't be ignored; it really was designed to resemble a crate and barrel, so before judging, cross the street and study its sleek shape created by the alternating glass and white-painted aluminum bands which are tied to the corner rotunda; then go inside the rotunda and look up to the glass dome. And, have you ever seen the underside of an escalator? Also visit the establishment after dark when it glistens like a mini–Crystal Palace. Four floors finished in natural wood contrast with the glassy exterior and provide plenty of light to gape at the housewares, kitchenware, glassware, and furniture. The roof treatment, however, adds that little extra element that spells the difference between a structure that would be merely eye-catching and one that is aesthetically pleasing.

The glassy, "supermodern" Crate and Barrel, on the southwest corner of E. Erie Street, is a singular and exciting addition to the Michigan Avenue streetscape. Designed to resemble its name, the housewares emporium which opened in 1990 glistens like a mini–Crystal Palace. (Photo by author)

Diagonally across E. Erie Street is an interesting pair of buildings, which appear contemporaneous, but are 41 years apart in age. The corner building, **663 N. Michigan Avenue,** was designed in 1925 from plans by the ubiquitous Philip B. Maher, and remodeled in 1966 by Holabird & Root; and **669 N. Michigan Avenue,** built from scratch in 1966, also by Holabird & Root. Originally a single specialty shop, and later joined together as Saks Fifth Avenue (until its move to Chicago Place, further north), the twins are now separated again, as the **Sony Gallery** (go inside and see the exhibits on several levels, and play with the myriad audio and video paraphernalia); and **Nike Town Chicago,** a mecca for the devotee of "cool sports stuff." The facade of the Nike building leaves nothing to the imagination about what's inside, as metallic sculptures of athletes doing their thing seem to leap from the wall. Go in, and if you can push your way past the hectic scene, look for the tropical fish swimming in a tank on the left wall, behind the (what else?) sneakers.

Directly across, **664 N. Michigan Avenue** (*1927, Philip B. Maher*) was the first Maher building on the Avenue. The 11-story Bedford limestone building is a pleasing combination of Art Deco and a smidgen of Beaux Arts. Like other buildings of his, this one too, boasts a mansard roof. Formerly known as the Farwell Building, it now houses offices of the adjacent Terra Museum, to which it was joined when the latter was reconstructed.

The **Terra Museum of American Art** (*1987, Booth/Hansen & Associates*), 666 N. Michigan Avenue, is named for Daniel J. Terra, a noted art collector who invented a revolutionary process for color printing, and who later founded the Lawter Chemical Company. He was appointed by President Reagan as Ambassador-at-Large for Cultural Affairs, and served until 1989. Housing one of the world's foremost collections of American masterworks from the 18th through the 20th centuries, the museum is dedicated to preserving and sharing American art through a wide variety of educational programs. The museum was originally established in Evanston, Illinois, but moved to the "Mag" Mile when its new building was renovated. The front of the five-story building is faced with white Vermont marble, framing a 45-foot-high glass "picture window" entrance. There is also a small bookshop. Be sure to return to spend some time with the permanent collection and the frequently changing exhibits. (Tuesday 12 to 8, Wednesday to Saturday 10 to 5, Sunday 12 to 5. Suggested donation: $4 adults, $2 seniors, students and children under 14 free; on Tuesday admission is free. Tours daily at noon and 2 P.M.)

In the adjacent 670 building was Stuart Brent Books, one of Chicago's old established bookstores and a mecca for booklovers, which was forced to close its doors in early 1996, unable to compete with the influx of mass-market discount bookstores.

Sharing the rest of the block is **City Place** (*1990, Loebl, Schlossman & Hackl*), 676 N. Michigan Avenue, whose bright red semicircular roof arch is a conspicuous and somewhat garish landmark. The 39-story tower faces sideways to Michigan Avenue, with its two-tone red and pink polished and matte granite facades facing north and south. Blue glass and striping highlight the details. Unlike most mixed-use skyscrapers, where the upper floors are usually

City Place (left) and the blocklong Chicago Place display an engaging geometric juxtaposition. City Place, at 676 N. Michigan Avenue, is a mixed-use 39-story skyscraper set at right angles to the avenue, with a conspicuous arched roof. In an unconventional arrangement, the lower 25 floors are occupied by the Omni Hotel, with the commercial floors above. Chicago Place, at 700 N. Michigan Avenue, rises one story higher in a tower set back from the building line behind an eight-level shopping atrium. (Photo by author)

reserved for hotel space, in City Place the upper 14 floors are occupied by offices and the lower 25 by the Omni Hotel.

In the next block north, on the same side of the avenue, and occupying the entire block from Huron to Superior streets, is **Chicago Place** (*1990, Skidmore, Owings & Merrill for the retail section; Solomon Cordwell Buenz & Associates for the tower*), 700 N. Michigan Avenue. Behind the eight-story front section, the marble and granite set-back skyscraper tower rises 40 stories. Unlike the skyscraper housing the Marriott Hotel, Chicago Place does not face the rear, but focuses its attention on Michigan Avenue, with a somewhat overscaled central glass arch atop a six-story glass bowfront, and differently styled corners. The curved south corner, with its somewhat tacky columns, is intended to recall the curved entrance rotunda of the Louis Sullivan-designed Carson Pirie Scott Store, while the flattened north corner is supposed to be reminiscent of Daniel Burnham's Marshall Field Store, both on State Street in the Loop. The eight-level atrium, however, is a more successful design, with some 80 specialty shops and the Saks Fifth Avenue flagship store.

On entering the lobby, note the murals on both walls depicting events in Chicago history, then go ahead into the eight-level atrium. Although influenced by the earlier Water Tower Place (to be seen later), this newer addition to "the battle of the atria" among the burgeoning group of mega-mixed-use skyscrapers has special features of its own: the four decorative and towering octagonal support columns sheathed in reddish faux-marbre that rise to the top, the seven rows of receding balconies, the array of free-standing crisscrossing escalators, and the two glass-enclosed elevators—together creating a dizzying and overwhelming effect. For those in need of a "pit stop," there is a tropical-garden food court on the eighth floor.

Directly across the avenue is one of Chicago's old-time favorite hostelries, the **Allerton Hotel** (*1924, Murgatroyd & Ogden, with Fugard & Knapp*), 140 E. Huron Street. The hotel was designed in a Northern Italian Renaissance style and boasts a conspicuous central tower topped by a lantern and surrounded by four smaller corner towers with arched windows set above a corbel table. The shape of the building reflects the 1923 zoning ordinance which dictated the use of setbacks in proportion to the building's volume or ground-floor "footprint." On the Huron Street side, the entrance is marked by a two-story trio of arches in the same limestone that surrounds the three-story-high base of the entire building. The dark-red-brick 25-story structure was the first major hotel built on North Michigan Avenue; it was actually under construction at the same time as the Chicago Tribune Tower. The Allerton was modeled on New York's Barbizon Hotel for Women (now the Barbizon), by the same architects, as part of a chain of residential "club hotels" for young professional singles. The hotel included many social and sports amenities, such as rooftop miniature golf, a handball court, exercise rooms, a library, plus scheduled weekly parties and dances. In keeping with the mores of the time, 14 floors were reserved for men and 6 for women, each served by a separate elevator bank.

In the middle of the west side of the block north of Superior Street, in stark contrast to the towering behemoths along the avenue, is **Banana Republic,** 744 N. Michigan Avenue, a two-story dark-gray structure that one might expect to come upon in the heart of a tropical jungle. Designed in 1991 by noted New York architect Robert A. M. Stern, who in his first commission in Chicago remodeled an undistinguished store into this attractive branch of the ubiquitous chain of casual clothing shops. The details are intended to imitate typical "bush" construction—bamboo support columns and sheet-tin walls, although these walls are made of lead-coated copper. Above is a barrel-vaulted roof with an "eyebrow" window peeking through. All that changes once inside, except perhaps for the large bowl of coconuts on the table and the unusual cable-supported central staircase whose balusters are made of leather. Plans are underway to wrap another mega-building around Banana Republic and other establishments on the block.

And speaking of contrasts, across the avenue is the striking postmodern **Neiman Marcus** (*1983, Skidmore, Owings & Merrill*), 737 N. Michigan Avenue, whose four-story two-tone polished brown-granite facade is dominated by a gigantic central arch. Although the keystone is replaced by a narrow translucent glass slit that connects with the curved glass roof, the grand entrance arch is nonetheless evocative of the Romanesque Revival style of Henry Hobson

(Left) Looking north on busy Michigan Avenue is one of Chicago's favorite moderate-priced hotels, the Allerton, 140 E. Huron Street, the first hostelry to be built on the avenue. Designed in a Northern Italian Renaissance style in 1924 as a "club hotel" for young professional singles, it was modeled on the Barbizon Hotel in New York by the same architects. When it opened, 14 floors were reserved for men, 6 for women. Alas, the Tip-Top-Tap with its superb panoramic views is no more, having succumbed to the need for more space. (Photo by author)

Richardson, or more likely, the colossal arched entrance to Adler & Sullivan's Stock Exchange (preserved behind the Art Institute). Unlike many of the newer towering giants that have invaded the "Mag" Mile, the four-story height of the Neiman Marcus section is respectful of the earlier scale of Michigan Avenue, which was more reminiscent of a Paris grand boulevard than a densely built American main street. Connected to the rear of Neiman Marcus is the skyscraper tower, which together with the Michigan Avenue store, form the complex called Olympia Center, which will be seen close at hand shortly.

Now cross Michigan Avenue to the little park at the northwest corner of Chicago Avenue.

From little Water Tower Square, there are good views of the surrounding buildings, but before examining the Water Tower itself, look across to the south side of Chicago Avenue to see how a fast-food establishment can fit harmoniously into the graceful surroundings of this pleasant square. **Arby's** (*renovation 1977, Stanley Tigerman & Associates*), 115 E. Chicago Avenue, uses a mere 20-foot-wide lot to create an interesting building whose infill facade of stucco and glass is used to develop a combination of curved and straight structural sections, both opaque and transparent. The unconventional remodeling of what formerly was a nondescript four-story structure purposely draws attention to the interior, where the management hopes to entice passersby to indulge their appetites.

The cast-iron street clock in the little park was donated by the First National Bank of Chicago, and is a reproduction of the once ubiquitous clocks that could be seen on sidewalks all over the country prior to the invention of the wristwatch around World War I. They were a great public amenity, but served primarily as advertisements for adjoining commercial establishments. Some of the little park's lampposts and railings were salvaged from the old Lake View Pumping Station before its demolition some years ago.

For many, the *pièce de résistance* of upper Michigan Avenue is the historic **Water Tower and Pumping Station** (*1866–1869, William W. Boyington*), 806 N. Michigan Avenue and 163 E. Pearson Street. The Water Tower, constructed two years before the Great Fire of 1871, was the only structure to survive it for miles around. Today it is probably Chicago's most cherished landmark, and stands as a memorial to the fire and its victims, as well as a symbol of the city's fierce drive to flourish with its "I Will" spirit. It is also the centerpiece of the **Old Chicago Water Tower Historic District,** designated by the City of Chicago Commission on Chicago Landmarks. So popular is this landmark that when

(Left) Although dwarfed by imposing skyscrapers, the Chicago Water Tower remains the city's most cherished landmark. As the only major structure to survive the Great Fire, it has come to symbolize Chicago's drive to survive and flourish. Constructed in 1869 from a plan by William W. Boyington, the yellow-sandstone 154-foot castellated Norman Gothic tower conceals a three-foot-diameter standpipe. In the base of the tower, the city maintains a Visitors' Center. To the right, further up Michigan Avenue, is No. 919 topped by four square cupolas. Known popularly as the "Bloomingdale Building," it houses the department store on five levels of selling space. Partially obscured is One Magnificent Mile with its three hexagonally shaped sections. (Photo by author)

Michigan Avenue (then called Pine Street) was widened in 1918, the city planners altered the street's path to accommodate the Water Tower and give it a monumental presence.

Built of yellowish Joliet (Illinois) sandstone, sometimes called "Athens marble," the 154-foot-high tower was designed to conceal a 138-foot-high standpipe three feet in diameter (since removed), which was used to even out the pumping surges and pulsations in the water to keep it flowing freely. Architect Boyington, noted for many Chicago buildings in the latter half of the 19th century, designed the tower and the pumping station (across Michigan Avenue) in what is generally described as a "castellated Gothic" style, although some wags say that it may have come instead from the drawing boards of the Walt Disney studios. According to the Chicago Water Department's rather fanciful description, "its saw-toothed towers were designed to recapture the romance of a medieval castle, the kind from which archers and crossbowmen defended themselves."

The Water Tower and the John Hancock Center—the old and the new—loom dramatically against a dark sky, exemplifying Chicago's respect for the past and vision for the future. (Photo by author)

When Oscar Wilde, who advocated "beauty for itself alone," visited Chicago, he was less than enthusiastic about the beauty of the Water Tower, and called it "a castellated monstrosity with salt and pepper boxes stuck all over it."

The octagonal tower rises in five sections from its square base to a crown of eight tourelles surmounted by a copper cupola, while at the top of the base section are so-called battlement towers at each corner. Each facade has huge arched doorways, flanked by typical Gothic pointed-arch windows topped by drip moldings. Each level displays small towers punctuated with lancet windows and surmounted by castellated crowns. Inside the Tower is a spiral staircase which encircles the space formerly occupied by the standpipe, and is still used occasionally to reach the cupola.

When the Water Tower was completed in 1869 it was supplied with water by a tunnel system which extended 2.5 miles out to an intake crib in Lake Michigan. Although the Tower is obsolete today, the equally elaborate Pumping Station, known officially as the Chicago Avenue Water Pumping Station, is still very much in use and supplies water to approximately 390,000 people in the near North Side. The Water Tower narrowly escaped demolition on several occasions—in 1906 when the interior standpipe was made obsolete, in 1918 when Pine Street (later renamed North Michigan Avenue) was widened, and in 1948 when the construction of an art center was proposed. On each occasion a vociferous public outcry dissuaded the city fathers from such ill-conceived plans. The first major renovation took place in 1962, and with its subsequent landmark designation, it has been carefully preserved. In 1969 it was designated by the American Water Works Association as "The First American Water Landmark because of its significance in the development of Chicago's water resources and its symbolic identity with the spirit of Chicago."

In front of the Tower is a cast-iron "multiple-use" drinking fountain, installed at the time by the Humane Society—an amusing holdover from the 19th century that also showcased Chicago's new public drinking water system. The upper part was for people, the middle trough for horses, and the little bottom bowl for dogs (or any little animal); birds still drink from all three. Take a moment to read the various commemorative plaques. Few such decorative water towers survive today in America; one notable exception is the landmark 175-foot-tall North Point Water Tower overlooking Lake Michigan, in Milwaukee.

The interior now serves as a **Visitors' Welcome Center,** open to the public daily 9:30 A.M. to 5:00 P.M., except holidays (telephone: 744-2400). Go inside and peruse the information racks and the exhibits, including early photographs of the Tower. Attendants are on duty to answer questions.

Cross Michigan Avenue to the Pumping Station.

The first-time visitor to Chicago will find **Here's Chicago** (*163 E. Pearson Street*), in the Pumping Station, an interesting and informative overview of the city's history. The one-hour audio-visual "sound and light" show also includes a narrated visit to the still-functioning water works. The show, which opened in

"Big John" (the John Hancock Center's popular nickname), the Chicago Avenue Water Pumping Station, and Water Tower Place offer fascinating contrasts in style, shape, color, and age, in this view looking northeast from Michigan and E. Chicago avenues. (Photo by author)

1983, is presented in two buildings that were the old boiler rooms and workshops and which survived the **Great Fire of 1871**—a holocaust that burned for three days, killed 300 people, and destroyed half of the city, leaving only 500 buildings where 17,450 once stood, and rendering at least 90,000 homeless. During the conflagration the roofs were burned off the Pumping Station, but within a week, the pumps were back in operation. When first installed, the original steam-driven machinery managed to pump eight million gallons per day; today the huge electric pumps have a capacity of 260 million gallons. As part of the show, visitors can observe the pumps in action from an overhead catwalk. There are also displays of historic memorabilia and a diorama of the St. Valentine's Day Massacre. (Performances every half-hour; adults $5.00, seniors and high school students $4.00, grade school students $3.00; 467-7114.)

On leaving the Pumping Station turn left, then left again on E. Chicago Avenue for a short detour east. Note another "multiple purpose" drinking fountain.

Across E. Chicago Avenue looms the 63-story **Olympia Center** (*1986, Skidmore, Owings & Merrill*), 161 E. Chicago Avenue. Immediately noticeable is the unusual profile of the skyscraper, clad in pink Swedish granite, which tapers gradually on the north and south sides. The sloping lower section was designed to create more office space, while the vertical upper part is reserved for condominium apartments. Observe how the fenestration changes to distinguish between the two divisions, thus providing broader vistas for the residents than for the office workers. Credit for the design of the tower and its four-story Neiman Marcus section on Michigan Avenue goes to SOM's Adrian Smith and the late Fazlur Khan.

At the end of the Pumping Station property and adjoining little Seneca Park, is the **Fire House** of Engine Company 98 and Ambulance Company 11. Designed in the same castellated Gothic style as the Water Tower and Pumping Station, it was erected in 1902 from plans by Chicago city architect Charles F. Hermann, and is a pleasant and harmonious addition to the Water Tower complex. To the left is a stone memorial in the form of a fireman's hat from Engine Company 98, honoring one of their fallen heroes.

Continue west to Mies van der Rohe Way.

Across the little street named for the great Bauhaus architect, who adopted Chicago and lived here from 1938 until his death in 1969, is the brand-new site of the **Museum of Contemporary Art,** which will move from its 237 E. Ontario Street location and open officially during the summer of 1996. The five-level museum building, at 234 E. Chicago Avenue, designed by German architect Josef Paul Kleihues (with A. Epstein and Sons International, associate architects and engineers), is four times the size of its former home, and its style is a fitting reflection of its mission. In a review of the plan, *Chicago Tribune* architecture critic, Paul Gapp, described Kleihues as having "designed a building of cool, quiet distinction . . . (that) is, in the most praiseworthy sense, an exercise in strongly gridded, back-to-basics modernism that could hardly be more at home than in Chicago." This is Kleihues's first American commission, and according to the Museum, "His design combines his poetic rationalist style with sensitivity to the site and Chicago's architectural history." The MCA, which many call Chicago's answer to New York's Museum of Modern Art, maintains one of the country's finest collections of contemporary painting, sculpture, prints, photographs, and drawings, and schedules special exhibitions on a regular basis. The new museum building, erected on the site of an Illinois National Guard Armory demolished in 1993, occupies 2.01 acres in a park-like setting between E. Pearson Street and E. Chicago Avenue, with Lake Shore Park on the east and Seneca Park on the west. Facing Lake Michigan is a one-acre sculpture garden. (Telephone: 280-5161.)

Stop for a moment in little **Seneca Park** and examine the unique sculpture of a horse, entitled *Ben,* by Deborah Butterfield (1989), a construction of chunks of bronze, cut to resemble random pieces of wood and logs, standing seven feet high.

Walk back along E. Chicago Avenue.

Halfway down the block on the south side, in the cavernous arcade to the right of the entrance to 211 E. Chicago Avenue (the American Dental Association Building), is a huge bronze sculpture, *The Family,* by Joseph J. O'Connell, depicting a mother, father, and child.

Return to Michigan Avenue and cross Water Tower Square to 814 N. Michigan Avenue, on the west side.

★   In consonance with the Gothic style of the Water Tower is the **Wally Findlay Galleries** (*1917, Perkins, Fellows & Hamilton*), 814 N. Michigan Avenue. The diminutive four-story freestanding building's red bricks have been painted white (many times!), and the delightful Gothic details that adorn the art gallery's facade, by sculptor Emil R. Zettler, are now somewhat obscured. The building was originally designed by the architects for their own offices and as a place to showcase their work.

Next door, at 820 N. Michigan Avenue, is **Loyola University–Lewis Towers** (*1927, Richard E. Schmidt and Garden & Martin*). The dark-red-brick building once housed the Illinois Women's Athletic Club, and was donated to the University by the philanthropist, Frank Lewis. It now serves as one of Loyola's Chicago campuses. Note the three broad Gothic arches (again in context with its surroundings). Among the bits of sculptural detail is *Diana*, above the entrance—but what is she tempting her guard dog with?

Across the avenue is the enormous blocklong **Water Tower Place** (*1976, Loebl, Schlossman & Hackl, with C. F. Murphy Associates; interior by Warren Platner*), 845 N. Michigan Avenue, the trendsetter of the mixed-use mega-skyscrapers that brought the suburban mall to the center of town. The completion of this building with its array of upscale shops dealt the Loop's State Street retailing center a devastating blow, as one by one, the fine stores began to "pull up stakes" and move to what would soon become a more chic shopping district, conveniently close to the "Gold Coast" and the wealthier northern suburbs. The tenants of Water Tower Place include the Ritz-Carlton Hotel (whose lobby is on the 12th floor), 200 luxury condominiums, office space, a

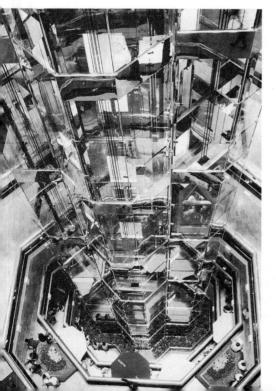

Taking a dizzying look down seven stories of the glass-enclosed, free-standing elevator shaft in the atrium of Water Tower Place is a popular activity for visitors. More than 100 stores and shops, including Marshall Field's and Lord & Taylor share space with the Ritz Carlton Hotel, commercial offices, and 200 luxury condominiums. (Photo by author)

shopping mall with more than 100 stores and shops that includes Marshall Field's and Lord & Taylor, plus restaurants and theatres. Marshall Field's, despite its glitzy store here, still maintains its famous flagship store on State Street (*see* pages 85–89).

The 62-story, 859-foot gray marble-clad tower and twelve-story base cover a reinforced concrete frame that until the completion of 311 S. Wacker Drive in 1991 (*see* pages 101 and 103) was the world's tallest concrete skyscraper. Despite the building's overall design which called for the setback of the tower, the Michigan Avenue facade is bland and uninviting, virtually without windows, and with blank walls seeming to turn their back on the great street.

Once inside, however, the picture changes dramatically. Take the escalator that glides past terraces filled with plants and cascading water to the large atrium. Ride up one of the centrally situated glassed-in elevators for a better view of the seven-story mall with its five courts, its vast array of shops, and especially the dazzling marble, glass, and chrome of the atrium's appointments. In 1986 the building was the recipient of an award by the Urban Land Institute for having "set a standard of excellence for Chicago's downtown" as a mixed-use complex. At that time the Water Tower Place atrium accounted for the lion's share of all retail sales in the city's North Michigan Avenue district.

Across Michigan Avenue at No. 835, is **F.A.O. Schwarz** (*1992, Lucien Lagrange & Associates*), with arguably the largest stuffed-animal menagerie in the world, while from the wide upper-story windows, the passing scene is observed by what may be the largest teddy bear anywhere. A children's paradise . . . so go in and enjoy yourself; and feel free to pet the animals. The adjoining building to the south, formerly the I. Magnin Store, is marred by the gaudy and inappropriate signs of Border's Bookstore, a subsidiary of the K Mart chain; while the recently arrived Filene's Basement is the first mass-market discount emporium to take its place among the more chi-chi establishments on North Michigan Avenue.

The three-story building extends to the corner of E. Chestnut Street as 840 N. Michigan Avenue, and is called **Plaza Escada.** The circular tower, flattened corner, wall clock, and French-style mansard roof of this postmodern structure are attractive, if not a bit pretentious touches. With its cream-colored limestone cladding, the overall effect is reminiscent of the scale of Michigan Avenue in former times and of the west side of the avenue today between Superior Street and Delaware Place. Sharing space in the building is Waterstone's Books & Music, another interesting emporium to explore.

The **John Hancock Center** (*1969, Skidmore, Owings & Merrill*), 875 N. Michigan Avenue, is Chicago's third tallest skyscraper (after the Sears Tower and the Amoco Building), and at this writing, the fifth tallest in the world (exceeded by New York's World Trade Center and the Empire State Building). Rising 1,127 feet, the 100-story giant, nicknamed "Big John," shares with the Sears Tower a dominant position on the Chicago skyline. The steel-frame building, sheathed in black anodized aluminum and tinted glass, tapers gently as it rises from its travertine marble base, measuring 265 feet by 165 feet, to a roof dimension of 100 feet by 160 feet. The larger floors are for office space,

On a clear day the 94th-floor Observatory of the John Hancock Center offers what many consider the finest overall view of Chicago and its suburbs, as well as an 80-mile view out on Lake Michigan and into four states. With its 1,127-foot-height, "Big John's" summit is often above low-lying clouds, as in this photo looking down on the Jardine Water Purification Plant, Navy Pier, Lake Point Tower, the Onterie Center, and a host of new high-rise residential towers. (Photo by author)

and the smaller upper spaces from floors 47 to 92 are for the condominium apartments. The tower was erected by the John Hancock Mutual Life Insurance Company, whose logo is the signature of the first signer of the Declaration of Independence, and the project became the company's largest single investment. The site had formerly been occupied by the one-third-mile-long dingy Pugh Warehouses.

Most noticeable on this lofty skyscraper is the distinctive cross-bracing, X-braces that are almost 18 stories long—which together with the exterior columns and horizontal beams, add significantly to its structural stiffness. With the frequent strong winds that blow in off the prairie and Lake Michigan, those braces are a virtual necessity. Even so, the building sways as much as 15 inches at the top, but only a sensitive instrument could detect it. Adding to the building's height are twin television antennas which add another 349 feet. For those statistically inclined, there are 11,459 window panes, and the framework consists of 46,000 tons of structural steel, supported by columns that weigh up to 105 tons each. Interestingly, both the John Hancock Center and the Sears Tower were designed by Bruce Graham and the late Fazlur R. Khan of Skidmore, Owings & Merrill, and were erected at approximately the same time. Graham and Khan designed a clever "braced tube" system, in which the exterior tubes are the supporting members, obviating the need for interior columns. So efficient was the system in carrying the loads downward, that one-third less steel was required than in comparable structures. For a first in building history, the tower was erected by means of crawling cranes, a technology formerly used only in the construction of bridges. In 1970 the John Hancock Center was presented with the Honor Award by the Chicago Chapter of the American Institute of Architects.

Take the time to visit the 94th-floor **Observatory.** The Center's elevators, considered the fastest in the world, make the ascent in just 39 seconds! On a clear day the view is spectacular, extending almost 80 miles, reaching as far as Wisconsin, Indiana, and Michigan. And the perspective of downtown Chicago is quite different from, but complementary to, that offered from the top of the Sears Tower. The views of the cityscape and the Lake Michigan shoreline change from hour to hour, but at sunset they are truly magnificent, as the city's lights begin to blink on and the western sky turns a brilliant scarlet. The bright band of light at the top of the tower was installed to prevent migrating birds that usually follow the Lake Michigan shoreline from crashing into the building. There are three restaurants in the building, but the one on the interconnected 95th and 96th floors claims to be the "highest in Chicago" (and close to that in price).

The base of the tower was the subject of some controversy in recent years when the owners planned to fill in the sunken plaza and build a three-story connecting retail atrium. Mayor Richard M. Daley expressed outrage at a design which would alter the shape of this treasured Chicago icon while destroying a favored public gathering place. Fortunately, the ill-conceived project was promptly abandoned. A new design, completed in 1994, changed the shape of the square plaza to an ellipse, and included a recessed outdoor amphitheater. There has also been some disagreement over the stark contrast between the dark-skinned building and its light-colored marble base. Writing in the *AIA Guide to Chicago,* architecture critic Blair Kamin compares it disparagingly to "a man in a tuxedo wearing white socks." And while "Big John" shattered the scale of the avenue, which soon became an "urban canyon of hulking blockbusters," Kamin does laud the usability by the public of the sunken plaza's open space. (The Observatory is open daily, 9:00 A.M. to midnight. Adults $4.75, seniors $4.00, students 5 to 17 years $3.25, children under 5 and servicemen and -women in uniform free.)

After your visit to "Big John," stop in at the **Chicago Architecture Foundation's Shop and Tour Center at the John Hancock Center,** located on the Concourse Level. Open 10:00 A.M. to 8:00 P.M. (later in the summer), the CAF recently opened this branch facility to offer daily tours and maintain a conveniently located book and gift shop.

Directly opposite the John Hancock Center is the splendid Gothic Revival–style **Fourth Presbyterian Church** (*1914, Ralph Adams Cram, with Howard Van Doren Shaw; Cloister, 1914, also by Shaw, as well as the Parish House, Blair Chapel, and Manse—added in 1925*), 866 N. Michigan Avenue. With most of its congregants residing in the nearby "Gold Coast," including the Cyrus McCormick family, the church could well afford the most distinguished architects of the day. They selected Cram, the nation's leading neo-Gothic Revival architect, whose reputation had been assured with New York's

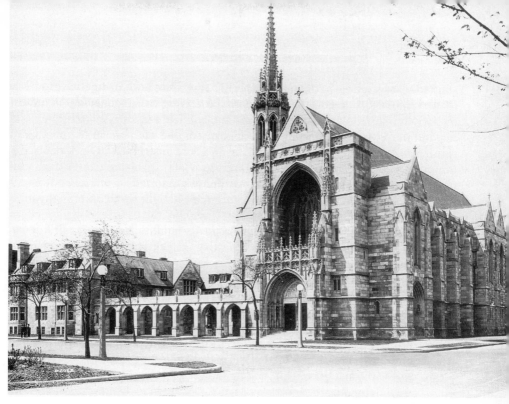

The elegant neo-Gothic-style Fourth Presbyterian Church, across Michigan Avenue from "Big John," was designed in 1914 by the nation's leading Gothic Revival architect, Ralph Adams Cram, with Howard Van Doren Shaw. It was the first major structure erected on Michigan Avenue after the Great Fire, and its parishioners included Cyrus H. McCormick and his large family. The photo, made in the late 1920s, shows a quieter, more sedate Michigan Avenue before the "great metamorphosis." (Courtesy of the Art Institute of Chicago)

Cathedral of St. John the Divine, the Chapel at the U.S. Military Academy at West Point, and the Princeton University Chapel. Designed in what is known as the "English Perpendicular Gothic Style," with all the attendant ornamentation—pinnacles, buttresses, stone spire, and window traceries—it offers a striking contrast to its skyscraper neighbors.

The complex of buildings surrounds a garth (courtyard), at the center of which is a large fountain donated to the church by supervising architect Howard Van Doren Shaw, who designed the parish buildings, but not the church building. To the left is the Manse, the residence of the senior pastor; and to the left rear, the parish house; directly opposite is Fellowship Hall. Blair Chapel and the Stone Chapel are behind the church and visible on the Delaware Street side. Enter the serene garth through the cloister that separates the complex from bustling Michigan Avenue. Then exit and visit the church (open Monday through Friday, 11:30 A.M. to 1:30 P.M.; Saturday, 11:00 A.M. to 2:00 P.M.; and Sunday, all day) and pick up a copy of the self-guided tour of the church.

The facade is of gray Bedford (Indiana) limestone and is composed of two enormous compound pointed arches, with the entrance in the lower arch and a stained-glass window in the upper. The 122-foot spire adds dramatic verticality to the plan. Once inside the sanctuary the feeling of spaciousness is almost overwhelming. Look up at the splendid and colorful ten-story-high timber ceiling and the 14 larger-than-life-sized angels atop the piers along the north and south walls of the nave. Each holds a different instrument symbolic of the importance of praising God through music. Walk down the center aisle and note the medieval-style stained-glass windows, painted in *grisaille,* or light-gray, "faded" style designed to admit more natural light while bathing the interior in soft colors. The windows were designed by Charles J. Connick of Boston, one of the finest masters of the art of stained glass. Look back at the east window with its depiction of the four evangelists. The chancel (at the head of the center aisle) displays an elaborately carved lectern; to the left is a black marble baptismal font, and to the right, the large octagonal stone pulpit. The choir loft and organist are located behind the large carved oak screen.

The Fourth Presbyterian Church was the first major structure built on N. Michigan Avenue after the Great Fire, and stood on what was then the shoreline of Lake Michigan before the area to the east was filled in. The original church building had been erected about a half-mile southwest, at the corner of Grand and Wabash. One day after it opened it was consumed in the Fire.

Occupying the entire block north, from Delaware to Walton streets, on the same side of the avenue, is the towering **900 N. Michigan Avenue** (*1989, Kohn Pedersen Fox, with Perkins & Will*). This huge limestone and glass mixed-use structure, although by the same developers as Water Tower Place, is a significant improvement. Instead of "snubbing" the pedestrians, this building invites them inside. As with the neighboring mixed-use skyscrapers, the 66-story tower rises 871 feet and is set back, with a six-level base of limestone, granite, and marble set in an eight-story cube. The dazzling Avenue Atrium with its neo–Art Deco decor, its soaring balconies and lofty bridges, houses approximately 100 shops and boutiques emphasizing European and out-of-town styles and designs. Dominating the huge atrium is Bloomingdale's, with five levels of departments located to the rear. Facing the second-level entrance to "Bloomies" is a square black-marble fountain. From the 8th to 28th floor, the building contains the Tower Offices. The 32nd to 46th floors are occupied by the Four Seasons Hotel (entrance on Delaware Street), and from the 48th to 66th are 106 luxury condos. There are also two theatres and, in the atrium, six restaurants.

The "Bloomingdale Building," as it's informally called, is topped by four square pavilions surmounted by illuminated lanterns, which give the building a distinct personality and make it a very noticeable addition to the skyline, visible day and night from a great distance. The structure is a bit controversial—some call it gaudy and tacky, others accept it as just another expression of passé postmodern tastes. The construction of the building combined two interesting structural systems. The lower 20 floors are of a conventional steel-framework design, while the upper 46 comprise a concrete tube, a technique which allows for more open space in the retailing areas.

Directly across the avenue, and facing north and south, is the Art Deco–style **919 N. Michigan Avenue** (*1929, Holabird & Root*). For 40 years it was the dominant landmark at the north end of Michigan Avenue, until the arrival of "Big John" in the late 60s. The prestigious location was deliberately selected by the Palmolive-Peet Company because of its proximity to the lakefront and the "Gold Coast." The building was known as the Palmolive Building for three decades, then as the Playboy Building in the 1980s, and now only by its street address. The Bedford limestone structure is almost a textbook example of the Art Deco style. Examining the building from its north or south side (which are essentially identical), what is immediately obvious are the series of symmetrical setbacks, which together with the three vertical channels than run the full height of the building, and the soaring ranks of windows separated by dark-colored spandrels, create a kind of harmonious vertical rhythm that draws the eye inexorably skyward. At night the sculptural effect is further heightened by floodlight illumination mounted on the setbacks. The 150-foot steel tower atop the building once supported an aircraft beacon, and was a gift to the city by Elmer Ambrose Sperry, of Brooklyn, N.Y. It was named in honor of Charles A. Lindbergh and installed just after his famous trans-Atlantic flight in 1927. The bright searchlight became obsolete and was turned off when more sophisticated aerial navigational aids were developed and also because the building was eclipsed in height by many of its neighbors. Residents in the upper floors of new nearby luxury condos had also complained about the powerful beacon shining into their windows.

Diagonally across Michigan Avenue and E. Walton Street is one of Skidmore, Owings & Merrill's more unusual skyscrapers, **One Magnificent Mile** (1983), 940–980 N. Michigan Avenue. The architects of the Sears Tower, "Big John," and Chicago Place came up with the "bundled tube" plan again (*see* Sears Tower, pages 100–102), originally developed by SOM's architect Bruce Graham and engineer Fazlur Khan. The architects were faced with several challenges in planning the structure: how to design an appropriately imposing "gateway" building to North Michigan Avenue's elegant shopping district, and one that would not cast a long shadow across diminutive Oak Street Park and Oak Beach; how such a building might withstand the wind pressures from Lake Michigan; and how the building would be contextual with its neighbors. The design called for three hexagonally shaped, conjoined concrete tubes sheathed in smooth pink granite, which as a bundled tube would resist the strong wind loads, and would also obviate the need for inner structural cores, thus allowing unimpeded interior space. The three hexagonal sections would be 21, 49, and 57 stories, respectively, with a five-story hexagonal entrance pavilion. The roof of the entrance pavilion would be slanted northeast toward the park, as would that of the tallest of the three towers. The result seems to have met those very demanding criteria. The mixed-use building is divided between retail space, office tower, and condominiums, with a two-story mechanical systems level at the 21st story dividing the offices from the living space. The change in fenestration also indicates this demarcation, with clear windows in the commercial section and reflective glass in the residential. The layout of the retail shops is not so successful. Its three rather small shopping levels do not fit together well, and finding one's way around can be confusing.

The Drake Hotel, at 140 E. Walton Street, has remained Chicago's "grande dame" through the years, displaying style and luxury since the day it opened in 1920. The hotel, designed by Benjamin H. Marshall, is considered the northern anchor of the avenue and the "real" gateway to the downtown shopping district. In this photo of the rear of the H-shaped building, which faces East Lake Shore Drive and cozy Oak Beach Park, the Drake's name is proclaimed in large Gothic letters—a familiar and longtime feature of the city's skyline. (Photo by author)

 The Drake Hotel (*1920, Marshall & Fox*), 140 E. Walton Street, in its dramatic position overlooking the lake, where N. Michigan Avenue meets E. Lake Shore Drive, at the portal to Chicago's "Gold Coast," has always been considered the anchor of the avenue and the "real" gateway to the downtown retail district (despite the claim of its pretentiously named neighbor, One Magnificent Mile). The hotel was completed shortly before the Michigan Avenue Bridge was opened, and for a time it stood in splendid isolation at the end of the newly widened avenue. It was built for two prominent hotelmen, brothers John B., Jr., and Tracy C. Drake, and opened on New Year's Eve 1920 with a supper party attended by 3,000 of the city's most prominent citizens. The Drake family came originally from England, and their family crest, which appears throughout the hotel, goes back many centuries. On their coat of arms, which displays a winged dragon and battle-ax, is the Latin phrase *Aquila Non Capit Muscas* ("an eagle does not catch flies"). The Drake, a member of the Hilton International chain, is considered by many to be Chicago's most prestigious hotel, and through the years it has been a symbol of "white-glove" elegance. Among its famous visitors were the Emperor of Japan, Sweden's King Gustavus, Denmark's Queen Margrethe, Great Britain's Queen Elizabeth and Prince Charles, Egypt's President Sadat, and Israel's Prime Minister Rabin.

The Drake's opulent Silver Forest Room was Chicago's most sumptuous dining and dancing rendezvous in the 1920s, and the favorite for receptions by visiting royalty. In more recent times, economics dictated that the elegant space be subdivided into smaller public rooms, the largest of which is now called the Gold Coast Ballroom; however the ornate columns and much of the original decor have remained intact. (Photo by the Chicago Architectural Photographing Company. Chicago Historical Society)

The 12-story Italian Renaissance–style building, sheathed in Bedford limestone, and adorned with a variety of period motifs, is built on an H-shaped plan, with its main public rooms on the raised main floor, or *piano nobile*. In the center is the luxurious Palm Court, and facing the lake, the opulent two-story Gold Coast Ballroom, with its richly adorned gilt columns, crystal chandeliers, and panoramic views. The Drake is the western anchor also of the **East Lake Shore Drive Historic District** designated as such by the city's Commission on Chicago Landmarks, and described in the following tour. Since the visit to the Drake brings us to the end of the "Mag" Mile tour, why not reward yourself with the hotel's delightful afternoon tea in the Palm Court, served from 3:00 P.M. to 5:30 P.M. daily. On leaving, note the plaque on the Walton Street side of the building, at the corner of Michigan Avenue, which recognizes the contributions of the design architect of the hotel, Benjamin H. Marshall.

End of tour. (Several bus routes return downtown along Michigan Avenue: Nos. 145, 146, 147, and 151.)

Tour 7: **East Lake Shore Drive to the Centennial Fountain**

Lake Shore Dr.

Start

The Drake

Bloomingdales

John Hancock Center

Water Tower Place

N. Mies van der Rohe Way

DeWitt Place

Water Tower

Pumping Station

Museum of Contemporary Art

Chicago Place

City Place

Lake Shore Playground and Softball Field

Northwestern University

Northwestern University

Lake Michigan

N

Northwestern Hospital

E. Huron St.

Lakeshore Place

E. Erie St.

E. Ontario St.

E. Ohio St.

N. Rush St.

N. Michigan

N. St. Clair St.

N. Columbus Dr.

E. Grand Ave.

N. McClurg Ct.

Peshtigo Ct.

Nav Pie

Lake Point Tower

Tribune Tower

Equitable Bldg.

Ogden Plaza

N. Fairbanks Ct.

North Pier Mall

Wrigley Building

Sun Times

N. Water St.

Sheraton Chicago

Centennial Fountain

Chicago River

E. Wacker Drive

One Illinois Center

Hyatt Regency

Swissôtel

0   250   500 F

7. East Lake Shore Drive to the Centennial Fountain

To reach the starting point of the tour from downtown, take any of the following bus routes that go north on Michigan Avenue: Nos. 145, 146, 147, or 151. Ask the driver to stop at the nearest street to E. Walton Street and the Drake Hotel.

This tour, which begins at the Drake Hotel, follows Lake Shore Drive and wends its way south through many of the streets in the area east of N. Michigan Avenue, close to the lakefront, visiting Navy Pier, and ending at the Centennial Fountain at the mouth of the Chicago River. It is recommended that the Magnificent Mile and Streeterville tour be taken first (or at least that the introduction on pages 213–214 first be read, as it includes useful information about the history and development of this neighborhood—a part of Chicago that was mostly under the waters of Lake Michigan until it was gradually filled in during the late 19th and early 20th centuries).

 The Drake Hotel (*1920, Marshall & Fox*), located at the point where Michigan Avenue disappears into Lake Shore Drive, is described in detail at the end of Tour 6. Begin the tour at its main entrance at 140 E. Walton Street, and refer to pages 246–247. The elegant Drake Hotel has been designated as the western anchor of the **East Lake Shore Drive Historic District** by the City of Chicago Commission on Chicago Landmarks, and the entire district will be seen shortly.

After leaving the Drake Hotel, turn right (north) on N. Michigan Avenue, and take the pedestrian underpass under E. Lake Shore Drive to little Oak Beach Park.

This 1981 panoramic view looking south from Lake Shore Drive encompasses the entire East Lake Shore Drive Historic District, and includes the Drake Hotel (right), the row of landmark apartment houses (Nos. 179–229 E. Lake Shore Drive), and tiny Oak Beach Park. (Photo by Bob Thall for the Commission on Chicago Landmarks)

Oak Beach Park, within the Historic District, is a pleasant little oasis and offers a convenient spot to view the north side of the Drake (note its name in large Gothic letters) and the row of apartment houses to the left, which will be viewed close at hand shortly. To the west, Lake Shore Drive swings northward along the lake, and for well over a mile the busy thoroughfare's west side is lined cheek-by-jowl with the luxury high-rise apartment houses with million-dollar views that characterize the eastern boundary of the "Gold Coast."

The first building on N. Michigan Avenue, named **Plaza 1000** (*1964, Sidney Morris and Associates*) for its address, is a steel-and-concrete condominium tower, rising a whopping 55 stories to offer its residents spectacular views of the Lake Michigan shoreline. Most of those behemoths were built from the 1950s to the 1980s, replacing earlier luxury apartment houses that had risen in the 1920s. They in turn had displaced many opulent 19th-century mansions that were forced to yield to the requirement for upscale, but smaller, more manageable living units. In the post–World War II era, as the demand for luxury housing increased again, land values skyrocketed, and economics dictated the construction of these blockbuster apartment houses. Many gracious villas, town houses, and early apartment houses still survive, however, and can be found within a few blocks to the west, particularly along N. Astor Street, and further north up the Drive. (This is the last address on N. Michigan Avenue; its neighbor to the north is also No. 1000, but on N. Lake Shore Drive.)

The original developer of the "Gold Coast" as the neighborhood of choice for Chicago's elite, was the influential socialite, Potter Palmer, the prime mover behind the State Street retail district (*see* page 78). Together with his wife Bertha, he built a magnificent castle-like mansion at 1350 N. Lake Shore Drive in what was then the "northern wilds"—a move that precipitated a "gold rush" to the lakeshore suburb by the city's "four hundred," and which the tycoon then turned to good advantage by speculating in the emerging land boom. Although the sumptuous mansion no longer stands (*see* photo on page 408), the Palmers established a trend which persists to this very day.

The uninterrupted row of luxury apartment houses along E. Lake Shore Drive, south of the park, all date from the second and third decades of the 20th century, and are included in a single encompassing designation as part of the East Lake Shore Drive Historic District. The buildings represent virtually every revival style, from Classic, Baroque, Renaissance, Georgian, Second Empire, to Beaux Arts; but together they present a unified and gracious appearance.

Before continuing the tour, you might want to walk down to sandy Oak Beach, a highly popular place for summer sunbathers and for those who would brave the chilly waters of Lake Michigan. Along the beach is a paved bicycle and jogging path which offers nice views of the lake, but don't take it for any distance, as it would be a while before you could get back across Lake Shore Drive. Then return via the underpass to the sidewalk along the row of apartment buildings, just to the left of the Drake Hotel.

Drake Tower Apartments (*1929, Benjamin H. Marshall*), 179 E. Lake Shore Drive, is a simple 26-story brick structure with a 2-story limestone base, with the top floor set back. Most of the buildings in the row were equipped with interior driveways to accommodate the luxury automobiles of the tenants, or to serve for deliveries. This building does not have such a driveway; however, it boasts a unique accoutrement, which although almost 70 years old, is just as practical today as when it was first installed: an automobile turntable. Take a peek in, and perhaps the doorman will demonstrate it for you. Instead of having to back out after dropping off a visitor or making a delivery, the turntable will rotate the vehicle 180 degrees so it can drive straight out. As far as is known, this is the only one of its kind in Chicago.

The Mayfair Regent Hotel (*1924, Fugard & Knapp*), 181 E. Lake Shore Drive, formerly a residential apartment house, later the Lake Shore Drive Hotel, and now an upscale hostelry, is joined to the Drake Tower Apartments in a "U" shape. The facade of the 17-story structure is Georgian, with the lower three floors of Indiana limestone and the shaft of dark-red brick. Note the Adamesque adornments (named for 18th-century Scottish architect Robert Adam), particularly the low-relief swags and urns. The parapets are embellished with balustrades and stone urns, and above are stone quoins and cornices.

199 E. Lake Shore Drive (*1915, Marshall & Fox*) displays many unusual touches. The entrance to this 11-story condominium is offset to the right with a curved oriel above an ornate two-story limestone base. The entry itself is almost a complete circle, flanked by a pair of classic columns, while above, one level of square bays is surmounted by one round.

209 E. Lake Shore Drive (*1924, Marshall & Fox*) is a 16-story condominium, with a rusticated facade below, a series of horizontal bands above, and a smooth surface at the top. The entrance door is crowned with a fanlight, and on either side are a pair of elegant iron lamp standards projecting from the wall. The driveway makes a complete U-turn around the entrance section, allowing for what would have then been a relatively unimpeded flow of traffic.

219 E. Lake Shore Drive (*1922, Fugard & Knapp*) illustrates the architects' interest in the Georgian Revival, with a typical split pediment over the entrance, and a limestone facade whose third floor is topped with a classic stone cornice, creating the impression of an 18th-century English mansion. The remainder of the 12 floors are of brick, interrupted by a stone balcony at the 10th floor. The top floor displays decorative low-relief panels between window groups.

229 E. Lake Shore Drive (*1919, Fugard & Knapp*) is an expression of northern Italian style in the shape of a Florentine *palazzo*. Because of its 11-story height, which would have been too tall even for the Medicis, the facade is divided into two sections. Above an elegant, but restrained, entrance the building rises five floors to a dentil course, then six more to a classic cornice. The ceilings in this building must be higher than in the previous building, since both have a common roofline, but this structure has one less story. This is the last building in the historic district.

999 N. Lake Shore Drive (*1912, Marshall & Fox*), the oldest in the row, is one of Marshall and Fox's earliest apartment houses. Both architects had made a name for themselves with the design of a number of theatres, and later with a wide variety of commissions. The Drake Hotel, with Benjamin H. Marshall as design architect, was probably their most famous assignment. Occupying a prominent corner position, No. 999 is also one of the most striking in the row. Most noticeable is the black mansard roof, punctuated with dormers. The facade of the 10-story building displays bands of red brick and white limestone trim, with a balustrade at the second floor level. Very interesting is the triple-arched entrance, placed at the corner, above which are two sets of shallow oriels, designed no doubt to provide tenants with sweeping views of the lake and shoreline. The entry has its own driveway, planned to permit the driver and passengers of horseless carriages to enter directly into the building. There is also a separate delivery driveway at the side to obviate the possibility of the high-class residents mixing with the tradesmen.

East Lake Shore Drive now becomes North Lake Shore Drive.

Just ahead is **990 N. Lake Shore Drive** (*1973, Barancik & Conte*), a 34-story white concrete structure with contrasting dark metal-frame windows. Note the split-faced concrete on the first two levels, then smooth texture above, with thin vertical striations.

Between Walton and Delaware streets stand the twin towers of **900** and **910 N. Lake Shore Drive** (*1956, Ludwig Mies van der Rohe; with Pace Associates and Holsman, Holsman, Klekamp & Taylor*). One of two pairs of Mies high-rises along the drive, the buildings are sited at right angles to each other, and at a 45-degree angle to the roadway, to provide the condominium residents with as broad and uninterrupted view as possible. The 29-story structures are fairly typical of the Miesian tinted-glass curtain-wall construction, but unlike most of his buildings, which are glass-sheathed steel-skeletons, Nos. 900 and 910 were erected on a flat-slab concrete frame which separates the skin from the structural members. The layout of the buildings also allows for pleasant landscaping, with the greenery contrasting with the rather somber towers.

Mies van der Rohe was one of the dominant figures in Germany's **Bauhaus School,** founded in Weimar in 1919. It included such notables in architecture and art as Walter Gropius, Marcel Breuer, Paul Klee, Lyonel Feininger, Wassily Kandinsky, and Laszlo Moholy-Nagy. The Bauhaus developed a new architecture that was intended to mirror the spirit of the age, and rejected traditional architecture as inappropriate. They sought to develop a universal architecture for all building types, regardless of location or function. By manipulating materials, forms and space, they created what they believed to be truly modern buildings.

As the leader of the modernist movement in America, Mies expounded the theory that *form should follow function*—a dictum that led to the development of a severely geometric, unadorned design which he employed in his unique glass-sheathed curtain-wall plan. Mies, who was elected president of the Bauhaus in 1930, became its major progenitor, and after the school was closed by the Nazis he came to America in 1937 and settled in Chicago. He was appointed director of the Armour Institute of Technology (which in a later merger became the Illinois Institute of Technology), where he planned a number of its campus buildings and also opened a private architecture practice for himself. In the late 1950s he received the commission for the neighboring 860 and 880 N. Lake Shore Drive, and the success of the project led to this slightly modified version. Promoters convinced urban developers that these modern "glass boxes" were economically efficient and easily accessible, and they soon became the prototype of a style that not only greatly influenced Chicago's residential communities, but gained tremendous universal popularity and lasted for several decades. (For further information about Mies, *see* the IBM Building in Tour 4, pages 150–151.)

In the block to the south, between E. Delaware and E. Chestnut streets, are **860** and **880 N. Lake Shore Drive** (*1951, Ludwig Mies van der Rohe; with Pace Associates and Holsman, Holsman, Klekamp & Taylor*). This pair of 28-story Mies-designed buildings constitutes the first and most influential example of his style. The steel-and-glass curtain wall became Mies's hallmark, and examples, both good and bad, can be seen in virtually every city in the world. From the 1950s through the 1970s it was the accepted design for the corporate headquarters tower as well as the ubiquitous luxury high-rise apartment

Nos. 860 and 880 N. Lake Shore Drive, designed by Mies van der Rohe in 1951, constitute the first and most influential examples of his style. The pair of 28-story apartment towers overlooking the lakefront were the forerunners of the typical corporate tower and the ubiquitous high-rise luxury apartment house for the next 25 years. (Photo by author)

house. A major aesthetic feature of the style was its strong verticality that resulted from narrow I-beams welded to the columns and mullions, creating an uninterrupted and upsweeping rhythm. In addition, the windows are divided into three groups of four on the narrow side of the building, and five groups on the wide side, creating "bays" separated by wider beams. Unlike 900 and 910, however, which display a solid dark-tinted glass wall, these buildings have contrasting aluminum window frames—a feature he wisely dropped in the later structures. Mies, himself, was a tenant, but reluctantly moved out, according to legend, because neighbors would frequently complain about routine maintenance to *him,* rather than to the management. He then settled at 200 E. Pearson Street, at the northeast corner of Mies van der Rohe Way, three blocks away, where he lived until his death in 1969. (The building, a 1916 Italianate six-story tan-brick apartment house, which except for its rusticated arched entrance, is of no great architectural merit, and can be seen at your leisure.)

On the opposite corner, the 18-story **Lake Shore Center–Northwestern University** (*1924, Jarvis Hunt*) is a reminder of the halcyon days of the area when the building housed the exclusive Lake Shore Athletic Club. The original clubhouse and apartments now serve as a dormitory of the University, and the resident student body still enjoys the club's old swimming pool and athletic facilities. The rather massive building has a neo-Classic base, but little ornament above. This is the first of a number of buildings of Northwestern University's architecturally significant Chicago Campus to be seen on this tour.

Walk west on E. Chestnut Street to the next block.

At the northwest corner of E. Chestnut Street and DeWitt Place is the towering **DeWitt-Chestnut Tower** (*1963, Skidmore, Owings & Merrill*), 860 N. DeWitt Place, a 46-story condominium apartment building. Unlike its nearby Miesian neighbors, this building has a reinforced concrete frame with a skin of travertine marble. While otherwise undistinguished, it does represent Chicago's first experiment with a tubular construction system. SOM's architect Bruce Graham and engineer Fazlur R. Khan, of Sears Tower and John Hancock Center fame, combined their talents to produce the structural design in which the building's load is borne by a screen wall of closely spaced exterior columns.

Turn left and walk one block south to E. Pearson Street, turn left (east) and walk on the Lake Shore Park side toward Lake Shore Drive.
    Note the rear of the Museum of Contemporary Art, facing Lake Shore Park, which is described in Tour 6 (*see* page 238).

In the middle of the block are a pair of buildings of distinct styles, but linked together by a three-story connecting structure. Both share the address 840 N. Lake Shore Drive, and are the headquarters of the **American Hospital Association** (*1961 and 1970, Schmidt, Garden & Erikson*). The westernmost 12-story structure and the earlier of the two, has recessed windows behind a full-facade concrete screen, a style popular in the 1960s; while the eastern 13-story twin has flush windows set in prominent aluminum frames. Both buildings, however, share white glazed-brick walls. At the Lake Shore Drive end is an open granite-columned arcade.

Turn right (south) on Lake Shore Drive one block to Chicago Avenue, and turn right (west).

We now enter the "Halls of Ivy" of the Northwestern University Chicago campus. Across Chicago Avenue and extending along Lake Shore Drive is the Northwestern University Law School and American Bar Center, which will be examined a little later.

Construction on the **Northwestern University Chicago Campus** began in 1926 and continues to this very day, with plans for further construction in the late 1990s. The campus includes the McGaw Medical Center and Medical School, School of Dentistry, and Law School. Although a variety of architectural styles are to be seen, the earliest and most enduring is the Collegiate Gothic, as created by James Gamble Rogers, a master of the neo-Gothic, whose reputation was firmly established with many of the Yale University buildings in New Haven, Connecticut, and New York City's Presbyterian Medical Center.

At mid-block is **Levy Meyer Hall** of the Northwestern University Law School (*1927, James Gamble Rogers, with Childs & Smith*), 357 E. Chicago Avenue, behind which is a pleasant courtyard, which unfortunately is not gen-

The imposing Montgomery Ward Memorial of Northwestern University, at 303–311 E. Chicago Avenue, was designed by the "dean of the Collegiate Gothic style," James Gamble Rogers, in 1926. Considered the first skyscraper built in that style, it rises 12 stories with a delicate four-story tower above. (Photo by author)

erally open to the public, the times being what they are; **Wieboldt Hall** of the School of Commerce (*1926, James Gamble Rogers, with Childs & Smith*), 339 E. Chicago Avenue, connected by a lovely arcade to the imposing **Montgomery Ward Memorial** (*1926, James Gamble Rogers, with Childs & Smith*), 303–311 E. Chicago Avenue. Considered the first skyscraper built in the Collegiate Gothic style, the main building rises 12 stories with a delicately designed four-story tower above.

Turn left (south) on Fairbanks Court (the extension of DeWitt Place) to Superior Street.

The 16-story **Tarry Medical Research & Education Building,** of the McGaw Medical Center of Northwestern University, on the corner (*1990, Perkins & Will*), 300 E. Superior Street, is a postmodern variation on the Gothic theme, particularly in the window treatment. Note the unusual combinations of window panes and the feeling of verticality created by the rows of narrow windows separated by dark-colored panels. Enter the glassed-in Method Atrium which cleverly links the Tarry Building with the Searle, Morton, and other buildings in the complex. One not immediately apparent feature of this and neighboring buildings in the medical complex is the gradual increase in height as they were built westward from the lakefront—an essential element in John Gamble Rogers's 1926 plan to provide a rising and balanced panorama of buildings.

Back at the corner, note the twin skybridges that cross both Superior Street and Fairbanks Court from the bland 15-story **Wesley Pavilion of Northwestern**

University Hospital (*1937–1941, Thielbar & Fugard*), 250 E. Superior Street. Directly across Superior Street is the **Passavant Pavilion** (Floyd E. Patterson Memorial Building). Note the ornate frieze above the Gothic-style entrance.

Continue left (east) along Superior Street.

After the Passavant Pavilion is the **Prentice Women's Hospital,** 333 E. Superior Street. The view from this angle gives no indication of what's in store for you very shortly. At 345 E. Superior Street, the Gothic yields to the modern, with C. F. Murphy's 1974 design for the **Rehabilitation Institute of Chicago.** The bronze-tinted curtain wall reveals its steel-frame construction, in sharp contrast to its older neighbors.

At the corner of Lake Shore Drive, and occupying the blockfront north to E. Chicago Avenue, is the striking Law School building, actually a pair of buildings: the **Arthur Rubloff Building,** 375 E. Chicago Avenue, and the **American Bar Center,** 750 N. Lake Shore Drive (*1984, Holabird & Root*). An interesting addition to the campus, the design of the pair is different, but harmonious. Observe the window arrangement of the southern, taller building, with its five bays of four windows, as opposed to its three-story neighbor, to which it is connected by a glassy atrium section. The Gary Law Library is located in the northern section. It was real estate tycoon Arthur Rubloff who coined the term "Magnificent Mile" in 1947.

Cross E. Superior Street and continue south along Lake Shore Drive.

On the right is **Abbott Hall** (*1939, Holabird & Root*), 710 N. Lake Shore Drive. A student residence hall, it also contains the University's book store. The smooth limestone building is otherwise undistinguished.

At the corner of E. Huron Street, and standing in splendid isolation, is a surviving artifact from the original campus, the decorative wrought-iron **McKinlock Memorial Gates.** Note how the handle of the bolt ends in a serpent's head grasping a ring.

Turn right (west) on E. Huron Street. Walk past McClurg Court.

The **Rehabilitation Institute of Chicago** (*1974, C. F. Murphy Associates*), 345 E. Huron Street, recalls the style of Mies van der Rohe in the technique of having the curtain wall express its steel-frame construction, as well as in the bronze-tinted reflective glass.

Then look to the left for a sensational view of:

The **Norman & Ida Stone Institute of Psychiatry,** 300–320 E. Huron Street (which is joined to the **Prentice Women's Hospital** on E. Superior Street). Designed in 1975 by Bertrand Goldberg Associates, it reflects the architect's iconoclastic approach to modern architecture, and is somewhat reminiscent of

The decorative McKinlock Memorial Gates, at the northwest corner of E. Huron Street and N. Lake Shore Drive, are preserved by Northwestern University as a memento and artifact from their original campus on the site. (Photo by author)

his circular design for Marina Towers and of his other hospital plans. A concrete "four-leaf clover" (actually two intersecting ovals) rises seven stories above the four-story rectilinear base which is of a conventional steel-framework and curtain-wall design. The rather astonishing design is the first of its kind in which the floors and the curtain wall are cantilevered out from a central core. The system permits clear, column-free space for patients' rooms above, with stairways and elevators in the core, while the doctors' and administrative offices and other hospital facilities are housed in the lower section. The plan also called for a separate nursing station at each of the wings, where patients could be grouped by medical needs. The oval-shaped windows were designed for energy efficiency and construction economy. This is arguably the most striking modern building on the campus and a triumph of architect Goldberg's creativity.

Across E. Huron Street is the **Veterans' Administration Lakeside Medical Center** (*1954, Schmidt, Garden & Erickson*), 333 E. Huron Street. The 17-story structure was the recipient in 1955 of an Excellence in Architecture Award by the Chicago Chapter of the American Institute of Architects and the Chicago Association of Commerce & Industry. The hospital, which is associated with

(Right) The astonishing concrete "four-leaf clover" of the Prentice Women's Hospital and Norman and Ida Stone Institute of Psychiatry was designed in 1975 by Bertrand Goldberg Associates. The unusual plan was the first of its kind in which the floors and curtain wall are cantilevered from a central core. The system permits clear, column-free space for patients' rooms and allows grouping by medical needs. The striking plan is a triumph of architect Goldberg's creativity, and was later applied to his Marina Towers, River City, and other hospital designs. (Courtesy Bertrand Goldberg)

Northwestern University's Medical and Dental School, and connected physically by a skybridge, is a rather austere example of the Art Moderne style. The vertical arrangement of windows with alternating dark-colored spandrels creates a feeling of height, and the block-of-four window pattern is repeated in the design of the intervening spandrels.

Walk back to McClurg Court and turn right (south) to E. Erie Street.

Occupying the entire blockfront on the west side of McClurg Court, south to E. Ontario Street is the surprising **CBS Building** (*1924, Rebori, Wentworth, Dewey & McCormick*), 630 N. McClurg Place. Built originally for the Chicago Riding Club, the unusual shape of the building with its line of windows set into the sloping roof allowed for maximum lighting and air circulation for the "horsey set," mainly from the nearby "Gold Coast," who came to practice the equestrian arts, put on horse shows and competitions, or enjoy riding in the heart of the city. Times changed and the horseback riders are now in the suburbs. The building now serves as studios and offices of the Columbia Broadcasting System's Chicago affiliate, WBBM-AM and FM radio, and TV Channel 2. McClurg Court is named for Alexander C. McClurg, a Chicago book salesman who enlisted in the Civil War as a private and returned as a brevet general, having distinguished himself in many battles. After the war he resumed his chosen profession.

Olive Park, on the lakefront near Ohio Beach, offers outstanding views of Streeterville and some of Chicago's notable skyscrapers. The building on the left, with the lavishly ornamented pyramidal tower (painted bright blue), is the former American Furniture Mart, where furniture dealers showed their wares until they moved their showrooms to the Merchandise Mart. The light-colored tower to the left of the John Hancock Center is Water Tower Place, and immediately to the right is One Magnificent Mile with its slanted roofs and hexagonal envelope. (Photo by author)

After a look at the CBS Building, return to E. Erie Street and turn right (east) toward Lake Shore Drive.

Filling the entire block from Huron to Erie streets and McClurg Court to Lake Shore Drive is the massive **Lake Shore Place,** whose official address is 680 Lake Shore Drive, although there are entrances on all four sides. The Gothic Revival–style building is actually two distinct structures, although it is almost impossible to see where they are joined. The east end (*1924, Henry Raeder Associates, with George C. Nimmons & Company and N. Max Dunning*) is 16 stories high and is built of reinforced concrete; whereas the western end, which faces McClurg Court (*1926, George C. Nimmons and N. Max Dunning*), is a steel-framed structure with a 20-story main section and a central tower that reaches a height of 30 stories. The building's bright-blue pyramidal tower, a major landmark along the lake shore, is, unfortunately, not visible from here, but will be seen later. It is said that the architects modeled the tower on the Houses of Parliament, although its bright-blue paint scheme would surely have raised some Londoners' eyebrows.

The building was originally designed for the American Furniture Mart, but when the industry ultimately became decentralized, many of the dealers and showrooms that filled the building later moved to the Merchandise Mart. The renamed structure was converted as a joint venture by Fujikawa, Conterato and Lohan, with Larocca Associates, in a four-year project completed in 1984, to a mixed-use building containing retail shops, offices, and three separate residential sections. The two-million-square-foot building became the largest adaptive reuse project to that time. Enter the building at its Erie Street entrance and note how the passageway leads directly through to Huron Street, but more interesting is the blocklong lengthwise corridor. Turn right at the "crossing" and walk through to Lake Shore Drive, noting the large wood-paneled lobby replete with Gothic details. Once out the door, turn around and observe the relief panels over the doorway illustrating the three main stages of furniture making, and also the Gothic detailing on the building's base and on the upper floors.

Turn right and walk south one block to E. Ontario Street.

At the corner is the towering 33-story **Days Inn** (*1964, William W. Bond, Jr. & Associates*), which was originally built as a Holiday Inn. Its ideal location provides superb views of Lake Michigan.

Turn right (west) on Ontario Street, and walk about 100 feet for a good view of the crisscross window treatment on the walls of the Onterie Center.

The **Onterie Center** (*1986, Skidmore, Owings & Merrill*), 446–448 E. Ontario Street, whose name is a too-obvious combination of Ontario and Erie, represents the last cooperative design plan between SOM's architect Bruce Graham and engineer Fazlur Khan. The 60-story building consists of a pair of

(Left) The Onterie Center, at 446–448 E. Ontario Street, is a Skidmore, Owings & Merrill building representing the last cooperative design plans of architect Bruce Graham and engineer Fazlur Khan. The crisscross pattern on the walls was created by deliberately sealing the windows which cover the structure's braces. Completed in 1986, it is a mixed-use building. To the right is the lofty 33-story Days Inn, built in 1964 as a Holiday Inn. (Photo by author)

reinforced-concrete tubes around a central core, with the crisscross braces outlined by the deliberately sealed windows. The cross-bracing is similar to that on the Hancock Center, and the tube construction like that on the Sears Tower (*see* pages 100–102). It is a mixed-use building, with office and retail space on the lower floors, and residential apartments above.

Enter at the Galleria atrium and note the attractive floor tiles that lead into the transverse hallway that penetrates to Erie Street. On the left wall is a terra-cotta memorial plaque to Fazlur Khan who died in 1982, before the Onterie Center was completed. Khan's quotation on the plaque is worth repeating: "The technological man must not be lost in his own technology. He must be able to appreciate life, and life is art, drama, music, and most importantly, people."

401 E. Ontario Street (*1990, Nagle, Hartray and Associates*) typifies the rapid development of an area that was once considered one of Chicago's "backwaters." With the building of mixed-use and residential towers, such as the Onterie Center and soon-to-be-seen Bancroft and Cityfront Place, the neighborhood has become one of the city's newest upscale "suburbs within a city." This 51-story finely detailed concrete apartment building is set on a base sheathed in striped precast concrete panels that are designed to look like granite and limestone, and is placed between two five-story parking structures. An interesting feature is the use of the rows of projecting triangular bays, which offer fine views for tenants and break up what would have been a bland vertical facade.

Continue west on E. Ontario Street to the southwest corner of McClurg Court.

The tall pair of apartment buildings with the rounded corners are the **McClurg Court Center** (*1971, Solomon Cordwell Buenz & Associates*), 333 E. Ontario Street. It was designed to be a self-contained complex, with retail shops and amenities, and the twin buildings were placed at right angles to each other to offer tenants unobstructed views.

Just ahead at the automobile entrance to the McClurg Court Center, turn around and look back for a view of the Onterie Center and a first glimpse of the Gothic tower of Lake Shore Place with its crowning pyramid topped by a lantern and surrounded by four stone spires.

Return to McClurg Court, turn right to E. Ohio Street, and turn left.

The neighborhood, nicknamed the "New Gold Coast," is now almost completely residential, as evidenced by the profusion of new apartment towers that have arisen in the last 15 years (i.e., 401 E. Ontario Street, mentioned on the previous block, and at the corner, the 50-story Bancroft, 400 E. Ohio Street, both with vertical rows of triangular bay windows zooming skyward; as well as the tan-brick 40-story 420 E. Ohio Street).

Continue east on Ohio Street to Lake Shore Drive. Stop for a moment and look back for another view of the Onterie Center's engaging "cross-braced" facade.

At Lake Shore Drive, cross Ohio Street and continue south along the pedestrian path, stopping for a brief look to the left at the dark-skin and curved facade of the soon-to-be-seen Lake Point Tower. Turn left at E. Grand Avenue and walk under Lake Shore Drive. Enter the park on the left and follow the pedestrian path along the water.

Olive Park, a delightful 10.5-acre oasis on the lake shore, is named for Vietnam War hero, Pfc. Milton Lee Olive, the first black Chicagoan to win the Congressional Medal of Honor. The award was bestowed posthumously in recognition of his bravery in having thrown himself on a grenade hurled at him and four other soldiers as they were moving together through the jungle. Look for the eight-foot-high monument that replaced an earlier one that had been vandalized.

Ohio Beach Park offers excellent views of Streeterville, N. Michigan Avenue skyscrapers, and Chicago's Outer Harbor, and is an attractive spot for Chicagoans seeking respite during the city's torrid summers. Dominating the skyline is "Big John's" dark slope-sided profile. (Photo by author)

Two miles out on the lake are four intake cribs for Chicago's water supply. In this ca. 1930 photo (taken from a not-too-steady small boat), the Chicago Avenue Crib, connected by an underwater tunnel to the Jardine Purification Plant, is visited by a tugboat that has just brought a barge to the site. (Photo by Valerian Ginter)

The park offers splendid views of the Chicago lakefront and a broad panorama of N. Michigan Avenue skyscrapers, which are seen to best advantage during the morning hours with the sun behind you over the lake. There are five large circular fountains representing the Great Lakes. To the left is diminutive **Ohio Beach Park,** facing the Outer Harbor, whose clean white sand attracts throngs of summer sunbathers and stalwart Chicagoans who brave the somewhat chilly Lake Michigan waters, much like at Oak Beach, seen earlier. Although it's a bit of a walk, on a clear day a stroll along the shady promenade to the end will offer rewarding vistas and refreshing lake breezes.

On leaving Olive Park, you will see a road to the left that leads to the entrance to the **Jardine Water Purification Plant,** 1000 E. Ohio Street, the largest facility of its kind in the world. Named for James W. Jardine, Commissioner of Chicago's Department of Water & Sewers and the city's first Chief Water Engineer, the plant occupies 51 acres and serves 5.1 million people. The buildings, of steel-frame curtain-wall style, were designed by C. F. Murphy Associates in cooperation with the Chicago City Engineer, and were constructed over a 12-year period, beginning in 1952. The facility is not open to the public, except by prearrangement for a group tour (telephone: 744-7001).

Look out on Lake Michigan. About two miles "out to sea" are two small structures that at first resemble distant ships. Set in water 32 to 35 feet deep, they are two of the four **intake cribs** for the Chicago water supply, and are connected by underwater tunnels to the Water Purification Plant. They were installed to bring in fresh drinking water subsequent to the reversal of the flow of the Chicago River, when the lake waters ceased to be so badly polluted (*see* pages 106–107).

★   To the right is one of Chicago's most popular sites, festive **Navy Pier** (*1916, Charles Sumner Frost; renovated 1976, Jerome R. Butler; renovation and recon- struction 1990–1995, Benjamin Thompson & Associates, with VOA Associates; rehabilitation of East Buildings 1992–1995, Bernheim & Kahn*), 600 E. Grand Avenue, reopened in the summer of 1995 after a major three-year renovation. The 3,000-foot-long pier, originally named Municipal Pier No. 2 (No. 1 was never built), was constructed to accommodate package-freight vessels and excursion steamers, warehouses, and also as a place of public entertainment, including such amenities as a dance hall, theatre, restaurant, Ferris wheel, and a variety of recreational facilities. It even had its own streetcar line. Built on 20,000 wooden pilings, it was the world's largest pier at the time. The construc- tion of the pier was a partial fulfillment of Daniel Burnham's 1909 Plan of Chicago, which had envisioned a similar long pier at the south end of a yacht harbor opposite Grant Park. By the 1930s, the rise of the motor age and the Depression combined to diminish its usefulness, and by World War II the pier was taken over by the U.S. Navy as a training facility, and its name was subse- quently changed.

    In 1946 the facility was acquired by the University of Illinois for their Chicago branch, and remained an academic center for the next nine years. A major renovation in 1976 restored the east buildings, and the pier was then reopened for public events. Then in 1989 the City of Chicago established the Metropolitan Pier & Expositic Authority to direct the reconstruction of Navy Pier, as well as McCormick F ce, and voted $150 million toward the conversion

In 1995 Navy Pier reopened jter a three-year-long renovation. The 3,000-foot-long pier once again assumes its role as Chicago's great place of public entertainment and culture. Among the many attractions is the 150-foot-tall Ferris wheel, a smaller version of George Washington Ferris's famous first wheel whose cabins carried 40 passengers at a time at the 1893 World's Columbian Exposition. The area in front is scheduled to be developed as Navy Pier Park. (Photo by author)

of the pier as a recreational and cultural center. The main features of the pier, the enormous ballroom at the east end and the headhouse at the west end, were restored, with the intervening buildings providing 170,000 square feet of exposition space and meeting rooms, as well as a huge entertainment center.

Although still incomplete at this writing, most of the facilities are now open, including the "Shops on the Dock," the Skyline Stage (a 1,500-seat outdoor theatre for major theatrical productions), a Family Pavilion, Crystal Gardens Indoor Botanical Park with 71 Mexican fan palm trees, Dockside Street Entertainment Area, a carousel, carnival-type rides, restaurants, food court, concessions, beer garden, Iwerks Theatre, the headquarters of public radio station WBEZ-FM, the Festival Hall Convention Center, and the Grand Ballroom. A boardwalk extends along the full length of the pier, but for the footsore a trolley-bus is also planned to shuttle visitors along its three-fifths-of-a-mile length.

Two major events are held annually in the 165,000 square feet of exhibition space of Festival Hall: In May, "Art 1996 Chicago" (with annual year change), America's largest international exposition of modern and contemporary art, with more than 90 U.S. and 85 international galleries represented; and Chicago's second annual exposition, "SOFA Chicago 1996" (*S*culpture, *O*bjects and *F*unctional *A*rt), which takes place in November, with a broad sweep of contemporary three-dimensional art. Scheduled to open later are a 1,500-seat performing arts center and a childrens' theatre, both under one roof.

One of the major attractions of Navy Pier is the wondrous new 150-foot-tall **Ferris wheel,** sponsored unmistakably by McDonald's. The continuously revolving six-seat cars present a built-in recorded history of Ferris wheels, and offer a brief, but breathtaking view of the city. The invention of George Washington Ferris, the first revolving wheel was the sensation of the 1893 World's Columbian Exposition. It was a much larger wheel, driven by a steam engine, with each compartment (not seat) holding 40 passengers, with one usually reserved for a brass band. The Ferris wheel at the Chicago Fair was later transported to the 1904 Louisiana Purchase Exposition in St. Louis.

At the east end of the pier is an anchor from the warship *Chicago,* commissioned in 1945, which saw service in Vietnam. New to the Pier is the **Chicago Children's Museum,** which moved from its former North Pier location and presents hands-on and interactive exhibits for children and their parents. It is said that the Museum has a collection of 200,000 Lego blocks. Cruise boats will also depart from Navy Pier, as they did 80 years ago.

Also planned is the reconstruction of what was formerly Navy Pier Park into Jane Addams Park, with a statue of the great social reformer in a landscaped area in front. But dominating the front traffic circle is the brand-new 200-foot-high geyser of **Navy Pier Fountain.**

Walk south along Streeter Drive (named for "Captain" George Wellington Streeter, the squatter who was the first settler of the area; *see* pages 213–214), past Lake Point Tower to the harbor at the mouth of the Chicago River.

The lakefront, looking south, presents excellent views of the Chicago skyline, including the Michigan Avenue "Cliff," and the skyscrapers of the Loop, as well as the Turning Basin—a widening of the mouth of the Chicago River, the lock, the Outer Drive Bridge, breakwater, and the landmark **Chicago Harbor Lighthouse,** which blinks red every five seconds at the south end of the north breakwater. On a clear day the Indiana shoreline with the smokestacks of the Hammond and Gary steel mills is clearly visible. Along the harbor are the docks of a number of sightseeing cruise lines. Look for the old steamboat *Captain Streeter,* tied up among the lake and river excursion boats.

This is a good opportunity to examine the striking **Lake Point Tower** (*1968, Schipporeit-Heinrich, with Graham, Anderson, Probst & White*), 505 N. Lake Shore Drive. This monumental metal-and-glass skyscraper was designed by two former students (and later, employees) of Ludwig Mies van der Rohe, George Schipporeit and John C. Heinrich, and is based on a 1921 sketch by Mies for a glass tower to be erected in Berlin. The revolutionary undulating curved-glass facade is somewhat different from the original unbuilt assymetrical plan, but as the young firm's first commission, it was a resounding success. As the world's first skyscraper with curving glass walls, the tower would become an enduring tribute to the "master" and his tradition of the metal and glass skyscraper. At 70 stories, it also was the world's tallest apartment building and probably the high-rise with the best uninterrupted lakefront views of the Chicago skyline.

The glistening three-lobed tower set at 120-degree angles, with its smooth fluid sweep and constantly changing light patterns, has been imitated many times, but never equalled. The bronze-toned aluminum and glass facade expresses the steel framework within, and when caught by the rays of early morning or late afternoon sunlight, the entire tower glows like an ethereal candle. In granting the building its Honor Award, the American Institute of Architects described the visual effect as "a highly refined, urbane interaction between translucent glass and light." However, whether intentional or not, the building is somewhat "unapproachable," constructed as it is on a podium several stories high, topped by a mini-park and containing parking facilities and some retail establishments exclusively for the tenants.

The open area near Lake Point Tower will soon be developed as Du Sable Park, in recognition of Chicago's first settler (*see* page 213).

Turn west on Illinois Street, pass under Lake Shore Drive, and at the other side of the Drive turn left and walk about 100 feet along the sidewalk to a staircase leading down to Ogden Slip, alongside the Chicago River.

(Right) Striking Lake Point Tower, at 505 N. Lake Shore Drive, a monumental 70-story metal-and-glass skyscraper apartment building, was designed by two former students of Mies van der Rohe, George Schipporeit and John C. Heinrich, and completed in 1968. The world's first high-rise with curving glass walls, it is an unmistakable landmark on the Chicago lakefront and an enduring tribute to the "master" and his tradition of the metal-and-glass skyscraper. (Photo by author)

North Pier Chicago, formerly a terminal warehouse and wholesale manufacturers' exhibition hall, was converted in 1990 to the North Pier Festival Market. Its prime location on Ogden Slip made it ideal for adaptive reuse for restaurants, cafes, fast-food shops, and a variety of specialty stores. It is a departure point for sightseeing boats, and also the home of the Bicycle Museum of America, located on the slip level. Towering over the complex at the rear is the grossly-out-of-scale North Pier Apartments. (Photo by author)

North Pier Chicago (*1905–1920, Christian Albert Eckstorm; renovation 1990, Booth/Hansen & Associates, with Austin Company*), 435 E. Illinois Street, has a long history. It was originally constructed as the North Pier Terminal Company, and later became the Pugh Terminal Warehouses. Through the years the structure was extended all the way to the lakefront. It first was the home of a number of wholesale manufacturers as a place to exhibit their wares. Later it became a storage warehouse complex when the Merchandise Mart and Furniture Mart moved into their own quarters. The location on Ogden Slip was very convenient to both Great Lakes shipping and railroad lines, and the area's warehouses extended westward almost to Michigan Avenue.

As a result of the renovation, the long red-brick building with its eight distinctive peaked towers has become one of the most popular spots in the city. Now dubbed the North Pier Festival Market, it houses on its three levels more than two dozen specialty and apparel shops, a variety of entertainment, plus a generous selection of dining and fast-food facilities. The conversion also includes four floors of office space. One of its attractions is the **Bicycle Museum of America,** on the slip level, with a collection of 140 bicycles from the 1800s to the present, a video presentation on the history of cycling, and a self-guided tour of the exhibits (admission $1.00; $2.00 for a guided tour). The museum's location in Chicago is significant. At the turn of the century Lake Street was termed "Bicycle Alley," because of the more than 60 manufacturers of bicycles and related components that were located within just one mile of each other.

During warm weather the outdoor cafes with their splendid views of the Chicago River and its rows of unusual buildings are a particularly favorite and lively gathering place. Look up at the pair of three-story glass galleries which adapt perfectly to the surroundings and whose functional rectilinear shape hearkens back to the old warehouse days. North Pier is also one of the departure points for Chicago River sightseeing boats, including one that offers an architectural/historical cruise.

New to North Pier is the **Chicago Academy of Sciences' Nature Museum,** which will remain here until a new building is completed at Fullerton Parkway and Cannon Drive in 1998. Among the exhibits are its Children's Gallery, the Water Works water quality testing laboratory, and "Energy: Choosing our Future," plus many changing exhibits. (Museum hours: Monday–Thursday 9:30 A.M.–4:30 P.M.; Friday to 8:00 P.M.; Saturday 10:00 A.M.–4:30 P.M.; Sunday 12:00 P.M.–4:30 P.M. Admission: $3.00 for adults, $2.00 for children ages 3–17 and seniors; children under three are free.)

After exploring North Pier, walk up to the second (street) level and exit on Illinois Street, and compare the facade with that on the river side. This side has a more finished appearance, since the other was merely the back side, and was not meant to impress. The warehouse loading docks were arranged along the Illinois Street side, and new, fan-shaped metal canopies have been added. Note the numbers above each former loading dock.

The 30-story former Time & Life Building (1968, Harry Weese & Associates), now known only by its street address, 541 N. Fairbanks Court, is easily recognized by its broad bands of bronze-tone mirrored glass windows framed in Cor-Ten steel. When completed, the building boasted the country's first bilevel elevators, designed to speed passenger loading and unloading. The system was later abandoned when flexible work hours were introduced. A major renovation by Perkins & Will was undertaken in 1989. (Photo by author)

Across Illinois Street, to the east, is the **Police Department Building,** formerly the Kraft-Phenix Cheese Company Building (*1938, Mundie, Jensen, Bourke & Havens*), whose entrance is around the far corner at 510 Peshtigo Court. The Kraft name is still visible on the tall smokestack. Incidentally, little Peshtigo Court is named for the town of Peshtigo, Wisconsin, where on the same day as Chicago's Great Fire of 1871, a much larger conflagration burned over much of six Wisconsin counties, destroying several towns in an unprecedented firestorm, and resulting in 1,152 deaths. (Just about 300 perished in the Chicago fire.)

Walk left to the end of North Pier, but before turning left again, look diagonally northwest to the modern building with the bright bronze-tinted ribbons of windows. At 541 N. Fairbanks Court, corner of E. Ohio Street, is the **former Time & Life Building** (*1968, Harry Weese & Associates; renovation 1989, Perkins & Will*), now known only by its street address. Seen from afar it is an imposing reinforced-concrete structure, with its mirrored glass windows framed in Cor-Ten steel, which has now weathered to a lush russet color. Note how the regular spacing of the seven bays and the horizontal arrangement of the windows is reminiscent of the Chicago school. While the building is beyond the itinerary of this tour, it is interesting to note that the 30-story building was the first in the country to install bilevel elevators, whose cabs were divided into an upper and lower section—the upper stopping on even-numbered floors and the lower on the odd-numbered. Access was from a two-story-high lobby. The plan was to decrease the number of elevator shafts by 30 percent without sacrificing the efficiency of service; however, the unique system was used only during rush hours. At other times the elevators would operate in the usual manner. Ultimately the double-decker plan was abandoned as flexible working hours became the rule.

Turn left on McClurg Court and walk around the end of Ogden Slip.

Take a moment to enjoy the view of North Pier again. Relax on one of the eight polished red-granite "chairs" of the sculpture *Seating for Eight,* by Scott Burton (1985). At the east end of North Pier is the high-rise **North Pier Apartment Tower,** (*1991, Dubin, Dubin & Moutoussamy, with Florian-Wierzbowski*), 474 N. Lake Shore Drive, a rather undistinguished 61-story building which was the first project in the Cityfront development project.

Turn around and examine **Cityfront Place** (*1991, Gelik Foran Associates*), 400, 440, and 480 N. McClurg Court, which represents a significant improvement in design. Directly across the street is the common entrance to the twin 12-story apartment buildings. At first glance it seems to disappear into the hill, but it connects to both Nos. 480 and 440. The twin midsize buildings are unusual for their circular multiwindow corner towers. Further south is the third member of the complex, No. 400, a 30-story dark-red brick and limestone-trim tower. It is set at a 45-degree angle from the street line in a rather remote site on a seven-story windowless "blind" podium, and its placement is somewhat reminiscent of the isolation of Lake Point Tower. This was the second major residential development of the Cityfront area—a project on 40 acres of riverfront land, which extends for several blocks to N. Michigan Avenue, described in Tour 6 (*see* pages 219–221). Note, too, the attractive street lighting that extends from North Pier and westward along the river. The design of these wrought-iron structures resembles miniature lighthouses or light buoys, and adds a lively nautical touch to the streetscape.

Continue in the same direction south along McClurg Court to the fountain overlooking the Chicago River.

The **Nicholas J. Melas Centennial Plaza, Fountain, and Water Arc** (*1989, Lohan Associates, George T. Kelly, supervising architectural planner*), according to the plaque, was dedicated by the employees of the Metropolitan Water Reclamation District of Greater Chicago, and honors its founding in 1889. It also memorializes the thousands of Chicagoans killed by epidemics in the days when the Chicago River carried raw sewage into the lake and polluted the drinking water supply. (*See* pages 106–107 to learn how the city performed the engineering feat of reversing the flow of the Chicago River.) The top of the red-granite pavilion symbolizes the point along the Chicago River at which the waters of the Chicago region flow east through the Great Lakes and the St. Lawrence River to the Atlantic Ocean, and just southwest of Chicago, at the

The famous Water Arc at Centennial Plaza shoots an 80-foot-high geyser across the 222-foot-wide Chicago River on a regular schedule from May to October. A collecting basin in the adjacent Centennial Fountain funnels water into a "cannon" that "fires" the stream with surprising intensity. Sightseeing boats plying the river must plan their schedules with some care to avoid drenching their passengers. Since the inauguration of the Centennial Fountain and Water Arc in 1989, it has become a major sightseeing attraction. (Photo by author)

The Sheraton Chicago Hotel & Towers, completed in 1992 from plans by Solomon Cordwell Buenz & Associates, occupies a prominent vantage point on the river. The facade expresses the steel structure in a simple grid pattern, and sheer walls of windows provide superb panoramic views for the 1,200 guest rooms. The unique curved tower sections are reminiscent of some of the early buildings of the Chicago school, such as the Loop's Old Colony Building. The hotel boasts the largest ballroom in the Midwest. In the foreground are Centennial Fountain's delightful cascades and pool. (Photo by author)

"continental divide," where the waters flow to the Mississippi River and the Gulf of Mexico. Linkage of these two great water systems at Chicago on the completion of the Chicago Sanitary and Ship Canal in 1900 attracted commerce, and destined the city to become a world metropolis. A collecting basin in the fountain funnels water into a "cannon" that "fires" an astonishing 80-foot-high Water Arc across the 222-foot-wide river on a regular schedule. The fountain operates from May 1 to October 27, from 10:00 A.M. to 12:10 A.M. The water arc is activated during the first 10 minutes of each hour (except 3:00 P.M. and 4:00 P.M., or during high winds).

According to Cityfront Center's master developer, Chicago Dock & Canal Trust, the riverwalk, or esplanade, will be extended further east when the vacant eight-acre parcel to the left is developed with apartment buildings.

To the east is the double-deck **Outer Drive Bridge** (*1937*), carrying Lake Shore Drive, the major north-south shorefront highway, over the Chicago River. Although the Chicago River enters Lake Michigan just beyond the harbor, its original path curved south, with the waters emptying into the lake about where Monroe Street is today. One of the engineers in charge of the challenging project to shift the mouth of the river to its present position was Jefferson Davis, then an officer in the U.S. Army, and later president of the Confederacy.

This is the end of the tour. Follow the scenic River Walk, past the Sheraton Chicago Hotel, to the base of the Michigan Avenue Bridge, where a staircase leads up to Pioneer Court, the grand plaza facing Michigan Avenue. Both northbound and southbound buses stop within a block.

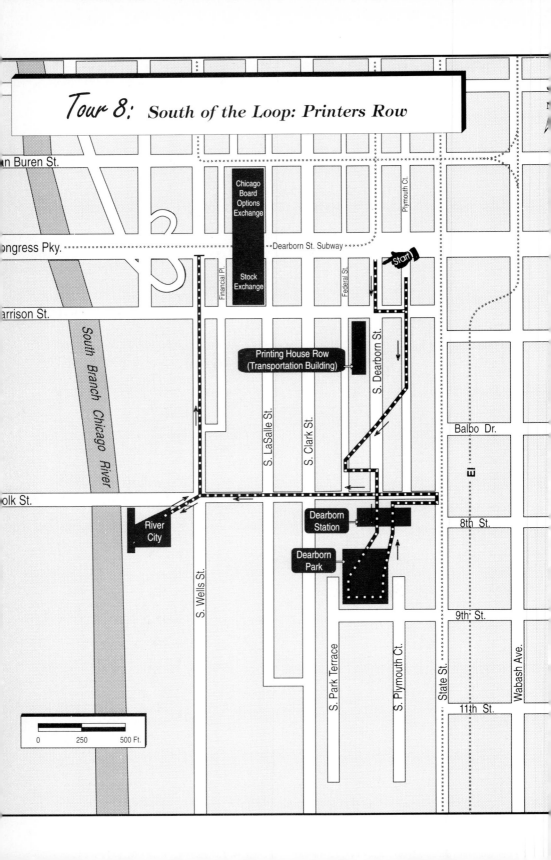

Tour 8: South of the Loop: Printers Row

an Buren St.

ongress Pky.

Chicago Board Options Exchange

Dearborn St. Subway

Start

arrison St.

Stock Exchange

Financial Pl.

Federal St.

S. Dearborn St.

South Branch Chicago River

Printing House Row
(Transportation Building)

S. LaSalle St.

S. Clark St.

Balbo Dr.

El

olk St.

River City

Dearborn Station

8th St.

Dearborn Park

9th St.

S. Wells St.

S. Park Terrace

S. Plymouth Ct.

State St.

Wabash Ave.

11th St.

Plymouth Ct.

0   250   500 Ft.

8. South of the Loop: Printers Row

The tour begins at the southwest corner of S. Dearborn Street and W. Congress Parkway, one block south of W. Van Buren Street, at the southern edge of the Loop. If you are walking south on Dearborn Street, you might want to refer to Tour 1, which includes a description of three particularly interesting buildings in the first block, the Old Colony, the Plymouth, and the Manhattan buildings (*see* pages 14–16).

The two blocks of Dearborn Street, from Congress Parkway to Polk Street, and the adjacent parallel Plymouth Court and Federal Street were the heart of the printing trades district from the mid-1880s through the late-1950s. The opening in 1885 of the Dearborn Street railroad station provided convenient street access to the loading docks of the terminal for delivery of paper, ink, typefaces, and other printing supplies, as well as for the outgoing finished publications. The buildings that were erected for the printing industry required strong load-bearing qualities to accommodate the heavy linotype machines and printing presses, as well as appropriate street space for loading and unloading delivery wagons, and their survival today is a tribute to the solidity of their construction. These buildings also required good lighting for the editorial staff's workrooms, as well as for the book binding, much of which was done by hand; hence the design of the structures also called for large expanses of windows. By the mid-1890s Chicago was recognized as the printing capital of America, and the narrow streets south of the Loop boasted the city's highest concentration of printing establishments, virtually all of which in recent years have been converted to residential buildings and office lofts.

Coincident with the nation's industrial growth and expansion during the last two decades of the 19th century, there developed a type of commercial architecture today referred to as "Industrial Romanesque Revival" that employed the recently developed steel-frame construction technology (invented, incidentally, here in Chicago by native architect, William LeBaron Jenney; *see* page 34). These new structures, no longer restricted in height by load-bearing walls, were often massive and quite tall. The influence of the Romanesque Revival movement, credited in large measure to Boston architect Henry Hobson Richardson, can readily be seen in many features of the buildings' facades—heavy rustication, massive bases, corbel tables, clustered colonettes, arched entrances, etc., with liberal use of broad expanses of dark-red brick adorned with ornamental terra cotta—often creating a castellated effect and giving these structures an imposing quality which is evident to this very day. The effective and influential use of the Romanesque Revival style is immediately apparent in the tower of the former Dearborn Street Station, which rises dramatically at the end of Dearborn Street and will be seen close at hand later in the tour.

With the widening of Congress Parkway in the decade 1945–1955 to complete an expressway link, and the resultant loss of a number of buildings on Dearborn and adjacent streets, together with the gradual shift of the printing industry to locations more appropriate to modern technology and truck transportation, the neighborhood went into rapid decline. The closing of the railroad terminal in 1971 was the final nail in the coffin. Then in the late 1970s an extensive real estate development called Dearborn Park, which included the Dearborn Station and the neighborhood to the south, sparked a major renaissance in the area to the north. One of the developers who took a big risk by investing in the former printing house district was architect Harry Weese, who understood the historic significance of the area and was convinced of its future viability through adaptive reuse. He prepared the nomination petition which led to the placement in 1978 of the **South Dearborn Street–Printing House Row Historic District** on the National Register of Historic Places. His gamble paid off, for the intervening years have witnessed a revitalization of the neighborhood for commercial and, for the first time, residential development. (The historic district includes an area roughly bounded by Taylor, Polk, Wells, and State streets, and Congress Parkway.)

Today, Printers Row has become a highly desirable and upscale place to live, and confidence in its future was confirmed by the recent remodeling of a group of former commercial structures on Dearborn Street by the Hyatt Corporation into an elegant hotel. In June, S. Dearborn Street between Harrison and Polk streets is the site of the annual Printers Row Book Fair, a festive event where book dealers display their wares, and demonstrations are given on the art of papermaking and bookbinding, accompanied by the usual aggregation of food vendors and street performers.

Begin the tour by walking south on the right (west) side of S. Dearborn Street.

The **Old Franklin Building** (*1887, Baumann & Lotz; renovation 1983, Booth/ Hansen & Associates*), 525 S. Dearborn Street, once home to the printing industry, has been adaptively remodeled as a multifamily residential building with commercial establishments on the ground floor. The typical dark-red brick facade is divided into seven bays of three windows each, separated by brick piers, with a central bay. Iron spandrels, supported by cast-iron columns which serve as mullions, separate the windows. A simple cornice sits above the conventional Romanesque Revival–style corbel table.

Immediately south is the **Terminals Building,** once the Ellsworth Building (*1892, John Mills Van Osdel & Company; renovation 1986, Community Resources Corporation, with Harry Weese & Associates*), 537 S. Dearborn Street. The 14-story building was the last one designed by Van Osdel, the architect who designed Chicago's first City Hall and many of the city's noteworthy buildings before and just after the Great Fire of 1871. Most noticeable is the very heavily rusticated base and the two rows of projecting oriels. Above the square entrance is an ornate carved lintel, unfortunately in a sadly deteriorating condition. The cornice, which would have added much to the building's recently spruced-up appearance, has been removed. Like its neighbor, it too has been remodeled for residential tenants and for ground-floor commercial use.

Across the street is an interesting adaptive reuse of two commercial buildings and the complete reconstruction of a third. From right to left: **500 S. Dearborn Street,** once the Morton Hotel (*1987, Booth/Hansen & Associates*), has modified Chicago windows set neatly into a tan concrete facade. **530 S. Dearborn Street,** the **Duplicator Building** (*1886, Edward P. Baumann; reconstruction 1987, Booth/Hansen & Associates*), a seven-story structure named for a former printing company, was a commercial loft building similar to the Old Franklin Building. The third member of the triumvirate, **538 S. Dearborn Street,** the **Morton Building** (*1896, Jenney & Mundie; renovation 1987, Booth/Hansen & Associates*), was built for the Morton Salt Company. Similar to the Terminals Building, it displays polygonal bays, but in this case they are supported by atlantes, or Atlas-like figures. The facade is of light-brown brick with splayed lintels above the windows. The two-story-high entrance is surmounted by an ornate arch. (Note that one of the partners in the design of the original building was the progenitor of the modern skyscraper, William LeBaron Jenney.) The 12-story building, unlike its neighbors, displays elements of the Renaissance Revival style, popularized by the World's Columbian Exposition of 1893. The Morton Company is still remembered for its boxes of salt with the picture of a little girl carrying an umbrella and spilling salt, with the immortal slogan, "When it rains, it pours."

In the 1986 renovation, all three buildings were joined together to form the **Hyatt on Printers Row.** Take a peek inside and note how the comfortable lobby, almost invisible from the street, runs across two buildings, with the ground floor of No. 500 occupied by the hotel's Prairie Restaurant.

Adjacent to the south is the landmark **Pontiac Building** (*1891, Holabird & Roche; renovation 1985, Booth/Hansen & Associates*), 542 S. Dearborn Street. The building has the distinction of being Holabird & Roche's oldest surviving structure in Chicago. With its vertical columns of oriels, it is vaguely reminiscent of Burnham & Root's Monadnock Block, a few blocks to the north; however this is a steel-framework structure, whereas the Burnham & Root half of the Monadnock is load-bearing. Note that the oriels, a novelty for Holabird & Roche, extend from the 3rd to the 13th floor and are three-windows wide and hide internal steel mullions necessary for support. A decorative terra-cotta band under the third floor gives the impression of support to the oriels. Also noticeable are the solid brick piers that mark each corner. The Booth/Hansen renovation also included replication of the original ground-floor storefronts. The Pontiac Building was also the site of the nation's first cafeteria, which was established in the Depression years of the 1890s by an organization called Noonday Rest, whose members were mostly women in the printing trades.

The nondescript two-story green building across the street, at the northeast corner of Harrison Street, which also accommodates an espresso bar, houses the offices of Booth/Hansen, the architects responsible for much of the Printers Row renovation.

Turn left (east) on Harrison Street one block to Plymouth Court, and turn left.

Just up from "Tom's Grill," at the corner, which we'll look at in a minute, is another former commercial building, adaptively reused as an apartment house. The former plant of the Merganthaler Linotype Company is now the **Merganthaler Loft Condominiums** (*1886, architect unknown; renovation 1917, Schmidt, Garden & Martin; renovation 1979, Kenneth A. Schroeder & Associates*), 531 S.

Talk about adaptive reuse! Tom's Grill, once a sandwich shop, was gutted by the developers of the adjacent Merganthaler Loft Condominium, and its skeleton incorporated into the site as a bit of avant-garde art (?). There is even a tree growing in the middle of it, and further to the right, a garage door without a garage, merely a rolltop door that provides access to the parking lot. The former Merganthaler Linotype Company, whose building was erected in 1886, was converted to a condo, along with the amusing additions, by Kenneth Schroeder & Associates in 1979. (Photo by author)

Plymouth Court. Ottmar Merganthaler, of New York, was the inventor of the linotype machine in 1884, the first mechanical typesetter. It revolutionized the printing trades by permitting lines of type to be produced instantly from molten lead by a machine operator working at a typewriter keyboard. In the renovation, Schroeder installed a red-painted post-and-lintel doorway that incorporates two vertical posts topped by an I-beam. He also restored the original brickwork, and installed four unusual wedge-shaped bay windows on the south side. In the lobby is a small "sculpture" made from various pieces of metal type. But a big attention-getter is not the building itself, but the humorous—some say "flaky"—incorporation of Tom's Grill into the site plan. Is it sculpture, avant-garde art, a put-on . . . ? Anyway, see for yourself what remains of the old sandwich shop and how the owner has fit its red-brick skeleton into the overall plan—it even has a tree growing in the middle—and how tenants drive into their fenced-in parking lot by raising a rolltop door that is not part of any building, but serves merely as a freestanding gate.

Cross W. Harrison Street and continue south on S. Plymouth Court.

Looking to the left (east), the white reinforced-concrete building on the next block (State Street) is the **William Jones Commercial High School** (*1965–1968, Perkins & Will*), 606 S. State Street, with its attached two-story gymnasium and auditorium building fronting on Plymouth Court.

A bit further down the block are a pair of turn-of-the-century commercial buildings, the **Moser Building** (*1909, Holabird & Roche; renovation 1987, Lisec & Biederman*), 621 S. Plymouth Court, and the **Pope Building** (*1904, H. G. Hodgkins; renovation 1986, Lisec & Biederman*), 633 S. Plymouth Court. The Moser Building, a nine-story red-brick structure. six bays wide with groups of three windows in each, was built for the Moser Paper Company, an important supplier for the printers in the neighborhood. Note the incised quadrangles in the spandrels and a stylized corbel table under a very minimal cornice. The company logo can still be seen in the lobby floor.

The adjacent Pope Building is 12 stories high with five bays, whose bright-green window frames, which were replaced in the renovation, create the impression of Chicago windows. The cornice, alas, was not replaced. Note the terra-cotta torches, a common symbol in the printing industry, atop the brick piers.

Turn right and walk directly through the parking lot toward Dearborn Street, and take another look at the Moser and Pope buildings, and continue to the west side of Dearborn Street.

On the west side of S. Dearborn Street is the **Transportation Building** (*1911, William Strippelman; renovation 1980, Booth/Hansen*), 600 S. Dearborn Street. At first glance this appears to be a blockbuster of a building with its length of 20 bays; however a look at its width from the mini-park at its south end reveals that it is only four bays wide, about 50 feet, since S. Federal Street is so close behind. The 22-story building, adaptively reused as a 294-apartment

The Transportation Building, at 600 S. Dearborn Street, is deceptively massive. Although it is a rather tall 22 stories high and 20 bays wide, because of its close proximity to S. Federal Street in the rear, it is only four bays wide! Erected in 1911, it was renovated in 1980 into a 294-apartment residential building. (Photo by author)

residence, was originally named because of its proximity to Dearborn Station and the many tenants whose business was related to the transportation industry. The tan-gray brickwork has been restored and cleaned, but the building's vertical divisions of rough brick still do not break up the oppressive horizontality. The conversion of the Transportation Building, as well as the nearby Borland Buildings three years later, provided significant impetus to the development of Printers Row.

Cut through the mini-park to S. Federal Street for a brief look at:

Printers Square, formerly the Borland Manufacturing Buildings (*1909, Frost & Granger; 1912, Charles S. Frost; 1928, Charles C. Henderson; renovation 1983, Louis Arthur Weiss*), 600–780 S. Federal Street, has its main entrance at No. 700. A group of five separate, but interconnected tan-brick loft buildings, they vary in height—the northern two are 8 stories high, the middle one 9, and the two at the south end, 12. They were constructed over a 19-year period, and converted in 1983 into a single 356-unit luxury apartment complex, with underground parking, plus some office and retail space.

Return through the little park to the near sidewalk on Dearborn Street.

Looking at the row of industrial buildings on the east side, left to right:
Grace Place (*ca. 1915, architect unknown*), 637 S. Dearborn Street, whose original industrial appearance belies its present purpose, is a converted church

shared by the Grace Episcopal Church and Christ the King Lutheran Church, whose individual congregations are too small to warrant a separate house of worship. Peek inside at the ground-floor meeting room which still retains the original wooden-beam ceiling. Upstairs, the sanctuary is encircled by a separate wall pierced with Gothic-style pointed-arch windows. Above, a skylight projects light onto the altar. Note how the sanctuary's cross behind the pulpit is formed by a sheet-metal bracket supporting the beam, a curious arrangement which did not escape the notice of Ira J. Bach, the late Landmarks Commissioner and author of *Chicago on Foot,* who commented, "Talk about melding form and function!"

The **Donohue Building** (*1883, Julius Speyer; renovation 1976, Harry Weese & Associates*), 701–721 S. Dearborn Street, was the first of the many printing industry buildings built in the area, and one of the first to be converted to residential apartments. The nine-bay-wide structure was erected in the typical Industrial Romanesque Revival style, and has a number of interesting features. Most notable is the impressive arched entranceway of granite and sandstone, with one-story arched arcade above. Unfortunately, the space above the doorway was replaced with a most unauthentic "mosaic." Also unfortunate is the missing tower above the central bay (the flagpole is an unworthy substitute), as well as what must have been a unifying cornice. The windows, in various arrangements, are punched out, with ornamental carved terra-cotta spandrels between many of them. The building leans ever so slightly, but that only adds to the sense of antiquity. Look into the lobby of the main entrance and notice the "birdcage" elevator, with a stated capacity of only four persons. Aptly named, it is a fascinating survivor, and its archaic motor can be heard even outside.

Note the doorstep of No. 711 which is actually a cast-iron vault cover. It displays the typical glass disks whose purpose was to allow light to penetrate into dimly lit basements, before the advent of electricity. The name of the iron foundry (Dauchy Co. Chicago) and its patent year (1883) are still clearly legible. The system was invented by Thaddeus Hyatt in 1845, in New York, for installation in sidewalk vaults, and although now rather rare, some vault covers still survive in Chicago, particularly in doorways. To the right, above the entrance to No. 721, note the black octagonal cast-iron counterweight at the end of the fire escape mechanism; it, too, is stamped with the name of the foundry, "J. T. Oowles & Co., established 1876, Chicago."

The adjacent **Donohue Building Annex** (*1913, Alfred S. Alschuler; renovation 1976, Harry Weese & Associates*), 727 S. Dearborn Street, was converted by the same architect as its neighbor. Although erected 30 years later, and revealing a simpler, more straightforward style, it is nonetheless harmonious with the Donohue Building.

Across Dearborn Street, at No. 714, is the **Rowe Building** (*ca. 1882 and attributed to William LeBaron Jenney; renovation 1980, Kenneth Schroeder, George Hinds, and Philip Kupritz*), a red-brick eight-story former loft building (with a modern addition on the roof), named for an early publishing establishment. The restoration was well executed, giving the building its original pristine appearance. In style it is Romanesque Revival, with three bays of two windows each. The mullions are of cast iron, as are the two central piers. At each end are rough-cut stone quoins. Below the third, fifth, and seventh floors, and the cornice, is a corbel table, and above the fifth floor are round arches, and at the seventh floor, paired columns supporting carved limestone blocks. Note the cast-iron counterweight at the base of the fire escape, as on the Donohue Building, but this one is smaller, and made by another foundry. You might want to explore Sandmeyer's Bookstore, the largest in the neighborhood, with an extensive Chicago stock, and a favorite local browsing spot.

To its left is the delightful **Second Franklin Building** (*1912, George C. Nimmons; renovation 1987, Lisec & Biederman*), 720 S. Dearborn Street, its 13-story dark-red brick facade adorned with a multitude of polychrome tile designs. Colorful tile ornamentation appears in every spandrel between triple windows. A gently-sloping gable, replete with colorful tilework, adds to the imposing appearance. Nine brick piers are set with tapering terra-cotta columnar designs terminating in small square ornamental "capitals." Above the ground-floor windows, colored tiles portray artisans working at the various printing trades, and above the entrance is a lovely terra-cotta mural entitled *The First Impression,* illustrating the initial "hot off the press" printing of a large document. Around the master printer and his obviously satisfied client in this medieval print shop, are the hand press, the font case, the pressman, and the printer's devil (the young man).

The entranceway is particularly charming, with the twin tile plaques announcing the Franklin Company: "Designing, Engraving, Electrotyping," and to the right, "Catalog and Booklet Printing." The entry is recessed and lined with colorful terra-cotta tiles, and over the door: "The Excellence of Every Art Must Consist in the Complete Accomplishment of its Purpose." The actual design for the terra-cotta tilework was done by Oskar Gross. Since architect Nimmons was particularly fond of the Prairie Style, which incorporated polychrome ornamentation, many such examples can be seen on his commercial buildings.

At Polk Street turn left (east) one block to Plymouth Court, and across the street, just to the left is:

The **former Lakeside Press Building,** now the Columbia College Residence Center, built as the Plymouth-Polk Building (*1897, 1902, Howard Van Doren Shaw, with Samuel A. Treat; renovation 1986, 1993, Lisec & Biederman*), 731 S. Plymouth Court. Between 1986 and 1993 the building was a residential apartment house. This is arguably the most elegant of the former printing plants in the area, and was designed by Shaw as his first commercial venture for R. R.

(Right) The charming entrance to the Second Franklin Building (1912, George C. Nimmons) displays the original tile plaques announcing the Franklin Company. There are also colorful tiles surrounding the portal as well as a superb terra-cotta mural above the door entitled The First Impression *that portrays a medieval print shop with a client looking approvingly at the initial printing of a large document. (Photo by author)*

THE FRANKLIN COMPANY

DESIGNING
ENGRAVING
ELECTROTYPING

THE·EXCELLENCE·OF·EVERY·ART
MUST·CONSIST·IN·THE·COMPLETE
ACCOMPLISHMENT·OF·ITS·PURPOSE

The colophon of the renowned Lakeside Press, in the form of a large terra-cotta plaque, adorns the upper facade of the former Lakeside Press Building, at 731 S. Plymouth Court. The Press has since been absorbed by R. R. Donnelley & Sons, the largest printing organization in the country. The plaque's motif represents a Potawatomi Indian chief against the background of Fort Dearborn, reiterating Lakeside Press's ties with the city of Chicago. The 1897 building has been adaptively reused as the Columbia College Residence Center. (Photo by author)

Donnelley & Sons, who were noted for the quality architecture of their printing plants, and who to this very day operate the largest printing organization in the country. (*See* their new striking skyscraper offices at 77 W. Wacker Drive, pages 146, 153, and 155). The bright-red-brick building is in pristine condition, with eight bays of three windows and cast-iron spandrels between floors three and six. Above the piers are oval plaques with an Indian chief and relief of Fort Dearborn, the colophon of the Lakeside Press. Above the top floor's arched windows are plaques illustrating famous historical printer's marks. The elaborately detailed facade is continued on the Polk Street side as well.

The broad entrance, two bays wide, also displays the Lakeside Press design, this time framed by a pair of rampant lions, and on the floor above, the windows are enframed with square limestone columns. Four large circular plaques represent the colophons of some of the most noteworthy presses in the history of American book printing, from left to right: McClurg (Chicago), De Vinne (New York), Riverside (Cambridge, Mass.), and Harper's (New York)—the latter with Harper's traditional torch and the Greek inscription, "Those bearing torches should pass them on to others."

Before crossing Polk Street, stand on the north side for a moment for an overall view of:

Dearborn Station (*1885, Cyrus L. W. Eidlitz; renovation and conversion 1983, Kaplan/McLaughlin/Diaz, with Hasbrouck Hunderman*). Now known as the Dearborn Station Galleria, this is the oldest surviving railroad station building in Chicago and the only one from the 19th century, when there were six major downtown railroad terminals and one at nearby Roosevelt Road. Train service ended in 1971, and the station was converted into a shopping mall in 1985. The rail yards and train shed were removed in 1976, and only the head-house of the former terminal remains. The clocktower stands as the center-piece of the neighborhood and the renovated station serves as a conspicuous transition between the renovated Printers Row district and the Dearborn Park development area to the south.

Although now a delightful "artifact," the former station remains a signifi-cant architectural landmark and a fine example of Italian Romanesque Revival style. The building suffered a disastrous fire in 1922 which burned off its distinctive peaked roof and destroyed the original Flemish Renaissance cupola. The rebuilt clocktower now rises like a Tuscan campanile, and in many ways symbolizes the rebirth of the neighborhood. The pressed red-brick facade is highlighted by horizontal courses of grooved bricks with considerable carved terra-cotta ornamentation. The base of the forward-projecting tower is of contrasting rough-cut granite, as are the arched entrances at each end. The third floor of the center section is an addition. The atmosphere of the old train station is still present—outside with the metal canopies over the entrances and the typical front plaza, and inside with old baggage wagons and a variety of railroad motifs and logos of some of the railroads that once served the Dear-born Station.

The central galleria, however, is a let-down. Its jarring "modern" aluminum and glass atrium was designed to recall the former station's main waiting room, but doesn't. From the rear, the pyramidal metal structure and rear "rotunda" are not harmonious with the elegant north facade. The result is just a banal shopping mall, with a handful of retail and business establishments. Walk through, and see for yourself. Then exit from the rear.

The master plan for **Dearborn Park,** by Skidmore, Owings & Merrill and a number of other architectural firms (including Booth/Hansen & Associates, Hammond, Beeby & Babka, and others), for the development of the area for-merly occupied by railroad yards and associated rail facilities south of Dear-born Station, dates to the mid-1970s. It was divided into two phases, with the 20-acre section north of Roosevelt Road to be developed first. The second phase was begun in 1988. The plan called for a mix of different size buildings, ranging from two- and three-story town houses, mid-rise buildings, to high-

(Pages 288–289) Dearborn Station, once one of Chicago's major railroad terminals, was converted in 1983 to the Dearborn Station Galleria, a shopping mall. As the oldest surviving railroad terminal building in the city, it was one of six downtown terminals. The structure (left photo), designed in 1885, suffered a disastrous fire in 1922 which destroyed the distinctive peaked roof and the original Flemish Renaissance cupola and clock of the 166-foot tower. The restored building's tower and rebuilt clock rises today like a Tuscan campanile. Before it closed, the terminal had been serving seven railroads, including the transcontinental trains of the Santa Fe and such major lines as the Erie, Wabash, and Grand Trunk. The last train departed Dearborn Station in 1971, and the tracks and platforms were removed. In their place in two phases beginning in 1988, rose a 1,200-unit complex called Dearborn Park, consisting of town houses and mid-rise apartment buildings surrounding an enclosed park. (Left, Chicago Historical Society; right, photo by author)

Polk Street Depot.

rises, all grouped around a central landscaped park. The approximately 1,200-unit development, with only limited access from outside streets, and with many internal cul-de-sacs, gives the impression of a self-contained, cohesive community. The tallest buildings, which are situated along the perimeter, further enhance the feeling of a private enclave. The success of the project is evident in the enthusiastic community life and active support by its multi-ethnic and economically diverse residents.

This tour will concern itself only briefly with the northern section of Dearborn Park, as it is well beyond the Printers Row district. Turn right on leaving from the rear of Dearborn Station and follow the roadway on what would have been the extension of S. Federal Street, counterclockwise around the park. To the right are red-brick eight-story mid-rise buildings, and further along are the two-story town houses, all painted white. The color contrast was done deliberately to add character and break up the traditional monotony of red-brick housing developments. Note the little courtyards created by the dead ends surrounded by the two- and three-story town houses, each with its own landscaping. The effect is one of a small uncrowded village. The park itself is obviously people-friendly and lends itself to rest and relaxation as well as to some limited recreation for youngsters. Note the concrete bird house (presently with tenants), as the road swings east toward the only entrance, at Ninth Street. A pair of 22-story high-rises bracket the street and mark the entrance to the community. Continue to follow the road as it swings north and back to Dearborn Station. The east side of the station is also well preserved, and with a little imagination, one can almost hear the sounds of the locomotives and train whistles on the other side of the building.

At W. Polk Street, turn right (east) and walk to the corner of S. State Street for a brief look at the high-rise that closes off Polk Street.

This 330-apartment behemoth across State Street, **Two East Eighth** (*1984, Seymour Goldstein*), named for its address, is a conventional steel-frame curtain-wall building with reflective glass, but its facade is interesting for its undulating wedge-shaped wall consisting of four sets of wedges with eight black-framed windows on each plane. The 27-story tower is capped by a flat concrete cornice, and the ground-level retail establishments are housed in a projecting glass-enclosed section, with an unusual arrangement of exterior neo-Classic columns.

In the mid-19th century the area south of the Loop became its most notorious red-light section. Known as the **Levee Vice District,** the neighborhood for several blocks south of Van Buren Street along State, Clark, and Wabash became the center for prostitution, gambling, crime, and political corruption. After the turn of the century the Levee, as it was called, moved further south before disappearing in the 1920s.

Return to Dearborn Station and continue west on W. Polk Street for a few short blocks to S. Wells Street, and turn left (south).

No visit to the Printers Row area would be complete without a visit to the striking **River City** apartment complex (*1986, Bertrand Goldberg Associates*), 800 S. Wells Street. The steel-reinforced cast-in-place concrete structure with its S-shape plan and distinctive clusters of semicircular bay windows is a conspicuous landmark on the city skyline. Rising like a cluster of cumulus clouds on the Chicago River, the curvilinear complex is set on concrete piers above a four-story base, incorporating 446 rental apartments and extensive commercial space. Within the 17-story building is a stunning 10-story atrium called "River Road," which snakes along a landscaped course between towering rows of balconies and under connecting skybridges, all gently lit from above by a slanted frosted-glass roof. Both within and without, the balconies and windows maintain their singular 12-foot-high "eyebrow" shape. On the river side is a 62-slip marina filled with yachts of all descriptions.

The gray-granite arcaded wall on the east side of the building on Wells Street is all that remains of a bridge that once crossed the tracks of the Baltimore & Ohio Railroad, which the architect adapted for the entrance into River City. Enter through the first large arch which opens into an oval driveway where the management maintains free shuttle buses to the Loop for its tenants. Enter the

The imposing River City apartment complex sits grandly on the Chicago River just south of the Loop. A conspicuous landmark on the city skyline since 1986, its revolutionary curvilinear design is a tribute to the creativity of architect Bertrand Goldberg. The steel-reinforced cast-in-place concrete structure, erected on an S-shaped plan, employs clusters of semicircular bay windows and balconies in a singular "eyebrow" shape, with the entire complex set on concrete piers above a 4-story base. The 17-story building incorporates 446 rental apartments and extensive commercial space, as well as a 62-slip marina. Within is a 10-story atrium called River Road whose path follows the serpentine pattern of the exterior. (Photo by author)

Chicago's Grand Central Station, designed by Solon S. Beman and completed in 1890, was considered the city's most beautiful railroad terminal. Its towering 250-foot campanile was visible for miles, and the massive and ornate structure was not only functional, but a monumental piece of architecture that exuded strength and dependability. The station, which stood at the southwest corner of S. Wells and W. Harrison streets, served the SOO Line, the Baltimore & Ohio, and the Chesapeake & Ohio railroads. Like the nearby Dearborn Station, it saw its last passenger train depart in 1971, but unlike Dearborn's fortunate survival, Grand Central was quickly demolished a few months afterward, with only a weed-strewn lot to mark the site. (Photo by Kaufman & Fabry, Chicago. State Historical Society of Wisconsin, Neg. No. Whi(X3)50129)

lobby and look out on the river. Even the huge sofa imitates the curving shape of the building. Visitors should remember that this is *not* a public space, so please be discreet; and if you wish to see the fascinating River Road upstairs, it will be necessary to have the receptionist call the Management Office for permission. Times being what they are, building security is quite tight. Afterward, you can walk around the complex and see the river and the marina close at hand. The project is another of architect Goldberg's typical "circular" designs. (*See* Marina Towers in Tour 4, pages 148–150, and the Prentice Women's Hospital–Northwestern University Institute of Psychiatry Building in Tour 7, pages 257–259.)

Return to S. Wells Street and walk north toward the Loop.

The corner of W. Harrison Street, one block north, is the **site of Grand Central Station** (*1890, Solon S. Beman*), one of Chicago's seven former major railroad terminals and now just a weed-strewn lot. Not a single trace remains of that imposing and once busy station that served the crack trains of the Baltimore & Ohio, Chesapeake & Ohio, and SOO Lines—railroads that were forced to abandon their passenger service as the result of America's love affair with the automobile. These railroads were merged into other railroad entities for freight service only. The last passenger train departed from Grand Central in 1971 the same year that saw the demise of Dearborn Station, and the ornate building—considered Chicago's most beautiful railroad terminal—was demolished a few months later; a somewhat melancholy note on which to end the tour.

End of the tour. Follow S. Wells Street two blocks north to the Loop.

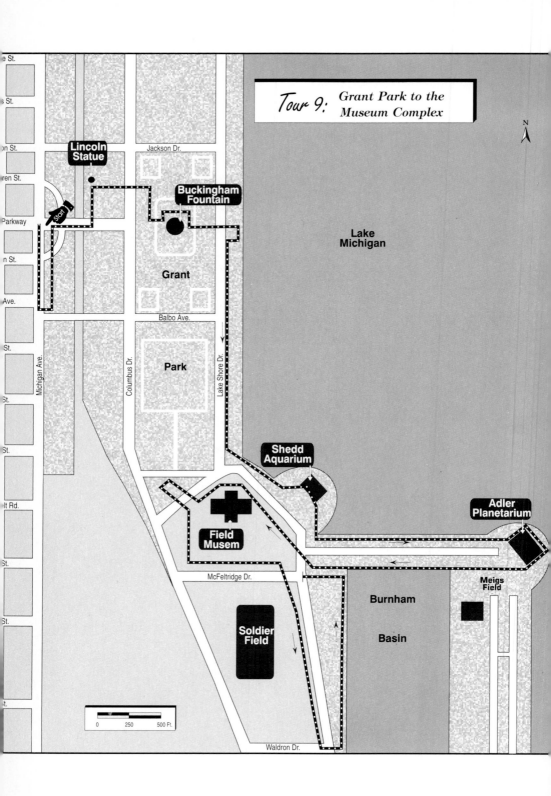

Tour 9: *Grant Park to the Museum Complex*

Lincoln Statue

Jackson Dr.

Buckingham Fountain

Lake Michigan

Start

Parkway

Grant

Balbo Ave.

Michigan Ave.

Columbus Dr.

Park

Lake Shore Dr.

Shedd Aquarium

Field Musem

Adler Planetarium

McFeltridge Dr.

Meigs Field

Burnham

Basin

Soldier Field

Waldron Dr.

0   250   500 Ft.

N

9. Grant Park to the Museum Complex

The tour begins at the Congress Parkway entrance to Grant Park on S. Michigan Avenue.

Grant Park, was named for the 18th president of the United States, Ulysses S. Grant, who before and after the Civil War lived in Galena, Illinois. The park, affectionately called "Chicago's front yard," graces the downtown lakefront with over 300 acres of lawns, gardens, trees, shrubs, and paths, built mostly on landfill. As early as 1835 the federal government ceded the land east of State Street south of the Chicago River to the Illinois & Michigan Canal Commission, which then began to develop the land by selling lots. Their 1836 subdivision map would have great impact on the future development of the park, as the area east of Michigan Avenue south of Randolph Street was designated to be a "public ground, forever to remain vacant of buildings," a requirement ignored, however, for more than half a century. Eleven years later the "public ground" was named Lake Park. In 1852, the Illinois Central Railroad obtained permission to build an offshore trestle to bring its commuter trains more directly into the city, in exchange for which they would construct a breakwater to prevent further shore erosion. As a result, natural land filling began as lake currents deposited sand in the intervening space. After the Great Fire of 1871 the area became a dumping ground for tons of rubble and debris to add further to the landfill. Little development took place in the next two decades, except for the construction of a pair of federal armories and a growing agglomeration of squatters' shacks, livery stables, plus the many tracks and sidings of the smoky ground-level Illinois Central Railroad.

Early in the 1890s, mail-order mogul Aaron Montgomery Ward, who had just moved his business to Michigan Avenue, was enraged by the abuse of the lakefront, and declared war on the city fathers with a legal battle to compel them to clean up the lakefront and protect its status as open land (*see* page 202). After a 21-year series of lawsuits, Ward ultimately prevailed, and all building incursions were removed, with the sole exception of the new Art Institute building whose construction had been agreed on in 1893. In the meantime the World's Columbian Exposition, planned for 1892 to celebrate the 400th anniversary of Columbus's arrival in the New World, opened a year late in the south end of the park, and was a stunning triumph. In 1906 a committee was appointed to develop a plan, not only for the park, but for the entire city.

Daniel H. Burnham, whose reputation had been firmly established as a progenitor of the Chicago school of architecture and as the principal designer of the Columbian Exposition, was called on to come up with the plan. Together with his associate, Edward H. Bennett, their famous Plan of Chicago was born. Three years later the city approved what would be recognized as the most influential city planning document ever produced, and its adoption in 1910 influenced the direction of city development nationwide for years afterward. The **1909 Plan of Chicago** envisioned a major east-west boulevard from the lake westward, a centrally located civic center, a greenbelt perimeter, the use of the Chicago River as a commercial waterway, a network of grand boulevards to relieve traffic congestion, and the construction of lakefront parks and beaches. "Make no little plans," advised Burnham, "they have no magic to stir men's blood and probably themselves will not be realized. Make big plans; aim high in hope and work, remembering that a noble logical diagram once recorded will never die, but long after we are gone will be a living thing, asserting with growing intensity."

The development of Lake Park, renamed Grant Park in 1901, and now under the aegis of the Chicago Park District, would finally take place. The commissioners then engaged the firm of Olmsted Brothers, whose father, Frederick Law Olmsted, had designed New York's Central and Prospect parks, Boston's Fenway, and a host of other parks nationwide, including Jackson and Washington parks in Chicago, to design a formal park to be based on the plan of the French Renaissance formal style, similar to the gardens of Versailles. The plan would include symmetrical spaces embodying formal rows of trees and hedges, tiered (hierarchical) structure of plant materials, promenades, classical architectural detail, sculpture, and a central fountain to serve as the focal point of the park. In 1919 a Lakefront Ordinance required the Illinois Central Railroad to electrify its shorefront line, and the company agreed to depress its right of way and even contribute a landfill site for the Field Museum at the south end of the park. A comprehensive development plan for the park was adopted by the commission in 1924, and by 1927 construction of the first section of Grant Park between Randolph Drive and 11th Place on Michigan Avenue was completed. The centerpiece of the park, the Buckingham Fountain, was completed later that year. Unfortunately, the onset of the Depression forestalled any further development for years to come.

In 1955 the park suffered a major intrusion with the extension of Congress Parkway to the lakefront, an error that was not rectified until 1995. On August 28, 1968, during the Democratic presidential nominating convention, the park was the site of a major confrontation between anti–Vietnam War protesters and an overzealous police force. In 1976 the Daley Bicentennial Plaza, with ice

Before the efforts of Aaron Montgomery Ward and others led to the removal of most structures from Grant Park (then Lake Park), there were a number of "intrusions," including an Armory, railroad yards, and this rather imposing structure on Michigan Avenue, the Exhibition Hall of the Inter-State Industrial Exposition of 1873. Designed by William W. Boyington, it was a cavernous iron-and-glass structure erected for the exhibition to show the world that Chicago had risen from the ashes of the Great Fire and had regained its prominence as the great city of the Midwest. The hall also hosted the Republican national conventions of 1880 and 1884. A few years later Dankmar Adler was commissioned to remodel the interior for a concert hall for the new Chicago Symphony Orchestra. The resultant 6,000-seat theatre with its excellent acoustics was so successful that it contributed to his selection with Louis Sullivan in 1886 to design the Auditorium Theatre. (Chicago Historical Society)

rink and field house, was added to the northern section; three parking lots bordering Michigan Avenue were eliminated and replaced by underground garages beneath the western edge of the park; and a small parcel of land was added to the northeast when Lake Shore Drive was realigned in 1986 at the point where it crosses the Chicago River on the Outer Drive Bridge. Today the park still remains true to its original purpose, as a park for the people—its great popularity evident by the throngs of Chicagoans who enjoy its delightful verdant lakeside atmosphere, the panoramic views of the city's unique skyline, the seasonal cultural events, the free summer concerts by the Grant Park Symphony in the Petrillo Bandshell, shows in the Goodman Theatre, the annual "Taste of Chicago," as well as the park's athletic facilities, its tree-lined walks, and the lakefront bike paths.

Before entering Grant Park, walk south along the park two blocks to the corner of Balbo Drive.

(Left) Just inside the park near Balbo Drive stands the 15-foot-tall Theodore Thomas Memorial *(1923), a monument to the founder and first musical director of the Chicago Symphony Orchestra. Sculptor Albin Polasek, a lover of classical music, designed the feminine figure which has just struck a chord on her lyre as she stands on a hemispherical base, to portray the "majesty and sweep of a symphony." (Photo by author)*

The standing bronze female statue is the *Theodore Thomas Memorial,* designed as a monument to the founder and first musical director of the Chicago Symphony Orchestra, and sculpted by Albin Polasek in 1923. The German-born Thomas served as conductor for 13 years while the orchestra performed in the Auditorium Theatre, but unhappy with the cavernous atmosphere of the theatre, he fought forcefully for a smaller, more permanent hall for the orchestra. Unfortunately, he died just three weeks after his much-sought-after Orchestra Hall was dedicated in 1905. According to the *Loop Sculpture Guide,* sculptor Albin Polasek loved classical music and wanted to personify "the majesty and sweep of a symphony . . . and be dignified, yet simple . . . assertive but not bold . . . a feminine figure . . . but not too feminine." The figure has just struck a chord on her lyre, and she stands on a hemispherical base "embellished with the power of music."

The statue has had a rather strange history. It once stood on the east side of Michigan Avenue just opposite Orchestra Hall, but was removed and relocated elsewhere in the park. In the meantime the exedra, or support, was removed and for some unexplained reason, tossed into Lake Michigan as landfill. Parts of it were discovered later and retrieved and incorporated into the present base when the 15-foot-tall statue was placed at this site a few years ago.

Return to the Congress Parkway entrance to Grant Park, and turn right.

A broad promenade, Congress Plaza, provides a grand entry to the park. After undergoing an extensive reconstruction and restoration in 1994–1995, which reversed a 1955 project that had pushed Congress Parkway into Grant Park, it now appears much as it did when the park was completed early in the century. On either side of the entrance are reflecting pools, each with a bronze *Eagle* grasping a fish in its beak, sculpted by Frederick Hibbard (1931). They were placed here as part of the park enhancement in recognition of the 1933–1934 Chicago Century of Progress Exhibition, and recently restored as part of the park improvement.

Underneath the park, close to Michigan Avenue, is the South Underground Garage (the North section is located to the north of the Art Institute), neatly hidden from the bucolic surroundings.

Guarding both sides of the plaza are a pair of splendid equestrian statues by Croatian sculptor Ivan Mestrovic, **The Bowman** and **The Spearman** (1928), which honor the Native American. The forceful 17-foot-tall statues were modeled in Chicago and cast in the sculptor's studio in Zagreb, in the former Yugoslavia. The tense and muscular figures represent the dynamism and energy of the New World, according to Mestrovic, who ultimately settled in the

The Spearman *together with its counterpart,* The Bowman, *are striking sculptures that guard the entrance to Grant Park at the Congress Parkway entrance. Created by Ivan Mestrovic in 1928, and recently restored, the tense and muscular figures are intended to represent the dynamism and energy of the New World. In both figures the sculptor leaves to the viewers' imagination the about-to-be-launched spear and arrow. In the background is the Congress Hotel. (Photo by author)*

United States, where he became sculptor-in-residence at Syracuse University and at Notre Dame. The sculptures were commissioned by the Ferguson Fund which has been responsible for considerable artwork in Chicago, as well as for the restoration and preservation of the city's public sculpture. In both figures the sculptor leaves to the viewers' imagination the about-to-be launched spear and arrow. Born of humble peasants, Mestrovic, Croatia's only internationally known sculptor, was a shepherd in his youth, but because of his artistic promise he was sent to Vienna for his studies. The two bronze sculptures are considered his greatest accomplishments.

Just beyond are twin pylons, also symbolizing the entrance into Grant Park. Of classic design, they are simple and unadorned, except for swags at the top.

The promenade next passes over a stone bridge across the tracks of Metra's Electric Division, formerly the Illinois Central Railroad commuter line into Chicago, and now part of the suburban rail system. The tracks are also used by the Chicago, South Shore & South Bend Railroad, serving northern Indiana commuters from the Randolph Street Station a half-mile to the north. The South Shore Line is the only surviving electric interurban rail line in the country.

Walk ahead a few yards, then turn left (north) to the open plaza framed by two tall columns, with the statue of Lincoln in the center.

The **Seated Abraham Lincoln** (1926) by Augustus Saint-Gaudens dominates the Court of Presidents, but Lincoln is the only president represented. A rather dour, introspective Lincoln looks down on the empty plaza. The statue is set on an eight-step-high platform bracketed by a pair of fluted Doric columns surmounted by carved stone braziers. Augustus Saint-Gaudens, considered America's greatest sculptor, had a long and enduring affection for Lincoln. Like

Just within the park are the submerged tracks of Metra's Electric Division, whose overhead bridges offer broad views of the Michigan Avenue "Cliff." From the bright-colored Santa Fe Center on the left to the Stone Container Building on the right, with its truncated diamond-shaped roof, the avenue provides a textbook example of virtually every building style by the finest Chicago architects. (Photo by author)

A rather dour Abraham Lincoln looks down on the empty Court of the Presidents, the only president for whom a statue was ever realized for this specially designated area. One of two Lincoln sculptures in Chicago, artist Augustus Saint-Gaudens has left an enduring memorial to the president he loved so much. The Seated Lincoln was completed in 1926, 39 years after his Standing Lincoln in Lincoln Park. The exedra (seat) was designed by Stanford White. (Photo by author)

many of his contemporaries, Saint-Gaudens used the very popular life masks of Lincoln's hands and face taken by Chicago sculptor Leonard Volk five years before the president's death to prepare the model for this work, but Saint-Gaudens did not live to see its final rendering because of the unexpected destruction of the model, his own lingering illness, and ultimate death in 1907. Likewise, Stanford White, of the New York firm of McKim, Mead & White, the architect of the exedra, or classical seat for the sculpture, did not live to see the work completed, as one year earlier he was the victim of a jealous madman who shot him while he was dining at the roof garden theatre of the White-designed Madison Square Garden. Saint-Gaudens and White had previously teamed up in a number of works, including the great masterpiece, *Standing Lincoln* (1887), in Chicago's Lincoln Park, behind the Chicago Historical Society. Saint-Gaudens also produced the dramatic equestrian statue of *General John Logan* (1897), located in Grant Park, four blocks south at Ninth Street and Michigan Avenue (a bit too far off the tour, but well worth a visit). In 1907, at the request of President Theodore Roosevelt, he designed the 10-dollar and 20-dollar gold-pieces (the latter still considered the most beautiful U.S. coin ever struck) that were in circulation until the nation went off the gold standard in 1932.

Turn right (east) to S. Columbus Drive and cross at the traffic signal, a short distance to the south.

Directly ahead is the **Clarence Buckingham Fountain,** a gift to the city of Chicago from Kate Sturges Buckingham, the daughter of a grain elevator mogul, in memory of her brother who had been a benefactor and trustee of the Art Institute of Chicago. It was dedicated in 1927 as the world's largest decorative fountain. Built of Georgia pink marble, it was designed by Marcel Francois Loyau (sculptor) and Jacques Lambert (engineer), of Paris; and Edward H. Bennett, of Bennett, Parsons & Frost, architects, of Chicago. The design is based on the Latona Fountain on the grounds of the Palace of Versailles, but is twice as large. The fountain consists of three concentric basins one above the other, each 24, 60, and 103 feet in diameter, mounted on a ground-level pool 280 feet wide. Together they hold 1.5 million gallons of water recirculating at a rate of 14,000 gallons per minute through 133 jets, with the central fountain spouting 137 feet high at regular intervals. The fountain itself, which is managed by the Art Institute of Chicago, symbolizes Lake Michigan, and the four identical pairs of 20-foot bronze sea horses represent the four states around it. In addition, there are bronze fish heads, shells, and cattails. The bronzes, which were cast in France, brought sculptor Loyau the Prix National at the 1927 salon.

The Buckingham Fountain figured in the 1909 Burnham Plan of Chicago, which envisaged the creation of a central focal point at the end of the Congress Parkway axis. Edward Bennett, the major design architect, was already at work on the park's landscaping when Kate Buckingham selected him for the commission. When the fountain was completed, one observer noted that "it is perhaps one of Chicago's greatest prides and in some ways its most distinctive artistic achievement." Note, too, the fountain's surrounding landscape design,

The Clarence Buckingham Fountain is the centerpiece of Grant Park, and in warm weather one of the most popular gathering places in the city. This photo, taken during the "Taste of Chicago" in early July, shows the newly restored fountain "doing its thing" on schedule by spouting a central jet of water 137 feet in the air. In the rear are some of the multicolored tents of the Windy City's "great gourmand event," while in the background is Chicago's world-famous skyscraper panorama. (Photo by author)

The Buckingham Fountain consists of three pink marble concentric basins mounted on a pool 280 feet wide. Together they hold 1.5 million gallons of water recirculating at the rate of 14,000 gallons per minute through 133 jets. The fountain symbolizes Lake Michigan, and the four pairs of bronze sea horses represent the four states around it. The fountain's design is based on the Latona Fountain at Versailles and its position as central focal point at the end of the Congress Parkway axis figured prominently in Daniel H. Burnham's 1909 Plan of Chicago. (Photo by author)

with a tiered canopy structure that begins with short hedges, then moves to small ornamental trees, and ends with tall, graceful shade trees.

The fountain recently underwent a painstaking rehabilitation by architects Uriel Schlair and Jerry McElvaine of Harry Weese & Associates at a cost of $2.9 million. From May 1 to October 1, major water-display shows take place on the hour from 10:00 A.M. to 11:00 P.M. At 10:00 A.M. there is a start-up sequence; then major displays that last 20 minutes at the start of each hour. Late afternoon is a good time to view the fountain, when wind blowing off the lake scatters the spray and rays of the setting sun produce brilliant rainbows. At 8:00 P.M. a static light display begins; then at 9:00 P.M. a spectacular light show, planned by theatrical designer John Culbert, featuring 15 different color sequences, is shown until 10:40 P.M., when shutdown begins. The system is controlled by two integrated computers alongside the pool—one for the fountain, the other for the lights. According to the Chicago Park District, the fountain attracts about four million spectators annually.

To the north and south of the Buckingham Fountain are the **Daniel H. Flaherty Rose Gardens,** planted in 1963 and named for a former Park District Superintendent, which feature over 150 different types of roses. At the ends closest to the fountain are pairs of fountain figures set in circular pools. The two to the north are *Fisher Boy* and *Crane Girl;* to the south are *Turtle Boy* and *Dove Girl* (1905), by sculptor Leonard Crunelle. They were placed in the present location in 1964.

After a few minutes enjoying the Buckingham Fountain (try to be there for the major display!), continue east to Lake Shore Drive, and cross over. (Wait for the traffic signal!)

At the water's edge is **Queen's Landing,** but don't wait for the royal barge to arrive. Rather this is a fine spot from which to take in much of the downtown Chicago waterfront, from Navy Pier to the north, to the museum complex to the south that includes the Adler Planetarium, Shedd Aquarium, and the Field Museum. The section of the lakefront immediately in front of you is called Monroe Harbor, and is protected by a pair of breakwaters which shield the shore from Lake Michigan's occasional wild storms. Looking out toward the horizon, one can see one of the four intake cribs of the city's water supply, about two miles distant.

Turn right (south) and follow the path along the shore toward the museum complex.

To the right, in the park, is Hutchinson Field, named for Charles L. Hutchinson, president of the Art Institute of Chicago in 1882, and a commissioner of the South Park District (which preceded the present Chicago Park District). The field was planted in the 1930s and 1940s and is surrounded by American elms, with flowering crab apples and lilacs on both sides of the walkways that overlook the athletic field.

The path ends at a staircase that leads up to a terrace in front of the Aquarium, where there is a splendid panoramic view of the city.

☆ The **John G. Shedd Aquarium** (*1929, Graham, Anderson, Probst & White*), 1200 S. Lake Shore Drive, is a Classic "temple" modeled after the Field Museum, across the drive, and erected 20 years later. The dazzling white marble building, with walls of smooth ashlar blocks, displays an impressive pediment supported by four Doric columns with acroteria along the roofline and an appropriate nautical wave design along the cornice. The Aquarium is named for a former president of Marshall Field and Company who donated $3 million for its construction.

(*Note:* Visits to the Shedd Aquarium, the Field Museum, and the Adler Planetarium are a must, and should be left for another time when their unique and impressive exhibits can be enjoyed at leisure. For now, read the brief descriptions and continue the tour; or if you can't resist a peek into one of the museums, save an hour for a quick overview of the Field Museum, later in the tour.)

The Shedd Aquarium, the largest in the world, has become, as they say, "the hottest ticket in town," since the opening of the spectacular **Oceanarium** in 1991. Designed by Lohan Associates, the modernistic marine mammal pavilion, on the east side of the building, has drawn tens of thousands of visitors, and long lines are always the rule. This unusual exhibit provides a "you are there" visit to the Pacific Northwest Coast, using the transparent back wall that opens

From the Museum Complex there is an incomparable vista of Chicago's skyline. At the left is the circular building housing the John G. Shedd Aquarium, with the windows of the Oceanarium facing the viewer. (Photo by author)

Monroe Basin, sheltered behind the breakwater, is popular with boats of all description. Among the more prominent buildings to be seen along the lakefront are, left to right, the Stone Container Building (with diamond-shaped sloping roof), both No. 1 and No. 2 Prudential Center buildings (the one on the right with pyramidal roof is "Two Pru"), the towering white Amoco Building, the buildings of Illinois Center, and to the far right, the curvilinear Lake Point Tower. (Photo by author)

The Oceanarium of the Shedd Aquarium has become "the hottest ticket in town" since its opening in 1991. The view through the glass front wall gives the impression that one is right on the lake and that the huge tank is an extension of Lake Michigan. In this photo taken during the Oceanarium demonstration, dolphins perform their usual tricks as part of a "you are there" visit to a Pacific Northwest Coast habitat. (Photo by author)

to Lake Michigan as a natural backdrop. Dolphins, beluga whales, harbor seals, otters, penguins, and other marine mammals frolic in re-created natural coastal environments visible from above and through underwater windows. Narrated presentations in the enclosed amphitheater are given five times daily in this world's largest indoor marine habitat.

Among the many special exhibits is the lifelike 90,000-gallon Tropical Coral Reef in the center of the building, into which a diver plunges every day to hand-feed sea turtles, nurse sharks, green moray eels, and an enormous variety of colorful tropical fish. Most of the Aquarium's exhibit areas are grouped around the coral reef, making a tour easy and convenient. There are also two aquarium gift shops. Even if you don't choose to visit the aquarium at this time, look into the foyer just beyond the main entrance to see the fine marble interior with its aquatic motifs on the walls, floor tiles, and clock, and even in the lovely coffered ceiling. (Open daily except Christmas and New Year's, 9:00 A.M. to 5:00 P.M., until 6:00 P.M. weekends and summer. Admission: adults $8, children (3–11) and seniors $6, children under 2 free. The fee includes a visit to the Oceanarium. Half the above prices without the Oceanarium. Admission to the building itself is free on Thursdays. Telephone: 939–2438.)

On exiting the building, descend the stairs in front, turn right and follow the lakeside path around the aquarium past the modern glass wall sheathed in marble of the oceanarium to the end, then climb the staircase and cross Solidarity Drive to the equestrian statue on the mall.

The imposing **Thaddeus Kosciuzsko Memorial** (*1904, Kasimir Chodsinski*) commemorates the service of the Polish general and military engineer who fought for the colonists in the American Revolution, then returned to Poland to take up the battle for the freedom of his own country from the domination of the Russian czars. The equestrian statue was erected by the Polish-American community of Chicago and was originally placed in Humboldt Park in the heart of their neighborhood; it was relocated here in 1978. (Just for the record, the pronunciation is Koh-SHIOOSH-koh.)

Solidarity Drive, named for Lech Walesa's "Solidarity," the independent trade union that helped overthrow the former Communist government of Poland in the 1980s, is situated on landfill connecting the mainland with **Northerly Island.** The island, also created artificially, was constructed between 1928 and 1930 and was part of the **site of the "Century of Progress,"** the 1933–1934 Chicago World's Fair, a huge extravaganza commemorating the centenary of the founding of the city. The fair also occupied the west side of the intervening waterway, now the Burnham Yacht Harbor. In the original Burnham Plan of Chicago in 1909, a chain of offshore islands was to be made into a park, but Northerly Island was the only part of the plan that was realized. During the World's Fair the island was linked by a temporary street and an overhead tramway in the middle of the island, called the Sky Ride, but afterward a more enduring roadway was built. In 1947–1948 Chicago staged its big Railroad Fair at the southerly end.

The equestrian statue of Thaddeus Kosciuzsko guards the west end of Solidarity Drive. The memorial sculpture (1904, Kasimir Chodsinski) was erected by the Polish-American community of Chicago, and moved here from its original site in Humboldt Park in 1978. In the background is the Adler Planetarium. (Photo by author)

Continue east along the mall to the:

Statue and Monument to Karel Havlicek (*statue, 1909, Joseph Strachovsky; monument, 1911, Anthony F. Rusy*), erected by the Bohemian-American community of Chicago to commemorate the poet and journalist of the country that is now the Czech Republic. The figure, dressed in military uniform and draped with a cape, stands with a boldly outstretched arm.

The third statue is that of **Nicolaus Copernicus,** by the Danish sculptor Bertel Thorvaldsen, set on eight polished granite blocks. It is a copy of the original which had stood in front of the Polish Academy of Science in Warsaw until it was destroyed in 1944. According to the Chicago Department of Cultural Affairs' *Loop Sculpture Guide,* the statue was replicated by Polish artist Bronislaw Koniuszy using Thorvaldsen's working model, which survives in the museum he founded in Copenhagen, and was placed here, appropriately near the Adler Planetarium, in 1973. Copernicus (1473–1543), considered the father of modern astronomy, was the first to theorize that the Earth and planets revolve around the sun, contrary to Ptolemy's previously accepted assertion that the Earth was the center of the universe. Dressed in contemporary Polish garb, Copernicus, looking wistfully skyward, holds a compass in his right hand and an armillary sphere (a model of the solar system) in his left. (At this writing the sphere has disappeared. One hopes that the Chicago Park District will commission a replacement.)

 Directly ahead is the "dark-glass box" (*1981, Lohan Associates*) which serves as the entrance to the **Adler Planetarium** (*1930, Ernest A. Grunsfeld, Jr.*), 1300 S. Lake Shore Drive, at the very end of the artificial peninsula. Before visiting the planetarium, note the intriguing Henry Moore "functional" sculp-

The landfill now occupied by Solidarity Drive, Meigs Field, Northerly Island, and the lakeshore for a mile south, was the site of the Century of Progress, Chicago's World's Fair of 1933–1934. In this aerial photo a blimp flies north along Lake Shore Drive, paralleling the many exhibit buildings. At the extreme north end are the twin towers of the fair's spectacular aerial "Sky Ride" that connected the mainland with Northerly Island. (Photo by Chicago Aerial Survey Company. Chicago Historical Society)

The Chrysler Building at night at the Century of Progress (above) creates a magical scene with modern lighting and tasteful building design enhanced by the water of the reflecting pool. This scene was artistically photographed by Kenneth H. Hedrich of Hedrich-Blessing. The Travel and Transportation Building (below) represented a major step forward in modern building design, demonstrating the endless possibilities available to the creative architect, and expressing the Chicago World's Fair's confidence in the "world of tomorrow." Compare the construction of this building with the North Building of McCormick Place, whose roof is similarly supported by cables strung from the top of steel pylons. (Both photos, Chicago Historical Society)

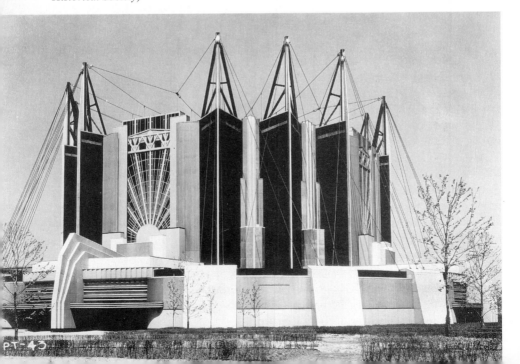

At the eastern end of the peninsula is the landmark Adler Planetarium, the nation's first. The twelve-sided building, 160-feet in diameter, is built of an attractive variegated rainbow granite, above which is a 68-foot-high dome. Within is the famous Kroc Universe Theatre, where its Zeiss projector creates the famous Sky Show. The Planetarium also presents a number of permanent and changing exhibits. In the foreground is the stunning Henry Moore Sundial *(1980). A "functional" sculpture, the 13-foot-tall bronze "timepiece" points to the hours along its horizontal curve, with an explanatory plaque below. (Photo by author)*

ture, *Sundial* (1980), a 13-foot bronze commissioned by the B. F. Ferguson Fund. A plaque relates that the sculpture was erected "in recognition of the revolutionary program of space exploration which was launched in the second half of the 20th century, making it possible for man to land on the moon and to send probes to Mercury, Venus, Mars, Jupiter, and Saturn." A second plaque explains how the sundial works. Check your watch, but subtract an hour if on daylight time.

The planetarium building, set on a raised platform, is twelve-sided and 160 feet in diameter, and built of an attractive variegated rainbow granite, surmounted by a prominent dome. Architect Grunsfeld's design won the 1930 Gold Medal from the Chicago Chapter of the American Institute of Architects. At each corner of the building are sculptured signs of the zodiac. The planetarium is named for its benefactor, philanthropist Max Adler, vice president and a director of Sears Roebuck, who gave $1 million toward the construction of the building. The centerpiece is, of course, the circular 430-seat Kroc Universe Theatre beneath the 68-foot-high dome where a Zeiss projector creates the famous Sky Show several times daily. The theatre is reached via the Stairway to the Stars, reputed to be the world's longest and fastest escalator. The Adler Planetarium was the first of its kind in the Western Hemisphere, and led the way for the building of others, such as the Hayden Planetarium in New York, and the Griffith Park Planetarium in Los Angeles. Most of the exhibits are underground and include a collection of antique astronomical instruments and manuscripts, second in the world only to that of Oxford, England, demonstrations on astronomical phenomena, space exploration, a "Planet Wall" with 3-D scale models of the planets and their moons, and a host of other displays that will fascinate adults and children alike. (Open daily 9:00 A.M. to 5:00 P.M., Friday until 9:00 P.M. Admission: $4 adults, $2 children age 17 and under, $2 seniors. Free on Tuesdays. Telephone: 922-STAR.)

Walk clockwise around the Adler Planetarium. To the rear, at the water's edge, is a small circular structure sheathed in split-faced concrete, the Doane Observatory Building. On Friday evenings following the Sky Show in the planetarium, the observatory's 20-inch computerized telescope projects images of the moon, planets, stars, and galaxies, into the planetarium theatre.

Take a moment to enjoy the spectacular Chicago skyline from this, the most favored vantage point in the city.

Walk to the end of Solidarity Drive and stay on the south side, as you walk back.

To the south is the extension of Northerly Island and the runway and terminal facilities of **Meigs Field,** Chicago's in-town general aviation airport, built in 1947 on part of the site of the 1933–1934 Century of Progress World's Fair. It was named for Merrill C. Meigs, a pilot and newspaper publisher who had pushed for an airport closer to his offices. The city approved the plan, despite its nonconformity with the original Burnham Plan which called for park land. The Air Traffic Control Tower was constructed in 1952 (*Consoer & Townsend*), and the Terminal Building in 1961 (*Consoer & Morgan*). It has always been a bit disquieting (figuratively and literally) to have airplanes, including the new, smaller private jets, and helicopters zoom over this otherwise tranquil and culturally vital complex, and even more worrisome for the tenants of the 70-story Lake Point Tower which stands two miles directly north of the runway. The concern is not entirely without validity, as strong crosswinds blowing from the lake and the prairie can be a serious threat. At this writing the city is planning to close Meigs Field when its lease runs out, with Northerly Island to be integrated into the city's park system. To the right of the airport is Burnham Harbor with its large marina.

Turn back on Solidarity Drive and bear to the right in front of the Shedd Aquarium. Take the pedestrian underpass, and on exiting turn right to the tall totem pole in front of the Field Museum. (As this book goes to press the city has announced plans to move Lake Shore Drive's northbound lane to the west of Soldier Field, thus opening the area as one continuous park linking the north lakefront parks with those of the south, and making this area much more pedestrian-friendly.)

The 65-foot-tall cedar totem pole, entitled *The Legend of Big Beaver,* was carved by Norman Tait on Vancouver Island, British Columbia, and was erected in a full Native American ceremony on the occasion of the opening of the Field Museum's exhibit, "Maritime Peoples of the Arctic and Northwest

Coast," in April 1982. Tait is a member of the Nishga Band of the Tsimshian tribe, one of the six major groups of Indians still living in the Pacific Northwest. All totem poles tell a story, and this one records a legend of a family of five brothers on a beaver hunt who kill all but two beavers who escape. The youngest brother follows the beavers to their lodge, discovers their spiritual power and adopts them as artists or totem animals of his family. The flying eagle at the top is the Tait family crest.

Directly behind the totem pole is the **Field Museum of Natural History** (*1909–1912, D. H. Burnham & Company; 1912–1917, Graham, Burnham & Company; 1917–1920, Graham, Anderson, Probst & White. Renovation 1977, Harry Weese & Associates*), Lake Shore Drive and E. Roosevelt Road. The Field Museum has an interesting history. Just prior to the closing of the 1893 World's Columbian Exposition in Jackson Park, the state of Illinois granted a charter to establish a Columbian Museum of Chicago to create a permanent home for the natural history collections gathered for the fair. Marshall Field donated $1 million toward its construction, and after his death left another $8 million. When it opened in 1894, the name was changed to the Field Columbian Museum in recognition of its benefactor. The site was the Palace of Fine Arts, one of the exposition's only permanent structures, which was renovated and

The exterior of the Field Museum of Natural History is closely patterned after the Erechtheium, one of the Acropolis temples. The neo-Classical-style museum, constructed of white Georgia marble, opened on May 2, 1921, to an overflow crowd. Eight caryatids, created by Henry Hering, embellish the exterior, with four tall fluted Ionic columns dominating the central section and supporting a simple architrave in the front and rear. The museum is named for major benefactor Marshall Field who favored the neo-Classical style. The museum originally opened in 1894 in the former Art Palace of the World's Columbian Exposition, a year after the great fair closed. (Photo by John Weinstein. Courtesy of the Field Museum, Chicago)

Opening day of the first building of the Columbian Museum, June 2, 1894, in the former Art Palace of the World's Columbian Exposition in Jackson Park. Rain did not seem to daunt the crowd of curious visitors anxious to see the variety of artifacts and collections from the fair. The building is now home to the Museum of Science and Industry. (Courtesy of the Field Museum, Chicago)

A view across the west end of the Main Basin at the World's Columbian Exposition, 1893, showing the "White City's" awesome variety of buildings, pools, and sculpture, which when night fell became a veritable fairyland of the newly perfected electric lighting. Daniel H. Burnham, considered the "father of the fair," was in charge of construction, with partner John Wellborn Root entrusted with the design, and Frederick Law Olmsted of New York hired as landscape architect. The fair, celebrating the 400th anniversary of the landing of Columbus in the New World, opened a year late. In this photo are (left to right) the Agricultural Building, Colonnade with Obelisk in front of it, Machinery Hall, and in the center foreground, the Columbian Fountain. After the fair closed a year later, every building was demolished (except the Art Palace, the only permanent structure). (Chicago Historical Society)

When the new Field Museum opened at its present location on May 2, 1921, a line of visitors over a quarter of a mile long gathered for the occasion. The neo-Classical museum building sits in splendid isolation on its landfill site, resembling a newly unearthed temple from Ancient Greece. (Courtesy of the Field Museum, Chicago)

today is the famous Museum of Science and Industry. It soon became evident that a new building was needed, and plans were drawn up by Daniel Burnham in 1906 along the lines of Marshall Field's favored neo-Classical style on a site that the architect, himself, had originally chosen for an imposing civic building in his original Plan of Chicago. The new landfill site was donated by the Illinois Central Railroad, but Burnham, sadly, did not live to see the Museum's construction, as he died in 1912. Construction on the present site was not begun until three years later and completed in 1921. Stanley Field, Marshall Field's nephew, was appointed as the unpaid president and later board chairman, and served for 42 years.

The building, set on a high stone platform, is a textbook example of the neo-Classic style in gleaming white Georgia marble. It is said that Marshall Field, who placed "cleanliness next to godliness," felt that, unlike marble, a white masonry facade would show the dirt, thus demanding constant attention by the museum staff to keep it clean and bright. Four Ionic columns dominate the central section and support a simple architrave, above which is a pediment adorned with an acroterion at each end and an anthemion at the peak. Two atlantean figures on each side support smaller pediments. The exterior is modeled after the Erechteium, one of the temples of the Acropolis complex in Athens. Each of the museum's wings displays 12 similar Ionic columns. Behind the entrance columns is a marble-clad vestibule with Greek motifs around the doorway. The style of the building was duplicated on a smaller scale in the Shedd Aquarium. The dramatic location of the museum, at the south end of a long stretch of Lake Shore Drive, presents one of the city's great vistas. Before entering, turn around and look back up Lake Shore Drive.

Spend a little while inside the building (even a short visit is worth the admission price!). On passing through the huge doorway one passes *under-*

Brightly lit Stanley Field Hall of the Field Museum is 360 feet long with a seven-arch arcade on each side and is an appropriately monumental space to house the mind-boggling 40-foot-tall, 75-foot-long brachiosaurus, the world's largest dinosaur, as well as two enormous stuffed African elephants, and twin Haida totem poles from the Canadian Northwest. (Photo by author)

neath the skeleton of the world's largest dinosaur on display anywhere, the brachiosaurus—40 feet tall, 75 feet long, which probably weighed between 50 and 80 tons! The incredible creature, which was excavated by a Field Museum paleontologist in 1900, roamed what is now Colorado in the late Jurassic Period, 150 million years ago. The majestic Stanley Field Hall, named for Marshall Field's nephew, is 360 feet long, with a seven-arch arcade on each side, brightly lit with natural light streaming through the coffered ceiling. For a good overall perspective, climb the double staircase at the south end. Dominating the center of the hall is the pair of enormous stuffed African elephants, and nearby are twin Haida totem poles from the Canadian Northwest, while at the north end is the mind-boggling dinosaur skeleton. Scattered about the museum are bronze sculptures entitled *The Races of Mankind,* by Malvina Hoffman, and a pair of lions by Carl Akeley (who also stuffed the huge African elephants). Be sure to pick up a map of the exhibit halls to plan your visit.

The Field Museum is one of the world's four greatest natural history museums. With a collection of over 20 million specimens from the fields of anthropology, botany, geology, and zoology, the Museum, a major research institution, explores life on earth from prehistoric times to the present. No musty artifact-strewn attic here. It is an exciting place with exhibits and displays to challenge the imagination of young and old. (For an excellent overview of and some interesting anecdotes and sidelights on the entire Grant Park museum complex, see *Norman Mark's Chicago,* Chicago Review Press, 1993.)

The museum is open daily 9:00 A.M. to 5:00 P.M. Admission: $5 adults; $3 children, seniors, and students with ID; $16 maximum for a family group; children age 2 and under, free; the museum is free on Wednesdays. Telephone: 922-9410. The museum complex is serviced daily by the CTA No. 146 bus.

With the completion of the Field Museum, the Shedd Aquarium, and the Adler Planetarium, plus the already established Michigan Avenue cultural institutions (Public Library—now the Cultural Center—Art Institute, Orchestra Hall, Fine Arts Building, and Auditorium Building), noted architectural historian Carl Condit referred to the entire complex as "the largest, oldest, and architecturally most impressive 'culture center' in the United States."

On exiting the museum turn left and walk around the building, following the pedestrian walk. At the traffic signal on Lake Shore Drive West, turn right and cross the drive. Bear right and cross Roosevelt Road. Just beyond is the Christopher Columbus statue.

The statue of *Christopher Columbus,* by sculptor Carl Brioschi was completed in 1933 as a gift to the Century of Progress Exposition by the Italian-American community of Chicago. The figure of the "Admiral of the Ocean Seas" was unveiled on Italian Day in August 1933 as a symbol of mutual respect and harmony between Italy and the United States. (The government of Italy, then under the fascist Benito Mussolini dictatorship, also presented the city with another soon-to-be-seen monument.) The figure of Columbus extends a visionary left arm while holding his charts in his right. On the 20-foot-high base are low-relief sculptures depicting his flagship, the Santa Maria; the city seal of Genoa, the explorer's home city; Amerigo Vespucci, whose name Columbus gave to the New World; and Columbus's tutor, Toscanelli, who is reputed to have taught him that the world was round.

Return to the pedestrian path along the Field Museum, turn right and continue to William McFetridge Drive.

Stop for a moment and look back at the rear facade of the Field Museum, and note that it is an exact copy of the front.

Across McFetridge Drive is the **Chicago Park District Administrative Building** (*1939, Holabird & Root*), 425 E. McFetridge Drive, headquarters of Chicago's parks, and alas, a most undistinguished building for such an important function. The four-story structure with its 24 square "columns" was doubtless designed to be somewhat harmonious with its surroundings (the Field Museum to the north and Soldier Field to the south), but it acts only as an insensitive and jarring intrusion.

Walk east past the front of the park headquarters, cut across the parking lot at the east end of the building, and follow Lake Shore Drive south.

To the west is the imposing **Soldier Field** (*1924, Holabird & Roche*), which is physically connected to the rear of the Park Administration Building. The $6 million neo-Classic stadium, home to the Chicago Bears football team ("Da Bears"), was designed to harmonize with the architecture of the Field Museum, but any visual connection has now been destroyed by the view-blocking park headquarters to the north. The huge athletic stadium, with its twin colonnades of twenty-two 100-foot-high Doric columns, plus four each in the pedimented corner pavilions, originally had a seating capacity of about 106,000, and conjures up visions of Ancient Rome where gladiators engaged in mortal combat to entertain the cheering multitudes. *Plus ça change,* the brutality continues today, only it's called professional football. The U-shaped structure was named to honor the fallen soldiers of World War I, and at the same time Municipal Pier was renamed Navy Pier to honor the sailors (*see* page 266). To see the interior of Soldier Field, you'll have to attend one of the regular sporting, musical, or religious events held here.

Continue to walk south in the parking lot, and follow the fence along Lake Shore Drive (which, as mentioned before, may now have been removed to the west side of Soldier Field) as far as E. Waldron Drive. There you can either wait for the traffic light to change (often as long as 10 minutes) or walk a bit further and cross over on the footbridge (which by now may have been removed).

E. Waldron Drive leads to **Burnham Harbor** and the marina. Walk in a short distance to see the marine activity and also to get a good view of Meigs Field's Administration Building and Control Tower. (The airport is accessible by road from Solidarity Drive, just south of the Adler Planetarium.)

The neo-Classical-style Soldier Field, Chicago's huge athletic stadium, conjures up visions of Ancient Rome where gladiators engaged in mortal combat to entertain cheering multitudes. Today the shouting is for "Da Bears," the city's celebrated football team, and for a variety of other events. Built in 1924 to honor the soldiers of World War I, the colossal colonnaded structure with twenty-two 100-foot-high Doric columns, was designed by Holabird & Roche. In the foreground is Burnham Yacht Harbor with its highly popular marina. (Photo by author)

Go back to Lake Shore Drive, and turn right (north) on the path. It is a bicycle path, so be careful and yield to bikers and skaters.

About one hundred yards north stands a solitary classic column to the right of the path. Named the **Balbo Monument,** it is one of Chicago's real oddities. The column, from the second century A.D., was presented by the Italian government during the 1933 Century of Progress Exposition, and is set on a square marble pedestal whose slowly fading bilingual inscription recalls another era, and today gives one pause for thought: "This column, twenty centuries old, was erected on the beach of Ostia, the port of Imperial Rome, to watch over the fortunes and victories of the Roman triremes. Fascist Italy, with the sponsorship of Benito Mussolini, presents to Chicago a symbol and memorial in honor of the Atlantic Squadron led by Balbo, which with Roman daring, flew across the ocean in the 11th year of the Fascist era."

Mussolini notwithstanding, the city of Chicago did name a major street for the intrepid pilot, Italo Balbo, for having led a squadron of 24 seaplanes on a 16-day series of hops across the Atlantic from Italy, landing on Lake Michigan near Navy Pier on July 16, 1933, in conjunction with the Century of Progress Exposition. During World War II, while flying for the Italian Air Force, Gen. Balbo lost his life when he was mistakenly shot down by friendly fire over Tobruk, Libya. So much for the fascist era, but the Roman column *is* appropriately situated in that part of town that so glorifies the neo-Classic architectural tradition.

The Balbo Monument is an odd holdover from the 1933 Century of Progress Exposition. The column, from Second Century A.D. Rome, was presented by the Italian government to honor Italo Balbo, an intrepid pilot who led a fleet of 24 seaplanes on a multihop flight from Italy to Chicago in conjunction with the fair. The fading inscription on the base describes the origin of the column and declares that "Fascist Italy, with the sponsorship of Benito Mussolini, presents to Chicago a symbol and memorial in honor of the Atlantic Squadron, led by Balbo, which with Roman daring, flew across the ocean in the 11th year of the Fascist era." Poor Balbo! During World War II he was shot down by accident by his own forces. His real memorial is the drive named for him. (Photo by author)

When viewed from the lakefront, the Buckingham Fountain is an impressive scene against the backdrop of Chicago's famous skyline. Whether in the late afternoon when the russet hues of the setting sun highlight the darkening buildings and create rainbows in the fountain's windblown spray, or in the bright morning light when the rising sun illuminates every sculptural detail, the stirring sight provides a memorable experience. (Photo by author)

Continue northward on the path as far as the traffic circle. Go past the Shedd Aquarium and the pedestrian underpass to the bus shelter. From here there are buses back to the Loop. Number 146 goes back up Michigan Avenue. For those who are still not foot weary, continue north, following this same path as earlier on the tour, and cross Lake Shore Drive into Grant Park at the traffic signal at E. Balbo Drive. Take a diagonal path northwestward which will end in the rose gardens adjacent to the Buckingham Fountain. Michigan Avenue is directly west.

End of tour.

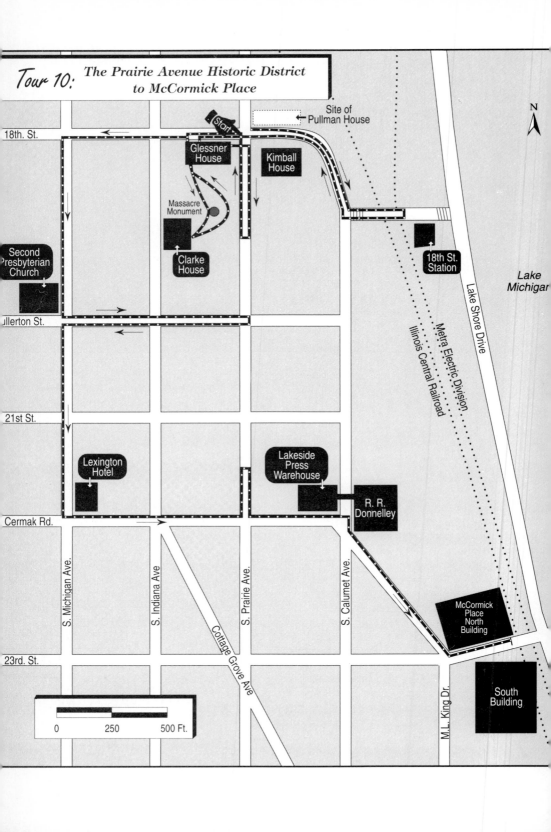

Tour 10: **The Prairie Avenue Historic District to McCormick Place**

Site of Pullman House

18th. St.

Start

Glessner House

Kimball House

Massacre Monument

Clarke House

Second Presbyterian Church

18th St. Station

ullerton St.

Lake Michigan

Lake Shore Drive

Metra Electric Division

Illinois Central Railroad

21st St.

Lexington Hotel

Lakeside Press Warehouse

R. R. Donnelley

Cermak Rd.

McCormick Place North Building

S. Michigan Ave.

S. Indiana Ave

Cottage Grove Ave

S. Prairie Ave.

S. Calumet Ave.

23rd. St.

M.L. King Dr.

South Building

0   250   500 Ft.

N

10. The Prairie Avenue Historic District to McCormick Place

The area of Prairie Avenue became the neighborhood of choice for the elite of Chicago by the mid-19th century thanks to the post–Civil War building boom, and it was already considered a "Gold Coast" even before the Great Fire of 1871. The raging fire obliterated most of the homes of the wealthy who lived in the area around the Loop, as well as their commercial enterprises in the center of the city. The rapid growth of industry downtown had already begun encroaching on their once-tranquil neighborhoods; therefore, following the fire, many of the burned-out well-to-do moved down to the wide-open spaces of the Prairie Avenue area and built grand new residences close to their more fortunate neighbors. The streets between 16th and 22nd from Michigan Avenue eastward were relatively close and accessible to the center of the city, and soon saw the arrival of such prominent Chicago industrialists and entrepreneurs as Marshall Field, George M. Pullman, Philip D. Armour, and William Kimball. The neighborhood became a major center of elite social activity and remained so for almost a half-century. Today, unfortunately, only eight of their once-sumptuous homes survive on Prairie Avenue, and none occupied by any descendants of the original families.

Many distinguished architects designed elegant residences for Chicago's "upper crust," among whom were Richard Morris Hunt, Henry Hobson

Richardson, Solon Spencer Beman, Burnham & Root, and Cobb & Frost. Although Prairie Avenue was little more than a cowpath in 1852 when brick manufacturer John N. Staples built the first house, within little over a decade the streets were paved, and scores of magnificent homes with marble fronts or brick-and-marble trim transformed the area into Chicago's most affluent neighborhood. The halcyon days of this "Neighborhood of Millionaires," as proclaimed by local guidebooks, were approximately 1870 to 1910, reaching its zenith at the time of the 1893 World's Columbian Exposition, after which it slowly declined, being superseded by the Near North Side, particularly the strip along Lake Shore Drive.

Among the most important factors that originally contributed to the development of Prairie Avenue was the construction of the Illinois Central and the Michigan Central railroads which laid their tracks nearby in 1852, providing a vital transportation link to the East. The Illinois Central made an agreement with the city of Chicago to allow it to construct a trestle just offshore in Lake Michigan in exchange for building a stone breakwater, thus stabilizing the shoreline and making possible the development of the intervening sandy marsh. The railroads also inaugurated commuter service from Chicago to suburban Hyde Park in 1856, bringing the downtown business area within minutes of Prairie Avenue. Another reason for the affluent to choose the South Side over the North was the problem of the lack of reliable bridges across the Chicago River; and there was also the advantage of newly arrived horse car lines along South Side avenues.

When the neighborhood fell into decline, many of the once-opulent mansions were converted into rooming houses or taken over by businesses, or demolished for the construction of printing plants and warehouses. Only a scant few of the descendants of the original families chose to remain. The area's former advantage of proximity to the Loop now became a disadvantage, as its close-in location attracted large-scale commercial development, with land becoming more valuable for industrial purposes. The year 1910 saw the first of the once fine residences fall under the wrecker's ball, the Robert Law house.

With the encroachment of commerce came all the nuisances of smoke, soot, and noise, and a burgeoning vice district gradually creeping down State Street, Wabash and Indiana avenues. Too, the formerly elegant houses were aging and considered old fashioned and had become much too expensive to maintain. The wealthy inhabitants had aged or died off, and their children sought smaller apartments in more desirable neighborhoods. Perhaps the greatest cause of the decline was the invention of the automobile. In the same length of time that it had taken to commute by carriage or horse car to the Loop, one could now travel quickly and easily by automobile to suburbs along the North Shore. Michigan Avenue during the period 1908–1910 became the center for automobile showrooms, and although most of the auto dealers have by now departed, their buildings still remain, and the emblems, logos, and heralds of many long-forgotten auto manufacturers can still be seen on the facades. In time, more warehouses intruded, particularly along Indiana Avenue after the Illinois Central Railroad built its large station to the north at Roosevelt Road in 1893.

Of those remaining mansions in the district, none has achieved greater fame and recognition than the one designed by Henry Hobson Richardson for John Jacob Glessner, the first house to be visited on the tour. Its survival is due to the valiant efforts of a group of citizens, including the architects Harry and Ben Weese, and Philip Johnson, who in 1966 founded the Chicago School of Architecture Foundation for the express purpose of saving the house from demolition. (The name was later shortened to Chicago Architecture Foundation.) In describing the dual nature of the CAF, Harry Weese wrote that the Glessner House could not only be a site for celebrating H. H. Richardson's genius, but also a place where "other educational programs and activities connected with the study, preservation, and interest in the Chicago School of Architecture will be encouraged and promoted."

The group then researched the house and the adjoining neighborhood, and prepared the nomination of the remaining houses to the National Register of Historic Places, providing the impetus for the inclusion of the **Prairie Avenue Historic District** on the National Register. The district, which is centered around the Fort Dearborn Massacre site, extends on both sides of 18th Street for one block in either direction. In 1976 the Commission on Chicago Landmarks designated the two square blocks centering on Prairie Avenue between 18th and Cullerton streets as a Chicago Landmark. In a joint effort, the City of Chicago and the CAF arranged to have Prairie Avenue closed off in the middle of the block south of 18th Street and made into a cul-de-sac, creating the new Prairie Avenue Promenade, a most attractive amenity for pedestrians. Antique lampposts were added, and along the fences on both sides, informative streetscape plaques were installed by the CAF between 1978 and 1987 describing each historic house as well as marking the sites of those that were demolished.

In 1977 the Henry B. Clarke House, Chicago's oldest structure, was moved into the district. Since 1995 both the Clarke and Glessner houses are administered by the Prairie House Museums, and offer regularly scheduled tours (*see* schedule below under each house). Take the time to read the interesting details on the various fence plaques, which give a fairly comprehensive history of the neighborhood, the houses and their architects, as well as the notable families that lived in this "citadel of social aristocracy" through the years. Tree-lined Prairie Avenue today, despite the loss of so many of its grand houses, is still a charming enclave, surviving as it does in stark contrast to a surrounding barren and desolate industrial area. When Oliver Wendell Holmes referred to Boston's Beacon Hill as "the sunny street that held the sifted few," the aphorism was applied in retrospect to Prairie Avenue after its decline.

(Assuming that you are reading this before sallying forth to explore the area, please take note that at present there are no nearby places to eat in the Prairie Avenue Historic area! *Take a bag lunch with you,* which you can eat in the Glessner House visitor's center or in the little park-like garden in the center of the block.)

Prairie Avenue Historic District

Prairie Avenue is one of Chicago's most historic neighborhoods. It was the site of the Fort Dearborn Massacre, where ninety-five settlers, soldiers and militia evacuating the fort on August 15, 1812 were ambushed by Indians from several tribes. Some forty-three escaped, aided by Indians who were friendly, mainly Potawatomis.

View of Prairie Avenue and 18th Street in the late 1800s, looking northwest. The large cottonwood tree in the street, enclosed by a fence, traditionally marked the site of the Massacre of 1812. The George M. Pullman mansion is seen on the right and the Hugh J. McBirney house in the background. In 1893, Pullman erected a monument a short distance away at 18th Street and Calumet Avenue to commemorate the Fort Dearborn Massacre. This monument is now located in the park south of Glessner House.

After the Great Fire of 1871 in Chicago, Prairie Avenue became the neighborhood of choice to Chicago's elite. Termed the "sunny street that held the sifted few," it was home to the Fields, Armours, Palmers, Kimballs, Pullmans, Searses, Glessners, and other prominent families, whose homes were designed by some of the nation's foremost architects as Richard Morris Hunt, H.H. Richardson, Solon S. Beman, John Wellborn Root and Daniel H. Burnham.

Today plaques along Prairie Avenue, starting at 18th Street, give the history of some of these wealthy families and mark the site of their fashionable nineteenth-century homes, most of which are no longer standing. Chicago's Gilded Age spanned approximately four decades.

The Prairie Avenue Historic District was so designated in 1974 by the City of Chicago. It is on the National Register of Historic Places.

On the other sides of this marker can be found tour information, a map of the Prairie Avenue Historic District, and a history of the Glessner and Clarke houses which are extant and now historic house museums.

(Left) The Prairie Avenue Historic District is centered around the Fort Dearborn Massacre Site and extends on both sides of 18th Street for one block in either direction. The informative sign stands adjacent to the Glessner House, where most tours begin. (Photo by author)

The tour begins at the intersection of E. 18th Street and Prairie Avenue. (To get there from the Loop, take CTA bus Nos. 1, 3, or 4 down Michigan Avenue. Number 1 begins at Union Station. Get off at E. 18th Street and walk east two short blocks. You can also take the Metra Electric Division train at Randolph Street Station and get off at the 18th Street Station; walk up the stairs, turn left along the wooden overpass, and walk west one block to Prairie Avenue. The only advantage is that it takes just six minutes. It will cost you around $1.75, and service is not very frequent, especially on Sundays.)

Before entering the Prairie Avenue Historic District, take a brief detour east along E. 18th Street to the end of the block where it joins S. Calumet Avenue. The corner is thought to be the approximate **site of the Fort Dearborn Massacre** and one of the darkest pages in the history of Chicago. More about that sad event later. Turn right and climb the wooden staircase leading up to the overpass. Walk out about 200 yards just about to the staircase leading down to the 18th Street Metra station, for a broad panorama of the lakeside area, the Chicago skyline to the north, and a sweeping view of **McCormick Place-on-the-Lake,** or simply McCormick Place, the gargantuan exposition and convention center to the south (to be seen at the end of the tour). Note the setting of the Center which extends from the shore of Lake Michigan over Lake Shore Drive and the many railroad tracks of the Metra Electric Division and the Illinois Central Railroad. From this vantage point, the East and North buildings of McCormick Place, connected by a pedestrian gangway over Lake Shore Drive, are clearly visible. Note how the roof of the North Building (on the right) is suspended on cables from concrete pylons to create a vast column-free interior space, while the earlier East Building's roof is cantilevered gracefully 75 feet beyond its supporting walls.

Return to the entrance to Prairie Avenue.

Standing at the northeast corner of Prairie Avenue and E. 18th Street, now a nondescript industrial area, is the **site of the George M. Pullman residence** (formerly No. 1729 Prairie Avenue), said to have been the most opulent of all the Prairie Avenue houses. In the early 1880s the founder of the Pullman Palace Car Company consolidated his sleeping-car manufacturing plants in Detroit and St. Louis into a model company town in the south Chicago suburb that he then named for himself. Earlier, in 1870, he had commissioned Chicago architect, Henry S. Jaffray, to design a large mansion for his family on Prairie Avenue. Construction took so long that they were unable to move in until six years later.

The house was described as being a three-story French Second Empire–style structure, topped by a mansard roof, with a porte-cochère, and according to

George M. Pullman's residence stood diagonally across Prairie Avenue from the Glessner House. The stately French Second Empire–style house was built for the sleeping-car magnate in 1870 and remained in the family until Mrs. Pullman's death in 1922, when the house was torn down. (Chicago Historical Society)

Mary Alice Molloy writing in *The Grand American Avenue,* "it was the first Prairie Avenue house to take its corner site seriously and to be clad on all sides in stone, a brownstone and not Athens marble. It was the Avenue's showiest place and meant for flamboyant lifestyle. . . . and incorporated a 200-seat theater, an organ, a bowling alley, and a billiard room in addition to at least three parlors and an extensive conservatory." In later additions, architect Solon S. Beman extended the house and added greenhouses and a palm court, including a greenhouse across 18th Street behind what is now the Kimball House. The mansion and its greenhouses were demolished after Mrs. Pullman's death in 1922. Pullman had also commissioned an office building on Michigan Avenue, downtown, which is also gone (*see* pages 189–190).

Space does not permit a detailed account of the vagaries of the Pullman Company's history, but his workers' "utopia" was anything but that. Pullman was a typical paternalistic company town of the 19th century, and factory workers had little to say about the conduct of their lives. After the Panic of 1893, Pullman lowered wages, but refused to lower rents and other charges, maintaining that the town was a separate business that needed to make a 6 percent profit no matter what, which ultimately led to the famous strike the following year. A nationwide boycott followed, and federal troops were summoned, ostensibly to protect the U.S. mail. The soldiers occupied the town, and the strike was broken; but in the end George Pullman was forced to sell the town's properties, and the Pullman Strike of 1894 is considered a major landmark event in the history of the labor movement.

A plaque on the present building indicates the Pullman house site as well as the location of the Fort Dearborn Massacre which is presumed to have occurred a bit further to the east. A cottonwood tree adjacent to the Pullman property was believed to have been there when the massacre took place, and it was regarded for years as a living testimonial to the event. When the tree finally died, the neighbors arranged for it to be moved to a court inside the Chicago Historical Society, which opened its new building on Dearborn and Ontario streets in 1893. Pullman then commissioned a large commemorative sculpture which was placed at the turn of Calumet Avenue, at the east end of his property. Pullman willed the statue to the Chicago Historical Society in trust for the City of Chicago. In 1931 it was moved to the Society's present building on N. Clark Street at E. North Avenue. It was brought back to its original neighborhood in 1987 and installed in the park-like garden behind the Glessner and Clarke houses, and will be seen later.

The first and most significant residence in the historic district is the Romanesque Revival–style house designed by Henry Hobson Richardson for farm implement manufacturer John Jacob Glessner. The **Glessner House,** built in 1887–1888 of rough-hewn granite, is unique for a number of reasons. It is the only surviving residence in Chicago designed by the famous Boston architect. His other residence and two commercial buildings, one of them the Marshall Field Wholesale Store, were demolished. Richardson's fortress-like designs, which to an extent employ motifs from French and Spanish sources, evoke great strength, solidity, and simplicity, and were copied so widely that the decades of the 1880s and 1890s are frequently referred to as the Richardsonian Romanesque era. Glessner's neighbors, however, were not impressed with the house, which they likened to a jail. It is said that his neighbor across the street, George M. Pullman, even tried to force Glessner to have the house remodeled.

Unfortunately, Richardson did not live to see his design carried out, as he died in 1886, leaving the completion of the house to his successors, Shepley, Rutan & Coolidge. The plan of the 35-room residence turned out to be one of the architect's best, as the primary living spaces face south, away from the chill winter winds, toward a quiet inner courtyard, with large windows to admit every last ray of winter sunshine. Interestingly, he "insulated" the main rooms by placing a servants' corridor along the north wall. The interior furnishings are mostly intact, including splendid carved wood furniture by Isaac E. Scott. The Glessners shared Richardson's great interest in the Arts and Crafts movement and its English pre-Raphaelite progenitors, John Ruskin, William Morris, and William De Morgan. Their ideal of reviving medieval craftsmanship is readily apparent throughout the house in the furniture, lamps, wallpaper, carpets, and ceramics.

Richardson's obsession with the medieval did not stop with architecture and design, as he would often dress in a monk's habit to amuse his friends or pose for photographs, which unfortunately, did not do much to conceal his portly 370-pound weight.

The Glessner House, at the southwest corner of 18th Street and Prairie Avenue, was designed by the noted Boston architect Henry Hobson Richardson, and built in 1887–1888. John Jacob Glessner conducted a successful farm machinery business, and his splendid archtypical Romanesque Revival–style residence is the architect's only surviving work in Chicago. The Glessner House now functions as a house museum. (Photo by author)

John Jacob Glessner's farm machinery business offered no real competition to Cyrus Hall McCormick, inventor of the famous reaper, nor to any of the other big giants in the industry, and his firm, known as Warder Bushnell & Glessner, was absorbed with the others in 1902 in a large merger which became the International Harvester Company.

The Glessners enjoyed many years in the house and entertained frequently. On their 25th wedding anniversary, the conductor of the Chicago Symphony Orchestra, Theodore Thomas, suggested to Glessner hiding members of the orchestra in the spacious house for a surprise concert for his wife, a stunt that was later repeated by the Glessner children. To this day the house retains a cozy, lived-in look, although family members have not been in residence for years. The last surviving Glessner grandchild died in 1994.

The exterior displays two distinct facades: the palazzo-like Prairie Avenue side draws upon the American Colonial period, while the 18th Street side is English in style. Note how the gray granite of the building blocks is highlighted by the use of a reddish mortar. The main entrance with a typical "Richardsonian" arch is symmetrical, while the servants' entrance on the 18th Street side resembles a sideways "G." In the gable above is a dovecote, and surmounting the peaked roof is a purple martin "apartment" house, both different birdhouses meant to attract a considerable population of pigeons, purple martins, and swallows—ostensibly the pigeons would devour any spilled grain around the stable. Several well-known architects were involved in the restoration of the house, including John Vinci, John Thorpe, and Wilbert Hasbrouck.

The Prairie Avenue side of the 35-room Glessner House displays a more Italian "palazzo" character, whereas the 18th Street side has a more sedate English-style facade. Richardson died before the house was finished, and his successor firm, Shepley, Rutan & Coolidge, completed the work. The fortress-like house, with its rough-hewn granite walls, is the hallmark of Richardson's style, and evokes strength and solidity, as well as simplicity. (Photo by author)

In 1976 the conservatory plus two large closets and a passageway on the second floor were gutted and remodeled as a conference center by Hammond, Beeby & Babka (the firm that planned the Harold Washington Library). Although a useful addition, the contrast of a starkly modern space alongside the richly furnished bedrooms is a bit startling. The brick-walled courtyard of the house is quite interesting, as that is where the main rooms face, away from the icy blasts of winter, where the family could enjoy year-round privacy, away from the eyes of disapproving neighbors.

The Glessner House, as a house museum, is open to the public Wednesday through Sunday from 1:00 to 3:00 P.M., with hourlong tours at 1:00, 2:00, and 3:00 P.M. Fee: $5.00 (CAF members free). A combination ticket to include the Clarke House is $8.00. Enter the house at the rear of the 18th Street side, into what was formerly the carriage house and stable. There is a small gift shop and also a few tables and chairs for your brown-bag lunch.

After your visit, cross to the southeast corner of Prairie Avenue and E. 18th Street.

The **William Wallace Kimball House** (*1890, Solon Spencer Beman*), 1801 S. Prairie Avenue, is one of the country's finest surviving examples of the "chateauesque" style. Architect Beman created a lavish exterior, following the

The "chateauesque" William Wallace Kimball House, across Prairie Avenue from the Glessner House, was designed in 1890 by Solon S. Beman for the famous dealer in and manufacturer of Kimball pianos and organs. The 29-room mansion, in Francis I style, is one of the finest examples of the genre in the country. (Photo by author)

style that became popular during the reign of French King Francis I (1515–1547). It is modeled after the Châteaux de Josselin in Brittany, in a style generally associated with the famous chateaux of the Loire Valley. The tall front bay is an expansion of the series of tall dormers on the French model. The house is reported to have cost one million dollars to build; it boasts 29 rooms, high ceilings, ornate plaster moldings, and is furnished with oak and mahogany paneling, cherry wainscoting, and onyx fireplaces. When occupied by the Kimballs, the house was filled with fine paintings and other art treasures that ultimately went to the Art Institute of Chicago. Perhaps impressed by the splendid chateaux designed at the time by Richard Morris Hunt for the Vanderbilts in New York City, the Kimballs engaged Beman to design a similar mansion, but on a smaller scale. Beman, a native of Brooklyn, N.Y., began his apprenticeship in the office of Richard Upjohn, and was later discovered by Pullman who brought him to Chicago to design his company town, one of the earliest planned industrial communities.

Kimball was a successful dealer in and manufacturer of pianos and organs which were renowned for superb craftsmanship and musical excellence. Theatre organs made by the Kimball Company are still to be found around the country, and the name is perpetuated today by a group of devotees and organ preservationists called the Kimball Theatre Organ Society.

Alongside the Kimball House is the **Joseph Griswold Coleman–Miner Thomas Ames House** (*1885, Henry Ives Cobb & Charles Sumner Frost*), 1811 S. Prairie Avenue. In strong contrast to the Kimball house, this rock-faced red sandstone building is a fine example of a *fin-de-siècle* elegant mansion. Although not purely Romanesque Revival in style, it retains many of its strong elements: round-headed arches set above short clustered columns at the right-side entrance, typical Romanesque foliated capitals with animal-head designs, a basket-handle arch over the windows in the gable, a second-story smooth-stone bay, and gabled dormer. Cobb & Frost was a highly respected Chicago partnership in the late 19th century. In the 1940s, the Kimball and Coleman-Ames coach houses were connected, creating a semi-enclosed courtyard which adds a bit of European-style charm to the setting. Like its neighbor, the Kimball House, it, too, has an elaborately furnished interior, with carved wood, oak panelling, onyx fireplaces, plus a grand staircase.

Joseph G. Coleman began his career as a harnessmaker, but soon turned to real estate and became one of Chicago's leading investors. He never completely abandoned his earlier interests, and parlayed them into a major hardware business. Upon the death of his wife in 1888, just three years after taking possession of the grand house, he sold it to Miner T. Ames, a major dealer in coal and a member of the board of directors of the Baltimore & Ohio Railroad. His occupancy was also short-lived, as he died two years later, leaving the property to his son. In the years that followed, the house passed to a number of different owners. Both this house and the Kimball House are presently owned by the Chicago Architecture Foundation and the Coleman-Ames House is currently occupied by offices of the U.S. Soccer Federation.

Continue south on Prairie Avenue.

On the west side of the street, and marked by one of the distinctive plaques placed by the Chicago Architecture Foundation, is the **site of the Osborn Rensselaer Keith House** (*1886, Cobb & Frost*), 1808 S. Prairie Avenue, razed in 1968. O. R. Keith, as he was known, and his two older brothers owned the largest millinery firm in the Midwest. The house, one of four built by Keith on Prairie Avenue, was acquired in 1901 by Stanley Field, nephew of Marshall Field and lifetime president of the Field Museum, who lived here until 1913.

Continuing along the Promenade we note the **site of the George Henry Wheeler House,** designed by Burnham & Root in 1885, at 1812 S. Prairie Avenue. The style of the house was 18th-century Dutch vernacular, and was designed for the builder of one of Chicago's first grain elevators. Wheeler later became president of the Chicago City Railway Company, which ran the city's extensive cable-car network. The house fell to the wrecker's ball in 1968.

Across the street is the **site of the Joseph Sears House** (*1881–1882, Burnham & Root*), 1815 S. Prairie Avenue, demolished in 1967. Sears made his fortune when he developed the process for using cottonseed oil for cooking.

Just a bit farther is the **site of the Thomas Dent House** (*1881, Burnham & Root*), 1819 S. Prairie Avenue, designed in pressed brick with a mansard roof. Dent was a popular lawyer known affectionately as "Judge" Dent. The house was sold to the Second Presbyterian Church in 1911 for use as its Manse. It was demolished in 1945.

Back across to the west side is the **site of the Charles M. Henderson House,** built in 1872 by an unknown architect, 1816 S. Prairie Avenue. Henderson made his fortune in shoe manufacturing, and became one of the largest dealers in the fabrication of rubber boots. The house was razed in the late 1920s.

The adjacent **site of the James A. Smith House,** 1824 S. Prairie Avenue, was built for Smith, a furrier, by an unknown architect in 1866. The house, one of the earliest built on Prairie Avenue, was later acquired by George B. Marsh, a lumber baron. Charles Schwartz, a partner in one of the largest grain and provisions companies in Chicago, was the next owner. The plaque recalls a visit by the renowned Polish pianist-composer Ignace Jan Paderewski, who had agreed to give a private concert for a fee of $1,000. According to the legend, Paderewski was drawn into a poker game afterward with his host, and he ended up gambling away more than his earnings.

A bit further is the **site of the Daniel B. Shipman House,** 1832 S. Prairie Avenue, erected after the land was purchased in 1873, and also designed by an unknown architect. Shipman headed the D. B. Shipman White Lead Works, the largest paint company in the Midwest. He was also noted for his involvement in the care for the incurably ill and his founding of the Chicago Home for Incurables. His wife, Louise Cady Shipman, like virtually all the Prairie Avenue wives, was active in the support of numerous charities. The house was demolished in 1936.

Crossing the street again, we find the **site of the John Wesley Doane House,** 1827 S. Prairie Avenue. Built in 1882 from plans by architect T. V. Wadskier, it was the first house in Chicago to be illuminated by electricity. Not surprising, since Doane was a founder of the Western Edison Light Company, a forerunner of Commonwealth Edison. Interestingly, Doane had his own power generating plant located in the basement of his coach house. He also maintained his own domestic steam laundry in his basement. His real fortune, however, derived from his wholesale tea and coffee importing business. According to the plaque, the architect employed renowned New York artist John La Farge to create the stained-glass windows for the house. The elegant house survived until 1936.

At 1901 S. Prairie is the **site of the O. R. Keith–Norman B. Ream House** (*1881, Lavall B. Dixon*). Ream hired Burnham & Root to make extensive changes in 1887 after he purchased the house from the original owner the year before. Ream, after many business failures, became a successful commission merchant, and ultimately a member of the Chicago Board of Trade and the New York Stock Exchange, in addition to playing an important role in the reorganization of the Baltimore & Ohio Railroad. The Ream House vanished in 1930.

Once more across to the west side of the street to the **site of the Fernando Jones House,** 1834 S. Prairie Avenue, one of the earliest homes to be erected on Prairie Avenue, was designed in 1866 by John M. Van Osdel, recognized as Chicago's first architect. Jones, a senior executive of the Chicago Title & Trust Company, had the distinction of living an unusually long life in Chicago, from its early Indian days until relatively modern times, dying at the ripe old age of 91. The house survived for 70 years and was razed in 1942.

Just beyond the fence-enclosed park, stands the **Elbridge G. Keith House** (*1870, John W. Roberts*), 1900 S. Prairie Avenue. The Keith House is the oldest

The Elbridge G. Keith House, 1900 S. Prairie Avenue, completed in 1870, is the oldest extant original residence on Prairie Avenue. The front facade is of Ohio sandstone in a modified Italianate style; the side walls, however, are of brick, as an economy measure. The mansard roof and dormers were added in the 1880s when the French Second-Empire style became all the rage. (Photo by author)

extant original residence on Prairie Avenue, and a typical three-story structure of the early 1870s in a modified Italiante style, with a facade of Ohio sandstone, a projecting bay that runs the full height of the house, a columned portico, carved lintels above the windows, and a traditional classic cornice. The side walls are brick, a typical economy measure. The roof with dormers is an 1880s addition. (When the French Second-Empire style came into vogue, it was not uncommon to see mansard roofs plopped atop classic and vernacular houses all across the country.) In the rear is the carriage house or stable. Elbridge Keith, a banker, and two brothers who also maintained residences on Prairie Avenue, were wholesale millinery merchants. It is said that they acquired merchandise salvaged from warehouses damaged in the Great Fire, and sold it from their carriage houses. The exterior has been lovingly restored by its present owner, who has opened an art gallery in the house.

Across Prairie Avenue (again!) is the once-elegant, but now woebegone **Marshall Field, Jr., House** (*1884, Solon S. Beman*), 1919 S. Prairie Avenue, designed in the then-popular Queen Anne style, in sandstone and brick. Young Mr. Field purchased the house for $65,000 shortly after his marriage in 1890, and resided there until his death in 1905. The years have not been kind to the integrity of the house, as additions and subtractions have left a rather muddled facade, and at present it is in dreadful condition and sealed. A little of its original style can be seen in the strong round-arch entryway with its stubby columns and foliated capitals.

In the lot to the left once stood the opulent **Marshall Field House,** 1905 S. Prairie Avenue, erected in 1871 for the merchant prince. This was the first major urban residence designed by Richard Morris Hunt, who some years later became the architect of choice of New York's multimillionaires, and designer of the base of the Statue of Liberty. One cannot but feel deep regret that it is the son's house that survived, rather than the far more beautiful and architecturally significant mansion of the father—a house said to be as important as the Glessner House. The mansion fell victim of the wrecker's ball in 1955.

Other lost homes on the west side of the street south of the Elbridge Keith House were the **Edson Keith House** (*1870, John W. Roberts*), 1906 S. Prairie Avenue; the **Byron Moulton House** (*1883, Treat & Foltz*), 1912 S. Prairie Avenue; and the **Daniel M. Thompson–Samuel W. Allerton House** (*1869, Lavall B. Dixon*), 1936 S. Prairie Avenue, the South Side's first $100,000 house, and the one that suddenly made Prairie Avenue famous! Thompson made his fortune as a grain elevator owner. On the east side were once the houses of Charles P. Kellogg, at No. 1923, immediately to the south, and George Armour, a bit further, at No. 1945.

It will now be necessary to retrace your steps to the Glessner House in order to enter the fenced-in park. Just beyond the house is a courtyard with entry gate (which is open only during the hours of the Glessner and Clarke houses).

On entering the park you will notice bits and pieces of masonry from demolished houses strewn about, creating the impression of an old cemetery, which in effect it is, with the scattered chunks of limestone as memorials to the once proud houses. At the south end are "slices" of fluted columns that once adorned the old Chicago Custom House and Post Office, designed by Henry Ives Cobb, built in 1905, and torn down in the late 1950s for the construction of the Chicago Federal Center.

Dominating this pleasant patch of green is the commemorative **Monument to the Fort Dearborn Massacre,** by sculptor Carl Rohl-Smith, and erected originally east of the supposed massacre site in 1893, at the corner of E. 18th Street and S. Calumet Avenue. Also known as *The Potawatomi Rescue,* it was commissioned by George M. Pullman, and moved here in 1987. Its original site was next to an old cottonwood tree that once stood in 18th street near Pullman's mansion and had witnessed the dread event in 1812. The grim and deeply moving statue, which the *AIA Guide to Chicago* claims has been giving children nightmares for years, depicts Potawatomi chief Black Partridge interrupting a tomahawk blow aimed at Margaret Helm, while Dr. Isaac Van Voorhees lies dying at their feet, and a terrified child with outstretched arms represents the 12 children killed in the massacre. The statue memorializes the assault on a group of settlers from Fort Dearborn, who in 1812, with about 100 men, women, and children had been ordered to abandon the fort to avoid a likely attack by the British and Indians.

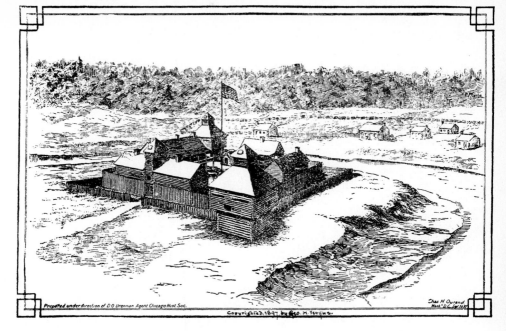

A sketch of Fort Dearborn in the first decade of the 19th century, before it was attacked and burned by local Indians. In 1812 the fort was abandoned and a group of settlers headed south in the hope of reaching Fort Wayne. They were set upon at a site thought to be about 100 yards east of what is today Prairie Avenue and 18th Street, at the intersection of Calumet Avenue, and 52 members of the band of 100 were brutally slaughtered. (Commission on Chicago Landmarks)

As they were fleeing south through an area known to be occupied by hostile Indians, they were set upon, and 52 were savagely slaughtered near this site.

On the west side of the park is the **Henry Brown Clarke House,** 1855 S. Indiana Avenue, built in 1836 and the oldest surviving house in Chicago. The architect is unknown; houses of that type were generally built by skilled carpenters who also served as local architects. The house was built originally on a 20-acre site for Henry and Caroline Clarke on what is now Michigan Avenue, between 16th and 17th streets. The property extended from the lakefront as far west as State Street. Henry fell victim to cholera in 1849, but his wife continued to live there until her death. In 1872 it was moved to 45th Street and Wabash Avenue and served for a time as a church meeting hall. When the house came up for sale in 1977, the City of Chicago bought it to have it restored as the city's oldest house, and had it moved to the present location in its original neighborhood. The move was not without major difficulties, however, since in the intervening years after the original move the city had built the Englewood-Jackson Park Elevated line which stood as an almost insurmountable barrier. In December 1977 the city solved the problem by hoisting the house over the El, thus allowing it to continue its journey northward.

The house, sometimes referred to as the Widow Clarke House, in addition to being the oldest structure in Chicago (although a house in the Norwood Park section makes a similar claim, but that area was not within the Chicago city limits at the time), is probably the only surviving Greek Revival–style house. The

(Left) The Monument to the Fort Dearborn Massacre, by sculptor Carl Rohl-Smith, was commissioned by George M. Pullman in 1893 and moved to this site in the little park behind the Glessner and Clarke houses in 1987. It had previously stood at what is thought to have been the actual massacre site. The grim and moving sculpture group depicts Potawatomi chief Black Partridge interrupting a tomahawk blow aimed at Margaret Helm, while Dr. Isaac Van Voorhees lies dying at their feet, and a terrified child with outstretched arms represents the 12 children killed in the attack. (Photo by author)

period of the Greek Revival in America was roughly 1825–1850, and throughout the country, houses of either wood or brick displayed the typical classic motifs of Doric-columned entrances, pedimented porticoes, panelled window lintels, peaked roofs, a raised basement, and a symmetrical building plan. The Clarke House is a larger, more elegant example of the style and incorporates a spacious and high-ceilinged interior, tall triple-hung windows, and a square tower. Greek Revival–style houses constructed of wood were invariably painted white, while those of brick often had their bricks laid in Flemish bond (alternating "headers," or short bricks, and "stretchers," or long bricks).

Tours of the Clarke House Museum are given Wednesday through Sunday, at 12 noon, 1:00 P.M., and 2:00 P.M., and depart from the Glessner House (see tour and fee information under Glessner House). Call 326–1480 for information.

The Henry Brown Clarke House, at 1855 S. Indiana Avenue, was built in 1836, and is the oldest surviving house in Chicago, and probably its last remaining Greek Revival–style house. The Clarke House has been moved twice, the last time by the City of Chicago, which purchased it, in an almost unsurmountable logistical challenge that involved hoisting it over an intervening El train line to bring it to this site. Like the Glessner House, the Clarke House is also a house museum, with both under the aegis of the Prairie Avenue House Museums. (Courtesy of the Prairie Avenue House Museums)

On leaving the museum grounds through the gate next to the Glessner House, turn left (west) to the corner of S. Indiana Avenue and E. 18th Street.

On the northeast corner is the **former Eastman Kodak Building** (*1905, Hill & Woltersdorf*). One of the earlier commercial "intrusions," it is typical of the factory buildings that gradually replaced the mansions of the wealthy. After Kodak left, the building was renovated into loft space and renamed Prairie District Lofts. The east end of the site also marks the location of the H. J. McBirney Residence, which was located at 1736 S. Prairie Avenue, and razed shortly after the turn of the 20th century.

Walk west one block to S. Michigan Avenue and turn left (south) one block to the church at the corner of E. Cullerton Street.

The **Second Presbyterian Church** (*1874, James Renwick; renovation 1900, Howard Van Doren Shaw*), 1936 S. Michigan Avenue, was designed by New York architect Renwick, who is considered one of the foremost exponents of the Gothic Revival style in America. He is noted for a number of famous Gothic Revival–style buildings, including St. Patrick's Cathedral and Grace Church in Manhattan, and the Smithsonian Institution "Castle" in Washington. Renwick had designed an earlier church for the congregation further uptown, but it was consumed in the Great Fire of 1871. This church too, suffered a fire in 1900, and much of the interior remodeling reflects Shaw's interest in the Arts and Crafts and Pre-Raphaelite movements. A number of exterior modifications were made as well, particularly in the large pointed arch window over the entrance and rectangular windows in place of Gothic pointed-arch windows in the clerestory. The church is built of a locally quarried limestone that is highlighted with dark speckling known as "bituminous mottling" and accented with dark horizontal bands of stone, said to be from the same quarry.

When the church was built, Michigan Avenue was lined with the homes of the city's most affluent citizens, as well as a number of churches of different denominations and a large synagogue. The Presbyterians were well represented among the upper-class settlers of early Chicago, as were Baptists, Episcopalians, Congregationalists, Unitarians, and Reform Jews. The list of the Second Presbyterian's wealthy congregants included such members of the Prairie Avenue elite as the Fields, Mary Todd Lincoln, wife of the president, and her son Robert Todd Lincoln, a corporation lawyer for railroad interests who served on the church's board of trustees and was president of the Pullman

(Right) The landmark Second Presbyterian Church, 1936 S. Michigan Avenue, the only surviving church in the Prairie Avenue neighborhood, was designed in 1874 by noted New York architect James Renwick, and renovated in 1900 by Howard Van Doren Shaw. Renwick's reputation for the Gothic Revival had already been established with his plans for St. Patrick's Cathedral and the Smithsonian Institution. The church was built of locally quarried limestone that is highlighted with dark speckling known as "bituminous mottling" and accented with dark horizontal bands of stone. (Photo by author)

The lavish interior of the Second Presbyterian Church boasts 22 Tiffany stained-glass windows, plus two smaller windows painted by the English pre-Raphaelite artist, Edward Burne-Jones and fabricated by William Morris. After a fire in 1900, architect Howard Van Doren Shaw transformed the nave of the church into what has been called "the crown jewel of the Arts and Crafts Movement in Chicago." In addition, there are several interesting murals by Chicago painter, Frederic Clay Bartlett. (Reproduced with permission of the publisher, Loyola University Press, from the book Chicago Churches and Synagogues, *by George Lane)*

Company from 1897 to 1911. Of all those many houses of worship, this is the only survivor left between 16th and 25th streets.

The outstanding feature of the church is its splendid interior which boasts no fewer than 22 exquisite stained-glass windows, 14 from the Louis Comfort Tiffany studio, including the one over the entrance. Two smaller windows were painted by the English pre-Raphaelite artist, Edward Burne-Jones, and fabricated by one of the most influential figures of the Arts and Crafts movement, William Morris. Architect Howard Van Doren Shaw succeeded in transforming the nave of the church into what has been called "the crown jewel of the Arts and Crafts movement in Chicago." In addition, there are several interesting murals executed by the distinguished Chicago painter, Frederic Clay Bartlett. (Note: Since the church is always closed, except for services, it would be wise to phone ahead to inquire about a tour; 225–4951.) Compare the Second Presbyterian Church with the Fourth Presbyterian Church on the Magnificent Mile, opposite the John Hancock Center. (*See* Tour 6, pages 242–244.)

Before continuing south on Michigan Avenue, take a brief detour left (east) along E. Cullerton Street toward Prairie Avenue again.

On the south side of the street, between Indiana and Prairie avenues, is an odd trio of houses, **Nos. 213, 215, and 217 E. Cullerton Street,** dating from the late 1860s to the early 1890s. The middle house, No. 215, recessed from its flanking pair, is the oldest and least remodeled, and was built in the then-popular Italianate style. No. 213 (1891) was remodeled in a Renaissance Revival style, and No. 217 was redesigned in Classic Revival style. It has a two-story projecting bay covered with sheet copper with an ornate terra-cotta entrance. The names of the architects are unknown, although No. 213 was designed by Thomas & Rapp for client Dr. Charles W. Purdy. What the two outer buildings may have looked like originally is also unknown, both having been added to over the years. This trio of houses was never in the same class as the houses seen earlier, and were doubtless constructed for somewhat less wealthy tenants. Although now dwarfed by the adjacent eight-story Atwell Building, they do give some idea of the scale of the old neighborhood. The **Atwell Building** (*1922, Alfred Alschuler*) was erected to house a printing company.

At the northwest corner of E. Cullerton Street and S. Prairie Avenue is the **Hump Hairpin Building** (*1915, Alfred Alschuler*), a commercial structure originally dedicated to the manufacture of ladies' hairpins, and the first factory to be built on Prairie Avenue. It replaced the 1869 Daniel M. Thompson–Samuel Allerton House, the first $100,000 house on the South Side. The one-story section of the factory was designed to be harmonious with its neighboring residences. In the 1930s, the lobby was redesigned with Art Deco adornments added and in 1939 a multistory addition was erected at the north end of the factory. The new section replaced a fine house once occupied by the Frank Lowdens, daughter and son-in-law of the Pullmans, and later by Mrs. Timothy Blackstone, whose earlier mansion on Michigan Avenue was demolished for the construction of the Blackstone Hotel, which bears the family name. Observe the interesting motifs above all the brick piers on both sides of the building. Note, too, the name of the company carved on both sides of the Prairie Avenue entrance. No longer a hairpin factory, at this writing it is vacant.

Now cross to the southeast corner.

At No. 2013 S. Prairie Avenue (east side), is the **William H. Reid House** (*1894, Beers, Clay & Dutton*). Surrounded by empty and desolate lots, where once similar elegant homes stood, the relatively narrow building is now the one survivor on the block, and is still occupied and preserved by its owner. Designed in Classic Revival style, the most noticeable features of this brick and masonry row house are the large third-floor Palladian window and the Ionic columned portico—vestiges of its once elegant past. Interesting is the wrought ironwork of the entrance balustrade and the fence which has unusually shaped twisted newel posts in the form of pineapples, the traditional symbol of welcome. The house has the distinction of being the first steel-frame residence in Chicago. Next door at No. 2009 once stood the **Max A. Meyer Residence** (*1888, Burnham & Root*) designed in French Gothic style with a prominent gable, and referred to as being the "most humane and lovely."

Return to Michigan Avenue.

At the southwest corner of S. Michigan Avenue and E. Cullerton Street is a three-story commercial building, **2000 S. Michigan Avenue** (*1909, Jenney, Mundie & Jensen*), built of concrete and red brick, and trimmed with terra cotta. Look above at the name in the parapet which reads "Locomobile," the brand name of a long-forgotten luxury automobile. The building is one of those along **Automobile Row,** which beginning in 1908, extended from Roosevelt Road south to 29th Street, and comprised an almost continuous line of automobile showrooms on both sides of Michigan Avenue that sprang up in the first decade of the 20th century. At least 40 buildings sold or serviced automobiles, with manufacturers vying with one another to market their horseless carriages to the clientele they had recently displaced. Michigan Avenue became the center for

The building at 2000 S. Michigan Avenue is one of a number of structures that were built as automobile showrooms during the first decade of the 20th century when S. Michigan Avenue from Roosevelt Road to 29th Street became known as "Automobile Row." At least 40 buildings sold or serviced the new "horseless carriages." The avenue was ideal for test drives, as it was wide, flat, and smoothly paved. Any mansions along the roadway were soon demolished as the character of S. Michigan Avenue gave way to the motor age. The Locomobile, now a long-forgotten name, was a luxury automobile that was manufactured well into the 1920s. (Photo by author)

auto sales in Chicago because it was wide, flat, and smoothly paved, and suitable for test drives. Too, the 200-foot-wide lots, of the by-then old-fashioned houses that had been sold or demolished, lent themselves to the construction of wide buildings needed for auto sales. These showrooms, typically three stories high, were at first purely functional, but by the 1920s, as Mary Alice Molloy writes in the *AIA Guide*, "designers began addressing the problem of how to effectively display indoors an item meant to be seen outdoors. Interiors, often with offices tucked away on mezzanines, were made to look like exteriors, with walls of stucco or stone. Mediterranean and California Spanish styling were deemed highly suitable." Now mostly all gone or converted to other purposes, a number of fanciful facades from their glory days still survive.

Take a stroll down Michigan Avenue as far as the 2200 block, look up and note the names and logos of such extinct auto makers as Hudson and Marmon, and several contemporary companies whose former logos are still clearly visible on their "movieland facades." There were a number of Chicago auto manufacturers during the first two decades of the 20th century—Amalgamated, Armac, Hertle, Hudson, Maxwell, and Marble-Swift—names that today have virtually faded from memory.

Walk south on Michigan Avenue two blocks to Cermak Road.

On the northeast corner stands the landmark **Lexington Hotel** (*1892, Clinton J. Warren*), 2135 S. Michigan Avenue, at this writing under a demolition order. Erected the year before the World's Columbian Exposition, the 10-story dark-red brick and terra-cotta building was built on a steel framework, with

Many of the automobile showrooms were quite stylish and ornate. This structure was a salesroom of Hudson Motors, a respected name in the industry that survived until well after World War II. Note the H in the circular plaques at the top. (Photo by author)

(Left and above) The Lexington Hotel, at 2135 S. Michigan Avenue at the corner of Cermak Road, was built in 1892, and was one of a number of hotels built to capitalize on the opening of the World's Columbian Exposition the following year by meeting the need for rooms for the millions of expected visitors. When the fair closed, so did most of the hotels, but the Lexington remained, and later achieved some "fame" as the favorite hangout of Al Capone, who maintained a six-room suite. Never more than a modest hotel, the somewhat retouched ca. 1920 photo on the left shows an attractive undulating facade and corner round tower, in the style of the Chicago school's Old Colony Building. After Capone was sent to jail in 1932, the management, in a move to upgrade the hotel's image, changed its name to the New Michigan. In a late 1995 view (above), the hotel stands vacant and gutted, and, at this writing, scheduled for demolition. (Left, Chicago Historical Society; above, photo by author)

rows of stacked bay windows and prominent rounded corners. It was one of several hundred hotels that were built to meet the demand for housing by the more than 26 million visitors who came to the Fair. Its only real claim to fame was that President Benjamin Harrison once spoke from its balcony. The depression of the 1890s sent many such hotels into bankruptcy, but the Lexington managed to survive.

In later years the hotel was the favorite hangout of "Scarface Al" Capone, who occupied a heavily guarded six-room suite in Salon 430, from 1928 until 1932 when the government finally sent him away to less luxurious accommodations. His early home had been about three miles south, at 7244 S. Prairie Avenue. It was during the notorious Capone era that the instrument known as the "Chicago piano" (the Thompson submachine gun) became the weapon of choice to "rub out" rival gang members. Some time after the imprisonment of Capone, the hotel management changed the name to the New Michigan Hotel, a move intended to upgrade its gangster-era image. It didn't work, and the establishment continued to stagger along for many years, sliding from bordello to flophouse to firetrap, finally breathing its last in 1980. In 1986 when workers discovered a 7- by 10-foot vault hidden in the recesses of the hotel, the thought that its contents might reveal a sensational treasure trove led TV personality Geraldo Rivera to stage a two-hour prime-time television event culminating with the opening of the enigmatic safe. However, after all the hype and hoopla, nothing was found inside except an empty and very dusty 60-year-old liquor bottle.

(As this book goes to press, the city announced that it had condemned the hotel as a public nuisance and safety hazard. The Commission on Chicago Landmarks also withdrew its landmark status, and a demolition contract had been issued, thus putting an end to the 103-year-old hotel. And as Donald Mulack, president of the Chicago Crime Commission declared, "Perhaps at last we can put to rest any misplaced nostalgia for the violence, crime and corruption of the past, and bury that image of Chicago once and for all.")

Turn left (east) on Cermak Road two blocks to Prairie Avenue.

Cermak Road, formerly 22nd Street, is named for former Chicago Mayor Anton J. Cermak, who is credited with presenting the city's first ethnically balanced election slate—a move that led to the growth of power of the city's Democratic Party. He served from 1931 to 1933, when he was gunned down in

The residential area of the city's affluent during the 1890s extended much farther south than the present Prairie Avenue historic area. In this view of S. Michigan Avenue (then Boulevard) looking south from 29th Street, an almost continuous row of solid and elegant town houses extends as far as the eye can see. (Chicago Historical Society)

Miami, Florida, while on the road with President Franklin D. Roosevelt. It was assumed that the assassin's bullet was meant for the President.

At Prairie Avenue turn left for just a short distance to **No. 2126 S. Prairie Avenue** (*1904, Mann, MacNeille and Lindeberg*), on the west side of the street. It is a rather large house, designed in a neo-Georgian style and is five bays wide, with four brick piers topped with Ionic capitals. The building, named Prairie House by a former restaurateur, is now a methadone clinic.

A bit further down the block is the **Harriet F. Rees House** (*1888, Cobb & Frost*), 2110 S. Prairie Avenue. Designed by the same architects as the Coleman-Ames House, it stands in "splendid isolation" and looks forlorn. The Richardsonian Romanesque house has a very smooth texture with a large two-story bow-front bay, an ornate colonnade at the third-floor level, a tall chimney, and a pointed gable surmounted by a Romanesque-style crocket. Also interesting are the ornate columns' capitals, the third-floor spandrels, and a band course above the first floor.

No need to walk further, but it should be mentioned that at the southwest corner of Prairie Avenue and 21st Street stood the mansion of millionaire John B. Sherman, known as the "Father of the Stock Yards." In 1874 he commissioned Daniel H. Burnham and John Wellborn Root to design his residence, which turned out to be the first important work of the two young architects. Alas, the imposing brick-and-masonry villa suffered the fate of so many of its contemporaries, and was torn down early in the 20th century.

While a bit off the tour's itinerary, the interesting Raymond Hilliard Center, 54 W. Cermak Road, of the Chicago Housing Authority, lies just a few blocks west. The low-income project, designed by Bertrand Goldberg Associates, and built by the CHA in 1966, bears the typical Goldberg stamp, with the curved walls and oval windows in monolithic concrete that recalls his River City and the Prentice Women's Hospital. The complex includes (left to right) a one-story community building, two 16-story buildings for the elderly, an amphitheater, and two 22-story family buildings. (Courtesy Bertrand Goldberg Associates)

Return to Cermak Road and turn left (east) two blocks to S. Prairie Avenue.

The red-brick and terra-cotta warehouse at 330 E. Cermak Road was built for the American Book Company (*1912, N. Max Dunning*), **330 E. Cermak Road,** and once was used for storage by the Lakeside Press Plant No. 3. One of the major quality printing houses that dates back to the late-19th century, the Lakeside Press is owned by the R. R. Donnelley Company, which had printing operations in the adjacent building, using this for warehouse purposes. (*See also* the former Lakeside Press Building in the Printers Row tour, pages 284 and 286.) Earlier in the century the area was home to a number of printing establishments. The four-story building is topped by a water tower, and over the entrance is the ABC logo of the American Book Company emblazoned above the second floor. An important tenant today is the Metropolitan Pier and Exposition Authority, the entity in charge of McCormick Place-on-the-Lake and Navy Pier.

Connected to a building to the rear of the former Lakeside Press building by a bridge across S. Calumet Avenue is the huge and imposing **former R. R. Donnelley & Company, Chicago Manufacturing Division Plant** (also known as the **Calumet Plant**) (*1912, Howard Van Doren Shaw; extensions periodically to 1925; additions 1929, Charles Z. Lauder*), 350 E. Cermak Road. The R. R. Donnelley Company, which moved its printing operations out of state after the demise of the Sears catalog, is the largest commercial printing house in the country. (The Sears catalog was printed in the newer addition to the rear of the Lakeside Press Building.) Telephone directories are just one of its many products. Shaw was also the architect of the Lakeside Press building mentioned above, on Plymouth Court, in Printers Row.

The plant is a truly outstanding example of the Gothic Revival style as applied to a large commercial building. Note how the brick piers, between symmetrical vertical rows of windows and topped by limestone arches, give a cathedral-like air to the building; and how the Gothic-style tower, designed by Lauder after the death of Shaw, adds a crowning medieval touch to the complex. Of particular interest are the historic stone medallions and terra-cotta plaques that depict printers' logos, or colophons, of many of the greatest book printers of all time: Johannes Gutenberg, Aldus Manutius, William Morris's Kelmscott Press, Riverside Press, William Caxton, and a host of others. There are also carved reliefs of an Indian chief, Lakeside's logo, and a frontiersman. The chief can be found even on the pushbars of the revolving entrance doors. R. R. Donnelley's headquarters building at 77 W. Wacker Drive, designed by Spanish architect Ricardo Bonfill, should not be missed (*see* Tour 4, pages 146, 153, and 155).

Directly to the east is the gargantuan exposition complex, **McCormick Place-on-the-Lake** (*East Building: 1971, C. F. Murphy Associates; North Building: 1986, Skidmore, Owings & Merrill; South Building: planned completion 1997, Thompson, Ventulett, Stainback & Associates*), 2300 S. Lake Shore Drive. McCormick Place, which comprises three connected mega-buildings, is the nation's largest exposition and convention center, and second in the world only to one in Cologne, Germany.

The former R. R. Donnelley & Company, Chicago Manufacturing Division Plant, also known as the Calumet Plant, 350 E. Cermak Road, was designed in 1912 by Howard Van Doren Shaw and now serves as a company warehouse. The plant is an outstanding example of the Gothic Revival as applied to a large industrial building, and has an almost medieval cathedral-like appearance that is enhanced by the graceful tower. (Photo by author)

Note: **Before exploring the McCormick Center, it is recommended that you read the following description, since it gives a brief chronological and architectural overview. You will have to enter the North Building first, which is described later. Also, it should be mentioned that the Center is not particularly visitor-friendly. It was designed solely for expositions and conventions, and the administration tends to discourage walking tours; however, you will not be stopped.**

The complex, still incomplete at this writing, was begun when the first McCormick Place was built in 1960 by Shaw, Metz & Associates. An earlier plan to be drawn up by Mies van der Rohe, would have sited the McCormick Place on the south side of Cermak Road between King Drive and Michigan Avenue; however, the Metropolitan Pier & Exposition Authority selected, over vigorous public protest, a site along the lakefront, east of the 23rd Street Viaduct. Chicagoans felt that by giving away a piece of municipally owned park land the city was thus betraying a promise to keep the lakefront "forever open, clear and free," as stipulated in Daniel Burnham's 1909 Plan of Chicago. The design would also deprive pedestrians and bikers of a mile of scenic shorefront paths.

Seven years later McCormick Place was destroyed by fire, and citizens hoped that City Hall would seize the opportunity to make amends and relocate the convention center further back from the lake. But economic and political pressure to get the much-needed center built as quickly as possible, plus the convenience of being able to use the former structure's foundations, persuaded the authorities to rebuild on the same site.

The North Building of McCormick Place, 450 E. 23rd Street, was constructed in 1986 from plans by Skidmore, Owings & Merrill, and is immediately recognizable by its unusual system of cables that support the roof from 12 concrete pylons—a novel system designed to resist Chicago's strong winds and temperature variations, as well as to provide added strength should any of the 450-strand cables fail. To maximize interior space for this world's largest exhibition complex, the heating and air-conditioning conduits were placed within the pylons. Along the east and west facades are fixed vertical tubes that help maintain the roof's stability in case of severe weather conditions. (Courtesy Metropolitan Pier and Exposition Authority)

The first of the three buildings to open was the **East Building,** on January 3, 1971, built on the site of the original McCormick Place building destroyed by the fire. A major feature of the design is that the 300,000-square-foot main exhibition hall, which at first glance resembles an enormous airplane hangar, has only eight visible columns. The roof, which measures 1,350 feet across, covers 19 acres and weighs 10,000 tons, and towers 50 feet above the main floor. It is cantilevered 75 feet beyond its supporting columns, providing all-around protection from rain and snow. The harmonious combination of the enormous trussed roof and glass walls are said to recall Mies van der Rohe's plan for the National Gallery in Berlin, which is not surprising, considering that C. F. Murphy's designer for the project was Gene R. Summers, who had been an associate of Mies from 1950 to 1966. While overwhelming to the casual visitor, it is carefully planned for efficient service to the city's important and burgeoning convention industry.

The East Building is connected to the nearby North Building by a two-level pedestrian bridge (*1986, Skidmore, Owings & Merrill*), the lower level enclosed for protection against Lake Michigan's wintry blasts, and an open upper level that offers nice views of both buildings as it crosses Lake Shore Drive. From the bridge one can appreciate the engineering feat of the East Building's cantilevered roof. The bridge also straddles the tracks of the Illinois Central Railroad as well as the Metra Electric Division, which has a commuter station underneath the center. One of the building's amenities is the huge **Arie**

The East Building of McCormick Place, 2301 S. Lake Shore Drive, designed by C. F. Murphy Associates and opened in 1971, was the first of the new three-building complex. It is connected to the North Building by a two-level pedestrian bridge which straddles the Illinois Central and Metra Electric railroad lines as well as Lake Shore Drive. The 300,000-square-foot main exhibition hall, which resembles an enormous airplane hangar, has only eight visible columns. The 50-foot-high roof, which measures 1,360 feet across, covers 19 acres, weighs 10,000 tons, and is cantilevered 75 feet beyond its supporting columns—a feature that, aside from its spectacular engineering achievement and distinctive architectural profile, also provides protection from rain and snow. (Courtesy Metropolitan Pier and Exposition Authority)

Crown Theatre, in the southern half of the building, with a seating capacity second only to the Auditorium Theatre.

The **North Building,** the first building to be visited, is markedly different. The roof trusses are supported by 72 four-inch, 450-strand cables, which hang from two rows of six huge concrete pylons, and are a conspicuous addition to the Chicago skyline. To maximize open space, the heating and air-conditioning conduits were placed within the pylons. Along the east and west facades are fixed vertical tubes which help maintain the roof's stability under severe weather conditions. The interior is quite similar to the East Building, but is furnished with very colorful and attractive carpeting throughout.

The **South Building,** located directly south of the North Building, is presently under construction, and is expected to be completed by 1997. Planned are over one million square feet of exhibition space, which would more than double the present capacity of McCormick Place.

After you have entered McCormick Place following the pedestrian access signs, and explored the cavernous center via the North Building, the Pedes-

trian Bridge, and the East Building, you will have to return to the intersection across from the R. R. Donnelley Plant (King Drive and 23rd Street, the extension of Cermak Road). At this writing there is no direct CTA bus service from within the center to the Loop, due to extensive construction around the center. But Metra Electric Division trains run about every 40 minutes on weekdays, hourly on Saturdays, and every two hours on Sundays, from the 23rd Street Station, located directly below the center. (Follow the signs.) The train takes seven or eight minutes to reach the Randolph Street Station, corner of Michigan Avenue, at the edge of the Loop.

End of tour.

To return to the Loop by bus from outside McCormick Place, cross (carefully!) to the intersection of King Drive and 23rd Street (the extension of Cermak Road), and take either CTA Bus No. 3 or No. 4 northbound.

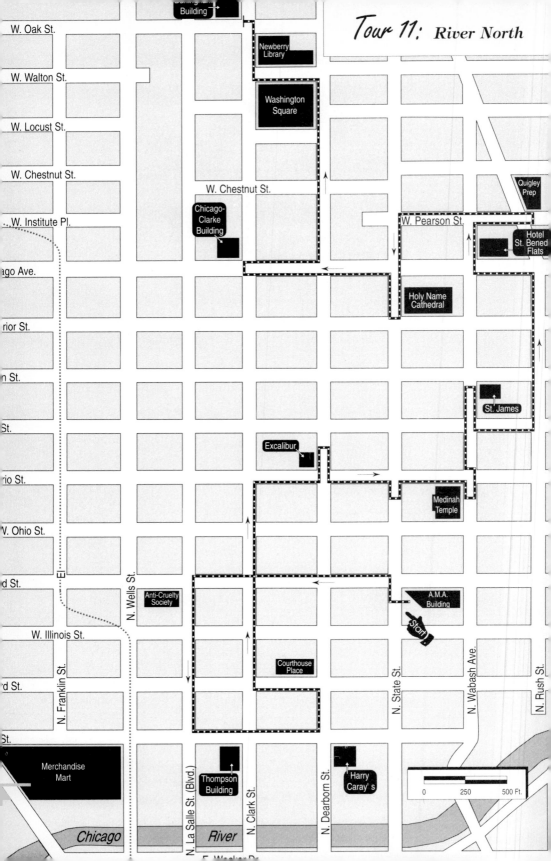

11. North of the Loop: The River North Neighborhood

The neighborhood to the north of the main branch of the Chicago River, between the north branch and Michigan Avenue, was the last downtown district to be developed. For most of the 19th century it had been a "backwater" and the place where the first Chicago industries got their start. Soon after Chicago's incorporation as a city in 1837, the area became the "portal to the city" for the poorest of the immigrant poor, and its unpaved streets were lined with an assortment of squatters' shacks, ramshackle buildings, and such local enterprises as slaughterhouses, soap and tallow works, glue factories, and an assortment of cottage industries. Of the new arrivals, the Irish made up the largest population, particularly after Ireland's Great Famine of 1846. At that time the only connection to the rest of the city was by the rickety Rush Street Bridge, built in 1850; later, two bridges in the western section, at Grand Avenue and Erie Street, provided additional links.

With the arrival of the Galena & Chicago Union Railroad in 1848, whose tracks ran along Kinzie Street to its terminal near the site of the present Merchandise Mart, the industrial role of River North took on much greater significance. New factories, warehouses, and brick and lumber yards sprang up, including many industries specifically designed to cater to the needs of the new railroad. Among other key industries were manufacturers of horse-drawn farm implement machinery. The shacks gradually disappeared, to be supplanted by rows of frame cottages to house the thousands of new immigrant laborers.

While the neighborhood was populated almost exclusively by the working poor, a few small enclaves of upscale residences sprang up, especially in the area along Rush Street above Grand Avenue, and later around Washington Square. Among the newly arrived wealthy were various members of the Cyrus McCormick clan, including Cyrus Hall McCormick, whose famous reaper revolutionized agricultural techniques worldwide. The McCormicks built elegant mansions and town houses, of which two still survive, but no longer as private residences.

When the Great Fire of 1871 spread its swath of devastation across downtown Chicago, the fleeing populace—rich and poor alike—assumed that once across the Chicago River they would be safe. A vain hope, for the windblown flames quickly leaped the river, and in a northeasterly route of destruction, sent the refugees onward, wiping out several square miles of buildings behind them before it burned itself out. Luckily, the path of the fire left many of the River North building industries unscathed, with the result that post-Fire reconstruction could begin almost immediately. And with Chicago's obsessive drive to rebuild, new jobs were created and more immigrant groups arrived—Swedes, Poles, and Italians—to find ready employment in one of history's greatest metropolitan rebirths.

The post-Fire boom continued to the turn of the century, bringing in more industrial development, and creating a growing ring of slums. The railroad, now the Chicago & Northwestern, abandoned its passenger station on Kinzie Street and moved west across the river to a new terminal on its present site. Further decline occurred after the opening in 1920 of the Michigan Avenue Bridge, and what remained of the once upscale enclaves deteriorated into an area of cheap rooming houses. While the neighborhood north of Michigan Avenue along Lake Shore Drive became Chicago's "Gold Coast," the district to the west stagnated. In the 1960s and early 1970s, there was a flurry of activity, as River North's inexpensive rents attracted many of the new bohemians. By the end of the decade the industrial pattern began to change, and most of the factories and warehouses either closed down or moved elsewhere.

In their place came artists, art galleries, trendy bars and restaurants, jazz clubs, discos, chic boutiques, and luxury high-rise apartment buildings. Much like the transformation that took place in New York's SoHo Cast-Iron District, River North became a desirable and interesting neighborhood to explore and live in. And like SoHo, its popularity soon became its undoing, as skyrocketing rents, expensive shops, and the construction of luxury apartment houses drove the artists to seek more affordable digs. On the heels of this development, office buildings and new hotels followed, particularly in the area east of State Street. In the western section, in the shadow of the Merchandise Mart, a new district developed, with dozens of shops specializing in interior design, antiques, lighting fixtures, and custom house furnishings—virtually an on-the-street extension of the Merchandise Mart itself.

Many of River North's older loft buildings, including a large number built just after the Great Fire, still survive, having undergone conversion to commercial and residential use. Too many, unfortunately, are now parking lots. On the other hand, a significant number of architecturally worthy buildings have been designated city landmarks and are listed on the National Register of Historic Places. While the neighborhood is by no means homogeneous in character, and shows little evidence of previous urban planning, much of its early character and scale still remains intact. And with its central location, its very special history, and its reputation as the "hottest place in town" for night life, River North is now firmly established as one of Chicago's most exciting and attractive areas.

The tour begins at the corner of N. State and E. Illinois streets, three blocks north of the Chicago River, and easily accessible from the Loop on foot, or by CTA State Street Bus No. 22, or by the State Street subway to the Grand Avenue Station (one block north).

Occupying the east side of the block from Illinois Street to Grand Avenue, is the towering, wedge-shaped **515 N. State Street** (*1990, Kenzo Tange; with Shaw & Associates*), the national headquarters building of the American Medical Association. The 29 stories are sheathed in glass and aluminum, with gray polished granite and marble trim on the lower floors and in the two-story glass wall enclosing the lobby. The lobby and the adjacent minipark are public amenities, hence open to visitors. Take a moment to explore the cheerful and expansive lobby, and note that the interior carries forth the wedge shape of the exterior. There is an art gallery in the rear. Outside are two black-marble pools, in the same wedge shape. But the big attraction of the building is its four-story cut-out section near the top—a unique trademark which serves as architect Kenzo Tange's "Welcome to Chicago" sign visible from afar. This unusual building has become a popular and familiar addition to Chicago's spectacular skyline.

On exiting the building (or minipark) on N. State Street, turn right to the corner of W. Grand Street and turn left (west). Continue beyond the post office to:

No. 57 W. Grand Avenue (*1912, Huehl & Schmid*), an eight-story loft building, of brick with limestone trim, is typical of the commercial structures built in the area around the turn of the century. It was erected for the Ramien & Kuhnert Company, a paint and wallpaper concern, whose initials can be seen above, below the roof.

(Note the banners on the lampposts announcing the "Courthouse District." The beautifully restored former court house—the pride of the neighborhood—will be seen shortly.)

Continue west on W. Grand Avenue to the corner of N. Clark Street.

On the southwest corner, **No. 101 W. Grand Avenue/516 N. Clark Street,** is an aggregation of buildings, the first pair dating from 1872 and 1873 by an unknown architect; adjacent are another pair from 1883 and 1884, by architect Cyrus P. Thomas. The entity began as a simple grocery store with attached loft space, then with the additions became within a decade a rather elegant hotel.

(Left) Wedge-shaped 515 N. State Street has become architect Kenzo Tange's "Welcome to Chicago!" sign. The eye-catching 29-story reflective-glass-and-aluminum tower's trademark is not so much its shiny triangular profile, but its novel four-story cut-out section near the top. Since the building's completion in 1990 the see-through perforation, clearly visible from afar, has made this structure a unique and interesting addition to the city skyline. The building serves as the national headquarters of the American Medical Association. (Photo by author)

In the 1880s it was the Grand Palace, in the next decade it became the St. Regis. Now it is a popular dining spot called The Corner Bakery. Note the galvanized metal sheathing on the bay windows. On the northwest corner is another group of buildings of the same era.

Continue west one more block to LaSalle Boulevard.

The unmistakable **Anti-Cruelty Society** (*1935, Leon Stanhope; addition on LaSalle Boulevard 1982, Stanley Tigerman Associates*), 157 W. Grand Avenue, is Chicago's equivalent of the Humane Society. The original Art Moderne limestone building is attached very tastefully to the International-style addition. Architect Stanhope once worked for Burnham & Root. This popular clinic and shelter for the city's four-legged homeless, which at first glance resembles a residential building, presents an eye-catching entrance with pairs of low-relief incised animal figures. Walk around the corner to enjoy the LaSalle Boulevard facade, a light-hearted architectural representation of what some might call a stylized doghouse, drawing potential pet buyers to inquire "how much is that doggie in the window?"

Further south at 500 N. LaSalle Drive is **Michael Jordan's Restaurant** ("He's back!"), in an 1890s vintage commercial loft building that was remodeled early in the century as a carbarn for the trolleycars. The restaurant is an enterprise of the Chicago Bulls' ace basketball player (in case you couldn't guess from the huge mural in front), and the team, of course, is just known as "Da Bulls."

A word about the confusion surrounding the name of the street: Some street signs say "Boulevard," others indicate "Drive," still others say "Street." After the Great Fire, LaSalle *Avenue* (to distinguish it from LaSalle Street, south of the river) was tree-lined and home to a number of wealthy Chicagoans. In 1930 the thoroughfare, already in decline, was widened, and all semblance to its halcyon days was obliterated. It was then renamed "Street." In 1978–1979 the city embarked on a multimillion-dollar revitalization program to upgrade the street and improve its seedy image, which led to another name change, "Boulevard" (Michael Jordan notwithstanding). Does this clarify the situation? Not by a long shot! The U.S. Post Office, in its infinite and inscrutable wisdom, has designated all street numbers from 300 to 1599 to be on LaSalle *Drive,* and numbers from 300 to 1598 on LaSalle *Street,* both in zip code 60610, and the street signs say either "Street" or "Boulevard." And what about those whose address is "300"? You figure it out!

Continue south to Illinois Street and look left (east) for a dramatic view of the A.M.A. Building against the high-rises along N. Michigan Avenue. Then continue to:

No. 442–444 N. LaSalle Boulevard. How does one explain an Art Deco terra-cotta facade on an 1880s-vintage warehouse? Simple. When LaSalle Street was widened by 14 feet on each side in 1930, it demanded the removal of all projecting building facades; so it was either remodel or demolish. The very attractive polychrome front was designed by George F. Lovdall.

Continue south past Hubbard Street to the southwest corner of Kinzie Street.

No. 350 N. LaSalle Boulevard (*1990, Loebl, Schlossman & Hackl, with Wojciech Lesnikowski*), by the architects of Water Tower Place, on N. Michigan Boulevard, is a modern reminder of the old Chicago school of architecture in its expression in the facade of the building's steel framework, only here it is with red brick rather than exposed metal, and the windows are of green glass. The curved corners and round towers are a neat addition to what might be just a routine postmodern building. To the rear, and at the edge of the Chicago River, is the harmonious Helene Curtis Building, remodeled six years earlier (*see* Tour 4, page 137). To the right of No. 350, along Kinzie Street, is an interesting row of post-Fire warehouses, with ornamented round-arch windows, and in its somewhat dingy state, re-creates the neighborhood atmosphere of a century ago.

Turn left (east) on W. Kinzie Street one block to the southwest corner of N. Clark Street.

The **John B. Thompson Building** (*1912, Alfred S. Alschuler*), 350 N. Clark Street, once housed the offices of the Thompson's Restaurant chain, branches of which could be found in every major city in the Midwest. Thompson's was the forerunner of the ubiquitous fast-food chains after World War I. The pristine creamy terra-cotta facade was a good advertisement for the now-defunct and sorely missed food establishment, and the proportions of the building were typical of the Chicago school at the time. Note how the tower dominates the building. The renovation into an office complex was executed in 1983 by Metz, Train & Youngren.

Continue east on W. Kinzie Street to N. Dearborn Street.

Holy Cow! What's that on the southeast corner? Is it the *Stadhuis* of a 17th-century Dutch town? No, it's **Harry Caray's** restaurant and bar (*1895, Henry Ives Cobb*), 33 W. Kinzie Street, where baseball is alive and well. Erected for the Chicago Varnish Company, which supplied the glossy finishes for railroad passenger cars, as well as for residences and office buildings, it was later the home of the Erhard Cheese Company. Today it is the establishment of Harry

The John B. Thompson Building, designed in 1912 by Alfred S. Alschuler, once housed the main office of the ubiquitous Thompson's Restaurant chain, an early forerunner of the fast-food industry. The Thompson name can be seen on the roof pavilion which hides the building's water tank. Many lamented the loss of these popular and inexpensive Midwest restaurants when the chain went out of business after World War II. (Photo by author)

This Dutch Renaissance Revival–style former factory building at 33 W. Kinzie Street is now "Holy Cow," the restaurant and bar of well-known Chicago Cubs radio announcer Harry Caray, and is acknowledged as the baseball "watering hole" in Chicago. Even the adjoining block of W. Kinzie Street is named for Caray. The charming building, originally a varnish factory, was designed in 1895 by Henry Ives Cobb. (Photo by author)

Caray, for years the well-known WGN radio announcer of Chicago Cubs games. Behind the banners and streamers is an excellent example of the Dutch Renaissance–Revival style, in red brick with limestone trim, with typical stepped gables, peaked roofline, quoins, and florid facade.

Turn left (north) on N. Dearborn Street one block to W. Hubbard Street, and turn left.

On the northwest corner is the "centerpiece" of the unofficial Courthouse District, **Courthouse Place** (*1892, Otto H. Matz, renovation 1986, Solomon Cordwell Buenz & Associates*), 54 W. Hubbard Street. Formerly the Cook County Criminal Courts Building, it is a fine example of the Romanesque Revival style. The six-story building was considered a model for court house design. The Cook County jail was conveniently located across the alley. When the building outlived its usefulness to the legal system in 1985, the city sold it to developers for adaptive reuse as an office development. Take a few minutes to examine the interesting rusticated Bedford limestone facade, dominated by the central bay. Note the different styles of window arches, the terra-cotta ped-

An excellent example of adaptive reuse is the impressive Courthouse Place (1892), formerly the Cook County Criminal Courts Building. Having outgrown its usefulness, the building was sold in 1986 to developers who contracted with Solomon Cordwell Buenz & Associates to convert it to an office complex. An attractive Romanesque Revival–style building, its forbidding fortress-like appearance must have seemed appropriate during the years of criminal trials that it witnessed, including the 1929 Leopold and Loeb child-murder case. The courtrooms also provided the grist for the reportage of Carl Sandburg, Charles MacArthur, and Ben Hecht. (Photo by author)

iment, and especially the elegant entrance. In the spandrels are sculptured figures of *Law* and *Justice,* and bracketing the entry arch are pairs of clustered columns with foliated capitals. The court house achieved national attention in 1929 when Clarence Darrow defended the notorious child-killers Leopold and Loeb. The courts also witnessed the reportage of such famous writers as Carl Sandburg, Charles MacArthur, and Ben Hecht. Al Capone was once brought in for questioning, but was released.

Walk west one block to N. Clark Street, and turn right (north).

On the left side of Clark Street, **Nos. 430, 432,** and **436** are a good study of post-Fire commercial/residential architecture. No. 430 was built of orange-colored brick in 1872 by an unknown architect. No. 432, in a harmonious modern style, was built considerably "post-Fire" (in 1988!). The initials in the gable, JAFA, stand for J. A. Friedman & Associates, the developer. The architectural firm was Florian-Wierzbowski. No. 436, in Italianate style, is seven bays wide and built of red brick with ornate window enframements. It was also designed in 1872, but by noted mid-19th century architect William W. Boyington (the architect of Chicago's Water Tower among other buildings, and first president of the American Institute of Architects). Note the change in window design on each succeeding floor. The east side of the block is another study in well-preserved post-Fire commercial/residential architecture.

At the southwest corner of W. Grand Avenue, take another look at No. 516 N. Clark Street, seen earlier on the tour. The tour itinerary now crosses our earlier route as we head north on Clark Street to W. Ohio Street.

In the block to the left, between W. Ohio and W. Ontario streets, is **the original "Rock 'n' Roll" McDonald's,** 600 N. Clark Street, designed in 1982 by Eugene Korbel. It is the first of the special series of the McDonald chain to celebrate the beginning of the Rock 'n' Roll era of the early 1950s, and is packed with reproduction memorabilia of the time.

Across the street is **Capone's Chicago,** 605 N. Clark Street, which invites visitors to "step back into Chicago's most glorious and infamous era, and 'Meet the Man, Scarface,' in a state-of-the-art Historical Family Show every 30 minutes." (*See also* his hangout at the Lexington Hotel, in Tour 10, The Prairie Avenue Historic District to McCormick Place, pages 345–348.) The group of fake-front buildings, which also includes a gift shop of Capone items, fits nicely in this "pop" culture district of River North. (Admission fee.)

Turn right (east) on W. Ontario Street.

The block to the right is shared by two unusual structures designed by Tigerman, Fugman, McCurry, the **Hard Rock Cafe** (*1985*), 65 W. Ontario Street, and the adjacent **Commonwealth Edison Ontario Street Substation** (*1987*). Always jammed with young people who come for the rock music, the

"Capone's Chicago," at 605 N. Clark Street, invites visitors to "step back into Chicago's most glorious and infamous era," and meet "Scarface" in this repeating 30-minute show. ("Glorious"? No! "Infamous"? Indeed!) The building fronts are all fake, as is the gift shop's plethora of Capone-era memorabilia and souvenirs, but the tourists love it, and it fits nicely into this "pop" culture section of the River North neighborhood. (Photo by author)

decor, and the T-shirts, but who scarcely notice the architecture, the Cafe's building was designed to harmonize with a former 1924 Com Ed substation next door that was due to be razed. The design is Classic Revival with a modern version of Palladian motifs. When Com Ed built its new substation, they chose to imitate the style of the neighboring Hard Rock Cafe, its earlier imitator. In the reconstruction, they rescued a number of the earlier building's adornments (plaques and medallions, even the old wrought-iron fence) and incorporated them into the new design. The electrical substation's "windows" are actually ventilation louvres. The building was erected, as the plaque indicates, on the 100th anniversary of the founding of the Commonwealth Edison Company.

Turn left (north) briefly on N. Dearborn Street.

On the northwest corner of N. Dearborn is the massive Richardsonian Romanesque building that was once the home of the **Chicago Historical Society** (*1892, Henry Ives Cobb*), 632 N. Dearborn Street. It now houses **Excalibur,** a popular night spot. The Society, which was founded in 1856, purchased the site nine years later. In 1868 they commissioned Burling & Whitehouse to build their first building. It lasted only three years until it was consumed in the Great Fire. Twenty-one years later the present building was constructed. The building has seen a number of tenants since the Historical Society moved out in 1931—a lodge of the Loyal Order of Moose, an office of the Works Progress

Harmonizing in style with the neo-Classical Commonwealth Edison substation at left is Chicago's edition of the Hard Rock Cafe, 65 W. Ontario Street, built in 1985. Interestingly, the Cafe's Palladian motifs were modeled after an earlier adjacent Com Ed powerhouse built in 1924. After the old substation was razed, the utility decided to commission a new building to match the style of the Hard Rock Cafe, and in 1987 the new Com Ed building was completed. Both the Hard Rock Cafe and the Com Ed substation were designed by the same architectural firm of Tigerman, Fugman, McCurry. The "windows" of the new substation are actually ventilation louvres. (Photo by author)

The former home of the Chicago Historical Society, on the northwest corner of W. Ontario and N. Dearborn streets, built in 1892 from plans by Henry Ives Cobb, is a striking example of Romanesque Revival architecture, but with many novel touches. Particularly interesting is the building's overall pyramidal shape and the massive entrance bracketed by a pair of heavy conical turrets surmounted by a pointed gable. A number of tenants have occupied the building since the CHS moved to larger quarters in 1931. Today it is home to the nightclub Excalibur. (Photo by author)

Administration, the Illinois Institute of Technology, *Gallery* Magazine, a school of design, a recording studio, the Limelight nightclub, and ultimately in 1989, the Excalibur.

The novel pyramidal-shaped structure of rough-hewn granite, with its conical turrets, arched and transomed windows, and massive entranceway convey the strength that is so typical of Richardson's style. (The Chicago Historical Society's new building is described in Tour 12, the Gold Coast.) Note the carved reliefs in the tympanum above the recessed entrance depicting Father Jacques Marquette and explorer Louis Joliet, the first Europeans to visit the area, in 1673.

Immediately to the right of the old Society building, **No. 642** N. Dearborn Street, built ca. 1872 by an unknown architect, is typical of what were called "marble front" residences. Sometimes called "Athens Marble," it was actually Joliet limestone which has the distinctive yellowish color. Note the carved window lintels.

At the corner is **The Raleigh** (*1891, architect unknown; renovation 1990, Berger & Associates*), 650 N. Dearborn Street. One of many hotels erected in anticipation of the throngs expected for the World's Columbian Exposition of 1893, this one in Queen Anne style, has an unusual facade of random ashlar of mottled-green serpentine stone (technically a mineral known as hydrous magnesium silicate, and relatively uncommon), with terra-cotta details. The base is battered, that is, it slopes outward. The building, which opened originally as the Hotel Vendome, has undergone many remodelings—one in 1912 that changed the top floor, another in 1952 after a major fire left 125 residents homeless, and finally the 1990 renovation.

Directly across the street is 641–649 N. Dearborn Street, the **telephone building,** one of a number of such buildings built in the 1920s to house local telephone exchanges throughout the city. This one, in a Classic Revival style, was built in 1923–1925 from plans by Holabird & Roche, in an era when the facade ranked close in importance to the building's function. Note the ornate bronze work in the two-story-high arches and the old Bell System plaque above the entrance. With the breakup of the Bell System, the local company became Illinois Bell, and more recently Ameritech.

Return to W. Ontario Street and turn left (east) one block to N. State Street.

On the east side of State Street, between Ontario and Ohio streets, are the exceptionally well-preserved **Lambert Tree Studios** (*1894, Parfitt Brothers; Bauer & Hill; and Hill & Woltersdorf*), 601–623 N. State Street. Another Columbian Exposition era building, the block-long row of studios and stores was planned by Judge Lambert Tree and erected behind his private residence in an act of cultural philanthropy for visiting artists who had been employed at the Fair, to entice them to stay in Chicago and continue to work in a conducive atmosphere. The long two-story Roman-brick building has a peaked roof and is divided into 12 sections which now house a variety of stores. Each section has pedimented bay windows, cast-iron arched storefront windows, terra-cotta

The telephone building at 641–649 N. Dearborn Street (1923–1925, Holabird & Roche) was one of a series of local exchanges built in the early 1920s by the Bell System. Most were designed with ornate facades, in keeping with the fashions of the times. The bronze panels in the windows and the delicate grill above the entrance are noteworthy. With the breakup of the Bell monopoly, the new company, recently Illinois Bell, is now part of Ameritech. (Photo by author)

decoration, and Queene Anne–style chimneys. At each end are peaked gables. An addition was constructed on the Ohio Street side in 1912, and another on the Ontario Street side. Look for Judge Tree's face in the stone trim surrounding the entrances. This is a particularly good example of the many low-rise blocks in River North that still preserve a human scale.

Skip the Ohio Street addition, cross State Street and walk east to the Lambert Tree Studios entrance at 3–5 E. Ontario Street. (State Street is the dividing line between east and west addresses.)

The main entrance to the former artists' studios is still impressive, and now serves the present tenants. The adjoining dark-red brick building, in a somewhat different style, **No. 7 E. Ontario Street,** displays extensive terra-cotta adornments, particularly in the high-relief plaque of three human figures, and the herald above, which proclaims that "Art is Long, Time is Fleeting," and the admonition "Be Up and Doing, Still Achieving, Still Pursuing." (Good advice!)

Directly across the street is one of a number of behemoths that have mushroomed in River North. **Ontario Place** (*1983, James Loewenberg*), 10 E. Ontario Street, rises 51 stories—more like a beanstalk than a mushroom—it has an atypical arrangement of windows and balconies that breaks up its verticality. The first six floors of this mixed-use building are reserved for commercial tenants, the rest are rental apartments. A short driveway leading to the porte-cochère prevents traffic backups, but the oval lobby is surprisingly small for such a huge building.

Continue east to N. Wabash Avenue, and cross to the east side.

The **Medinah Temple** (*1913, Huehl & Schmid; renovation 1924*), 600 N. Wabash Avenue, was built as the local headquarters of the Shriners. It consists primarily of a 4,000-seat grand auditorium for conventions, circus performances, symphony concerts, marching bands, and a host of other spectaculars as well as for the Temple's fraternal, social, and business activities. So excellent are the acoustics that the Chicago Symphony Orchestra records here regularly. Harris W. Huehl and Richard G. Schmid, themselves Shriner "nobles," were known for the florid Moorish-style buildings that were commissioned by the Shriners; this is reputed to be among their largest surviving examples. The Temple is named for the city in what is now Saudi Arabia, to which the Prophet Muhammad made his famous flight (the hegira) from Mecca in 622 A.D.

Take a moment to study the elaborate ornamentation, Arabic calligraphy, and excellent Flemish-bond brickwork. Most of the brickwork and terra cotta is brown, but monotony is effectively avoided by the use of yellow, red, blue, white, and gold applied with the boldness characteristic of Arabic design. Around the

The astonishing Medinah Temple, at 600 N. Wabash Avenue, was erected in 1913 by Huehl and Schmid for the local headquarters of the Shriners. The elaborate exterior is heavily adorned with Mahometal designs, including Arabic calligraphy and polychrome designs. Unfortunately, the splendid onion domes are no more, having fallen victim to 40 years of exposure to the extremes of Chicago weather, and were removed in 1995. The spacious interior contains the offices of the Shriners and a 4,000-seat auditorium that is used for a wide variety of events, including conventions, circuses, and Chicago Symphony Orchestra recording sessions. (Photo by Bob Peak)

main entrance is the inscription "There is no God but Allah," repeated as a border ornament. All forms of arch common to Mahometal architecture—the semi-circular, horseshoe, pointed, and keel—are employed in the exterior. Until recently the building was easily recognizable from afar by its imposing twin onion domes. Alas, the domes are no more. The original pair, made of terra cotta, were removed in the 1930s. Replacements made of sheet copper on a metal framework were installed in 1954, but after more than 40 years of exposure to the extremes of Chicago weather, they rusted through and had to be taken down in 1995, leaving the famous building bereft of its famous icons. (*See also* the Hotel Inter-Continental, formerly the Medinah Athletic Club, in Tour 6, The Magnificent Mile and Streeterville, pages 224–225.) The Medinah Temple and its compact, but spacious and elaborate, auditorium is open to the public weekdays, 9:00 A.M.–4:30 P.M., but it is best to phone ahead: 266-5000.

Walk north on Wabash Avenue one block to E. Erie Street.

On the southwest corner, in the shadow of the Cass Hotel (*1925, Oldefest & Williams*), is the magnificent **former Ransom R. Cable Mansion** (*1886, Cobb & Frost*), 25 E. Erie Street, now occupied by Driehaus Capital Management, Inc., and Driehaus Securities Corp. The structure is a fine example of Richard-

Almost overshadowed by the Hotel Cass is the charming former Ransom R. Cable Mansion, at the southwest corner of N. Wabash Avenue and E. Erie Street. A textbook exemplar of the Romanesque Revival—the popular style of choice of so many residents in River North—it was designed in 1886 by Cobb & Frost, and incorporates virtually every feature of the style: rough-hewn masonry, a corner tower, peaked roof and dormers, heavy columns with foliated capitals, and an arched corner entrance. The building now houses Driehaus, a financial management and securities corporation. (Photo by author)

sonian Romanesque Revival style, with its rock-faced Kasota stone, peaked roof and dormers, corner tower, center gable, heavy columns with foliated capitals, a triple-arched corner entrance, and neo-Byzantine carving. To the west is a charming garden with a variety of sculpture (unfortunately closed to the public), and in the rear, a delightful medieval carriage house, which is a perfect match to the main house, connected inconspicuously by a later addition. The whole is surrounded by a tall iron fence, which also embraces the next building, a ca. 1875 remodeled town house, not part of the property.

Diagonally across Wabash Avenue on the northeast corner, is the striking **Samuel M. Nickerson House** (*1883, Edward J. Burling, of Burling & Whitehouse; restored 1991*), 40 E. Erie Street, now the R. H. Love Galleries. The 30-room sandstone Italianate palazzo was built for Nickerson by the same architect as St. James Cathedral, next door. Nickerson was a banker and financier who founded Chicago's first bank to get a national charter. The family had lost their first home in the Great Fire, and apparently spared nothing to create what was later called "Nickerson's Marble Palace." According to the

The Samuel M. Nickerson House, diagonally across from the Cable Mansion, on the northeast corner of N. Wabash Avenue and E. Erie Street, is a striking Italianate palazzo, built in 1883. Nickerson, a prominent banker, lost his first home in the Great Fire of 1871, and built this opulent 30-room mansion, sparing no expense with the interior fittings. No fewer than 27 varieties of marble went into the construction, which gave rise to the house being called "Nickerson's Marble Palace." So massive was the stone and its two-foot thick bearing walls that the house required additional foundations and shoring. The exterior, though, is of sandstone, and through the years it has darkened to an almost black hue. When the Nickerson family departed in 1919, the house was acquired by the American College of Surgeons which used it as their headquarters until a new building was constructed across the street. The ACS still owns it, and at present it is leased to the R. H. Love Galleries. (Photo by author)

historic marker near the entrance, the Nickerson House "was designed to reflect the wisdom and taste of the original owner, who was prominent in Chicago's financial community and in the city's developing cultural life. The home is a unique reminder of the opulence that characterized many upper-class residences at the end of the 19th century."

Although not visible from the outside, the interior boasts no fewer than 27 varieties of marble, plus alabaster and onyx fireplaces. The tremendous weight of so much stone required special foundations with pilings driven down to hardpan (the subsoil compacted clay), and four 2-foot-thick brick bearing walls. When the family gave up the mansion to move out of state in 1919, it was acquired by the nearby American College of Surgeons as their main office until the completion of their building across the street in 1963. The house is still owned by the ACS. The R. H. Love Gallery presents frequent public exhibitions—a fine opportunity to view the lavish interior as well as the art.

Before walking east on Erie Street, go back around the corner and a short distance north to **St. James Episcopal Cathedral** (*1857, Burling & Bacchus; reconstruction 1875, Edward J. Burling*). A fine example of English Gothic Revival–style architecture, built of "Athens Marble" (the yellowish Joliet limestone), its real treasure is the interior, whose stencilled nave presents an overwhelming riot of 26 different colors which are highlighted by the crisscross wood vault trusses that virtually lift one's eyes to the peaked ceiling. The designer, New York architect Edward J. Neville Stent, a master of the pre-Raphaelite school and exponent of the Arts and Crafts movement, was a student of the movement's English founder, William Morris, and executed the work in 1888.

St. James Episcopal Cathedral, on N. Wabash Avenue, just north of E. Erie Street, was built in 1857 of "Athens Marble" (yellow Joliet sandstone) and is a fine example of English Gothic Revival. The parish was founded in 1834 and is the oldest in the city. The church was raised to the status of cathedral of the Diocese of Chicago in 1955. Inside, the nave displays a treasure of Arts-and-Crafts-movement stencilling together with dramatic wooden crisscross ceiling vaults. On the lower level is the 1913 Chapel of St. Andrew, which is a "must see." The church escaped most of the devastation of the Great Fire, but scars still remain on the tower. (Photo by author)

The Chapel of St. Andrew, on the level below the sanctuary, was designed in 1913 by Cram, Goodhue & Ferguson, from plans by Bertram Grosvenor Goodhue, architect of New York's famous St. Thomas' Church and the Nebraska State Capital. It was in this chapel, modeled after an ancient Scottish abbey chapel, that the international Brotherhood of St. Andrew was founded by James L. Houghteling in 1883. The architectural firm also designed the Goodhue Memorial narthex in 1928. A splendid sympathetic restoration was completed in 1985 by Holabird & Root. St. James, founded in 1834, was the first Episcopal parish in Chicago, the oldest in the city, and one of the oldest in the state, and became the cathedral of the Diocese of Chicago in 1955. On leaving the church, look up at the tower and note the scars left by the Great Fire of 1871.

Return to E. Erie Street and turn left (east).

On the south side is the **headquarters of the American College of Surgeons** (*1963, Skidmore, Owings & Merrill; addition 1983, Graham, Anderson, Probst & White*), an unremarkable building by two of Chicago's most distinguished architectural firms.

Across the street again, and in striking contrast to both the ACS Building and the Nickerson House, No. 50 E. Erie Street, evokes virtually every Classic motif. The **John B. Murphy Memorial Auditorium** of the American College of Surgeons (*1922–1926, Marshall & Fox*), which stands on what was the yard of the Nickerson House, serves not only as an auditorium, but as a library and meeting hall as well. The curving stairs of this lavish French Classical structure lead to a columned and pedimented entrance portico, behind which are ornate bronze doors executed by the Tiffany Studios. The building is said to be modeled after the Chapelle de Notre-Dame de Consolation in Paris, designed ca. 1900 by Albert Guilbert.

Continuing east, the next building, a former coach house, had been the editorial offices of the journal *Surgery, Gynecology and Obstetrics*. It was renamed the Franklin H. Martin Building, in honor of the founder of the ACS.

The next building, No. 54 E. Erie Street, was the **former coach house and stable of the Robert Hall McCormick Mansion,** to the east. It was remodeled for ACS editorial offices in 1924 and modernized in 1980.

The adjoining building at the northwest corner of N. Rush Street, now Chez Paul restaurant, was the **former Robert Hall McCormick House,** 660 N. Rush Street, designed by an unknown architect in 1875. The McCormick family chose to settle in this neighborhood, rather than along Prairie Avenue, as did many of their wealthy contemporaries. So many members of the clan built their homes in this immediate area that it was later referred to as "McCormickville." The paterfamilias, Cyrus Hall McCormick, was the inventor of the famous reaper, a horse-drawn harvesting machine that revolutionized agricultural methods worldwide. Cyrus's sumptuous mansion, at 675 Rush Street, was modeled after a pavilion of the Louvre and completed in 1879; L. Hamilton McCormick's mansion went up at 631 Rush Street in the early 1890s; and about a half-mile to the east, Edith Rockefeller McCormick's palatial residence set new standards

Gracing the northwest corner of E. Erie and N. Rush is the former Robert Hall McCormick House, designed in 1875. The numerous McCormicks chose this neighborhood to build their homes, and all were located within a few blocks of each other. The sumptuous mansion of reaper-inventor Cyrus H. McCormick is long-since gone, as are all the other McCormicks, with the exception of the house built for Robert Hall (although a small wall section does remain of the L. Hamilton McCormick house, now incorporated into the much-remodeled Lawry's restaurant). Today, Robert Hall McCormick's house still exudes an aura of elegance, and survives as the Chez Paul restaurant. (Photo by author)

of opulence, at 1000 N. Lake Shore Drive. Only the Robert Hall McCormick mansion and the much remodeled L. Hamilton McCormick Renaissance palazzo, now Lawry's Restaurant, survive today. The present McCormick house, built for Cyrus's brother, Robert Hall, still maintains an aura of elegance. Note the columned and pedimented entrance.

A bit of trivia associated with the inventor of the reaper: As a sales tool, he would often sponsor contests pitting his farm machines against competitors'. These daylong affairs often deteriorated into drunken plowboy brawls, but the name survives in American slang as a general term for an alfresco free-for-all, called "Field Days."

Rush Street was named for the late-19th century physician, Dr. Benjamin Rush, who served as a surgeon in the Revolutionary War and was a signer of the Declaration of Independence. Chicago's Rush–Presbyterian–St. Luke's Medical Center was also named for him.

Continuing north on N. Rush Street, we note the **St. James Cathedral– Episcopal Church Center** (*1968, Hammond & Roesch*), 65 E. Huron Street, which is back-to-back with St. James Cathedral on Wabash Avenue. Its steel-and-glass facade rising above an open ground-floor space is reminiscent of the landmark pioneer in this glass-box style, Lever House, in New York, and is in stark contrast to the ornate chapel around the corner.

On the southeast corner of Huron Street is the back of the towering **City Place** and **Hotel Omni** (*1990, Loebl, Schlossman & Hackl*), whose front faces N. Michigan Avenue, and which is described in Tour 6, The Magnificent Mile and Streeterville (*see* page 229). The hotel occupies the first 25 of its 39 floors. On the northeast corner is the back of 40-story **Chicago Place** (*1990, Skidmore, Owings & Merrill*), similarly facing N. Michigan Avenue (*see* pages 230–231).

Situated across Huron Street on the northwest corner is the headquarters of the **National Congress of Parents & Teachers** (*1954, Holabird & Roche*), 700 N. Rush Street. Typical of the simple style and solid materials used in the 1950s, the "PTA Building" remains a fine example of that decade. It was built through contributions that poured in from PTA members around the country, in amounts as little as 10 cents, during the organization's campaign to erect an appropriate headquarters building, whose slogan was "Quarters for Head-quarters." Look into the large window on the Rush Street side to see the sculp-tures of *Teacher, Mother,* and *Father,* by Milton Horn.

A short distance west on Huron Street, at No. 50, is the office of the **American Library Association** (*1954, Holabird & Root*), appropriately named McCormick House, since it occupies the site of the Cyrus H. McCormick II mansion, which was used by the ALA from 1945 until the old house was razed in 1954 for the construction of the association's present building. Historic preservation, alas, was still in its infancy.

Return to N. Rush Street, turn left (north) and proceed to E. Chicago Avenue.

On the southwest corner, and best viewed later at a distance, is the 37-story high-rise apartment building **The Chicagoan** (*1990, Solomon Cordwell Buenz & Associates*), 750 N. Rush Street. The sharply delineated framework high-lights a somewhat round central shaft, to which are affixed a pair of octagonal bays, one at each of two corners. The result is six apartments per floor with sweeping 180-degree panoramic views.

Turn left (west) on E. Chicago Avenue.

On the north side of Chicago Avenue and extending half the block to Wabash Avenue is the **Hotel St. Benedict Flats** (*1882, James J. Egan*), 42–50 E. Chicago Avenue and 801 N. Wabash Avenue. The row of connected houses is typical of what were known as "French flats" in the early 1880s. As the wealthy found that maintaining a mansion and its required staff could be quite bur-densome, the popularity of the luxury multiple-dwelling house became all the rage. One such example is the Dakota in New York, which attracted some of the city's most affluent tenants. No small apartments these, 15 rooms was not uncommon, with servants' quarters in another part of the building, usually the top floor. The St. Benedict displays the florid combination of both Queen Anne and French Second-Empire styles. At this writing it is in a sad state of neglect with the stained-glass transom windows replaced by plywood sheets and the entire building rather woebegone in appearance.

The Hotel St. Benedict Flats was built in 1882 as a residential hotel for affluent tenants unwilling to support the increasing burden of maintaining a private mansion. The row of attached houses, each for a separate family, were known as "French Flats," and were rather common in big cities throughout the country in the 1880s. The wealthy tenants suffered little hardship moving into these smaller buildings, as the flats had as many as 15 rooms plus servants' quarters. The St. Benedict, recently listed on the National Register, displays a combination of Queen Anne and French Second-Empire styles. Unfortunately, time and neglect have taken their toll, and the decaying row is in urgent need of rehabilitation. (Photo by author)

Turn right (north) on N. Wabash Avenue, one block to E. Pearson Street. Turn right again and walk one block to N. Rush Street (for a very rewarding detour).

On the northeast corner, and extending all the way to E. Chestnut Street, is the **Archbishop Quigley Preparatory Seminary and Chapel of St. James** (*1917, Gustav Steinbeck and Zachary Taylor Davis*), 831 N. Rush Street, Chicago's finest example of the French Gothic style. The seminary building on the left with its highly ornate stone facade and its carved buttresses, is a fine counterpart to the Chapel. Steinbeck, a New York architect is said to have based his design on the Sainte Chapelle, in Paris, noted for its extensive and dazzling panes of stained glass. The building boasts an astonishing collection of English antique glass, the work of Robert T. Giles. Looking through the gate to the inner courtyard seems much like a glimpse into the Middle Ages. The facade of the St. James Chapel displays splendid carvings on both sides of the entry and a rose window with ornate traceries, above which are sculptures of Mary and the Four Disciples set at the base of the high-pitched gable. The Seminary was organized in 1905 by Archbishop James E. Quigley, but he died before construction could begin, and the task was taken over by the noted George Cardinal Mundelein. It serves as a high-school-level seminary for the Archdiocese of Chicago. A statue of Archbishop Quigley can be found on the corner of Chestnut Street.

Chicago's finest example of the French Gothic style is Archbishop Quigley Preparatory Seminary and Chapel of St. James, designed in 1917 by Gustav Steinbeck and Zachary Taylor Davis. On the left is the Seminary building with a finely detailed facade; and on the right, the Chapel, said to be modeled on the Sainte Chapelle in Paris. The large gate of the Seminary opens into a Medieval-style inner courtyard. Among the splendid carvings on the Chapel's facade are Mary and the Four Disciples set above the delicate traceries of the rose window and beneath the high-pitched gable. The two buildings are slightly "folded" toward each other to accommodate the northwest bend of Rush Street. (Photo by author)

Return (west) on E. Pearson Street to N. Wabash Avenue, noting the number and variety of Loyola University buildings on both sides of the street and on the following blocks. Cross Wabash Avenue and continue west.

Midway down the block, on the north side, Nos. 14 and 16 are an attractive pair of three-story Queen Anne–style structures, the **Edwin S. Hartwell Houses** (*1885, Julius H. Huber; renovation 1980, Bauhs & Dring*). The pair are identical and look much as they did the day they were built, thanks to good preservation and an architecturally accurate renovation. Look above the first floor at the pair of sculptured heads that emerge from roundels at each end. Since Hartwell built the twin houses for his son and daughter, what better way to perpetuate their memory than to have their heads sculpted and placed on the facade as a permanent graphic memento of the original inhabitants.

Continue west to N. State Street and turn left (south) one-and-a-half blocks to:

Holy Name Cathedral (*1875, Patrick Charles Keeley*), 735 N. State Street, was designed in a late Victorian Gothic style, and has been the seat of the Roman Catholic Archdiocese of Chicago since it was erected. The Brooklyn-born architect designed more Catholic churches throughout the country— over 200—than any other architect. An earlier church on the site, built in 1854, was destroyed in the Great Fire. Built of Lemont limestone, with a prominent steeple that rises 210 feet, and displaying fairly simple Gothic detailing throughout, the cathedral has endured a number of remodelings through the years, with an addition in 1915 by Henry J. Schlacks, and a major renovation in 1969 by C. F. Murphy Associates.

The interior, far more elaborate than the exterior, is richly furnished in Gothic detail, and is open daily. The focal point of the sanctuary is the free-standing granite altar. The stained-glass windows, progressively brighter toward the front, are abstract in style, and were fabricated in Milan. Don't overlook the ornate ribbed and vaulted ceiling above the altar, and note the four wide-brimmed red hats, called *galeros,* which belonged to the former cardinal-archbishops of Chicago: Mundelein, Stritch, Meyer, and Cody. Hanging the cardinal's official hat after his death is a custom dating back to the 13th century. The massive bronze cathedral doors, designed by Albert Friscia, weigh over 1,200 pounds, and are opened by an unusual hydraulic power-assist system.

This was a "busy" spot during the notorious Capone era of the 1920s. Directly across from the Cathedral, early Chicago mobster Dion O'Bannion, who as a young boy had served in the church as an acolyte, maintained a flower shop at 738 N. State Street as a respectable front for his dealings in illegal booze. In revenge for cutting in on the dealings of Al Capone, he was gunned down in his shop in November 1924 by members of Al Capone's gang. Two years later, O'Bannion's successor, Hymie Weiss, was likewise "rubbed out" by Capone's triggermen in a hail of submachinegun bullets directly in front of the Cathedral, as repayment for Weiss's earlier attempt on Capone's life, in retaliation for a still earlier Capone shooting. The Cathedral sustained a few chipped stones (since repaired), and the flower shop was demolished in 1960 when the parking lot was built across the street.

Return to Chicago Avenue and turn left (west).

On the north side of W. Chicago Avenue, about halfway down the block is the **Victor F. Lawson Department, YMCA** (*1930–1934, Perkins, Chatten & Hammond*), 30 W. Chicago Avenue. Built during the Art Deco era, it is a typical brick and limestone high-rise of the time. Look at the variety of Art Deco ornament in the spandrels, as well as the low-relief carvings of athletes above the entrance. The "Y" is being rehabilitated by the city, and in addition to its renovated lodging facilities it will provide a wide variety of on-site social services for the needy. With its 580 units it is Chicago's largest SRO (single-room occupancy) hotel.

At the next corner (N. Dearborn Street), look diagonally southwest to the tall apartment building, whose multilevel garage extends to Chicago Avenue: **Asbury Plaza** (*1981, George Schipporeit*), 750 N. Dearborn Street. Schipporeit was a student of Mies van der Rohe, and the innovative style of his protégé is quite apparent. The design of this concrete tower is an amazing example of applied solid geometry. With its variety of angles and uneven massing, the result is a maximum number of panoramic views within a minimum building envelope.

Take another brief detour to see one of Chicago's unique mixed-use buildings by continuing west along the south side of W. Chicago Avenue one block further to N. Clark Street.

(Left) Holy Name Cathedral, at 735 N. State Street, has been the seat of the Roman Catholic Archdiocese of Chicago since it was built in 1875. Brooklyn-born architect Patrick Charles Keeley, who designed more than 200 Catholic churches throughout the country, employed his favored Gothic Revival style, building the church of Lemont limestone and adding a prominent 210-foot steeple. In contrast with the simplicity of the exterior, the sanctuary is ornate and elegant and boasts a free-standing granite altar, excellent stained glass, and a decorative vaulted ceiling. An earlier church on the site, built in 1854, was consumed in the Great Fire. The present church has undergone two major remodelings, the most recent by C. F. Murphy Associates in 1969. (Photo by author)

On the northwest corner is the massive **Chicago-Clark Building** (*1901, J.E.O. Pridmore*), 100 W. Chicago Avenue. Built for the Bush Temple of Music, it had everything a music school was supposed to have: teaching studios, practice rooms, various size rehearsal rooms, and a large concert hall. The theatre was also popular with German troupes and musicians. In more recent times, economics dictated a remodeling for first-floor retail establishments, offices, and residences above. An enormous building with a dominant black mansard roof, it presents a strange spectacle on this marginal commercial street.

Across Clark Street, on the northeast corner, is the former Cosmopolitan State Bank, now the **Cosmopolitan National Bank of Chicago** (*1920, Schmidt, Garden & Martin*), 801 N. Clark Street. In an era when a bank's strength was often judged by the massiveness of its Classic columns, the architects here created a much simpler design, with only a few so-called Classic touches (in the

The massive Chicago-Clark Building, 100 W. Chicago Avenue, named for the two streets on whose intersection it stands, was erected in 1901 for the Bush Temple of Music, a self-contained music establishment, with school, rehearsal rooms, and concert hall. The building's sounds of music are long-since silenced, replaced by ground-floor retail establishments and residences above. The huge brick and limestone structure is topped by an oversize black mansard roof, giving it a unique and domineering profile. (Photo by author)

two arches) and a pleasing use of light-red brick trimmed with unadorned limestone.

Return to N. Dearborn Street and turn left (north).

Along the west side of N. Dearborn Street, **Nos. 802–812** present a particularly fine row of Italianate houses, probably designed by the same unknown architect, all with uniform roof and porch lines. The windows, too, are similar and their lintels are incised in typical Neo-Grec style. The large trees that have grown up in recent years add much to the rather pleasant atmosphere. No. 816 displays many differences, as does 818 with its rough-cut, rather than smooth limestone facade.

Across the street, **Nos. 827–833** (*1878, Frederick H. Waescher*) present a fairly uniform line with smooth-brick facades and unusual window lintels decorated with rows of arrow points. The original entrances were all removed in favor of basement entries, to allow for subdivision into more apartments. The strange, and certainly not original, rudely constructed brick wall, meant to fence in the little front gardens (or to keep out strangers), boasts two sculpted portrait rondelles taken from Adler & Sullivan's 1892 Schiller Building, demolished in 1960 (*see* pages 51–52).

At the end of the row, the corner building, built at the same time and by the same architect, once served as Grant's Seminary for Young Ladies. Now called **Newberry House,** after the original owners of the estate, it too has been subdivided into smaller apartment units. The style of the red-brick building, however, is quite different from the rest of the row, and is reminiscent of the work of Philadelphia architect Frank Furness, particularly in the treatment of the bays and columns.

At the southwest corner of W. Chestnut Street, looms **John Fewkes Tower** (*1967, Harry Weese & Associates*), 55 W. Chestnut Street. While an apparent intrusion on the scale of the immediate neighborhood, the 30-story high-rise in soft-red brick has some unusual redeeming characteristics, and perhaps should be called "Trapezoid Towers." The bays, which rise the full height of the tower, are in the shape of trapezoids, alternating with bands of masonry, while the corners of the building are chamfered by the use of narrow windows. Architect Harry Weese, an active preservationist, has designed many important Chicago buildings and has offices in River North, at 10 W. Hubbard Street, in an 1880s-vintage loft building which he remodeled. The area is now home to a number of architectural firms (Bertrand Goldberg Associates; Graham, Anderson, Probst & White; Hammond, Beeby & Babka, Inc.; Solomon Cordwell Buenz & Associates; John Vinci, and others).

Continuing north, stop in front of No. 863 N. Dearborn Street, the **Robert N. Tooker House** (*1886, William LeBaron Jenney & William A. Otis*). The house is built of rough-cut pink granite, with a two-story projecting bay and a conspicuous gable with three windows. Note diminutive E. Tooker Place.

 Just ahead on the left is **Washington Square,** Chicago's oldest park. The land was donated by developer Orsamus Bushnell, and by the turn of the century it had become an upscale gathering place for the wealthy residents whose mansions and town houses surrounded the square or were nearby. Unity Church (now the Scottish Rite Cathedral), which had dominated the enclave, was acquired by the Oriental Consistory of the Masonic Order, which also purchased the town houses along the east side. By the beginning of the second decade of the 20th century the "upper crust" denizens had left for the "Gold Coast" or the suburbs, and their once-sumptuous homes were divided into rooming houses. During the 1920s Washington Square became the favorite hangout of the New Bohemia, and with its reputation for political debate, poetry readings, and just plain talk, it soon acquired the sobriquet "Bughouse Square," the "outdoor forum of garrulous hobohemia." The city, which leases the square to the Park District, requires that it still be a place of public forum. A fountain which once burbled in the center was replaced in 1985 by the present concrete platform. Except for occasional outdoor concerts or the annual Newberry Library debates, little public discussion goes on, except perhaps by some of the transients who debate sleeping rights on the adjacent park benches. Particularly attractive, however, is the peaceful atmosphere enhanced by the lush variety of trees that provide a shady retreat. Interestingly, the park's history and role is remarkably similar to that of New York City's Washington Square, and not unlike the one in Philadelphia, or even Dubuque.

★   The park and some of its neighbors have been designated the **Washington Square Historic District** by the City of Chicago, which in addition to the park includes the Newberry Library and Nos. 915–929 N. Dearborn Street.

Note the trio of town houses on the east side, No. 915 N. Dearborn Street, the former **John Howland Thompson House** (*1888, Cobb & Frost*), No. 919, the **George H. Taylor House** (*1895, Treat & Foltz*), and No. 925, the **George B. Carpenter House,** by the same architects. The Thompson House, designed by the same pair of architects as the previously seen Ransom R. Cable House, is a really splendid example of Richardsonian Romanesque, and according to the *AIA Guide to Chicago* is second only to the masonry design of Richardson's Glessner House (*see* pages 329–331). The building is constructed of Lake Superior sandstone whose characteristic reddish-brown color gives it texture while not overwhelming with its size. Note particularly on the Delaware Place side the steeply pitched slate roof punctuated with turrets and gables; and in front, the bundled columns with rock-faced lintels bracketing the tripartite entrance, and above, a panel of foliated diaperwork.

The adjacent pair (919 and 925) are quite different in style from each other, but reveal certain similarities. The Carpenter House boasts a rough-cut facade on its bay, but a smooth dark-red brick wall with Georgian-style windows. Its neighbor is mostly Georgian in appearance. Both betray the affluence, if not the refined architectural taste, of their original owners, and are overshadowed by the quality of the Thompson House.

Adjacent is the **Scottish Rite Cathedral** (*1867, Theodore Vigo Wadskier; reconstructed 1873, Edward J. Burling & Dankmar Adler*), 929 N. Dearborn Street). When the former Gothic Revival–style Unity Church was severely damaged in the Great Fire, it lost everything combustible, including the wooden

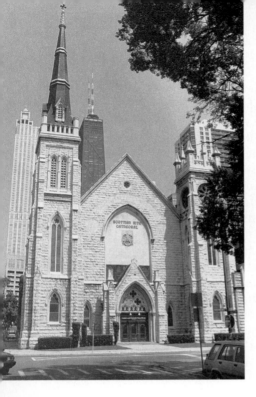

The Scottish Rite Cathedral, at 929 N. Dearborn Street facing Washington Square, was built in 1867 in Gothic Revival style and suffered severe damage in the Great Fire. Erected at the time for the Unity Church, all that was left after the holocaust were its scorched Joliet limestone walls. In the 1873 reconstruction by Burling and Adler, it was the younger partner, Dankmar Adler, who was called on to perform his first commission, to design the church's acoustics by planning the seating arrangement. The success of the plan helped launch a career which reached its zenith with the acoustical design of the Auditorium Theatre. The Scottish Rite, connected with the Masonic Fraternal Organization, has occupied the building since 1910. (Photo by author)

towers and steeples, roof, and most of the interior furnishings, leaving just the scorched Joliet limestone walls. In the Burling and Adler reconstruction, young Dankmar Adler took on his first commission in designing the acoustics of an interior, in this case with the planning of the church's seating arrangement—the beginning of a career that culminated in the acoustical design of the Auditorium Theatre. In 1882 the South Tower was rebuilt by Frederick B. Townsend. The Scottish Rite is connected with the Masonic Fraternal Organization and has occupied the building since 1910 after the Medinah Temple, which had used the church for the previous 15 years, outgrew the site and built their ornate temple at 600 N. Wabash Avenue, seen earlier on the tour. The offices of the Cathedral are located a few doors south at No. 915.

Dominating the north side of Washington Square is the venerable **Newberry Library** (*1890–1893, Henry Ives Cobb; addition 1981, Harry Weese & Associates*), 60 W. Walton Street. Housed in a magnificent Richardsonian Romanesque–style edifice, the Newberry Library, founded in 1887, and one of Chicago's great treasures, is one of the nation's preeminent research libraries. Cobb, who was an exponent of H. H. Richardson's work, also designed the old Chicago Historical Society building (now the Excalibur), seen earlier, and a host of other buildings throughout the city. Although in partnership with Charles S. Frost, he worked alone on this commission. The splendid legacy, which benefactor Walter Loomis Newberry called the "uncommon collection of uncommon collections," was originally planned to be placed in a much larger structure, a matter which was not resolved until 1981, when an addition to the rear was designed by Harry Weese. It is interesting to note that the library stands on the site of the Mahlon D. Ogden Residence, the only house in the path of the Great Fire of 1871 that was not burned.

The venerable Newberry Library, one of the nation's great research libraries, dominates the north side of Washington Square. Designed in 1890, it is one of architect Henry Ives Cobb's finest works. In his favorite Romanesque Revival style, Cobb, an exponent of H. H. Richardson, created this superb example of a more restrained, somewhat Italianate, and less fortress-like plan, unlike the designs made during his partnership with Charles S. Frost for the Chicago Historical Society and a number of mansions in River North. The stunning triple-arched entrance is attributed to Cobb's designer, Louis C. Mullgardt, and is based on the Romanesque 12th-century French church of Saint-Gilles-du-Gard. (Courtesy of the Art Institute of Chicago)

The impressive entrance, with its triple arches, is said to have been inspired by the Romanesque 12th-century French church of Saint-Gilles-du-Gard, and is attributed to Cobb's designer Louis C. Mullgardt. The window arrangement of the facade is especially attractive, with each of the four floors in a different style—square, transomed, bifora, and arcaded, with the front elevation divided into three distinct bays, and the entire structure capped by a low peaked roof. The plan of the interior, drawn up by the Newberry's first librarian, William C. Poole, called for extra-wide corridors to provide a sound-dampening barrier between the reading rooms. The Newberry was also one of the first buildings in the city to be illuminated by electricity. Go into the restored lobby and note the chandelier (a replica) whose bulbs do not point upward, as did all gas fixtures, but downward as do electric bulbs. Do spend some time exploring this delightful building.

Walk around the west end (on N. Clark Street) to see the modern brick addition tastefully hidden at the rear, which is eight stories high plus two below ground level. On the brick facade it displays a few motifs of the main facade, particularly in the restrained incised low-relief arches. A round tower at each corner contains a staircase and plumbing stacks. The new facility is now a

The unusual Burlingham Building, at 1000 N. Clark Street, dates from 1883, with two stories added in 1887. It would appear that architect Alfred Smith drew on every feature of the Queen Anne–style lexicon to embellish his design: bay windows with cast-iron piers, a corner cast-iron turret, slate spandrels, and stained-glass windows. Note that in the curved bay windows, the outer pair are wide, and the central pane is narrow—just the opposite of the usual convention. The six-story mixed-use building is in a surprisingly good state of preservation; even the ground floor—usually the first section to be "modernized"—is intact, except for two blind bricked-up windows. (Photo by author)

repository for over 21 miles of books and manuscripts housed in an additional 80,000 square feet of shelves and stacks, in a climate-controlled environment.

Time for one last building? Walk north one block on N. Clark Street to the northwest corner of Oak Street.

A rather unusual mixed-use structure, the **Burlingham Building** (*1883, Alfred Smith; two-story addition 1897*), 1000 N. Clark Street, displays an odd conglomeration of Queen Anne–style features: bays with cast-iron piers; a corner turret, also of cast iron; spandrels made of slate; and stained-glass windows. The fenestration is also unusual, with the bays having wide side windows and the central windows narrow—the opposite of the normal arrangement. The upper two floors were added by the same architect. An interesting survivor, it is in a good state of preservation, and is listed on the National Register of Historic Places.

End of tour. To return to the Loop, take CTA Bus No. 22 southbound on Clark Street.

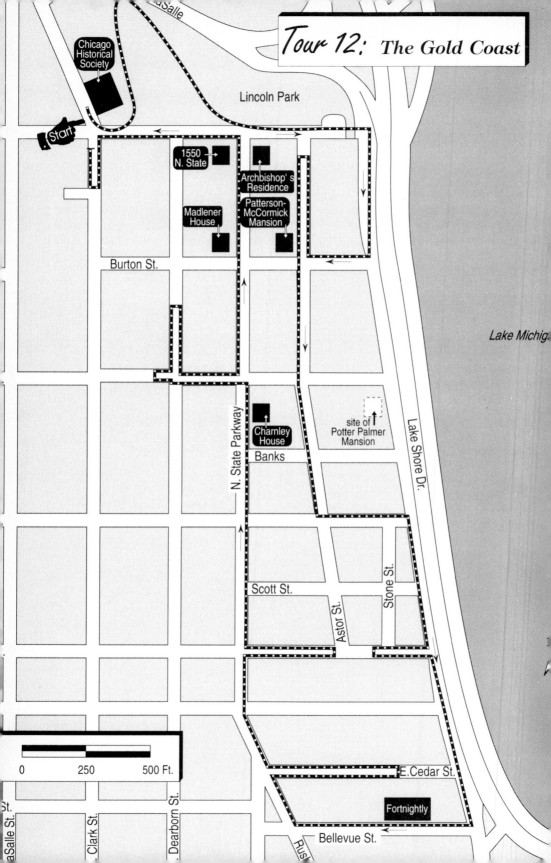

Tour 12: The Gold Coast

Chicago Historical Society

Lincoln Park

Start

1550 N. State

Archbishop's Residence

Madlener House

Patterson-McCormick Mansion

Burton St.

N. State Parkway

Charnley House

Banks

site of Potter Palmer Mansion

Lake Shore Dr.

Lake Michig.

Scott St.

Astor St.

Stone St.

0   250   500 Ft.

E. Cedar St.

Fortnightly

LaSalle St.

Clark St.

Dearborn St.

Rush

Bellevue St.

12. The Gold Coast

The area bounded by Oak Street on the south, N. LaSalle Boulevard on the west, E. North Avenue on the north, and Lake Michigan on the east today comprises what is known as Chicago's Gold Coast. It was developed shortly after the Great Fire of 1871, and as the name implies, was an enclave settled by the city's affluent. For a time the area vied with the Prairie Avenue neighborhood for status as the "real" Gold Coast. Eventually this relatively convenient lakefront district won out, and as Prairie Avenue became industrialized and fell into decline, Chicago's elite settled here. In 1978 the area roughly bounded by North Avenue, Lake Shore Drive, and Clark and Oak streets was placed on the National Register and designated the **Gold Coast Historic District.**

To this very day the Gold Coast remains Chicago's most affluent residential area, in spite of the loss of so many of its once-sumptuous mansions. Through the years they were replaced first by elegant apartment houses, then by towering high-rises. Yet a surprising number of town houses survive, most now subdivided into smaller units or converted to institutional offices, and can be seen along N. Astor Street, N. State Parkway, N. Lake Shore Drive, N. Dearborn Parkway, and on adjacent side streets. Space just does not permit detailing every significant house; those covered in this walking tour are the selections of most Chicago architectural historians, plus some additional buildings which the writer felt should be included as well.

The first luxury apartment houses began to appear in the 1890s, but the big boom in multifamily housing took place in the 1910s with exclusive elegant apartment houses, whose graceful facades often imitated the styles of the mansions they replaced. With the skyrocketing demand for apartments in the 1950s and 1960s, new high-rises proliferated, particularly along Lake Shore Drive, disrupting the scale of the neighborhood and wiping out virtually every vestige of the former spectacular row of mansions that lined the drive.

Credit for the original development of the Gold Coast must go to retail tycoon, hotelier, and creator of the State Street shopping district, Potter Palmer, who with his wife Bertha, queen of Chicago's social elite, were the first of Chicago's affluent to settle in the area. In 1882 Palmer engaged Henry Ives Cobb to design what would become the most luxurious and ostentatious "castle" ever seen in the Midwest, setting a trend which persisted well into the 20th century. After the turn of the century the trend was away from large Romanesque Revival mansions to the neo-Classical and Georgian Revival–style town house, many of which survive today in pristine condition and are among the most desirable (and expensive) housing in Chicago. While the Gold Coast is no longer as exclusive and fashionable as it once was, a stroll along these quiet, shady thoroughfares offers an unexcelled opportunity to experience much of the atmosphere of the past, while enjoying a seemingly endless variety of architectural styles, fads, and fancies in a neighborhood that still retains the charm of its halcyon days.

The tour begins at the Chicago Historical Society building, at the corner of N. Clark Street and North Avenue, about a mile-and-a-half north of the Loop. Take CTA bus No. 22 northbound on Clark Street to North Avenue.

The **Chicago Historical Society** (*1932, Graham, Anderson, Probst & White; addition 1971, Alfred Shaw & Associates; addition 1988, Hammond, Beeby & Babka*), N. Clark Street at North Avenue, is situated at the southwest corner of Lincoln Park, and is a splendid museum of Chicago history and a "must see." You will need several hours for just an overview, so plan a return visit at leisure, and allow time for lunch at their very pleasant Big Shoulders Cafe, located in the glassed-in circular section at the south end of the building. Entrance to the cafe is through the imposing stone arch designed by Daniel H.

The Chicago Historical Society, on N. Clark Street at North Avenue, is the primary guardian and repository of Chicago's history. It presents a variety of interesting exhibits, and maintains a library and research center. This view of the front facade of the CHS is the 1988 Daniel F. and Ada L. Rice Pavilion, designed by Hammond, Beeby & Babka—a major addition to the original 1932 Graham, Anderson, Probst & White building. The eye-catching hi-tech facade is dominated by the curved glass-and-aluminum wing that houses the Big Shoulders Cafe. (Photo by author)

Burnham for an early building of the Stock Yards Bank & Trust Company, which was located on W. Exchange Avenue and S. Halsted Street, opposite the now-vanished, famous Union Stock Yards. Later, take a few moments to explore the Society's well-stocked book store.

This is the fourth home of the CHS—the first was destroyed in the Great Fire five years after the Society was founded in 1856. The collection then reposed temporarily at the office of a former president, but in 1874 it was again the victim of a destructive fire. In 1892 architect Henry Ives Cobb was commissioned to design its first and more permanent (and more fireproof) building. A massive Richardsonian Romanesque Revival–style structure, it housed the collections until the present, larger building was completed in 1932. The former CHS building still stands at 632 N. Dearborn Street, as the Excalibur nightclub, and is described in the River North Tour 11, on pages 366–368. When Charles F. Gunther, the inventor of caramel candy, died in 1920, the CHS purchased his private collection of historical artifacts, which he had had on display above his candy store downtown. The collection, which included Lincoln's death bed, was so extensive that this single acquisition demanded the construction of the present building for the Society. The idiosyncratic Gunther had even purchased the former Confederate Libby Prison from the city of Richmond, Virginia, and had it reconstructed on S. Wabash Avenue (only fragments survive today).

The main section of the Chicago Historical Society building was erected in a neo-Georgian style, however the Clark Street facade underwent two major renovations which replaced the main entrance and extended it. The 1971 addition was much criticized for its lack of architectural integrity and was remodeled in 1988. The present addition, known as the Daniel F. and Ada L. Rice Pavilion now contains the main entrance to the building. To get an idea of the original Georgian facade, look at the Doric portico at the rear of the building later in the tour. The new front, a pleasant mixture of high-tech with the building's red-brick facade, is an eye-catching, albeit architectural anomaly. Many have acclaimed the open, pedimented, and gridded metal entrance as reflective of the Society's new more up-to-date image.

At the Chicago Historical Society the city's dramatic history will unfold in all its glorious dimensions. You can step into an early fur trader's cabin; climb aboard the *Pioneer,* Chicago's first locomotive (which required breaking out the wall to install); relive a visit to the 1893 World's Columbian Exposition; re-create the sounds of a 1930s radio show; see the flames of the Great Chicago Fire flicker before your eyes; and much, much more. Do not miss the famous "Chicago History Dioramas," the Chicago History Galleries, and the exhibit "A House Divided: America in the Age of Lincoln." (Hours: Monday–Saturday, 9:30 P.M.–4:30 P.M.; Sunday, noon–5:00 P.M. Adults $3.00, students and seniors $2.00, children 6–16 $1.00, children under 6 free. Admission free on Monday.)

On leaving the Chicago Historical Society, turn left (south).

The rear of the Chicago Historical Society reveals the contrasting Georgian Revival style of the original building. The CHS moved from its former location at 632 N. Dearborn Street in 1932, and now occupies its fourth site since its founding in 1856. (Photo by author)

What appears to be an overturned aluminum tower next to the Chicago Historical Society building is sculptor Sheila Klein's Commemorative Ground Ring *(1989), designed to recall many familiar landmarks of Chicago's architectural history which are listed on a plaque below. (Photo by author)*

Near the corner is a most unusual sculpture, at first glance it appears to be an overturned aluminum tower. But according to sculptor Sheila Klein, *Commemorative Ground Ring* (1989) was designed in the shape of a gigantic ring incorporating references to familiar landmarks of Chicago's rich architectural heritage: a prairie-style roof; the facade of the Louis Sullivan–designed Getty Tomb in Graceland Cemetery (1890); the facade of the Wrigley Building, by Graham, Anderson, Probst & White (1921); Holabird & Root's 333 N. Michigan Avenue Building (1928); and a Chicago school–style window. Take a closer look!

Walk around to the rear of the CHS building, past the Lincoln statue, and continue about 50 yards north to a clump of trees surrounding a low stone structure near where LaSalle Drive meets Stockton Street.

In the 19th century, the area which is now **Lincoln Park** was a public burial ground. As the city's population moved northward after the Civil War, the cemetery was closed and most of the remains reburied elsewhere by 1895. Strangely, only one tomb remains, the **Couch Mausoleum.** No one knows for sure why it is still there, although according to municipal records, the family had donated the former cemetery grounds to the city, but objected strenuously to the tomb's removal, and fought what was apparently a successful legal battle to keep it there. It is also not known how many bodies repose in the 100-ton crypt. Ira Couch was one of the owners of the Tremont House, an elegant hotel

Behind the CHS and just within Lincoln Park is the Couch Mausoleum, a lone surviving tomb from when this part of Lincoln Park was a public burial ground. The influential Couch family objected to its removal when the cemetery was closed after the Civil War, and the city agreed to leave it. No one seems to know how many bodies repose in the 100-ton crypt. (Photo by author)

that was destroyed in the Great Fire. There is another burial a few blocks further north, marked by a boulder, that of David Kennison, a survivor of the Boston Tea Party who died in 1852, purportedly at the age of 115.

Return to the statue of Abraham Lincoln.

The Lincoln Park **statue of Abraham Lincoln** (1887) is a much more pleasant representation of the president than the seated Lincoln in Grant Park, which has a rather dour expression. Both were executed by America's greatest sculptor, Augustus Saint-Gaudens (who preferred his Grant Park rendition), and both exedrae, or seats, were the design of Stanford White. On the pink granite base are quotes from Lincoln's Gettysburg address and from his Second Inaugural. Smaller copies can be found in London and Mexico City.

Now cut diagonally across the park in a southeasterly direction toward North Avenue, and cross North Avenue to the corner of Astor Street. Note the Astor Street Historic District plaque.

Between N. State Parkway and N. Astor Street is the largest private house in the Gold Coast, the **Residence of the Roman Catholic Archbishop of Chicago** (*1880, Alfred F. Pashley*), 1555 N. State Parkway. The sprawling Queen Anne–style mansion was erected on the site of a large Catholic cemetery, and upon completion, the adjoining former burial grounds were subdivided into lots for sale to Chicago's well-to-do. The house was also the first major residence constructed in the area, and was built of red brick with Bedford limestone trim. Note, too the floral carvings in the terra-cotta spandrels, and the imposing driveway and porte-cochère. The mansion, now the residence of Archbishop Joseph Cardinal Bernadin, boasts no fewer than 19 chimneys, giving the peaks and gables of its roofline a picturesque flavor, enhanced by the shady curtain of the grounds' surrounding trees. Among its distinguished visitors were President Franklin D. Roosevelt and Pope Pius XII.

Before crossing back across E. North Avenue to the monument just to the east, note the plaque on the small pylon commemorating the Astor Street Historic District, which will be seen shortly.

The bronze **statue of Dr. Greene Vardiman Black** (*1918, Frederick C. Hibbard, sculptor*) honors the "Father of Modern Dentistry." According to the inscription in the base he was recognized as the foremost scientific investigator of his time in his profession, and before his death in 1915 he was the author of more than 500 books and papers, and invented over 100 different dentist's instruments.

(Right) The famous Standing Lincoln, *by Augustus Saint-Gaudens (1887), in Lincoln Park is one of two Lincoln sculptures in Chicago by the famous artist (the other, the* Seated Lincoln, *is in Grant Park). The exedrae (seats) of both were executed by Stanford White. (Photo by author)*

The sprawling Queen Anne–style residence of the Roman Catholic Archbishop of Chicago, at 1550 N. State Parkway, was built in 1880 on the site of an early Catholic burial ground. The house is constructed of red brick with limestone trim, and has a particularly picturesque flavor with its roofline of peaks and gables, an imposing porte-cochère, and no fewer than 19 tall chimneys. (Photo by author)

Walk east on E. North Avenue to the cul-de-sac, and follow the sidewalk to Lake Shore Drive. There is an underpass to the lake shore, but leave that for another time. Turn right (south) to the second building.

1540 N. Lake Shore Drive (*1925, Huszagh & Hill*) is rather typical of the refined town houses built early in the 20th century. The upper part of this red-brick and limestone-trim building is interesting with its three tourelles, giving it a definite chateauesque appearance. The more modern porte-cochère is a detraction.

1530 N. Lake Shore Drive (*1916, Benjamin H. Marshall*), originally the Bernard A. Eckhart House, is now the residence of the Polish Consulate General. The style is that of a Florentine villa, with a rusticated first floor, a pair of Palladian columned windows on the second floor, and an ornate cornice above the fourth floor.

1524 N. Lake Shore Drive (*1917, Howard Van Doren Shaw*), the former Eleanor Robinson Countiss House, together with its neighbor to the south, **No. 1516** (*1914, McKim, Mead & White*), are now owned by the International College of Surgeons, founded in 1935 in Geneva by Dr. Max Thorek, which maintains this **International College of Surgeons Museum.** The four-story limestone building was modeled after the smaller Petit Trianon at Versailles. Note the prominent fluted Corinthian pilasters. In front is the sculpture *Hope and Help,* depicting a surgeon holding a sick patient. This unique museum boasts one of the most complete medical collections in the world, with contributions to modern surgery shown from every country and every civilization, relating the culture of a people with their science, and with their religion and their method of treating the sick.

Go inside (ring the bell for entry) and make a short visit. The ground floor exhibit of early surgical instruments is particularly interesting. Other rooms depict the growth and perfection of many surgical specialties. The Hall of Immortals with its twelve imposing eight-foot-high stone-cast sculptures lining the room looks as though it had been chosen as a conference site by these medical giants. Climb the massive stone staircase to the second-floor panelled library. See the Inca skulls showing the earliest examples of trephining, around 2000 B.C., among other fascinating exhibits, and pick up a copy of the pamphlet *Medicine Man to Modern Surgeon . . . A History,* for much more than a dollar's worth of interesting information and a guide to the exhibits. The museum is open Tuesday–Saturday, 10:00 A.M.–4:00 P.M.; and Sunday, 11:00 A.M.–5:00 P.M. Although admission is free, a $2.00 donation would be appreciated.

Continue south to E. Burton Place and turn right (west) to N. Astor Street.

The Elinor Patterson–Cyrus H. McCormick Mansion, at 20 E. Burton Place, is generally known only by its around-the-corner street address, 1500 N. Astor Street. The splendid four-story Italian Renaissance palazzo, built of orange-colored Roman brick with terra-cotta trim, was designed by noted architect Stanford White in 1893 for Joseph Medill, publisher of the Chicago Tribune, *as a wedding present for his daughter "Cissy," who married Robert A. Patterson. The mansion was later acquired by Cyrus Hall McCormick II who had a perfectly harmonious addition built at the north end. Note the splendid second-story Ionic-columned portico, carved window enframements, and classic cornice. In 1978 the huge house was subdivided into condos. (Photo by author)*

Dominating the northwest corner is the **Elinor Patterson–Cyrus H. McCormick Mansion** (*1893, McKim, Mead & White; addition 1927, David Adler*), 20 E. Burton Place, known now by its 1500 N. Astor Street address. Designed by famed architect Stanford White, it follows his predilection for the Italian Renaissance palazzo. The splendid four-story mansion (converted to residential condominiums in 1978 by Nagle, Hartray & Associates, with Wilbert R. Hasbrouck, after many years of gradual decay) is built of orange-color Roman brick with terra-cotta trim. It boasts a second-story Ionic-columned portico, ornately carved window enframements, and a classic cornice—the building and grounds surrounded by a beautiful wrought-iron fence with sandstone pillars and highly decorative gate.

The house, the largest on Astor Street, was commissioned by *Chicago Tribune* publisher Joseph Medill as a wedding present for his daughter "Cissy" and new son-in-law Robert A. Patterson. Years later the house was acquired by Cyrus Hall McCormick II who engaged David Adler to build the huge and almost undistinguishable addition to the north. In more recent times, before its conversion to condos it housed a private school.

Astor Street was named for fur tycoon John Jacob Astor. The enormous profits he reaped from the Chicago-based American Fur Company were later used for his immensely profitable real estate ventures. The six blocks of Astor Street, between North and Division avenues is designated the **Astor Street Historic District.**

Across Astor Street, on the northeast corner, at **40 E. Burton Street/1501 N. Astor Street,** erected in 1909, is a neat red-brick Georgian-style house. Built for John G. Shortall, who according to *Norman Mark's Chicago* (a treasure-trove of interesting historical minutia), became a hero of the Great Fire of 1871 when he saved 20 years of real estate records. His brave act allowed the city to rebuild quickly and without lengthy legal battles as to whose property ended where. The building now houses the offices of the Greek Orthodox Diocese of Chicago.

Alongside, **No. 1505 N. Astor Street** (*1911, Jenney, Mundie & Jensen*) is a well-proportioned Georgian-style house, whose ground floor is of limestone and the upper three floors of traditional red brick. Note how each floor's three windows are evenly stacked above those beneath, with each succeeding level slightly shorter than the one below. A *piano nobile,* on the second floor reveals the principal space within. Capping the trim structure is a typical Georgian balustrade.

Continue north on Astor Street.

No. 1525 N. Astor Street (*1916, architect unknown*) is another variation on the Georgian theme, with arched windows on the first floor, pedimented windows on the second floor, and square-headed windows on the third. The entry

(Right) North Astor Street presents a variety of town house architecture in a leafy setting along nicely landscaped sidewalks, and represents the finest in Gold Coast living, within minutes of downtown Chicago. (Photo by author)

is also arched, with a wrought-iron door grille. Another typical feature of the style is the two shades of red brick, which adds texture and elegance to the facade.

Cross N. Astor Street to the west side and turn left (south) to examine the houses on the west side.

An interesting oddity: note that the alley behind the Archbishop's Residence is paved with sawn wooden logs set vertically in the ground.

No. 1524 N. Astor Street (*1968, I. W. Colburn & Associates*) at first glance resembles its early-20th-century neighbors. It is actually a contextual addition with its corner "tower" almost hidden behind a cloak of English ivy. Walk around the right side of the building and notice how the center of the building, now unabashedly modern, has an open second story with huge windows on the inside of the U-shaped open area. Alas, the front door is completely out of context.

No. 1520 N. Astor Street (*1911, Jeremiah K. Cady*), connected by a continuous brick wall to **No. 1524** and **No. 1518** (*1911, Jenney, Mundie & Jensen*), both three stories high, are another set of the then-popular Georgian Revival–style houses. Note the typical swag above the entrance to No. 1518 and the curved bay running the full height of the building.

No. 1519 N. Astor Street is of more interest historically than architecturally. It was once the home of Robert Todd Lincoln, the only surviving son of the president and his wife, Mary Todd Lincoln. The youngest son of Abraham Lincoln, he became a lawyer after the Civil War and lived in Chicago most of his life serving railroad corporation interests. He also held several government posts, including Secretary of War and minister to Great Britain. Upon the death of George M. Pullman in 1897, Lincoln took over the presidency of the Pullman Palace Car Company.

Continue south on N. Astor Street, to E. Burton Street, to the southeast corner.

No. 1451 N. Astor Street (*1910, Howard Van Doren Shaw*) in Tudor Revival style, is a pleasant "country house" fairly typical of the English Revival styles so favored by Shaw. The dark red-brick and limestone house was built for John L. Fortune, and displays twin trapezoidal bays, plus carved fruit baskets above strapwork panels on both sides of the Astor Street entry.

No. 1449 N. Astor Street (*1899, architect unknown*) is an impressive Gothic-style chateau squeezed in between its neighbors. The entire facade is almost overwhelmed by the massive entry porch. The attic, however, is rather incongruous. Note the shell design in the frieze with strange, twisted half-columns at each end.

No. 1443 N. Astor Street (*1891, Joseph Lyman Silsbee*) was designed for Horatio N. May. It is a massive Romanesque Revival–style rock-faced granite structure, three stories high, plus an attic in the gable, with a huge arched doorway. Note the decorative carved panels flanking the entrance.

No. 1443 N. Astor Street is a massive Romanesque Revival–style town house. Built in 1891 its rock-faced granite facade, arched doorway, and pointed gable are evidence of the affluence of its original owner, Horation N. May. (Photo by author)

Cross to the west side.

No. 1444 N. Astor Street (*1929, Holabird & Root*), known as the Edward P. Russell House, is an archtypical Art Deco–style structure, made of stone quarried in Lens, France, and trimmed in black granite around the entrance and along the base. Four stories high, it has a gently curved three-story metal-sheathed bay with incised floral designs. There are a variety of window shapes, some with leaded glass. The *AIA Guide to Chicago* rhapsodically describes it as "sleek, urbane, sophisticated, and very French . . . timeless and unique."

No. 1442 N. Astor Street (*1891, Pond & Pond*) was built for C. Vallette Kasson, and consists of rough-hewn stone on the lower floor and Roman brick with limestone trim on the second and third floors. Most notable is the pointed-stone-arch entrance, with the door offset to the right and the same arch design traced in the brick above.

Cross back to the east side.

No. 1431 N. Astor Street (*1894, Holabird & Roche*), the George W. Meeker House, was originally designed in Federal style, but has suffered a number of inappropriate accretions, such as the pedimented porch with Ionic columns, oversize shutters, and the appalling black paint scheme. Look up to the roof and note the ornate cornice decorated with garlands of balls. At one time the house was occupied by Edward Ryerson, chairman of the Inland Steel Corporation.

No. 1429 N. Astor Street (*1891, Pond & Pond*), the Eugene R. Hutchins House, is a strange confection of styles, but with a romantic medieval atmo-

(Left) One of the most charming town houses in the neighborhood is No. 1429 N. Astor Street, the Eugene R. Hutchins House. Eclectic in style, it presents an almost medieval atmosphere with its mixture of Romanesque and Gothic features, particularly in the peaked roof and dormers with leaded glass. (Photo by author)

sphere. The first two stories are faced with rough-hewn stone, in a Romanesque style, while the arch above the door and small, leaded-glass windows lend a Gothic touch. The main feature, however, is the steeply pitched projecting roof with peaked dormers and unusual adornments.

No. 1427 N. Astor Street (*1889, William LeBaron Jenney*) was commissioned by Rensselaer W. Cox. This otherwise rather dull structure is sheathed in unusual rock-faced red brick with limestone trim. More notable, perhaps, is the architect, who is recognized as the father of the modern skyscraper.

No. 1425 N. Astor Street was built in 1895 for city controller William D. Kerfoot, who is credited with erecting the first building (a shanty) after the Great Fire of 1871. Demonstrating the typical Chicago "We Can" attitude, he is said to have built his house on the still smoldering ruins, with a sign reading "Wm. D. Kerfoot is at 53 Onion Park Place/All gone but wife children AND energy." A photograph of his shanty and sign can be seen in the Chicago Fire exhibit at the Chicago Historical Society. The building is quite large, resembling an Italian villa. It is three stories high plus an attic, with twin bays and rusticated ground floor. The arched entrance is extra wide with a pair of ornate arched windows above. Note the oval windows in the attic with swags below the classic cornice.

Cross back to the west side.

No. 1416 N. Astor Street (*Arthur Heun, 1917*) is a simple Georgian Revival–style house with fine brickwork laid in Flemish bond, built for William McCormick Blair. In 1952 Adlai Stevenson was a guest at the house when he received word that the Democratic Party had designated him as the presidential candidate.

No. 1412 N. Astor Street (*1892, Douglas S. Pentecost*) is known as the Thomas W. Hinde House. A limestone and yellow-brick structure, it displays a number of unusual English Renaissance motifs, although many details were lost in an early remodeling. Note the various medieval features and the diamond-pane windows.

No. 1406 N. Astor Street (*1922, David Adler; addition 1931, also by David Adler*) was designed for Joseph T. Ryerson, Jr., grandson of the founder of Ryerson & Son, now part of Inland Steel. An impressive French Renaissance–style town house, it has many noteworthy details: the second-floor balcony and third-floor windows with wrought-iron balustrades, ornate stonework around the windows which are different on each floor, a mansarded fourth floor, a decorative iron fence, and Ryerson's initials in florid wrought iron in the transom of the entrance door.

No. 1412 N. Astor Street, the Thomas W. Hinde House, displays a number of interesting English Renaissance details. Note the diamond-pane leaded glass in the transomed windows and the elaborate terra-cotta work above. (Photo by author)

No. 1400 N. Astor Street (*1887, Cobb & Frost; addition 1991, Hammond, Beeby & Babka*), the **Perry H. Smith House**, is a large structure with fine Romanesque Revival details, particularly in the forceful arch on the Schiller Street side. The recent addition at the rear by HB&B fits so harmoniously that it is virtually impossible to find the place where it joins the original house.

At E. Schiller Street look east along the north side of the street at the fine row of Queen Anne–style town houses; then continue south on N. Astor Street, noting how the street jogs slightly to the right. Stay on the east side of the street.

No. 1365 N. Astor Street, the **James Charnley House** (*1892, Dankmar Adler & Louis Sullivan; renovation 1980, John Vinci, restoration 1988, Skidmore, Owings & Merrill*), is one of the most significant residences in the area, and now the **national headquarters of the Society of Architectural Historians.** The actual designer was 23-year-old Frank Lloyd Wright, who at the outset of his career was an apprentice at the firm of Adler & Sullivan. The house has a distinctly modern appearance and contains hints of the future Prairie house designs that would later be Wright's hallmark. Built for lumber baron James Charnley, the house displays Sullivan's ornamental style as well, particularly in the decorative wooden balcony, the leaded-glass windows, and the copper cornice. Invisible from the exterior, the house contains a 30-foot-tall central light well, a Sullivan-designed fireplace, and 11 wood-paneled rooms. The structure is built of a tawny Roman brick over a limestone basement.

Occupied as a single-family home until the 1970s, it was purchased in 1986 by the Skidmore, Owings & Merrill Foundation for its headquarters, and a

The north side of Schiller Street between N. Astor Street and N. Lake Shore Drive is a pleasant row of Queen Anne–style town houses—all with a variety of peaked gables and facades, and dating from ca. 1890. (Photo by author)

The James Charnley House, 1365 N. Astor Street, was built in 1892 by Adler & Sullivan, but credit for the design goes to Frank Lloyd Wright, a young apprentice in the firm. Built for lumber baron James Charnley, the house displays Sullivan's ornamental style in the balcony ornament, copper cornice, and leaded-glass windows; but there is no mistaking the hints of the Prairie Style that would later be Wright's hallmark. The house was recently donated to the Society of Architectural Historians for their national headquarters. (Photo by author)

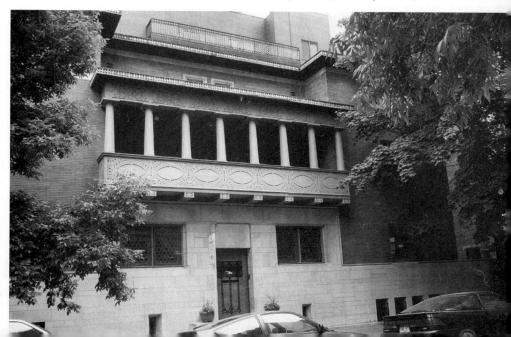

three-year restoration program was undertaken, thus saving the house as a unique and invaluable architectural landmark. In 1994 the house was purchased for $1,650,000 by Seymour H. Persky, an active preservationist and supporter of religious organizations and a board member of the Society of Architectural Historians, who had hoped that the house would be a suitable showcase for his collection of Sullivan and Wright artifacts. But because the structure would have to be damaged with elevators and new staircases, he decided instead—in an unprecedented act of generosity—to donate the Charnley House to the SAH, provided they move their headquarters from Philadelphia to Chicago. In a recent interview in *Preservation News,* the magazine of the National Trust for Historic Preservation, Persky was asked, "Why Chicago?" "Because American architecture originated here, as did all the great architects," he replied.

For information about the Society of Architectural Historians and its program of tours, call 573-1365 (same four digits as the address).

No. 1353–1355 N. Astor Street, "Astor Court" (*1914, Howard Van Doren Shaw*), was commissioned by lumber magnate William O. Goodman. It was Goodman who donated the theatre named for him in Grant Park as a memorial to his son, a lieutenant in the U.S. Navy, who was killed in World War I. A lovely Georgian-style house, it is one of the largest in the area—seven bays wide—and built of high-quality brick laid in a variety of bonds. The ground

"Astor Court," No. 1353-1355 N. Astor Street, was designed in 1914 by Howard Van Doren Shaw for lumber magnate William O. Goodman. It is one of the largest Georgian-style houses in the Gold Coast, seven bays wide, with a ground floor faced with limestone, a high-quality brick facade, stately pilasters, and a roof balustrade. Behind the iron gate on the right is a passageway leading into a large inner court. Note the keystones above the third-floor windows which display animal skulls. (Photo by author)

floor is of limestone, and rising from the second floor to the cornice are limestone pilasters framing windows on the *piano nobile* floor that are topped by
carved arches. A roof balustrade completes the Georgian composition. Note
the keystones above the third-floor windows which display animal skulls surmounted by fruit baskets. On both sides of the central second-floor window are
carved stacked urns.

At the south end of the building, once a driveway, a passageway leads to an
inner landscaped court. Look through the large iron gate, and note the polished brass door knockers in the shape of hands delicately grasping an apple.
Some have disappeared over the years, yet the yard is still known as the Court
of the Golden Hands.

No. 1345 N. Astor Street (*1887, Treat & Foltz*), the Edwin J. Gardiner
House, is a Romanesque Revival–style town house whose distinguishing feature is the polychrome sandstone facade of bright red and orange which was
quarried in Dunreith, Ohio. The front elevation displays twin arches—one for
the entry, the other as a window with peaked gable.

No. 1325 N. Astor Street is a 14-story apartment house designed in 1928 by
Andrew M. Rebori. One of the early high-rises in the neighborhood, it once
boasted luxury apartments with as many as 11 rooms, 4 baths, and 2 wood-
burning fireplaces.

At E. Banks Street cross to the southwest corner.

Nos. 1316–1322 N. Astor Street and **25 E. Banks Street** (*1889, Charles M.
Palmer*) are known as the Houses for Potter Palmer, since they were built as a
speculative investment by the noted retailing, real estate, and hotel
entrepreneur. Although there are many differences between the individual
town houses, they form a uniform and harmonious row. Some exhibit rough-
cut stone facades with prominent horizontal banding. Note the arched and
recessed doorways, the bartizan on No. 1318, and the carved foliation on Nos.
1324, 1318, and 1316. No. 1320 is built of dark-red sandstone with pronounced
bands.

Potter Palmer had begun buying large tracts of land in this area in the
early 1880s, which he then drained, improved, and sold to wealthy families. He
built his own mansion in 1882 on nearby Lake Shore Drive, just north of
Schiller Street, which resembled a Norman Gothic castle (*see* photo), which
soon gave impetus to the move by Chicago's elite to the Gold Coast. It survived until 1950 and was replaced by twin high-rises at 1350–1360 N. Lake
Shore Drive.

Nos. 1308–1312 N. Astor Street (*1887–1888, Burnham & Root*) are a row of
four town houses (No. 1306 was razed), designated the **James L. Houghteling
Houses.** The actual architect was John Wellborn Root, who lived in No. 1310
until his untimely death in 1891 at the age of 41. The houses, which vary stylisti-
cally, but form a homogeneous assemblage are built of rough-cut sandstone on
the ground floor, with Roman brick above. The roofline is particularly interesting, showing Gothic details, with a sharply steep slate roof, a variety of peaked

The Norman Gothic–style "Castle" built by Potter Palmer in 1882 on Lake Shore Drive gave impetus to Chicago's elite to move north of the river along the lakefront. Designed by Henry Ives Cobb and Charles Sumner Frost, it was probably the most imposing mansion ever built in Chicago. Palmer, a real estate tycoon and entrepreneur, was responsible for developing the State Street shopping area, helping Marshall Field begin his career, building the famous Palmer House hotel, and buying, draining, and improving the land in this area for resale to the wealthy. The majestic "fortress" survived until 1950 when it fell victim to latter-day developers who built the twin tower apartments on the site at 1350–1360 N. Lake Shore Drive. (Courtesy of the Art Institute of Chicago)

gables, a corner tower sheathed in sheet metal and topped with a cupola, and carved terra-cotta panels. After Root's death, his widow remained for a number of years, and his sister-in-law, Harriet Monroe, founder of the magazine *Poetry,* also lived in the house until her death in 1936.

Continue to the corner of E. Goethe Street.

On the northeast and southwest corners are twin 14-story apartment towers, built two years apart, **No. 1301 N. Astor Street** and **No. 1260 N. Astor Street,** the former in 1932, the latter in 1930, and both designed by architect Philip B. Maher. Similar in appearance, they are good examples of the Art Moderne style, so popular in the early 1930s, and typical of Maher's Art Moderne and Art Deco buildings. The pair were early arrivals on Astor Street, as less space became available for high-rise construction on nearby Lake Shore Drive.

Potter Palmer and his wife Bertha were perhaps the most influential members of Chicago's high society, and their lifestyle showed it. Here a pair of liveried coachmen attend the Palmers' elegant carriage near the entrance to the "Castle" in this ca. 1885 photo. (Courtesy of the Art Institute of Chicago)

This pair of 22-story towers, erected in 1949–1951 from plans by Loebl, Schlossman & Bennett, replaced the Potter Palmer "Castle." One of the first new high-rise constructions on Lake Shore Drive, it gave birth to a new generation of development that virtually wiped out all traces of the drive's past glory, with only a small handful of mansions surviving. The irregular plan of the facade with its projecting rows of windows was designed to provide all tenants with broad views of Lake Michigan. (Photo by author)

Originally the Astor Tower Hotel, this "high-rise on stilts" at 1300 N. Astor Street, was designed by Bertrand Goldberg in 1963. Now a condo, its first four floors are reserved for the elevator core and mechanical systems. The building was planned to "rise above" the neighboring town houses and provide panoramic views for the hotel guests. (Photo by author)

On the northwest corner is a rather different style high-rise, **No. 1300 N. Astor Street** (*1963, Bertrand Goldberg*). Built originally as the Astor Tower Hotel, it appears to be standing on stilts, providing tenants with views above neighboring rooftops. The first four floors are for the mechanical systems and services, and floors 5–28 are now condominium apartments. When still a hotel, the Astor Tower was the favorite haunt of many traveling shows and entertainment personalities, and its basement restaurant, Maxim's, was a gourmet landmark in Chicago. At this writing all windows are covered with fixed metal louvres, whose original purpose was to obviate the need for venetian blinds, however complaints from dissatisfied tenants have elicited promises from the management to remove them.

On the southeast corner is **Goudy Square Park,** a special children's play park, richly endowed with an assortment of facilities to provide lots of fun for the under-12 set. The pleasant amenity is under the jurisdiction of the Chicago Park District.

Turn left (east) on E. Goethe Street to Lake Shore Drive, and turn right (south). (Chicagoans often have their own unique pronunciation for names of foreign origin. The great German writer's name is pronounced "GO-thee," with a hard "th.")

★   **No. 1260 N. Lake Shore Drive** (*1911, Holabird & Roche*), the Lawrence D. Rockwell House, is a simple Classic-style house, typical of the era, whose covered stone entrance faces Goethe Street. Note the quoins at the ends of the building and a keystone over every window.

✱   **No. 1258 N. Lake Shore Drive** (*1896, Holabird & Roche*), the Arthur T. Aldis House, presents a striking example of Venetian Gothic style. The three-story palazzo has a limestone ground floor and brick-facing above, with limestone trim. The ornate balcony with decorative pointed-arch windows is particularly attractive. On the next level are twin balconies, and supporting the cornice are consoles in the form of gargoyles. Look for the date in the plaque above.

✱   **No. 1254 N. Lake Shore Drive** (*1889, Gustave Hallberg*), the Mason Brayman Starring House, as well as its neighbor to the south, offer textbook examples of a variety of Richardsonian Romanesque details: the rock-faced granite facade, recessed arched entry with stubby columns and elaborate foliated capitals (look for the smiling face in one of them!), and ornate carving in the peaked gable. In 1990 the building was connected to its neighbor and both were subdivided into four large apartments. Note the plaque from the Landmarks Preservation Council of Illinois.

✱   **No. 1250 N. Lake Shore Drive** (*1890, Frank B. Abbott*), the Carl C. Heisen House, has a pink granite facade highlighted by reddish mortar. Probably the most dazzling of the row because of its round tower and open belfry, recessed balconies on the first and second floors, arched entry, broad entrance stairway, and peaked roof, the Heisen House resembles a miniature castle. Note, too, the columns made of square-cut (on the first floor) and round-cut (on the second)

Nos. 1250, 1254, and 1258 N. Lake Shore Drive (plus 1260, not visible at right) are a delightful row of town houses that somehow escaped the onslaught of the developers. All designated city landmarks, each has its own characteristics and style. No. 1250 (1890) with the round tower and open belfry is the "queen" of the row; 1254 (1889) is a fine example of Richardsonian Romanesque; while 1258 (1896) is an interesting example of a Venetian Gothic palazzo. (Photo by author)

granite, unlike the smoothly polished columns with elaborately carved capitals on No. 1254. Now diminished by the neighboring high-rise, the house was doubtless a major attraction on the drive.

Continue south on N. Lake Shore Drive past E. Scott Street to the northwest corner of E. Division Street.

The entrance to **No. 1200 N. Lake Shore Drive** (*1913, Marshall & Fox*), known as the Stewart Apartments, is on E. Division Street. The building typifies the growing trend of the elite early in the 20th century to move from spacious town houses to almost equally spacious apartments. The 13-story yellow-brick Georgian-style high-rise "mansion" has large rounded projecting bays on the Lake Shore Drive side, with smaller bays facing Division Street, and is adorned with many Adamesque swags. When built, this luxury multi-family building housed the servant staffs on the lower two floors, and had playrooms for the children, as well as additional maids' quarters, on the top floor. Most apartments had 18 rooms with as many as six bathrooms, and all had uninterrupted lake views (without the traffic noise!).

Turn right (west) on E. Division Street to No. 57.

No. 57 E. Division Street, on the south side, is a typical Queen Anne–style house of dark-red brick with limestone trim, sporting a prominent peaked roof with dormer and a large gable. Note the incised carving over the center windows, but ignore the unauthentic carriage lamps. (A century from now, will residents adorn their mid-20th-century homes with automobile headlights to give them "atmosphere"?)

Look too, at **Nos. 45–51 E. Division Street,** a pleasant row of Queen Anne– and Romanesque Revival–style town houses.

Return to N. Lake Shore Drive, turn right (south) one block to the northwest corner of E. Elm Street.

No. 1130 N. Lake Shore Drive (*1911, Howard Van Doren Shaw*), whose entrance is at 90 E. Elm Street, is a nine-story Tudor-style apartment building—one of the first to rise along the drive and also one of the first cooperatives. It is constructed of red brick with limestone window enframements, and the treatment of the windows is typically Tudor. As mentioned earlier, Shaw favored English medieval styles, especially Tudor Gothic, and he backed up his predilections by purchasing one of the co-op apartments for himself. The facade exhibits many medieval motifs; look at the ground floor on the lake side, with its pointed-arch windows, above which are terra-cotta adornments.

Continue walking south, past E. Cedar Street to the southwest corner of E. Bellevue Place.

The lofty 24-story high-rise **No. 1000 N. Lake Shore Drive** (*1954, Sidney Morris & Associates*), a concrete structure sheathed in brick and glass, displays a unique array of balconies of punched concrete on the Bellevue Place side. This was the site of the palatial residence of Edith Rockefeller McCormick, which was said to have set new standards of opulence, even for the super-rich.

Turn right (west) on E. Bellevue Place.

On the north side, **No. 50 E. Bellevue Place** (*1892, McKim, Mead & White; restoration 1992, Perkins & Will*) is the **former Bryan Lathrop House,** and since 1922 the women's literary club, "The Fortnightly of Chicago." Designed in what was to become the favorite style of the Gold Coast, the Georgian Revival, it is a graceful and symmetrical mansion, with prominent twin semicircular bays, erected from plans by Charles Follen McKim, of the famous New York architectural firm, who was also a major architect of the World's Columbian Exposition of 1893. According to the Chicago Landmarks plaque, McKim drew inspiration from the neo-classical styles of the 18th century and "the clarity and simplicity of its facade make the Lathrop House one of the finest examples of Georgian Revival architecture in this country."

Across the street is a fine row of town houses, among which **No. 115** is in Queen Anne style and adjacent **No. 113** is Tudor. Further west, look at **No. 65**

At 50 E. Bellevue Place stands the splendid Georgian Revival–style former Bryan Lathrop House, since 1922 the women's literary club, "Fortnightly of Chicago." Designed by Charles Follen McKim of the famous New York architectural firm of McKim, Mead & (Stanford) White, it is considered one of the finest examples of the style in the country. With McKim's introduction of the Georgian Revival to the Gold Coast, it quickly became the style of choice for the neighborhood's wealthy homeowners. (Photo by author)

with its second-floor wooden bay window, and the triangular bay on **No. 63.**
The exterior iron spiral staircase on No. 59 is a later addition to conform to fire
codes. **Nos. 49** and **47,** with rock-faced facades, have prominent half-circle bays
with ornate carved bands above. Both have splendid rooflines.

Nos. 45 and **43,** designed in 1892 by Charles M. Palmer for the real estate
investments of tycoon Potter Palmer, are fairly large town houses. Note how
the facade's rustication on this pair of Romanesque Revival–style houses is
reduced on each succeeding floor. Alas, the cornice has been removed.

No. 33 (*1911, Richard E. Schmidt, Garden & Martin*) is a huge Georgian
Revival–style apartment house. Called the Chandler Apartments, it lacks
nothing for refinement and boasts a number of interesting touches: iron window balconies, an attractive upper floor with mini-balustrades above each of
the four windows; the lintels and keystones, particularly on the fifth floor, display carvings, and on the second floor, at each end of the building, are carved
faces. The brickwork, laid in Flemish bond, adds more elegance.

Across the street again, **Nos. 34** and **32** are worthy of notice. No. 32 (*1887,
Burnham & Root*) with its peaked gable, odd dormer with finials, with a circle
design in the pediment and above the entrance, presents an unusual appearance, partly hidden by English ivy. It is a delightful surviving design of architect
John Wellborn Root. Further down the street, **No. 29** has a large, round corner
bay and peaked dormer.

Walk to N. Rush Street, at the end of the block.

The triangular mini-park formed by the confluence of N. Rush Street and
N. State Parkway, between E. Bellevue Place and E. Cedar Street, is called
Mariano Park. Cross to the shelter in front of the fountain. It was designed by
Birch Burdette Long, a member of the staff of Frank Lloyd Wright and later a
noted architectural renderer. His plan for this charming little structure won the
design competition in 1895. In 1979 it was restored by the Park District. Go
inside and admire the detail of the singular polychrome columns which have a
certain "Wrightian" flavor.

Walk north one block to E. Cedar Street.

Before turning right into E. Cedar Street, look left across N. State Parkway
at the **Cedar Hotel,** 1118 N. State Parkway, and its broad and flamboyant white
terra-cotta frieze and cornice, as well as the paneling between the windows at
the south end. North State Parkway is the extension of N. State Street, but was
elevated to parkway status more appropriate to the classy residential district it
slices through.

Turn right into Cedar Street and note the red-brick Gothic-style apartment
house on the north side, **No. 20 E. Cedar Street** (*1924, Fugard & Knapp*). Particularly interesting are the limestone Gothic terra-cotta window enframements which encompass the pairs of duplex apartments in this 18-story
building. The 12th floor has projecting bays, and the topmost floor is recessed
and resembles a castellated terrace.

The little shelter in Mariano Park, at the confluence of N. Rush Street and N. State Parkway, was designed by Birch Burdette Long, a member of Frank Lloyd Wright's staff, who won the competition for the design of this cozy little Prairie-style structure in 1895. Note the morning-glory design on the columns which erupt into delicate flowers in the capitals and along the frieze. The shelter was restored by the Park District in 1979. (Photo by author)

Across N. State Parkway from Mariano Park is the Cedar Hotel with an astonishingly ornate terra-cotta frieze, cornice, and spandrels on the south end of the building. (Photo by author)

(Left) Nos. 42–48 E. Cedar Street is a row of town houses built speculatively for Potter Palmer in 1896. The Romanesque Revival–style limestone houses are quite symmetrical, with a peaked gable at each end of the row. (Photo by author)

Nos. 42–48 (*1896, Charles M. Palmer*) is another row of town houses built for Potter Palmer's real estate interests. The row of Romanesque Revival–style limestone houses is quite symmetrical, except for the addition atop No. 42 (said to contain a ballroom), with recessed entrances and round-arch windows on the third floor. The houses at each end have an ornate peaked gable, each with a different floral design.

Nos. 50–54 (*1892, L. Gustav Hallberg*) is another group of Romanesque Revival–style houses, with similar entrances, all of which have single columns supporting the entrance canopies, but each with a different design in the foliate capitals. The center building, No. 52, has a semicircular bay.

Across the street, **No. 49** (*1908, Marshall & Fox*) is an attractive small apartment house, with a distinguishing semicircular bay, that is rather different from the architects' 1200 N. Lake Shore Drive building. Here the house is designed in Georgian Revival style, with Flemish bond brickwork emphasized by the use of dark-brown headers alternating with red-brick stretchers. Marshall & Fox are also remembered for their designs for the Drake Hotel, the Blackstone Hotel, and a number of apartment houses in the E. Lake Shore Drive Historic District, among others.

Surprising **No. 60** (*1890, Curd H. Gottig*) seems to include every possible attribute of the Romanesque Revival style: rock-faced exterior (in this case

No. 60 E. Cedar Street (1890) is another "textbook" exemplar of the Richardsonian Romanesque, with its powerful recessed entrance, squat columns with foliate capitals, projecting bays, a half-round window, ornate peaked gable set off-center, and oriel attached to the left corner. Oddly, the side wall is of dark-red brick. (Photo by author)

Georgia marble), a powerful and dramatic recessed entrance, squat support columns with foliate capitals, projecting bays with carving underneath, a half-round window above, an ornate peaked gable offset to the right, copper trim above, and a bartizan or oriel attached to the left corner. The side walls, however, are of dark-red brick.

Other town houses meriting more than a cursory glance are **No. 66** in dark-brown sandstone designed in a quasi-Italianate style, with carving in its bell gable. Note the house number carved above the first floor. Take a brief glimpse at the unusual cornice line and detailing on **Nos. 67–79** across the street, including the stone entrance arch of No. 71. Although the cornice designs vary, the effect is harmonious.

Return to N. State Parkway, and turn right (north) past E. Elm Street to E. Division Street. Turn right (east) for a brief detour of one block to the northwest corner of N. Astor Street.

No. 1200 N. Astor Street (*1897, Holabird & Roche*) was formerly the McConnell Apartments, and is now the Renaissance Condominiums. The seven-story orange-brick apartment house built on a ground floor of limestone has a classic-style cornice and "punched out" windows over a simple sill. The main feature of the building is its conspicuous rounded corner bay, reminiscent of the firm's 1894 Old Colony Building in the Loop (*see* pages 15–16), and is typical of the Chicago school of architecture.

No. 1200 N. Astor Street, formerly the McConnell Apartments, designed in 1897 by Holabird & Roche, was remodeled as the Renaissance Condominiums. The outstanding feature of this seven-story orange-brick apartment house is its conspicuous rounded corner bay, reminiscent of the architects' 1894 Old Colony Building in the Loop. (Photo by author)

Return to N. State Parkway and turn right (north).

One can't miss **No. 1209 N. State Parkway** (*1937, Andrew N. Rebori*), the Frank Fisher Apartments, in its bright white coat of paint. Designed in an Art Moderne style complete with the then-popular glass-brick wall treatment, it is an interesting addition to the streetscape. Peek through the side gate into the narrow garden which has the entrances to 13 duplex apartments. The terra-cotta plaques on the front wall were done by Edgar Miller.

Continue north past E. Scott Street.

Nos. 1234–1252, known as the "Fairbanks Row Houses," is a symmetrical and attractive group, most constructed of "Athens marble," or Joliet yellow limestone. All have had their entrances removed and lowered to the basement floor.

Across the street, diminutive **No. 1241,** a one-and-a-half story brick house, seemingly out of place in this neighborhood, is one of its oldest, built shortly after the Great Fire, ca. 1874.

No. 1243–1245, is a double house that was built in 1880 by an unknown architect for Charles Henry Hulburd and Charles C. Yoe. It displays French Second-Empire characteristics with its mansard roof and neo-Grec carving over the windows. Two types of stone were used, one for the walls and a con-

The row of town houses, Nos. 1234–1252 N. State Parkway, built ca. 1885, is a symmetrical group, set back with attractive front landscaping. Known as the "Fairbanks Row Houses," they were uniformly constructed of "Athens Marble," or Joliet yellow limestone. Unfortunately all have had their main-floor entrances removed, with entry now at the basement level, ostensibly to provide more rooms after the buildings were converted from one-family residences to multifamily homes. (Photo by author)

trasting color for the horizontal bands that join window heads and sills. Above the trapezoidal bays are rows of iron cresting.

Continue north to the southeast corner of E. Goethe Street.

Read the plaque on the corner of the building that designates this as "Churchill Corner."

On the northeast and northwest corners are the 17-story **Omni Ambassador East Hotel,** No. 1301 N. State Parkway, and the 12-story **Radisson Plaza–Ambassador West Hotel,** No. 1300 N. State Parkway, the former with a Georgian-style facade, the latter in a modified Federal style. They are linked together by an underground passage, although the formerly single establishment is now operated by two separate organizations. The East building was designed in 1926 by Robert S. DeGolyer, the West by Schmidt, Garden & Martin in 1919. The Ambassador East is noted for its famous Pump Room, where the rich and famous have dined and danced for generations. Go inside and look at the display of photos of the celebrities who have been guests and those who ate at the prestigious Booth One, just to the left of the entrance to the dining room. According to *Norman Mark's Chicago,* the tradition was begun by actress Gertrude Lawrence in 1938, when she ate in Booth One for 90 straight days. Other celebrities have dined there too, including Lauren Bacall with Humphrey Bogart, Elizabeth Taylor, Margaret O'Brien, Frank Sinatra, Salvador Dali, and a host of others, even Morris the Cat, although Mark says that Lassie was refused service. The Ambassador East also figured in a scene from the Hollywood film *North by Northwest,* starring Gregory Peck.

No. 1328 N. State Parkway (*1928, Andrew N. Rebori; remodeled 1956, Bertrand Goldberg*), on the west side of the street directly opposite E. Banks Street, and sometimes called the Florsheim Town Houses, is another Rebori Art Moderne conversion. Note the curved glass-brick entrance wall—a forerunner of the streamlining motif that would become so popular in the 1930s, and would be applied to so many examples of modern technology of the day, from kitchen appliances, to automobiles, and especially to streamline trains. Observe how the lines of dark-red brick form a huge zig-zag as they rise from the left side of the entrance, then swing over it, and climb to the right above the glass wall. In the remodeling, Goldberg connected the adjoining houses to create a second-floor studio for his mother-in-law, sculptor Lillian Florsheim.

No. 1340 N. State Parkway (*1899, James Gamble Rogers*) was built at a cost of $100,000 for the socially prominent physician Dr. George Snow Isham, and is one of the largest French Renaissance–style mansions in Chicago. The facade is divided into three sections: the outer two are three bays wide and the center, just one. The entrance, whose door is embellished with carvings, is framed with Doric columns which support an entablature. The brickwork is laid in Flemish bond, with the headers yellow (now darkened with age) to contrast with the red stretchers. Three very ornate dormers grace the steep slate roof, and a pair of tall chimneys rise above.

No. 1340 N. State Parkway, designed in 1899 by James Gamble Rogers, was built for prominent physician Dr. George Snow Isham, but is still remembered as the "Playboy Mansion." The splendid French Renaissance–style mansion, one of the largest in Chicago, is in pristine condition although it has gone through a long and varied line of owners. In 1959 it was purchased by Hugh Hefner for the frolic of his Playboy bunnies, then in 1984 it became a dormitory for the students of the School of the Art Institute of Chicago, and a few years later it was auctioned by Sotheby's to a developer who subdivided the 72-room mansion into just seven condominium apartments. (Photo by author)

The house has had a rather unusual and varied history. After the departure of the original owner it served as a distinguished dancing school for the upper crust, and a later owner played live chess on the black and white marble squares of the 60-foot-long oak-panelled ballroom using people and horses for the "pieces." In 1959 Hugh Hefner purchased it for his **Playboy** Mansion and "bunny warren." Then in 1984, after the bunnies scampered off to California, the Art Institute of Chicago acquired it for use as a dormitory, naming it Hefner Hall. In more recent times it was sold at auction by Sotheby's to a developer who subdivided the 72-room manor house into seven condominium apartments.

Continue north to E. Schiller Street, named for Johann Christoph Freidrich von Schiller, the great German literary figure, considered the founder of modern German literature, and turn left (west) for a brief detour to N. Dearborn Street.

No. 1401 N. Dearborn Street, designed in 1877 by an unknown architect, is a delightful and rather early Queen Anne–style house. The rotated corner bay is in pleasant counterpoint to the varied planes of the facade. Note the amusing carved stone plaques, particularly the crouching griffin set in a recessed niche under the chimney.

Across the street stands **St. Chrysostom's Episcopal Church** (*1913, Brown & Walcott; additions 1922, 1925; remodeling 1925*), 1424 N. Dearborn Street. The lovely church hearkens back to the English country Gothic tradition. The belfry was added in 1925 together with an addition to the church building and parish house. The sanctuary has a mosaic of St. John, a replica of a 10th-century original in Hagia Sophia, in Constantinople (now Istanbul).

Nos. 1434 and **1450** are interesting examples of the French Second-Empire style, with mansard roofs and delicate detailing. No. 1434, the Philo R. King House, was built in 1876; and No. 1450, the John P. Wilson House, a year later, both by unknown architects.

No. 1454 N. Dearborn Street (*1877, Edbrooke & Burnham*), the Joseph C. Bullock House, is by far the best French Second-Empire example of the three town houses. It includes the typical mansard roof, shingled in slate, and fine ornamentation. Note how the entrance bay is set back and how the north corner stands out with its incised quoins and pilasters.

Turn back to E. Schiller Street and go left (east), returning to the corner of N. State Parkway.

On the northeast corner of E. Schiller Street stands **No. 1411 N. State Parkway** (*1914, Andrew Sandegren*), whose entrance at the north end of the building is surprisingly inconspicuous. The rather large red-brick house with smooth limestone window enframements was designed in a modified Tudor style with large balconies at each end, peaked gables, and a Spanish-tile roof. Another entrance is at 10 E. Schiller Street.

The George A. Weiss House, **No. 1428 N. State Parkway** (*1886, Harold M. Hansen*), presents a veritable fantasy of architectural adornment. Set against its rock-faced pink Georgia marble facade are carvings on the second-floor bay and in the stepped gable; a wooden porch canopy; copper crockets on the pyramidal cupola, crests, and parapet; a prominent protruding gargoyle; and an attractive pair of cast-iron entrance-stairway newel posts and balustrade. The side walls are of dark-red brick.

The Charles K. Miller House, **No. 1432 N. State Parkway** (*1884, A.M.F. Colton*), displays a wide variety of Queen Anne–style elements, from its wooden porch canopy with carved balusters, large stained-glass window in the left-hand bay window, unusual circular window on the second floor, steeply pitched slate roof, to its twin asymmetrical bays—the right-hand one with an ornate curved cornice. Note the unusual terra-cotta plaque above the circular window which portrays a flaming brazier pouring out long tongues of flame.

At the northwest corner of W. Burton Place is the former **Albert F. Madlener House,** commissioned by a major brewer and wholesale liquor distributor, and now the home of the **Graham Foundation for Advanced Studies in the Fine Arts** (*1902, Richard E. Schmidt; restoration 1963, Brenner, Danforth & Rockwell*), No. 4 W. Burton Place. The design of the large house, including the ornament that surrounds the doorway, was designed by Hugh M. G. Garden, who later became a partner of Schmidt. The solid three-story brick structure is noteworthy for the banding or stringcourses between the windows on the ground floor, the limestone window enframements that are particularly bold on the second floor, and for the less conspicuous bands connecting the third-floor windows. A simple, but substantial cornice surmounts the building. However, many consider Garden's ornate frame around the entrance to be the "crown jewel" of the house, with its Sullivanian motifs (architect Garden called it "Gardenesque") in stark juxtaposition with the rather severe lines of the building.

In its landmark designation, the Commission on Chicago Landmarks praises the "clarity, simplicity, and order of the Madlener House [that] make it an outstanding residence in the tradition of the Chicago and Prairie schools of architecture. It has the massing, logic, and dignity of a Renaissance palace, yet is a thoroughly modern design." The Graham Foundation is broadly interested in educational areas directly concerned with architecture.

In the rear of the building is a pleasant little garden designed by John Vinci and Philip Hamp in 1986 to display a collection of architectural fragments rescued from significant Chicago buildings that were demolished over the years.

The former Albert F. Madlener House, at the northwest corner of N. State Parkway and E. Burton Street, is now the home of the Graham Foundation for Advanced Studies in the Fine Arts. Designed in 1902 by Richard E. Schmidt, the elegant house was restored in 1963. The design for the house, including the delicate ornament around the entrance, was executed by Hugh M. G. Garden, who later became a partner of Schmidt's. Noteworthy are the stringcourses between the ground-floor windows, the limestone window enframements, and the unusual treatment of the third floor. The highlight of the design is the imposing entrance, framed by a wide and delicate pattern. The Landmarks Commission praised its plan as being in the tradition of the Chicago and Prairie schools, with the dignity of a Renaissance palace, yet thoroughly modern in design. (Photo by author)

*A closer look at the unusual and ornate entrance of the Madlener House reveals
"Sullivanian" design motifs that contrast strongly with the fairly severe lines of the building.
The pair of masonry blocks topped with planters that frame the entry add strength to the
overall plan. (Photo by author)*

The idea for the collection dates from the early 1960s and was the suggestion
of Daniel Brenner, the architect commissioned to remodel the Madlener
House for the Graham Foundation. While the collection has artifacts representative of a number of Chicago architects, there are so many pieces by Louis
Sullivan, that it is a virtual encapsulation of his brilliant but tragic career.
Included as well are fragments from buildings by Dankmar Adler (in cooperation with Sullivan), Richard Elmslie, H. H. Richardson, Frank Lloyd Wright,
and other notable architects.

The garden is open to the public Monday to Thursday, 9:00 A.M. to 4:00 P.M.
(Be sure to purchase the explanatory catalog, *Collection of Architectural Fragments from Famous Chicago Buildings,* available for $1.00.) Enter through the
building's main entrance, and note the rich wood paneling of the interior.

If the building is closed, you can get a little glimpse of the collection
through the iron gate at the west end.

Continue north on N. State Parkway.

*(Right) The C. A. Mair House, 1515 N. State Parkway (1893), boasts a prominent
multicolumned loggia on the piano nobile floor and repeated round-arch windows—shorter
on each successive floor—to create a feeling of greater height. The entrance is framed with
twin Corinthian columns, and the wrought-iron fence and front landscaping add charm to
the Italianate design. (Photo by author)*

The entrance to 1520 N. State Parkway is striking, with a rococo terra-cotta entrance that contrasts strongly with the simple Roman brick facade. (Photo by author)

   No. 1515 N. State Parkway, the C. A. Mair House (*1893, Frederick W. Perkins*), recently added to the National Register of Historic Places, has a smooth, rusticated limestone facade, with a prominent loggia on the *piano nobile* floor above which are triple round-arch windows. The arched windows are repeated on the third and fourth floors with Ionic columns and pilasters. The entrance columns are adorned with ornate capitals. A decorative iron fence screens the front.

At the end of the block, on the southwest corner of E. North Avenue, **No. 1550 N. State Parkway** (*1912, Marshall & Fox*) represents what was doubtless the height of luxury apartment-house living in the early years of the 20th century and is still one of the city's most posh addresses. Designed in an opulent French Beaux Arts style, with each of the full-floor, 9000-square-foot, high-ceiling, 15-room apartments on each of the 12 floors, sporting its own French name. The apartments all had their own *orangerie,* in true French palatial custom, that faced Lincoln Park; and a *grand salon,* or large living room, occupy-

(Right) Dominating the southwest corner of North Avenue is No. 1550 N. State Parkway, arguably the most elegant and luxurious apartment building in the neighborhood, if not in the entire city. Designed in 1912 by Marshall & Fox in a French Beaux Arts style, it represented the height of posh living in the early years of the 20th century, a tradition which to a great extent, it still maintains today. Each of the 12 floors boasted a 15-room apartment, with a grand salon, or living room, extending into the round corner bay, each window having its own decorative wrought-iron balcony and railing. Most apartments still have superb views of the lake and Lincoln Park. In its halcyon days, the least desirable corner of each apartment (facing southwest) was reserved for the servants' quarters. (Photo by author)

ing one of the two round corner bays that offered excellent lake and park views. Every window is still furnished with its own iron balcony and decorative railing—the third floor having the most ornate. All building services were conducted at the rear, and the servants' quarters were relegated to the southwest corner of the building.

Turn left (west) on E. North Avenue two blocks to the southeast corner of E. North Avenue and N. Clark Street. (For a better view, cross N. Clark Street, carefully!)

The **Latin School of Chicago** (*1969, Harry Weese & Associates*), 59 W. North Avenue, a private academic secondary school, houses the upper grades in this building, while the lower grades meet at 1531 N. Dearborn Street. The massive five-story structure, of concrete and red brick, has a covered loggia at the entrance with a broad two-level gallery. In addition to full facilities for its 450 students, there is an outdoor terrace on the fourth floor and a recreation area and botanical laboratory on the roof. The school was founded in 1888 and has maintained an enviable tradition of academic excellence through the years. The construction of the Latin School required the demolition of the old Plaza Hotel, built in 1892.

Although outside the unofficial boundaries of the Gold Coast, the **Germania Club,** across the street, must have caught your eye. Built in 1888 from plans by August Fiedler, the exuberantly ornate building was the busy center of local German social life at the turn of the century. The nearby Old Town Triangle witnessed the arrival of German immigrants to the area as early as the late 1840s, particularly after the failed liberal revolution of 1848, and the construction of the building was undertaken by the *Germania Maennerchor,* a singing society that had been organized to present a requiem for President Abraham Lincoln when he lay in state in Chicago. The florid decorations include appropriate lyres attached to the capitals of the Ionic columns. As the German population moved on and the neighborhood changed, the building fell into decline and was empty for years. In more recent times the structure was renovated (*1992–1993, Harold D. Rider and Nidata, Inc.*), and a bank took over much of the ground floor; a restaurant followed, and now there are a variety of tenants, all of whom seem to take pride in the preservation of the venerable building. Walk around to the Germania Place facade to see the elaborate entrance. During banking hours, enter the lobby and admire the stained-glass windows.

End of tour. To return to the Loop, take CTA bus No. 22, southbound on N. Clark Street, on the same side of the street.

The Pedway: Chicago's Downtown Underground Walkway System

A convenient and quick way to get to see many of downtown Chicago's landmarks in inclement weather, this pedestrianway system consists of a core network of underground tunnels and overhead bridges linking over 40 blocks in the central business district. These walkways, built over a 40-year period, connect public and private buildings, rapid transit stations, and commuter rail facilities.

Development of the pedestrianway system began in 1951 when the City of Chicago built one-block tunnels connecting the State Street and Dearborn Street subways at Washington Street and Jackson Boulevard. Private developers later expanded the Pedway network to provide amenities for future tenants. A large-scale example of such private development is Illinois Center (*see* Tour 4). This complex provides pedestrianway access to office, hotel, and residential buildings east of Michigan Avenue and south of Wacker Drive, and offers a wide variety of shopping, restaurants, and other services. Other developers have provided more modest links in the system.

The city, with private sector cooperation, has planned and completed a number of Pedway links in recent years. One such project is the Randolph Street Pedestrianway, which opened in 1988 and runs between State Street and Michigan Avenue. It links the Chicago Transit Authority's State Street Subway

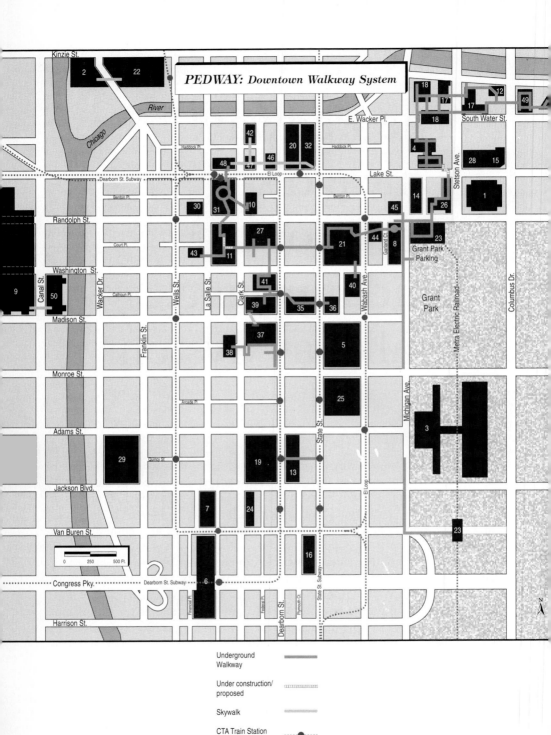

PEDWAY: *Downtown Walkway System*

Underground
Walkway

Under construction/
proposed

Skywalk

CTA Train Station
Entrance

with Metra's Randolph Street Station, and passes through lower levels of Marshall Field's, 139 N. Wabash Avenue, and the Chicago Cultural Center. Another Pedway project coordinated by the city opened in 1992, and runs in an east-west direction under LaSalle Street between City Hall and 120 N. LaSalle Street. The City of Chicago Department of Transportation is currently planning additional Pedway links downtown and continues to encourage private pedestrianway development and improved Pedway access for people with disabilities.

Pedway Map Legend

1. Amoco Building
2. Apparel Mart
3. Art Institute of Chicago
4. Boulevard Towers
5. Carson Pirie Scott & Co.
6. Chicago Board Options Exchange/LaSalle Street Station
7. Chicago Board of Trade
8. Chicago Cultural Center
9. Chicago & North Western Station
10. Chicago Title & Trust Center
11. County Building/Chicago City Hall
12. Columbus Plaza
13. Dirksen Federal Building
14. Doral Plaza
15. Fairmont Hotel
16. Harold Washington Library
17. Hyatt Regency Chicago
18. Illinois Center
19. Kluczynski Federal Building
20. Leo Burnett Building
21. Marshall Field's
22. Merchandise Mart
23. Metra Electric Railroad Station
24. Metcalfe Federal Building
25. Palmer House Hilton
26. Prudential Center
27. Richard J. Daley Center
28. The Sporting Club
29. Sears Tower
30. State of Illinois Building
31. James R. Thompson Center (State of Illinois Center)
32. Stouffer Riviere Hotel
33. Swissôtel Chicago
34. Union Station
35. One N. Dearborn Street
36. One N. State Street
37. One First National Plaza
38. Two First National Plaza
39. Three First National Plaza
40. 25 E. Washington Street
41. 69 W. Washington Street
42. 77 W. Wacker Drive
43. 120 N. LaSalle Street
44. 139 N. Wabash Avenue
45. 150 N. Michigan Avenue
46. 200 N. Dearborn Apartments
47. 201 N. Clark Street
48. 203 N. LaSalle Street
49. 303 E. Wacker Drive
50. 400 W. Madison Street

Glossary of Architectural Terms

ACANTHUS LEAF, the leaf of a Mediterranean prickly herb whose characteristic spike edges were used for classical design elements, such as on Corinthian capitals (the shape derives from the Greek for "bear's-foot")

ACROTERION, a decorative ornament at the top or at the corners of a cornice, often in the shape of an acanthus leaf (plural *acroteria*)

ANTHEMION, a conventional leaf motif based on a honeysuckle or palmette form, originating in Greek ornamental forms

ARCADE, a row of curved structural members spanning an opening and serving as a support for a wall

ARCHITRAVE [*see* ENTABLATURE]

ART DECO, the decorative style that originated with the *Exposition Internationale des Arts Décoratifs et Industriels Modernes,* which was held in Paris in 1925, and is characterized by smooth verticality, slender geometric and stylized floral forms, and a sleekness expressive of the emerging modern technology. Art Deco–style buildings are almost always sheathed in light-colored masonry.

ASHLAR, blocks of square stone laid horizontally, with vertical joints

ATRIUM, a large, interior space of a building which may be open to the sky (*see* LIGHT COURT) or illuminated by artifical light from above

BALUSTER, the vertical element or spindle in a balustrade [*see* BALUSTRADE]

BALUSTRADE, a row of baluster columns topped by a railing, forming a parapet, usually set on a cornice or in front of a window

BAROQUE, from the highly ornamental style that achieved great popularity in Europe during the 17th and early 18th centuries

BARTIZAN, a small turret or oriel projecting from the corner of a building; originally a lookout for defense on a fortress or castle

BATTER (*noun*), the receding upward slope of the outer face of a wall or other structure; BATTER (*verb*), to give a receding upward slope

BAUHAUS, the school of art and architecture founded in Weimar, Germany, in 1919, headed by Walter Gropius, and included among its faculty Paul Klee, Wassily Kandinsky, Laszlo Moholy-Nagy, and Marcel Breuer. In 1930 Mies van der Rohe became director; in 1933 the school was closed by the Nazis. The highly influential style emphasized a minimalist and industrial aesthetic.

BAY, the general term for the window section

BEARING WALL, a wall upon which the structural load of a building rests

BEAUX ARTS, a style derived from the *Ecole des Beaux-Arts* in Paris during the late 19th century, where classical motifs were expressed on a large scale; the school was a mecca for many American architects such as Richard Morris Hunt and Louis H. Sullivan.

BRACKET, a projecting L- or S-shaped support used frequently in the form of an S-shaped curve to support a cornice

CAISSON, a watertight chamber used in construction work under water or soft clay. These box-like forms were usually filled with concrete to support the foundation of a building.

CANTILEVER, a projecting beam supported only at one end

CAPITAL, the element at the top of a column [*see* CLASSICAL ORDERS]

CARYATID, a decorative column usually in the form of a female figure

CAST-IRON CONSTRUCTION [*see* pages 75–76 for a complete description]

CHAMFERED CORNER, the flattened or curved corner of a building

CHICAGO WINDOW, a window which occupies the full width of a bay of a steel-framed building and which is divided into three sections—a wide, fixed center pane with a narrower movable sash at each side

CLASSICAL ORDERS (with reference to the capitals atop columns):

CORINTHIAN, a capital embellished with carved acanthus leaves

COMPOSITE, a capital combining volutes and acanthus leaves (a composite of the Ionic and Corinthian orders

DORIC, a relatively simple capital with a flat topmost member

IONIC, a capital with spiral volutes beneath its topmost member

COFFERED CEILING, refers to a ceiling with ornamental recessed panels forming a pattern of squares

COLONNADE, a series of columns set at regular intervals, usually supporting the base of a roof structure

COLONNETTE, a small, thin column, with a decorative rather than supporting function

CONSOLE BRACKET [*see* BRACKET]

CORBEL, an architectural member that projects from within a wall and supports a weight. It is usually stepped upward and outward from a vertical surface.

CORNICE [*see* ENTABLATURE]

COR-TEN STEEL, a type of steel whose surface has been sealed and protected by natural oxidation. It eventually turns rust-colored, but does not deteriorate.

CRUCIFORM, in the shape of a cross, sometimes referring to a building layout

CUPOLA, a small structure built atop a roof, which can be circular or square in shape

CURTAIN WALL, an exterior wall, separate from the structural framework, that supports only its own weight

DENTIL COURSE, a row of small block-like projections, usually underneath the cornice, forming part of a molding (from the French *dent,* tooth)

DORMER, a window that projects from a sloping roof

ENTABLATURE, the group of horizontal members directly above the column capitals. It consists of:

ARCHITRAVE, the lowest member resting upon the column capitals. An architrave is also occasionally extended to enframe the sides of a door or window opening that is topped by an entablature.

FRIEZE, the middle member of an entablature, which in 19th-century architectural styles is frequently embellished by panels or medallions, and interrupted by large cornice brackets; 19th- and early 20th-century adaptations of classical orders often combine a frieze and cornice without an architrave.

CORNICE, the horizontally projecting topmost member of an entablature. It is frequently found by itself as the crowning motif of a facade.

EXEDRA, a classical "chair" or seating fixture; sometimes in a niche, or free-standing, as with the chair for a seated statue.

FACADE, the front of a building, usually given special architectural treatment

FANLIGHT, a semicircular window placed over a door, with bars radiating from its center like spokes of a fan

FAUX MARBRE, a surface painted to imitate marble, from the French "false marble"

FINIAL, an ornamental form at the top of a pediment, spire, pinnacle, etc.

FLUTED, refers to the vertical parallel grooves usually in a column or pilaster

FOOTPRINT, the outline of a building on the ground

FRIEZE [*see* ENTABLATURE]

GABLE, the upper part of a front wall from cornice or eaves to ridge; it can be triangular, stepped, or curved

GEORGIAN STYLE, the style developed during the 18th and early 19th centuries, corresponding with the reigns of English kings George I–IV. As used here, the style is more accurately called "neo-Georgian."

GOTHIC STYLE, refers to the European architectural style, primarily of churches and public buildings erected during the Middle Ages, from the middle of the 12th to the early 16th century, and characterized by the convergence of weights and strains at isolated points upon slender vertical piers and counterbalancing buttresses and by pointed arches, rib vaulting, and stone traceries. As used here, the style is more accurately called "neo-Gothic."

KEYSTONE, the central voussoir (block) of an arch

LIGHT COURT, a large interior courtyard of a building, usually open to the sky, but may be covered by a translucent roof

LINTEL, a horizontal member placed over a window or door to support the superstructure

LOAD-BEARING, a wall, pier, or column that supports the weight (load) of a building

MACHICOLATIONS, the openings between the corbels of a projecting parapet or in the roof of a portal; originally a defense mechanism found on medieval castles to permit the discharge of missiles upon assailants below

MANSARD ROOF, a roof having two slopes on all sides, with the lower slope steeper than the upper one; named for French architect François Mansart (1598–1666)

MIESIAN, referring to the style developed by Ludwig Mies van der Rohe

MULLION, a slender vertical pier between window panes or doors

NARTHEX, the vestibule leading to the nave of a church

NAVE, the long central hall of a church

NEO-CLASSICAL, the revival of the use of Greek and Roman architectural principles and motifs

ORIEL, a projecting bay window or vertical grouping of bay windows supported on brackets or consoles

PALAZZO, an Italian "palace," usually associated with those from the Renaissance; any large, impressive building whose style was derived from the Italian Renaissance

PARAPET, a low retaining wall usually at the edge of a roof, platform, or bridge

PEDIMENT, a low, usually triangular gable constructed in a classical style that is often filled by sculpture and framed by a cornice. It is used decoratively to crown central bays, porticoes, and important windows of a facade, and is sometimes segmental in shape or broken away in the center.

PIANO NOBILE, the main floor of a house (from the Italian "noble floor"). It is usually higher than the other floors, with a basement or ground floor below, and is used for receptions and gala events. The *piano nobile* can be identified from outside by its often taller windows.

PIER, in masonry architecture, an upright supporting member carrying a structural load

PILASTER, a shallow, flat engaged (attached) column, normally serving only a decorative function

PORTICO, a colonnade or covered entrance porch

PRAIRIE STYLE, an early 20th-century movement centered in Chicago and based on Frank Lloyd Wright's theories of a true Midwest "natural" environment, as opposed to traditional revival styles

QUOIN, large square stones used to reinforce a corner or salient angle of a building

REINFORCED CONCRETE, building forms into which poured concrete surrounds steel reinforcing bars or netting to add strength to the structure

ROMANESQUE STYLE, the style popular in western Europe from approximately the 12th to 15th centuries which employed Roman and Byzantine architectural motifs and was characterized by heavy rusticated masonry walls and round arches; the Romanesque *Revival* style was influenced by Boston architect Henry Hobson Richardson toward the end of the 19th century.

RUSTICATION, in masonry architecture, an emphasis of individual (usually large) stones by recessing their connecting parts, creating the appearance of large individually cut stones

SEGMENTAL ARCH, an arch in which the curvature is a segment of a circle, but less than a semicircle

SPANDREL, the wall panel between the head of one window and the sill of a window directly above it; the space between the outer curve of an arch and its rectangular enframement

STRINGCOURSE (sometimes called a bandcourse), a horizontal band of stone or bricks on the facade of a building

TEMPIETTO, a miniature "temple" in classic style

TERMINAL BLOCK, a decorative block placed at the extreme ends of a cornice between floor levels, thus interrupting the quoin lines or flanking piers of a facade

TERRA COTTA, a glazed or unglazed fired clay, used primarily for ornamentation [*see* page 80 for a complete description]

TOURELLE, a miniature ornamental tower or turret projecting from a wall or tower and supported by brackets or corbels

TRAVERTINE, a light-colored, porous and less expensive marble used primarily for floors and walls, and popular with International-style buildings

TRUSS, a structure made up of an assemblage of rigid support members, usually iron or steel beams

VAULT, an arched masonry structure usually forming a roof or ceiling

VOLUTE, a spiral or scroll-like form, as with the Ionic capital

VOUSSOIR, a wedge-shaped stone forming part of a masonry arch

Resource Organizations and Institutions Related to Chicago Architecture and History

American Institute of Architects,
  Chicago Chapter
222 Merchandise Mart Plaza
Chicago, IL 60654
(312) 670-7770

Burnham and Ryerson Libraries
Art Institute of Chicago
S. Michigan Ave. & E. Adams St.
Chicago, IL 60604
(312) 443-3336

Chicago Architecture Foundation
224 S. Michigan Ave.
Chicago, IL 60604
(312) 922-1742

Chicago Historical Society
1601 N. Clark St.
Chicago, IL 60614
(312) 642-4600

City of Chicago, Commission on
  Chicago Landmarks
320 N. Clark St.
Chicago, IL 60610
(312) 744-3200

Frank Lloyd Wright Home & Studio
951 Chicago Ave.
Oak Park, IL 60302
(708) 848-1500

Friends of the Chicago River
407 S. Dearborn St.
Chicago, IL 60605
(312) 939-0490

Harold Washington Library Center
Chicago Public Library
Central Library—Main Branch
400 S. State St.
Chicago, IL 60605
(312) 747-4300

Landmarks Preservation Council of
  Illinois
53 W. Jackson Blvd., Ste. 752
Chicago, IL 60603
(312) 922-1742

Newberry Library
60 W. Walton St.
Chicago, IL 60610
(312) 943-9090

Prairie Avenue House Museums
1800 S. Prairie Ave.
Chicago, IL 60616
(312) 922-3432

Society of Architectural Historians,
  Chicago Chapter
James Charney House
1365 N. Astor St.
Chicago, IL 60610
(312) 573-1365

Recommended Readings

The following list of titles provides background only on the history and architecture of the tour areas of downtown Chicago as discussed in this book, and are not to be considered an overall bibliography on the city. There are many excellent books currently in print on Chicago's political and social history as well as on its suburbs and ethnic neighborhoods. There are also many distinguished works of literature by famous Chicago writers. All the titles below can be obtained at local bookstores or are available at your local public library.

ALLEN, TED and KEVIN O. MOONEY, photographer. "Raging Boul," in *Chicago* magazine. June 1995, p. 76 et seq.

ANDREAS, ALFRED THEODORE. *A History of Chicago: From the Earliest Period to the Present Time.* Chicago: A. T. Andreas, 1884–1886.

ANDREW, DAVID S. *Louis Sullivan and the Polemics of Modern Architecture.* Urbana: University of Illinois Press, 1985.

ANDREWS, WAYNE. *Architecture in Chicago and Mid-America.* New York: Harper & Row Icon Editions, 1973.

APPELBAUM, STANLEY. *Chicago World's Fair of 1893: A Photographic Record.* Photographs from the collection of the Avery Library of Columbia University. New York: Dover, 1980.

ART INSTITUTE OF CHICAGO. Burnham Library of Architecture, *The Plan of Chicago, 1909–1979.* Chicago: Art Institute of Chicago, 1979.

———. *Burnham, Sullivan, Roark, and the Myth of the Heroic Architect,* Ross Miller. *No Little Plans: The Achievement of Daniel Burnham,* Thomas S. Hines. *Small Blessings: The Burnham Library's Louis H. Sullivan Collection,* Robert Twombly. *A Selection of Architectural Photographs from the Burnham Library,* Richard Pare. *Museum Studies* 13, No. 2 (1988).

———. *The Art Institute of Chicago Buildings 1879–1988: A Chronology, Museum Studies* 14, No. 1 (1988).

———. *Chicago Architecture and Design, 1923–1933.* Catalog for the Exhibition (1993).

BACH, IRA J. and SUSAN WOLFSON. *Chicago on Foot: Walking Tours of Chicago Architecture,* 5th ed. Chicago: Chicago Review Press, 1994.

———, and MARY LACKRITZ GRAY, *Chicago's Public Sculpture.* Chicago: University of Chicago Press, 1984.

————, SUSAN WOLFSON, and CHARLES E. GREGERSON. *A Guide to Chicago's Train Stations, Present and Past.* Athens: Ohio University Press, 1986.

BERGER, MILES L. *They Built Chicago: Entrepreneurs Who Shaped a Great City's Architecture.* Chicago: Bonus Books, 1992.

BLUESTONE, DANIEL. *Constructing Chicago.* New Haven: Yale University Press, 1991.

BOLOTIN, NORMAN and CHRISTINE LAING. *The World's Columbian Exposition.* Washington: National Trust for Historic Preservation/The Preservation Press, 1992.

BREEN, ANN and DICK RIGBY. *Waterfronts: Cities Reclaim Their Edge.* New York: McGraw-Hill, 1994.

BROOKS, H. ALLEN. *The Prairie School: Frank Lloyd Wright and His Midwest Contemporaries.* New York: George Braziller, 1984.

BRUEGMANN, ROBERT. *Holabird & Roche and Holabird & Root: An Illustrated Catalog of Works, 1880–1940.* New York: Garland, 1991.

BURNHAM, DANIEL H. and EDWARD H. BENNETT. *The Plan of Chicago.* New York: Da Capo Press, 1970. (An unabridged republication of the first edition, published in Chicago in 1909.)

CAHAN, RICHARD. *They All Fall Down: Richard Nickel's Struggle to Save America's Architecture.* Washington: National Trust for Historic Preservation/The Preservation Press, 1994.

CALLAHAN, CAROL J. "Glessner House, Chicago, Illinois." *The Magazine Antiques,* 139, May 1991, pp. 970–983.

CAMERON, ROBERT. *Above Chicago.* San Francisco: Cameron & Co., 1992.

CASARI, MAURIZIO and VINCENZO PAVAN, eds. *New Chicago Architecture: Beyond the International Style.* New York: Rizzoli International Publications, 1981.

CHAPPELL, SALLY. *Architecture and Planning of Graham, Anderson, Probst and White, 1912–1936: Transforming Tradition.* Chicago: University of Chicago Press, 1992.

CHRIST-JANER, ALBERT. *Eliel Saarinen—Finnish-American Architect and Educator,* rev. ed. Chicago: University of Chicago Press, 1979.

CIGLIANO, JAN and SARAH BRADFORD LANDAU, eds. *The Grand American Avenue, 1850–1920.* The Museum of The American Architectural Foundation. San Francisco: Pomegranate Art Books, 1994.

COHEN, STUART E. *Chicago Architects.* Chicago: Swallow Press, 1976.

CONDIT, CARL W. *The Chicago School of Architecture: A History of Commercial and Public Building in the Chicago Area, 1875–1925.* Chicago: University of Chicago Press, 1964.

————. *The Rise of the Skyscraper.* Chicago: University of Chicago Press, 1952.

CONWAY, W. FRED. *Fire Fighting Lore: Strange But True Stories from Firefighting History,* New Albany, Ind.: Fire Buff House Publishers (no date).

CROMIE, ROBERT. *The Great Chicago Fire.* Nashville: Rutledge Hill Press, 1994.

————. *A Short History of Chicago.* San Francisco: Lexikos, 1984.

CRONON, WILLIAM. *Nature's Metropolis: Chicago and the Great West.* New York: W. W. Norton, 1991.

CUDAHY, BRIAN J. *Destination: Loop—the Story of Rapid Transit Railroading In and Around Chicago.* Brattleboro, Vt. and Lexington, Mass.: The Stephen Greene Press, 1982.

CUTLER, IRVING. *Chicago: Metropolis of the Mid-Continent.* Dubuque: Kendall/Hunt, 1982.

DARLING, SHARON S. *Architectural Terra Cotta in Chicago.* New York: Assopiastrelle—The Italian Tile Center (no date).

FINDING, JOHN E. *Chicago's Great World's Fairs.* Manchester, England and New York: Manchester University Press, 1994.

FLEMING, JOHN, HUGH HONOUR, and NIKOLAUS PEVSNER. *The Penguin Dictionary of Architecture,* 4th ed. New York and London: Penguin Group, 1991.

FRAZIER, NANCY. *Louis Sullivan and the Chicago School.* Greenwich, Conn.: Brompton Books, 1991.

GIEDION, SIGFRIED. *Space, Time and Architecture.* 6th ed. Cambridge, Mass.: Harvard University Press, 1946.

GILBERT, JAMES. *Perfect Cities: Chicago's Utopias of 1892.* Chicago: University of Chicago Press, 1991.

GILL, BRENDAN. *Many Masks: A Life of Frank Lloyd Wright.* New York: G. P. Putnam's Sons, 1987.

GLESSNER, JOHN J. *The Story of a House: H. H. Richardson's Glessner House.* Chicago: Chicago Architecture Foundation, 1979, 1992.

GLIBOTA, ANTE. *Helmut Jahn.* Paris: Paris Art Center, 1987.

GREGERSEN, CHARLES E. *Dankmar Adler: His Theaters and Auditoriums.* Athens, Ohio: Swallow Press, University of Ohio Press, 1991.

GRESE, ROBERT E. *Jens Jensen: Maker of Natural Parks and Gardens.* Baltimore: Johns Hopkins University Press, 1992.

HARRIS, NEIL. *Chicago's Dream, a World Treasure: The Art Institute of Chicago, 1893–1993.* Chicago: Art Institute of Chicago, 1993.

———, WIM DE WIT, JAMES GILBERT, and ROBERT W. RYDELL. *Grand Illusion: The Chicago World's Fair of 1893.* Catalog for the 1993–1994 exhibition at the Chicago Historical Society. Chicago: Chicago Historical Society, 1993.

HAYNER, DON and TOM MCNAMEE. *Metro Chicago Almanac: Fascinating Facts and Offbeat Offerings about the Windy City,* rev. ed. Chicago: Chicago Sun-Times/Bonus Books, 1993.

———. *Streetwise Chicago: A History of Chicago Street Names.* Chicago: Loyola University Press, 1988.

HEINZ, THOMAS A. *Frank Lloyd Wright: Chicagoland.* Layton, Utah: Gibbs Smith Publishers, 1994.

HILTON, GEORGE W. EASTLAND. *Legacy of the Titanic.* Stanford: Stanford University Press, 1995.

HINES, THOMAS S. *Burnham of Chicago: Architect and Planner.* New York: Oxford University Press, 1974.

HITCHCOCK, HENRY-RUSSELL. *The Architecture of H. H. Richardson and His Times,* rev. ed. Cambridge, Mass.: The MIT Press, 1961.

HOFFMAN, DONALD. *The Architecture of John Wellborn Root.* Baltimore: Johns Hopkins University Press, 1973.

HOLT, GLEN E. and DOMINIC A. PACYGA. *Chicago: A Historical Guide to the Neighborhoods: The Loop and South Side.* Chicago: Chicago Historical Society, 1979.

HONES, THOMAS S. *Burnham of Chicago: Architect and Planner.* Chicago: University of Chicago Press, 1979.

INGLES, J. DAVID. "Still the Railroad Capital," and "Metra: The Best 'Commuter Trains' in the U.S." *TRAINS* magazine, Vol. 53, No. 7, July 1993, p. 34 et seq.

International Competition for a New Administration Building for the Chicago Tribune, MCMXXII, The. Containing all the Designs Submitted in Response to the Chicago Tribune's $100,000 Offer Commemorating Its 75th Anniversary, June 10, 1922. Chicago: The Tribune Company, 1923.

JACOBS, AMANDA B., ed. *Fodor's '92 Chicago.* New York: Fodor's Travel Publications, 1992.

JOEDICHE, JOACHIM. *Helmut Jahn: Design of a New Architecture.* New York: Nichols Publishing Company, 1987.

KAUFMAN, MERVYN. *Father of Skyscrapers: A Biography of Louis Sullivan.* Boston: Little, Brown, 1969.

KENT, CHERYL. "Street of Dreams: Chicago's North Michigan Avenue." *Historic Preservation,* March/April 1996.

KOGAN, HERMAN and LLOYD WENDT. Chicago: *A Pictorial History.* New York: Bonanza Books, 1958.

LANE, GEORGE A. Photographs by Algimantas Kezys and George A. Lane. *Chicago's Churches and Synagogues: An Architectural Pilgrimage.* Chicago: Loyola University Press, 1981.

LARSON, GEORGE A. and JAY PRIDMORE. Photography by Hedrich-Blessing. *Chicago Architecture and Design.* New York: Harry A. Abrams, 1993.

LARSON, PAUL CLIFFORD, ed. with Susan M. Brown. *The Spirit of H. H. Richardson on the Midland Prairies: Regional Transformation of an Architectural Style.* Ames: Iowa State University Press, 1988.

Loop Sculpture Guide. City of Chicago, Department of Cultural Affairs, 1990.

LOWE, DAVID GARRARD. *Lost Chicago.* New York: Wings Books, 1975.

———. *The Great Chicago Fire.* New York: Dover Publications, 1979.

MANSON, GRANT CARPENTER. *Frank Lloyd Wright to 1910—The First Golden Age.* New York: Van Nostrand Reinhold, 1958.

MARK, NORMAN. *Norman Mark's Chicago,* 4th ed. Chicago: Chicago Review Press, 1993.

MAYER, HAROLD M. and RICHARD C. WADE. *Chicago: Growth of a Metropolis.* Chicago: University of Chicago Press, 1969.

MOFFAT, BRUCE. *Forty Feet Below: The Story of Chicago's Freight Tunnels.* Glendale, Calif.: Interurban Press, 1981.

———. *The "L": The Development of Chicago's Rapid Transit System, 1888–1932.* Chicago: Central Electric Railfans' Association, 1995.

MOLLOY, MARY ALICE. *Chicago: A Guide to New Downtown Buildings Since the Sears Tower,* rev. ed. Chicago: Inland Architect Press, 1992.

———. *Prairie Avenue Servants: Behind the Scenes in Chicago's Mansions, 1870–1920.* St. Clair Shores, Mich.: Palindrome Press, 1994.

MUSEUM OF SCIENCE AND INDUSTRY. *A Guide to 150 Years of Chicago Architecture.* Chicago: Chicago Review Press, 1985.

PAUL, SHERMAN. *Louis Sullivan: An Architect in American Thought.* Englewood Cliffs, N.J.: Prentice Hall Spectrum Books, 1962.

PEISCH, MARK L. *The Chicago School of Architecture: Early Followers of Sullivan and Wright.* New York: Random House, 1964.

RANDALL, FRANK A. *History of the Development of Building Construction in Chicago.* Urbana: University of Illinois Press, 1949.

REGNERY, HENRY. *The Cliff Dwellers: The History of a Chicago Cultural Institution.* Chicago: Chicago Historical Bookworks, 1990.

ROOT, JOHN WELLBORN. *The Meanings of Architecture, Buildings and Writings by John Wellborn Root.* New York, Horizon Press, 1967.

RYDELL, ROBERT W. *World of Fairs.* Chicago: University of Chicago Press, 1993.

SALIGA, PAULINE, ed. *The Sky's the Limit: A Century of Chicago Skyscrapers.* New York: Rizzoli International Publications, 1990.

SCHNEDLER, JACK and ZBIGNIEW BZDAK, photographer. *Chicago.* Oakland, Calif.: Compass American Guides, 1993.

SCHULZE, FRANZ. *Mies van der Rohe: A Critical Biography.* Chicago: University of Chicago Press, 1985.

———, and KEVIN HARRINGTON. *Chicago's Famous Buildings,* 4th ed. Chicago: University of Chicago Press, 1993.

SCROGGS, MARILEE MUNGER. *A Light in the City—The Fourth Presbyterian Church of Chicago.* Chicago: The Fourth Presbyterian Church, 1990.

SIMMERLING, JACK and WAYNE WOLF. *Chicago Homes: Facts and Fables.* New York: McGraw-Hill, 1995.

SINKEVICH, ALICE, ed. *AIA Guide to Chicago.* American Institute of Architects, Chicago Architecture Foundation, Landmarks Preservation Council of Illinois, Commission on Chicago Landmarks. New York: Harcourt Brace & Company, 1993.

SIRY, JOSEPH. *Carson Pirie Scott: Louis Sullivan and the Chicago Department Store.* Chicago: University of Chicago Press, 1988.

SLATON, DEBORAH, ed. *Wild Onions: A Brief Guide to Landmarks and Lesser-Known Structures in Chicago's Loop.* Chicago: Association for Preservation Technology, 1989.

STAMPER, JOHN W. *Chicago's North Michigan Avenue: Planning and Development, 1900–1930.* Chicago: University of Chicago Press, 1991.

STERN, ROBERT A. M. *Pride of Place: Building the American Dream,* Boston: Houghton Mifflin, 1986.

STORRER, WILLIAM ALLIN. *The Frank Lloyd Wright Companion.* Chicago: University of Chicago Press, 1993.

SULLIVAN, LOUIS H. *The Autobiography of an Idea.* New York: Press of the American Institute of Architects, 1924; reprinted New York: Dover Publications, 1956.

SZARKOWSKI, JOHN. *The Idea of Louis Sullivan.* Minneapolis: University of Minnesota Press, 1956.

TERKEL, STUDS. *Chicago.* New York: Pantheon Books, 1986.

THALL, BOB. *The Perfect City.* Baltimore: Johns Hopkins University Press, 1994.

THORNDIKE, JOSEPH J., JR., ed. *Three Centuries of Notable American Architects.* New York: American Heritage Publishing Company, 1981.

TIGERMAN, STANLEY, and STUART E. COHEN. *Chicago Tribune Tower Competition and Late Entries.* New York: Rizzoli International Publications, 1980.

TWOMBLY, ROBERT. *Louis Sullivan: His Life and Work.* Chicago: University of Chicago Press, 1987.

UHL, MICHAEL. *Frommer's Walking Tours—Chicago.* New York: Prentice Hall Travel, 1994.

VAN RENSSELAER, MARIANA GRISWOLD. *Henry Hobson Richardson and His Works.* New York: Dover Publications, 1969.

VINCI, JOHN. *The Trading Room: Louis Sullivan and the Chicago Stock Exchange.* Chicago: Art Institute of Chicago, 1989.

WILLE, LOIS. *Forever Open, Free, and Clear: The Struggle for Chicago's Lakefront,* 2nd ed. Chicago: University of Chicago Press, 1991.

DE WIT, WIM, ed. *Louis Sullivan: The Function of Ornament.* New York: W. W. Norton, 1986. (Catalog for an exhibition organized by the Chicago Historical Society and the St. Louis Art Museum.)

WOLFE, GERARD R. *New York: A Guide to the Metropolis,* Walking Tours of Architecture and History, 2nd ed. New York: McGraw-Hill, 1994.

WRIGHT, FRANK LLOYD. *An Autobiography,* 3rd ed., rev. New York: Horizon Press, 1977.

ZUKOWSKY, JOHN, ed. *Chicago Architecture 1872–1922: Birth of a Metropolis.* Chicago and Munich: Art Institute of Chicago and Prestel Verlag, 1987.

———, ed. *Architecture and Design 1923–1993: Reconfiguration of an American Metropolis.* Chicago and Munich: Art Institute of Chicago and Prestel Verlag, 1993.

Recommended Videotapes

MOFFAT, BRUCE. *Forty Feet Below* (video version of the book, with 1992 flood update). Pasadena: Pentrex, 1992.

SKYLINE CHICAGO series, with accompanying guidebooks: (I) *Chicago's Riverfront: Where the Present Meets the Past;* (II) *The Loop: Where the Skyscraper Began;* (III) *Michigan Avenue: From Museums to the Magnificent Mile;* (IV) *The Lakefront: Parks and Plans;* (V) *Chicago: A City of Neighborhoods.* Guidebook text by Judith Paine McBrien, illustrations by Victoria Behm and John DeSalvo. Willmette, Ill.: Perspectives International, 1991–1996.

Index

Whistler, James McNeill, 162
Whistler, Captain John, 162
White, Stanford, 301, 302, 394, 397, 398
"White City," 186, 314
Widow Clarke House, 337–339
Wieboldt's Department Store (former), 77, 84
Wigwam (razed), 132
Wilde, Oscar, 236
William B. Tabler Architects, 153
William H. Reid House, 343–344
William J. Campbell U.S. Courthouse Annex, 18
William Jones Commercial High School, 281
William W. Bond, Jr. & Associates, 261
William Wallace Kimball House, 331–332
Willoughby Tower, 201
Wilson (John P.) House, 422
WLS radio station, 96
WLS-TV, 96
WMAQ radio station, 221
Wolf Point, 128
Wolf Tavern, 128
Women's Athletic Club, 228
Works Progress Administration, 366, 368
World's Columbian Exposition of 1893, 9, 11, 26,
    31, 61, 75, 86, 151, 165, 178, 186, 192, 193, 205,
    266, 267, 279, 296, 313, 314, 368, 391, 413
World's Congress Auxiliary, World's Columbian
    Exposition of 1893, 193

World's Fair of 1933–1934, 94, 165, 299, 307, 309,
    310, 317, 319
World Trade Center (New York), 100, 240
World Trade Center Chicago, 133
Wright, Frank Lloyd, 3, 11, 30, 31, 32, 34, 182, 188,
    404, 405, 424
Wright, Steve, 169
Wrigley, William K., Jr., 217
Wrigley Building, 23, 159, 165, 168, 214, 215–217,
    218, 393
    Annex, 217, 218
Wrigley Field, 217

Xerox Center, 65, 67

Yale University, 255
Yerkes, Charles T., 11
YMCA:
    Central YMCA Building, 38
    Victor F. Lawson Department, 379
Yoe, Charles C., 419
Young, Hugh, 163
Zettler, Emil R., 239
Zhou, Da Huang, 189
Zhou, Shan Zuo, 189

About the Author

Gerard R. Wolfe has written a number of acclaimed books, including the best-selling *New York: A Guide to the Metropolis,* called by the city's Landmarks Commission the finest walking tour guide to the "Big Apple." Director of the Arts and Liberal Studies Program at the University of Wisconsin—Milwaukee, Professor Wolfe holds a doctorate in American Studies. He has led walking tours for more than 25 years and is proud of his long-standing love affair with Chicago and its fabled architecture.